THE

BODY

THESAURUS

A FICTION WRITER'S SOURCEBOOK OF WORDS AND PHRASES TO DESCRIBE CHARACTERS

DAHLIA EVANS

For Mum

Contents

40. Wrist(s)

Also by Dahlia Evans

Introduction

So, what's a body thesaurus, anyway? Simply put, it's a book that is arranged alphabetically by body part and includes all the adjectives, verbs, and noun phrases that have been used with said body part in published fiction. Meaning, these collocations (word groupings) come up again and again in all popular fiction.

Using textual analysis, I was able to extract this information from a huge body of texts and in turn save you countless hours racking your brain trying to think up a word to use. After all, every word you think of has probably already been used with that particular body part, and is thus part of this thesaurus. This way you'll save yourself time and a possible headache, not to mention get ideas you wouldn't have thought of.

How This Book Is Organized

The book is broken up into 40 chapters. Each chapter covers a single body part.

Each body part is further categorized by part of speech; adjectives, verbs and phrasal verbs, and noun phrases. The words and phrases in these categories are arranged in alphabetical order.

Example sentences are added at the end of each chapter to give you an idea of how to use an entry in a sentence. Entries are italicized for clarity.

Lastly, a note about entries. Verbs are listed in their past tense form. Also, American spelling is used, with a few British forms where that spelling is popular internationally.

How to Use This Book

1) Table of Contents

You know you want to describe your character but need ideas about what to describe. Check the Table of Contents for a list of body parts and let your imagination follow.

2) Adjectives

You know what part of the character you want to describe, now you just need a list of words to use. Go to the Adjective section and find one or more that fit your needs.

3) Verbs

You want to describe your character's movements. Go to the Verbs and Phrasal Verbs section and find a ton of verbs that can be used with that part of the body and end the use of cliché verbs once and for all.

4) Noun Phrases

You want to use a variation of the noun or describe an aspect of that noun (body part). Go to the Noun Phrases section and find many phrases to use instead.

This book was a big project. It took the better part of six months to finish. The thing that kept me going was knowing how valuable a resource this would be for writers of genre-based fiction - no matter what genre you write, I believe you'll find this book immensely helpful when writing character descriptions or describing actions.

As an aside, you may have purchased my other book 'Thinking Like a Romance Writer' and want to know how this book differs. Well, first and foremost, this book is for all fiction writers, and includes many words that are not needed or used in romance. That being said, that particular book was written a few years ago. Since then, I have expanded my romance database quite a bit. So romance writers can expect a 2nd Edition of 'Thinking Like a Romance Writer' in the near future.

In closing, I want to say thank you for your investment. I hope this thesaurus comes in handy with all your future writing projects.

Warm Wishes,
Dahlia Evans

1
ANKLE(S)

Adjectives in Alphabetical Order

aching; aging; attenuated; bad; bandaged; bare; beautiful; bird-slim; biting; black; blasted; blistered; bloody; blue; bluish; bone-cold; bony; booted; bound; bright-pink; broken; brown; bruised; busted; chubby; cold; cool; cracking; crossed; crushed; dainty; delicate; delicate-looking; dirty; dusty; elegant; enormous; excessive; exposed; fabulous; fair; fat; fine; fleshy; fractured; full; gimpy; good; gouty; grayish; hairy; hard; heavy; high; high-heeled; hurt; hyper-extended; injured; inner; knobby; knotted; knotty; laced; lacy; lame; left; little; lovely; low; lower; mottled; muddy; naked; narrow; nice; nimble; opposite; other; outer; painful; pale; pallid; pasty; plump; pretty; purple; purple-socked; red; resprained; retwisted; right; severed; shapely; shattered; short; silken; skinny; skirted; slender; slight; slim; small; sodden; soft; sore; spindly; sprained; stiff; still; still-slim; still-sore; stockinged; strong; swelling; swinging; swollen; tanned; tapered; tattooed; thick; thickish; thin; throbbing; tight; tingling; tiny; trim; turned; turning; twisted; twisting; ugly; unstable; varicose; warm; weak; weary; white.

Verbs and Phrasal Verbs in Alphabetical Order

ached; appeared; arrayed in; attached to; balanced; balanced on; banded together; bared; became; began; bent; bent at; bled; bloated; bobbled; bore; bothered; bound; bound by; bound in; bound to; bound up; broke; buckled; buckled beneath; caked in; caught; caught in; caused; clamped; clamped by; clutched; coated; coated in; covered; covered in; cracked; creaked; crossed; crossed against; crossed over; crushed; crushed in; cuffed; disappeared; disappeared into; dislocated; drenched; drenched in; elevated; encased in; exposed; fell; fell against; felt; fixed; flashed; flexed; folded; folded beneath; folded inward; freed; freed from; gave out; gripped; healed; held; held fast; held up; hooked; hooked around; hooked behind; hooked under; hung; hurt; itched; jarred; jerked; jostled; jutted out; knocked; knocked together; lashed together; locked; locked around; looked; loosened; peeked out; peeped from beneath; peeped out; perched on; played with; pointed through; poked out; poked through; popped; pressed; pressed against; prickled; prickled with; propped on; protested; protruded; protruded from; pulled; pulled up; quivered; rapped; remained; replaced; rested; rested on; rested sideways; returned; revealed; roasted; roasted by; rotated; rotated inward; sat in; sat on; scraped; scraped against; shackled; shaved; shocked; shook; shook with; shot through; showed;

showed between; skated; slapped; slapped by; slid; slid up; slipped; snagged; snagged in; spattered with; sprained; spread apart; started to; stopped; strapped; strapped to; stretched; stuck out; stuck together; supported; supported by; swelled; swelled up; tattooed; tattooed with; throbbed; tied; tied to; tied together; tingled; touched; tucked in; turned; turned away; turned inward; turned on; twinged; twisted; twisted beneath; wobbled; wobbled over; worked; worked out; wrapped; wrapped in; wrenched.

Noun Phrases

area of the ankle(s); back of the ankle(s); ball of the ankle(s); bend of the ankle(s); bone(s) of the ankle(s); center of the ankle(s); crossing of the ankles; curve of the ankle(s); dislocation of the ankle(s); edge of the ankle(s); extension of the ankle(s); flesh of the ankle(s); fracture of the ankle(s); glimpse of the ankle(s); grip of the ankle(s); hold of the ankle(s); injury of the ankle(s); instability of the ankle(s); joints of the ankle(s); line of the ankle(s); motion of the ankle(s); movement of the ankle(s); muscles of the ankle(s); pair of ankles; part of the ankle(s); position of the ankle(s); region of the ankle(s); rise of the ankle(s); shape of the ankle(s); side of the ankle(s); skin of the ankle(s); slimness of the ankle(s); sprain of the ankle(s); stability of the ankle(s); strength of the ankle(s); stumps of the ankle(s); surface of the ankle(s); top of the ankle(s); turn of the ankle(s); view of the ankle(s).

USAGE EXAMPLES

Tommy's *swollen ankle gave out* when he tried to put his full weight on it.

The *flesh of her ankle was pale*, having not seen the sun for many months.

Both her *ankles throbbed* as she climbed yet another step on the way to the summit.

As she walked down the red carpet, Beth's *bad ankle twisted*, making her lose her balance and fall.

All he could see was *a pair of exposed ankles peeking out* from beneath a sparkling blue dress.

2
ARM(S)

Adjectives in Alphabetical Order

A - L

absent; abused; aching; active; adjacent; age-bruised; agile; albino-white; allusive; amputated; angry; angular; anxious; ape-like/apelike; arthritic; articulated; artificial; ashy-brown; athletic; authoritative; average; awkward; baby-oiled; bad; baggy; balanced; bandaged; bare; bared; basic; battered; bearish; bearlike; beautiful; beefy; bent; best; better; big; bionic; birdlike; black; black-cloaked; black-skinned; black-sweatered; blackened; bleeding; blighted; blistered; bloated; blood-streaked; bloody; blubbery; blue; blue-gray; blue-jerseyed; blue-shirted; blue-veined; blurred; blustery; bone-thin; boneless; bony; bound; boyish; brawny; brazen; bright; bright-white; broad; broken; brown; brown-black; brown-tweed; browned; bruise-blackened; bruised; bruising; brutal; brutish; budding; bulbous; bulky; bunched-up; burgundy; burly; burned/burnt; burning; burnished; busted; busy; capable; caped; captive; careful; careless; caring; carved; chalk-white; chicken-bone; childish; chilled; chiseled; chocolate-brown; chubby; chunky; clammy; claw-like; clinging; cloaked; cloth-wrapped; clumsy; coated; cocked; cold; collective; colored; colorful; combat-trained; combined; comfortable; comforting; compact; compassionate; competent; considerable; consoling; cool; corded; costumed; counter-balanced; courtly; crablike; cradling; crane-like/cranelike; creamy; creamy-white; crimson; crooked; crossed; cruel; cuffed; curled; curved; curving; cushiony; dainty; damaged; damp; dark; dark-brown; dark-clothed; deadly; decisive; defensive; deformed; deft; delicate; desperate; destructive; detached; developed; dimpled; dipping; dirt-covered; dirty; disabled; disgusted; disgusting; distended; diverging; divine; dominant; double-jointed; doughy; downy; dreadful; drooping; droopy; dry; eager; eighteen-year-old; elegant; elevated; elongated; emaciated; empty; encircling; endless; enfolding; engulfing; enormous; entire; entwined; ethereal; excellent; expansive; exposed; extended; extensive; extra; extraordinary; fabled; fair; faithful; faithless; familiar; fat; fatherly; fatigued; favored; favorite; feeble; feeble-fleshed; female; feminine; fiery; fine; firm; flabby; flaccid; flailing; flannel-shirted; flapping; flappy; flat; fleshless; fleshy; flexible; flexing; floppy; fluttering; fluttery; flying; folded; fond; foolish; forgiving; formidable; fractured; fragile; fragrant; frail; frantic; freckled; free; friendly; frightened; frozen; full; functional; functioning; funny-looking; fur-cloaked; fur-covered; furred; furry; gangling; gangly; garish; gaunt; gawky; generous; gentle; gentleman's; gesturing; ghostly; giant; gigantic; gleaming; glistening; glittering; glorious; glove-covered; gloved; glowing; gnarled; good; goose-fleshed; goosebumped; gorgeous; grabbing; graceful; gracious; grappling;

grasping; grazed; greasy; great; Grecian; grimy; groping; grounded; grown-up; gym-toned; hairless; hairy; half-lifted; hamlike; hammy; handcuffed; hard; hard-muscled; haughty; health-club; healthy; heavenly; heavily-muscled; heavy; hefty; helpful; heroic; hidden; high-raised; horizontal; horrid; hospitable; hostile; huge; hulking; human; hungry; hurt; hypnotic; icy; immovable; imperial; imperious; impressive; inadequate; inert; infamous; injured; inked; inner; innocent; innumerable; inquiring; insectlike; interlocked; intertwined; invincible; invisible; iron-hard; irresistible; itchy; javelin-like; jerky; jiggly; joined; jointed; kindling-thin; knife-wielding; knightly; knobby; knotty; lace-covered; lacerated; lacy; languid; lanky; large; lazy; leaden; lean; leathered; left; legendary; leisurely; lifeless; light; limber; limp; linked; lithe; little; liver-spotted; loaded; lobster-like; locked; lone; long; long-boned; long-fingered; longish; loose; lovely; loving; lower; lumbering; lumpy; lusty.

M - Y

magnificent; male; mangled; manly; marked; marvelous; masculine; massive; matching; maternal; meaty; mechanical; merciless; metallic; midget-size; mighty; milky; missing; moist; monstrous; motherly; mournful; moving; multiple; muscled; muscular; mutilated; naked; narrow; natural; nerveless; nervous; nervy; nice; noble; now-empty; now-folded; numb; numerous; old; open; opened; opposite; ordinary; other; out-flung; out-reaching; out-spread; out-stretched; outer; over-developed; over-hanging; over-muscled; overworked; painted; pale; paralyzed; paternal; patient; pendulous; pink; pious; pipe-cleaner; pithless; pivoting; pleading; pliant; plump; plush; pointing; poor; possessive; potent; powerful; powerful-looking; pressing; pretty; pricked; prickly; prominent; prosthetic; protecting; protective; protesting; protruding; proud; pudding-soft; pudgy; puny; purple; quivering; raging; rail-thin; raised; rangy; rash-covered; reaching; ready; reassuring; rebellious; recognizable; red; red-orange; reddened; reedy; regular-sized; relaxed; relentless; remaining; responsible; restrained; restraining; right; rigid; rippling; robed; robotic; robust; rod-like; ropy; rotating; rotund; rough; rubbery; rugged; ruthless; safe; sagging; saggy; saintly; satiny; scarred; scornful; scraggly; scraped; scratched; scratched-up; scrawny; sculpted; severed; sexual; shadowy; shaggy; shaky; shaped; shapely; shattered; sheltering; shining; shiny; shirtless; short; shriveled; shrunken; shuddering; sickly; silent; silken; silky; similar; simple; sinewy; single; sinister; sinuous; skeletal; skinny; skinny-ass; slack; sleepy; sleeved; sleeveless; slender; slight; slim; small; smelly; smooth; snowy; soaring; soft; soiled; sole; solid; soothing; sore; spare; spastic; spear-like/spearlike; speckled; spidery; spiked; spindly; splendid; splinted; spotted; stained; stalwart; steady; steadying; steely; stick-figure; stick-like/sticklike; stick-thin; sticky; stiff; stiffened; stiffening; still-throbbing; stirring; stocky; stout; straight; stray; stretched; stretching; striated; striking; stringy; striped; strong; struggling; strumming; stubby; stumpy; stunned; stupid; sturdy; substantial; suited; sun-baked; sun-browned; sun-dark; sun-darkened; sun-roughed; sunburned/sunburnt; sunstroked; suntanned; superior; supple; supporting; sure; sweatered; sweaty; swinging; swollen; tan; tangled; tanned; tattoo-laced; tattooed; teenaged; tender;

tendon-torn; tense; tentacle-like; tentacular; tentative; terrible; thick; thickish; thin; throbbing; thrusting; tight; tightly-muscled; tiny; tired; too-long; torn-off; tortured; touching; trailing; trained; trapped; trembling; triumphant; tubular; tuxedoed; twiggy; twisted; twisted-up; twisting; unbandaged; unbendable; unburned; uncertain; underdeveloped; undernourished; unfeeling; ungainly; uniformed; uninjured; unlifted; unmoving; unresisting; unruly; unseen; unwieldy; upflung; uplifted; upper; upraised; upstretched; useful; useless; valiant; various; vast; veiny; vengeful; vertical; victorious; vigorous; visible; voluminous; waiting; wandering; wanting; warm; wary; wasted; water-slick; waving; waxen; waxy; weak; weak-looking; weak-muscled; weakening; weary; weedy; weight-lifter; weighted; weightless; welcoming; well-defined; well-muscled; well-placed; well-sculpted; well-shaped; wet; whip-thin; white; white-gloved; white-sleeved; whole; wide; wide-spread; wiggling; wild; willful; willing; willowy; wiry; wispy; withered; wizened; wobbly; womanly; wonderful; wonky; woolly; work-roughened; worked-out; wounded; wrapped; wretched; wriggly; wrinkled; wrinkly; young; youthful.

Verbs and Phrasal Verbs in Alphabetical Order

A - C

accentuated; ached; ached after; ached for; ached from; ached with; achieved; acted; added; adjusted; adopted; adorned with; affixed to; aimed; aimed at; allowed; amazed; amputated; angled; angled downward; appeared; applied; applied pressure; approached; arced; arched; arose; arranged; arranged in; arrayed; arrayed up; arrested; arrested in; arrived; arrived at; arrowed; arrowed down; articulated; asprawl; assembled; assigned; assumed; attached; attached to; attended; attracted; attributed; awakened; backhanded; balanced; bandaged; bandaged up; banded around; banded together; bared; bathed; bathed in; beat; beat at; beat down; became; beckoned; began; began to; belonged to; belted; bent; bent across; bent around; bent at; bent back; bent behind; bent forward; bent in; bent into; bent on; bent out; bent over; bent upward; betrayed; blazed; blazed with; bled; blew off; blocked; bloomed; bloomed with; blurred; bore; bound; bound across; bound around; bound behind; bound tightly; bound to; bound up; bound with; braced; braced against; braced on; braced over; brandished; brimmed with; bristled; bristled with; broke; broke away; broke out; broke through; brought down; brought up; browned; bruised; brushed; brushed against; brushed past; brushed together; buckled; built; built up; bulged; bulged from; bulged out; bulged under; bulged with; bumped; bumped into; buried; buried in; buried inside; burned/burnt; burst from; burst through; busted; busted in; busted through; buzzed; caked with; called for; calmed; came around; came at; came back; came down; came forward; came from; came in; came into; came loose; came out; came past; came through; came up; captured; carried; carried away; carried off; carried upward; carved; cast; caught; caught in; caused; ceased; charged; charged with; chopped; chopped at; chopped off; chopped out; churned; cinched; circled; circled around; circled over; circled under; circulated;

claimed; clamped; clamped across; clamped around; clamped down; clamped tightly; clapped; clapped across; clashed; clashed with; clasped; clasped across; clasped around; clasped behind; clasped over; clasped securely; clasped tightly; clasped to; clawed; clawed at; clawed upward; cleaned; cleaved; clenched; clenched around; clicked; clicked back; climbed; cloaked; cloaked by; closed; closed around; closed on; closed over; closed tightly; clung; clung to; clutched; clutched around; coated; coated in; coated with; cocked; cocked back; cocooned; coddled; coiled; coiled around; collapsed; collapsed onto; collected; combed; combined; combined with; commenced; concealed; concealed behind; concealed beneath; concealed in; concealed under; connected; connected to; connected with; consisted; consisted of; contained; continued; contracted; controlled; conveyed; convinced; copied; corresponded to; covered; covered in; covered with; cracked; crackled; crackled with; cradled; cradled against; cradled around; cradled in; cramped; cranked; cranked up; crashed; crashed into; crawled; crawled into; crawled through; created; crept; crept across; crept around; crested; crossed; crossed above; crossed against; crossed around; crossed behind; crossed beneath; crossed defensively; crossed firmly; crossed inside; crossed loosely; crossed nonchalantly; crossed on; crossed over; crossed overhead; crossed stoically; crossed tight(ly); crossed under; crowded; crowded over; crowned with; crumpled; crushed; crushed against; cuddled; cuddled against; cupped; curled; curled against; curled around; curled up; curved; curved down; curved downward; curved in; curved into; curved out; curved over; curved up; curved upward; cut; cut down; cut off; cut through.

D - G

dampened; danced; dangled; dangled between; dangled down; dangled from; dangled in; dangled limply; dangled loosely; dangled off; dangled on; dangled out; dangled over; dangled straight; darted; darted down; darted out; darted up; decorated with; defended; delivered; deposited; deprived; descended; detained; dipped; dipped into; directed; disappeared; disappeared into; disguised; disguised beneath; dismembered; displayed; diverted; dodged; dragged; dragged back; dragged down; draped; draped across; draped around; draped down; draped on; draped over; dressed; drew back; drew close; drew in; drew near; drew up; dried out; drifted; drifted into; drifted up; dripped; dripped with; drooped; drooped over; dropped; dropped across; dropped away; dropped back; dropped down; dropped from; dropped onto; dropped to; drowned in; dug; dug into; dulled; dumped; dwarfed; dwindled; eased; eased around; eased together; eclipsed; elevated; elicited; embraced; emerged; emerged from; emptied; encased in; encircled; enclosed; encumbered by; encumbered with; enfolded; engaged; engaged in; engulfed; enjoyed; enmeshed; entangled; entangled in; entered; entered through; entwined; entwined across; entwined around; entwined with; enveloped; erupted from; erupted through; escaped; exercised; exerted; expanded; exposed; extended; extended above; extended across; extended along; extended down; extended forward; extended horizontally; extended out; extended outward; extended over; extended parallel; extended straight; extended to; extended toward; extended upward; faced forward; failed to; fanned;

fastened; fastened behind; fatigued; fell; fell across; fell against; fell at; fell away; fell back; fell between; fell by; fell down; fell from; fell into; fell off; fell on; fell out; fell over; fell to; felt; felt as; felt like; festered; filled with; fired out; fit into; fixed on; flagged down; flailed; flailed about; flailed against; flailed behind; flailed out; flanked; flapped; flapped in; flapped like; flapped up; flared; flared beneath; flared with; flashed; flashed back; flashed forward; flashed out; flattened; fled; flew; flew around; flew in; flew into; flew out; flew over; flew through; flew up; flew upward; flexed; flexed around; flexed beneath; flipped down; flitted; floated; floated above; floated in; floated up; flopped; flopped at; flopped down; flopped out; flopped over; flung about; flung above; flung across; flung around; flung back; flung out; flung outward; flung over; flung up; fluttered; folded; folded across; folded against; folded around; folded behind; folded beneath; folded in; folded over; folded under; folded underneath; folded up; followed; forced; forked out; formed; found; framed; freed; freed from; froze; froze in; furnished by; furnished with; fused together; fused with; gained; gave; gave out; gave up; gestured; gleamed; gleamed with; glided; glided around; glided past; glinted; glinted with; glistened; glistened with; glowed; glued to; grabbed; grabbed at; grasped; grasped around; grasped at; grazed; grew; grew tired; gripped; groped; groped toward; guarded; guarded against.

H - P

hammered; hammered at; handcuffed; handcuffed to; handed; hauled; headed for; healed; heaped with; heaved; held; held above; held aloft; held at; held away; held by; held down; held in; held onto; held out; held over; held tight(ly); held up; helped; hid; hid behind; hid in; hid under; hinted at; hit; hoisted; hooked; hooked around; hooked behind; hooked onto; hooked over; hooked through; hooked to; hooked up; hovered; hovered over; hugged; hugged to; hung; hung at; hung by; hung down; hung on; hung over; hurt; hurt from; immobilized; impaled; impeded; impressed; imprisoned; included; increased; indicated; injected with; inserted; intended; interlaced; interlocked; intersected; intertwined; intrigued; itched; jabbed; jammed; jammed against; jerked; jerked back; jerked forward; jerked out; jerked sideways; jerked with; jiggled; jingled; joined; jolted; jolted upward; jumped; jutted; jutted from; jutted out; knocked; knotted; knotted in; labored; laced with; laden with; laid; laid across; laid around; laid aside; laid by; laid down; laid out; laid over; landed; landed across; landed on; lashed; lashed out; latched around; latched onto; leaned; leaned against; leaned into; leaned on; leaned out; leaped into; leaped out; leaped/leapt; led; led by; left in; lengthened; lent; let; levered; lifted; lifted up; lingered; linked; linked around; linked together; loaded; loaded down; loaded with; locked; locked across; locked against; locked around; locked behind; locked together; locked up; lofted; lolled; longed for; looked; looped; looped about; looped around; looped between; looped through; loosened; lopped off; lost; lowered; lurched; lurched forward; lurched toward; marked; marked by; marked with; mashed; mashed together; met; met with; mimed; mingled with; mirrored; missed; mocked; motioned; motioned for; motioned to; moved; moved along; moved around; moved away; moved back; moved down; moved forward; moved from; moved further; moved in; moved like; moved over; moved toward; moved up; moved with; needed; obeyed; obtained; offered; offered to; opened; opened wide; operated; opposed; orchestrated; ordered; ornamented with; outraised; outreached; outstreched; overflowed with; overrided; paddled; pained; painted; paraded; paralyzed; parted; passed; passed through; peeked out; pendulumed; pendulumed up; perched on; perched up; performed; persisted; picked up; piled with; pinioned; pinioned behind; pinned; pinned above; pinned behind; pinned beneath; pinned to; pivoted; pivoted on; placed; placed against; placed around; placed at; placed in; placed on; placed over; played; plopped on; plucked; plucked up in; pointed; pointed out; pointed straight; pointed through; pointed to; poised; poised for; poised high; poked; poked out; poked through; poked up; popped; popped out; popped through; positioned; positioned at; positioned on; positioned under; possessed; prepared; prepared for; presented; pressed; pressed across; pressed against; pressed into; prevailed; prickled; prickled from; prickled with; proceeded; procured; produced; projected; projected forward; projected from; propped against; propped behind; propped on; propped up; protected; protested; protruded; protruded from; protruded out; proved; provided; pulled; pulled above; pulled against; pulled around; pulled away; pulled back; pulled down; pulled in; pulled out; pulled up; pumped; pumped up; punctured; punctured with; pushed; pushed back; pushed in; pushed out; pushed up; put in; put into; put on; put out.

Q - S

quivered; quivered like; quivered with; raced; radiated; raised; raised above; raised against; raised aloft; raised over; raised toward; raised up; reached; reached across; reached around; reached back; reached behind; reached down; reached for; reached into; reached out; reached over; reached to; reached toward; reached up; reappeared; received; reclined; reclined upon; reflected; reflected in; refused; relaxed; released; remained; removed; removed from; rendered; required; resembled; rested; rested across; rested against; rested around; rested at; rested in; rested on; rested over; rested upon; restrained; retained; retracted; retreated; retrieved; returned; revealed; revolved; riddled with; ripped from; ripped open; rippled; rippled through; rippled under; rippled with; rocked; rocked slightly; rolled; rolled beneath; rolled over; rose; rose above; rose from; rose to; rose toward; rose up; rotated; rounded; rounded with; rowed; rubbed; rubbed against; rushed; rustled; rustled in; sagged; saluted; sank; sank in; sank to; saved; scissored; scooped up; scooped up in; scrambled; scrambled for; scraped; scraped around; scraped by; scraped over; scratched; scrubbed; searched; secured; seemed; seized; seized by; seized up; sent; separated; served; set; set down; set in; settled; severed; shattered; shielded; shifted; shivered; shivered with; shone; shook; shook from; shook when; shook with; shortened; shot across; shot back; shot down; shot forward; shot out; shot through; shot up; shouldered; shoved; shoved inside; showed; showed through; shrank; shrank back; shrouded; shrouded by; signaled; signaled toward; signified; sizzled; sizzled in; skimmed; skimmed past; slackened; slammed across; slammed against; slammed around; slammed down; slammed into; slammed onto;

slammed over; slanted; slanted back; slapped; slapped on; slashed; slashed through; sliced; sliced through; slid; slid across; slid around; slid down; slid off; slid out; slid over; slid up; slipped; slipped around; slipped beneath; slipped from; slipped into; slipped off; slipped out; slipped through; slithered; slithered past; slithered up; slowed; slumped; slumped on; slung across; slung around; slung down; slung over; slung through; smacked; smashed; smeared; smeared with; smelled; smelled of; smuggled; snaked across; snaked around; snaked in; snaked out; snapped; snapped across; snapped back; snapped forward; snapped to; snapped up; snatched; sneaked; sounded like; spanned; sparkled; sparkled with; spasmed; spasmed from; spattered with; speared; speared up; splashed; splashed on; splatted; splatted down; splayed; splayed across; splayed out; split; sported; sprang; sprang back; sprang forward; sprang out; sprang up; sprawled; spread; spread across; spread along; spread on; spread out; spread wide; sprouted from; spun; squeezed; squeezed around; squirmed in; stamped; stamped in; stamped on; started; started to; startled; stayed; steadied; steamed; steamed in; stiffened; stiffened with; stirred; stole around; stomped; stood; stood at; stood behind; stood out; stood up; stopped; straightened; straightened out; strained; strained against; strained under; strained with; strapped; strapped to; streaked with; strengthened; stretched; stretched above; stretched across; stretched along; stretched around; stretched behind; stretched down; stretched forward; stretched out; stretched over; stretched straight; stretched through; stretched to; stretched toward; stretched up; stripped; stroked; struck; struggled; stuck; stuck in; stuck out; stuck under; stuffed; stung; submerged; submerged in; suffered; suggested; suggested otherwise; suited; summoned; summoned up; supplied; supported; supported against; supported by; supported on; surrendered; surrounded; surrounded by; surrounded with; suspended; suspended from; suspended in; suspended out; suspended over; sustained; swaddled in; swam; swam through; swathed down; swayed; swayed in; swayed together; swelled up; swept across; swept back; swept forward; swept out; swept round; swept through; swept to; swept toward; swept up; swiped; swirled around; swished; swooped; swooped on; swung; swung about; swung around; swung at; swung back; swung down; swung freely; swung out; swung overhead; swung round; swung up; swung upward.

T - Y

tackled; tangled; tangled in; tanned; tattooed; teetered; teetered out; tended to; tensed; tensed with; tentacled around; thrashed; thrashed at; thrashed out; threaded around; threatened; threw; threw around; threw back; threw onto; threw out; threw over; threw up; threw upwards; throbbed; thrust back; thrust forward; thrust into; thrust out; thrust through; thrust upward; tied; tied around; tied behind; tied to; tied together; tied up; tied with; tightened across; tightened around; tightened on; tingled; tired; took; took in; took on; took up; tore; tore from; tore off; tossed around; tossed up; touched; traced; trailed; trained; trapped; trapped beneath; trapped in; trapped under; traveled; traveled around; trembled; trembled beneath; trembled from; trembled in; trembled with; tried; triggered; triumphed; triumphed over; tucked away; tucked in; tucked inside;

tucked under; tugged; tugged on; turned; turned toward; twined; twined about; twined around; twined behind; twined between; twinged; twirled; twisted; twisted around; twisted back; twisted behind; twitched; unbent; unfolded; unfurled; united; unsettled; upheld; uplifted; upraised; used for; used to; vanished; veered; vibrated; wagged; waggled; waited; waited for; wandered; wandered over; warmed; washed; waved; waved about; waved in; waved up; weakened; wedged beneath; weighed; weighed down; went around; went down; went in; went into; went limp; went on; went out; went over; went straight; went to; went up; whacked; whacked against; wheeled around; whipped; whipped forward; whipped through; whipped up; whirled; wielded; willed; winded around; windmilled; withdrew; wobbled; wore; wore out; worked; wound around; wounded; wrapped; wrapped about; wrapped across; wrapped around; wrapped beneath; wrapped in; wrapped over; wrapped under; wrapped up; wrenched; wrestled; wrestled for; wriggled; wriggled in; wriggled under; yanked; yearned for.

Noun Phrases

action of the arm(s); aid of the arm(s); amputation of the arm(s); angle of the arm(s); appendage of the arm; archway of arms; area of the arm(s); array of arms; assistance of the arm(s); back(s) of the arm(s); bandage on the arm(s); bend of the arm(s); bit(s) of arm(s); blur of arms; bone(s) of the arm(s); bounce of the arm(s); brush of the arm(s); bundle of arms; circle of arms; clash of arms; clatter of arms; clutch of arms; comfort of the arms; contours of the arm(s); corner of the arm(s); couple of arms; cradle of the arm(s); crook of the arm(s); curve of the arm(s); cushion of the arm(s); drape of the arm(s); effort of the arm(s); end(s) of the arm(s); exercise of the arm(s); extension of the arm(s); extent of the arm(s); feel of arms; feel of the arm(s); flash of arms; flesh of the arm(s); flourish of the arm(s); flurry of arms; flutter of the arm(s); fold of the arm(s); force of the arm(s); forest of arms; front of the arm(s); fury of the arm(s); gesture of arms; gesture of the arm(s); grasp of the arm(s); grip of the arm(s); hair(s) of the arm(s); hardness of the arm(s); hold of the arm(s); inside(s) of the arm(s); jerk of the arm(s); jerking of the arm(s); joints of the arm(s); jumble of arms; kind of arm(s); length of the arm(s); lift of the arm(s); limit of the arm(s); line of the arm(s); loop of the arm(s); loss of the arm(s); lot of arms; meat of the arm(s); mess of arms; might of the arm(s); motion(s) of the arm(s); movement(s) of the arm(s); muscle(s) of the arm(s); nerves of the arm(s); number of arms; orgy of arms; outline of the arm(s); pair of arms; part(s) of the arm(s); pillow of the arm(s); pit(s) of the arm(s); portion(s) of the arm(s); position of the arm(s); possessiveness of the arms; power of the arm(s); press of the arm(s)s; pressure of the arm(s); protection of the arm(s); prowess of the arm(s); pull of the arm(s); pump of the arm(s); raising of the arm(s); range of the arm(s); reassurance of the arm(s); reflection of the arm(s); rest of the arm(s); rhythm of the arm(s); rows of arms; safety of the arms; salute of arms; sea of arms; set(s) of arms; shake of the arm(s); shape of the arm(s); shelter of the

12

arms; shield of the arm(s); show of arms; side of the arm(s); sight of the arm(s); silhouettes of arms; sinews of the arms; size of the arm(s); skin of the arm(s); smell of the arm(s); smoothness of the arm(s); snap of the arm(s); span of the arm(s); splendor of the arm(s); spread of the arm(s); spring of the arm(s); strength of the arm(s); stretch of the arm(s); stringiness of the arm(s); stroke of the arm(s); stump of the arm(s); support of the arm(s); sway of the arm(s); sweep of the arm(s); swing of the arm(s); swirl of the arm(s); swoop of the arm(s); tan of the arm(s); tangle of arms; tendons of the arm(s); thrust of the arm(s); top(s) of the arm(s); touch of the arm(s); twist of the arm(s); underbelly of the arm(s); underpart of the arm(s); underside(s) of the arm(s); use of the arm(s); veins of the arm(s); vigor of the arm(s); wall of arms; warmth of the arms; wave of the arm(s); weakness of the arm(s); web of arms; weight of the arm(s); whirl of arms; white of the arm(s); whiteness of the arm(s); wisps of arms; wrap of the arm(s).

USAGE EXAMPLES

A row of arms caught her after she was flung off the stage.

Henry *pinned the boy beneath his heavily-muscle arms*.

When Jack touched her, he couldn't help but admire the *smoothness of her creamy white arms*.

Nancy struggled for breathe as the tall guard *locked his lean arms around* her torso and began to squeeze.

The swimmer's *tanned arms gleamed* in the sun.

3

BACK

Adjectives in Alphabetical Order

A - L

able; abundant; aching; adequate; admirable; ailing; alternating; amber; ample; ancient; angled; angular; arched; arching; arcing; armored; arrogant; arthritic; artificial; asleep; attractive; average; awful; bad; bad-smelling; baggy; banged-up; bared; battered; beaten; beautiful; belted; bent; best; better; big; billowy; black; blackened; bleeding; bloated; bloody; blue; bluish; bold; bony; bouncing; bowed; braced-up; brawny; brilliant; bristly; broad; broad-shouldered; broken; bronzed; brown; browned; brownish; bruised; burly; burned/burnt; burning; busted; captivating; carved; ceaseless; cherry-red; clean; clear; cold; collective; colored; comfortable; comfy; compact; compressed; concave; condensed; confident; considerable; contorted; convex; cool; covered; cramped; crawling; creaking; creaky; creamy; crooked; crushing; cursed; curvaceous; curved; curvy; damn; damned; damp; dark; darkened; darn; dashing; defenseless; defensive; deformed; delicate; denim-covered; departing; developed; dirty; disabled; disappearing; distant; dominant; downy; dramatic; drooping; dropped; dry; eight-year-old; elastic; elegant; elevated; elongated; endless; enormous; entire; erect; ever-so-flexible; excellent; excessive; exhausted; exposed; extensive; failing; fair; falling; familiar; faraway; fast; fast-disappearing; fat; faulty; fear-stricken; feline; feminine; fetching; filthy; fine; fine-boned; flat; flawless; fleeing; fleshy; flexible; formidable; fragile; frail; freckled; freezing; frozen; full; furry; gargantuan; gaunt; gentle; giant; glazed; gleaming; glistening; glittering; glossy; goddamn; good; graceful; grand; greasy; great; growing; hairy; half-turned; halfway-decent; handsome; hanging; hard; hardened; healthy; heated; heavy; hidden; high; high-class; hot; huge; humble; humped; humpy; hunched; icy; ideal; immense; imposing; impossible; impressive; inclined; incredible; inner; innocent; invisible; involved; itchy; jerky; khaki-clad; kind; kindly; lace-clad; lacerated; lame; large; laughable; lazy; lean; leather-clad; level; little; long; loose; loosened; lovely; lower; lowered; lumbering; lunging; lush.

M - Y

magnificent; majestic; mangled; mangy; manly; masculine; massive; meager; mighty; modest; moist; molten; monstrous; moonlit; motionless; mud-splattered; muddy; muscled; muscular; mysterious; mystical; naked; narrow; natural; nice; noble; normal; obscure; old; olive; ordinary; outer; outrageous; overhanging; oversized; overstrained; pain-free; painful; pale; perfect; perpendicular; pink; plain; pliant; plump; poor; powerful; pretty; prickly; prominent; proud; puffing;

pulled; puny; purple; ramrod-straight; raw; reclining; red; relaxed; reliable; restless; rickety; rigid; rippling; rosy; rough; ruddy; rugged; s-shaped; salmon-colored; sandy; scabbed; scarlet; scarred; scraped; scrawny; sculpted; seductive; sensitive; sexy; shaded; shadowed; shadowy; shady; shapely; shaven; shimmering; shiny; shitless; short; shy; silken; silky; simmering; sinewy; sizzling; skinny; slack; slanted; sleek; slender; slick; slicked; sliding; slight; slim; slippery; sloped; sloping; small; smooth; snow-covered; snug; sodden; soft; soiled; solid; sopping-wet; sore; speckled; spindly; spiny; splendid; sprained; squared; squat; squatting; squishy; stable; steady; steaming; steely; sticky; stiff; stooped; stout; straight; strained; striking; striped; strong; struggling; stubborn; sturdy; substantial; sun-damaged; sunburned/sunburnt; sunken; super; superior; supple; supportive; sweat-dampened; sweat-soaked; sweaty; sweeping; sweet; t-shirted; tall; tan; tanned; tapering; tender; tense; tensed; terrible; thick; thin; throbbing; thrusting; tight; tilting; timid; tiny; tired; tough; tremendous; trim; turned; twisting; ugly; unguarded; uniformed; unlit; unprotected; unsuspecting; unzippered; upper; valiant; vanishing; vast; velvety; vertical; vulnerable; warm; weak; weary; weathered; weedy; well-defined; well-developed; well-muscled; wet; white; white-shirted; whole; wide; wonderful; wooden; woolly; wounded; wretched; wriggling; wrinkled; young; youthful.

Verbs and Phrasal Verbs in Alphabetical Order

A - L

ached; ached for; ached from; ached like; acted up; added; admired; adorned with; affected; agitated; aimed at; allowed; altered; amplified; appeared; appraised; arched; arched back; arched forward; arched over; ascended; assumed; astounded; attached to; attempted; attended; banged; bared; beat; beat with; became; began; began to; begged for; belonged to; bent; bent at; bent over; betrayed; bit; bled; blew out; blinded by; blocked; bobbed; bobbed along; boosted; bore; bothered; bound; bound up; bowed; braced; braced against; brandished; bristled; bristled with; broke; brushed; brushed against; bubbled with; bucked; buckled; bulged; burned with; burned/burnt; buzzed; came down; came out; came up; carried; cast; catapulted; caught; caused; ceased; changed; charged; charged with; chased by; checked; chilled; clapped; clasped; climbed; clipped on; clothed; clung to; clutched; clutched at; collapsed onto; colored; complained about; connected with; continued; contorted; contracted; cooled off; covered; covered by; covered in; covered with; cracked; cradled; cradled by; cramped; craned; crashed into; crawled on; crept up; crippled; crossed; crowned with; crunched; crushed; curled; curved; curved inwards; cut; damaged; danced; decorated with; deepened; demanded; depended on; depressed; descended; dipped; disappeared; disappeared around; disappeared into; dislodged; displayed; dragged; drained; drenched; drenched with; dressed; dressed in; drew up; dried; drooped; dropped; dropped onto; drove into; dug into; emphasized; enabled; enhanced; enjoyed; enriched; entered; erupted in; escaped; exhausted; exhausted by; exhausted from; expanded; exposed; extended; faced; faced down; faced forward; faded; faded away; faded into; fastened onto; fastened to; fell; fell on; fell onto; felt; felt cool; felt like; felt relieved; filled with; fitted; fixed; flared; flayed; fled; flew; flexed; flip over; flipped; flipped onto; floated; flushed; flushed with; followed; followed by; formed; found; framed; freed; gained; gave out; gleamed; glinted; glinted in; glistened; glistened in; glistened with; greased; grew; hammered; hauled up onto; healed; heaved; heaved up; held; helped; hesitated; hesitated on; hid; hit; huddled; hunched; hunched forward; hunched over; hung; hurt; hurt from; hurt like; ignited; imbued with; impressed; improved; indicated; injured; inscribed on; itched; jerked; jumped; kept; kissed; knocked against; knocked over; knotted; laid down on; laid on; lashed; leaned; leaned against; leaned forward; leaned on; leaned over; leaned up against; let out; lifted; lifted off; lifted onto; lined; lit by; lit up; loaded with; locked; locked up; looked; lowered.

M - W

marked with; massaged; matted with; met; missed; mounted; moved; muddied; needed; neglected; nestled against; nipped; numbed; obscured; occupied; offered; oozed; outfitted with; outlined; overcame; paddled on; pained; passed; pat; perched atop; pierced; pillowed against; pinched; pinned; pinned by; placed; planted; planted against; played with; pointed to; popped; positioned; presented; pressed; pressed against; pressed into; pressed to; pressed up against; prevented; pricked; prickled; prickled with; propelled; propped against; propped on; propped up; protected; proved; provided; pulled; pushed; quivered; quivered with; radiated heat; raised; raised up; ran; reached; rebounded; received; reclined; recoiled; recovered; reeked of; reflected; reflected in; registered; relaxed; relaxed against; remained; required; resembled; rested; rested against; retreated; returned; revealed; riddled with; rippled; rippled with; roasted in; rode on; rolled onto; rolled over on; rose; rubbed; sagged; sat; scarred; scraped; scraped against; scratched; seemed; seized up; set; set against; set up; settled; shaded; shaped; shattered; shed; shielded; shifted; shifted against; shivered; shone; shook; shot up; shoved; showed; shuddered; silhouetted; silhouetted against; skimmed; slammed; slammed into; slapped; slashed; slept on; slid against; slid along; slid down; slid off; slid on; slid up; slithered on; sloped; sloped downward; slumped; smarted; smelled; smelled like; snapped; snuggled against; soaked in; spasmed; spiked; spooned; spooned against; spread out; squeaked; stabbed; staggered; started; stayed; stiffened; stiffened up; stirred; stood; stood up; stooped; stopped; straightened; straightened up; strained; strapped onto; streaked with; strengthened; stretched; stretched out onto; struck; struggled; stuck; stumbled; stung; suffered; suggested; supported; supported against; supported by; suspended; sustained; swayed; sweat; swelled; swung; talked to; tanned; tapered; tapered down; tapped on; taunted; tended to; tensed; thickened; threatened to; threw out; throbbed; thrust; tightened; tinged with; tingled; tired; took; took on; took up; touched; traced; trailed; transformed; trembled; tried; tumbled onto; turned onto; twinged; twisted; twitched; uncovered; used to; vanished; vanished into; wanted; warmed; warmed up;

washed; went out; went tight; went up; widened; wiped; withdrew; wobbled; woke on; wore; worked; wounded; wriggled; writhed.

Noun Phrases

account of the back; ache in the back; action of the back; angle of the back; appearance of the back; arch of the back; area of the back; axis of the back; base of the back; beginning of the back; bone(s) of the back; bottom of the back; breadth of the back; bristles of the back; center of the back; color of the back; comfort of the back; condition of the back; contour of the back; contraction of the back; corners of the back; crack of the back; cradle of the back; crease of the back; curvature of the back; curve(s) of the back; deformity of the back; diameter of the back; direction of the back; edge of the back; elevation of the back; entirety of the back; examination of the back; expanse of the back; extension of the back; extent of the back; extremity of the back; face of the back; fall of the back; flat of the back; flatness of the back; flesh of the back; form of the back; function of the back; fur of the back; glimpse of the back; hair(s) of the back; heat of the back; height of the back; hold of the back; hollow of the back; hump of the back; hunch of the back; idling in the back; inclination of the back; injury of the back; inside of the back; inspection of the back; jab in the back; knee in the back; knot(s) in the back; length of the back; level of the back; ligaments of the back; line(s) of the back; look of the back; magnificence of the back; meadows of the back; meat of the back; middle of the back; midline of the back; midpoint of the back; midsection of the back; movement of the back; muscles of the back; musculature of the back; nerves of the back; outline of the back; pain in the back; part of the back; pinch of the back; plane of the back; portion of the back; position of the back; power of the back; pressure of the back; profile of the back; region of the back; remainder of the back; rest of the back; ridge of the back; rigidity of the back; rigidness of the back; rotation of the back; scar on the back; section of the back; shade of the back; shadows of the back; shape of the back; shelter of the back; shove in the back; side(s) of the back; sight of the back; silkiness of the back; size of the back; skin of the back; slope of the back; spine of the back; stiffening of the back; stiffness in the back; stillness of the back; stimulation of the back; sting of the back; straightness of the back; strain of the back; strength of the back; structure of the back; summit of the back; surface of the back; sway of the back; tendons of the back; tension in the back; thickness of the back; throbbing in the back; top of the back; turn of the back; veins of the back; view of the back; wall of the back; weakness of the back; weight of the back; width of the back; wound in the back.

USAGE EXAMPLES

Samantha watched on as her former friend *rubbed lotion on* Samantha's ex-husband's *bronzed back.*

Her *beautiful arching back* felt amazing beneath his hands.

My grandfather has suffered with a *bad back* since his youth.

All he could see in the distance was *the profile of a back positioned* in line with the setting sun.

The *shimmering back* of a dead naked man *bobbed* in the water.

4
BODY

Adjectives in Alphabetical Order

A - L

140-pound; 200-plus-pound; 45-year-old; able; abnormal; abused; acceptable; aching; achy; active; adaptable; addict-thin; adequate; adjacent; admirable; adolescent; advancing; age-stiffened; age-worn; aged; ageing/aging; agile; agitated; agreeable; ailing; alabaster-white; alien; amazing; ample; ancient; angular; animated; appealing; apprehensive; arched; aristocratic; armored; arthritic; artificial; assaulted; astral; Athena-like; athletic; attractive; average; awesome; awkward; bad; baggy; balanced; banged-up; banging; barbie-doll; bare; barrel-like; barrel-shaped; barren; bathing-suited; battered; battle-ready; bear-like; bearish; beaten; beauteous; beautiful; bedraggled; beefy; beloved; bent; best; better; better-built; big; big-boned; black; black-clad; black-shrouded; blackened; blanket-wrapped; bleeding; blemished; blissful; bloated; blocky; blood-caked; blood-soaked; blood-stained; bloodied; bloodless; bloody; bludgeoned; blue; blushing; bobbing; bony; bouncing; bountiful; bowed; boxy; boyish; brave; breastless; breathless; brilliant; broad; broad-shouldered; broken; bronzed; brown; brownish; bruised; brutalized; brutish; budding; buff; bulbous; bulky; bullet-ridden; bullet-riddled; buried; burly; burned/burnt; burning; burning-hot; busty; busy; butchered; calm; carnal; cartoon-flexible; cartoonish; chalk-white; changing; charred; chaste; child-like; childish; chilled; chiseled; chubby; chunky; circular; clad; classic; classical; clean; clenched; cloaked; cloned; clothed; clumsy; cold; colored; colorless; comatose; comfortable; compact; competent; compliant; compressed; concealed; conscious; considerable; contorted; contoured; convulsing; cool; corruptible; covered; cracking; cradling; cramped; creaking; creaky; creamy; crimson; crippled; critical; crooked; crouched; crouching; crushed; cumbersome; curled; curvaceous; curved; curvy; cute; damaged; damp; dangerous; dangling; dark; dark-skinned; dazzling; dead; decapitated; decayed; decaying; decent; declining; decomposed; decomposing; decrepit; deformed; delicate; delicious; demanding; dense; departing; depressed; desiccated; desirable; developing; diminutive; disabled; disappointing; disciplined; disemboweled; disfigured; disgusting; dismembered; distant; distinct; distinctive; distinguished; distorted; disturbing; divine; docile; doll-like; dominant; doughy; drained; dried; dried-up; drifting; drooping; drop-dead-gorgeous; drowned; dry; dummy; dumped; dumpy; dying; eager; earth-toned; earthly; earthy; efficient; eight-year-old; eighty-three-year-old; elastic; elderly; electrocuted; elegant; elemental; elevated; elongated; emaciated; embryonic; emerging; eminent; emotional; empty; energetic; enhanced; enlarged; enlightened; enormous; enthusiastic; enticing; entire; erotic;

eternal; ethereal; excellent; exceptional; excessive; excited; exhausted; exposed; expressive; exquisite; extended; extensive; exterior; external; extraordinary; extraterrestrial; extravagant; extreme; failing; fair; fairskinned; fake; fallen; false; faltering; familiar; fantastic; fashionable; fat; fat-filled; fatigued; fatty; feather-light; feeble; female; feminine; fetal; fever-hot; fierce; fine; fine-boned; firm; first-rate; fit; five-foot-ten-inch; flabby; flaccid; flailing; flat; flat-chested; flattened; flawed; flesh-and-blood; flesh-and-bone; fleshy; flexible; flexing; flirtatious; floating; floppy-legged; flourishing; flush; flying; folded; formidable; fragile; frail; free; freezing; fresh; frosty; frozen; full; full-breasted; full-length; fully-functioning; functional; funny; furred; furry; gallant; gangling; gangly; gaunt; generous; gentle; ghostly; giant; gigantic; girlish; glamorous; glistening; globular; glorious; glowing; gnarled; god-given; goddamn; gold-brown; gold-skinned; golden-brown; golden-hued; good; good-size; gorgeous; gory; graceful; graceless; grand; greased; great; great-looking; gross; grotesque; growing; grown-up; gutted; gym-built; hairless; hairy; half-clad; half-dead; half-naked; half-rotted; handless; handsome; hanging; hard; hard-muscled; hard-trained; hardworked; hardy; headless; healing; healthy; heavenly; heavy; heavy-boned; heavy-breasted; hefty; helpless; hidden; hideous; holy; horizontal; hormonal; hormone-driven; horrible; hostile; hot; hourglass-shaped; huddled; huge; hulking; human; human-looking; human-sized; humanoid; humble; humiliating; hunched; hungover; hungry; hunky; hurt; icy; ideal; idealized; identical; identifiable; idle; immaculate; immense; immobile; immobilized; immortal; immovable; immune; imperfect; imposing; impressive; improved; inactive; inadequate; incredible; inert; inferior; infirm; injured; inner; innocent; intact; intelligent; intense; interesting; internal; intriguing; invincible; inviting; irregular; jittery; jiving; juvenile; lacerated; languid; lanky; large; lean; leather-clad; leathery; leggy; legless; lethal; lifeless; light; lightly-clothed; lightweight; limber; limbless; limp; lissome; listless; lithe; little; lively; living; loathsome; lonely; long; long-abused; long-hipped; long-legged; looming; loose; loose-jointed; lousy; lovely; lower; lumbering; luminous; lumpy; lush; lusty; luxurious.

M - Y

magnetic; magnificent; male; malformed; malnourished; mangled; manly; mannish; marble-white; marvelous; masculine; massive; mature; meager; melted; middle-aged; mighty; military; military-style; minute; miserable; misshapen; missing; mobile; model-thin; moderate; modern; moist; monstrous; mortal; motionless; moving; mummified; murdered; muscle-bound; muscled; muscular; mutilated; mysterious; mystical; naked; narrow; nasty; natural; near-lifeless; near-nude; nearby; neighboring; nerveless; nervous; new; newborn; nice; nightgowned; normal; not-so-awful; nude; numb; nut-brown; obese; obscene; obscure; odd; odorous; offensive; oiled; oily; old; once-white; one-armed; opaque; ordinary; out-of-shape; outer; outlined; outrageous; outstanding; outstretched; oval; over-tall; overgrown; overlarge; overpowering; oversized; overweight; overwhelming; pain-free; pain-racked/pain-wracked; pale; pallid; palpitating; paltry; panicked; panting; paper-thin; paralyzed; paralyzing; passive;

pasty; paunchy; pear-shaped; pearl-colored; peculiar; perfect; perspiring; petite; phenomenal; pierced; pigmy; pillowy; pink; pinned; pitiful; plain; pleasing; pliant; plump; poor; portly; possessed; powerful; precious; pregnant; preteen; pretty; prime-condition; primitive; pristine; prized; proud; pubescent; pudgy; puffy; pulpy; pulsing; pumped-up; pungent-smelling; puny; pure; purified; purple; putrid; quick; quilt-covered; quivering; radiant; radiating; radioactive; rag-doll; rage-stiffened; raging; rail-thin; rangy; ravaged; ravenous; raw; rawboned; real; realistic; reasonable; reclining; red; red-robed; reed-thin; regular; rejuvenated; relaxed; remarkable; renewed; resolute; respectable; responsive; rested; restless; restrained; resurrected; revealed; rigid; ripe; ripped; rippling; rising; robe-draped; robotic; robust; rock-hard; rock-solid; roly-poly; Roman; rotten; rotting; rotund; rough; round; rubbed-raw; rubbery; rugged; ruined; sacred; sad; sandy; satin-clad; satisfactory; scaly; scarecrow-thin; scarlet; scarred; scented; scorched; scrawny; sculpted; seated; sedated; semi-conscious; senseless; sensitive; sensual; sensuous; sentient; serpentine; severed; sexual; sexualized; sexy; shadowlike; shaggy; shameful; shapeless; shapely; sharp; shattered; sheet-covered; shifting; shimmering; shining; shiny; shirtless; shivering; short; shredded; shriveled; shrouded; shuddering; sick; sickly; siesta-softened; silk-robed; silk-sheathed; silken; silky; similar; simple; sinewy; sinful; six-foot-tall; sixteen-year-old; sizable/sizeable; skeletal; skinny; skirted; slack; sleek; sleep-stiff; sleep-warmed; sleeping; slender; slender-boned; slick; slight; slim; slim-hipped; slimy; slippery; slow; sluggish; slumbering; slumping; small; small-breasted; smashing; smoldering; smooth; smothering; snagged; snaky; soaked; soapy; soft; soft-in-the-belly; soft-yet-solid; soiled; solid; sore; sore-covered; soulless; sparkling; sparse; spasming; spasmodic; special; spectacular; specter-like; spectral; spherical; spindly; spineless; spinning; spiritual; splayed; splendid; spongy; sprawled; sprawling; square; squarish; squat; squirming; stable; starvation-thin; starved; starving; static; stationary; stick-shaped; stick-thin; stiff; stiffened; still; still-breathing; still-living; still-slim; still-twitching; still-unconscious; still-unidentified; still-voluptuous; still-warm; still-wet; stocky; stooped; storklike; stout; straight; strange; strangled; strapping; stretched; stretched-out; stricken; striking; stringy; stringy-muscled; stripped; strong; struggling; stubborn; stubby; stuffed; stunted; sturdy; substantial; subtle; suited; sunburned/sunburnt; superb; superior; supersized; supple; supreme; surfer-dude; swaddled; swaggering; swathed; swaying; sweat-drenched; sweat-slick; sweat-soaked; sweating; sweaty; sweet; swift; swimmer-type; swinging; swollen; sylphlike; symmetrical; synthetic; tactile; tall; tan; tanned; tapering; tattooed; taut; tawny; teenage; teeny; ten-month-old; tender; tense; terrific; thick; thick-chested; thickset; thin; thinning; three-hundred-pound; thrusting; tight; tilting; timeless; timeworn; timid; tiny; tired; tomboyish; toned; too-lean; too-thin; topless; tortured; tough; towel-wrapped; towering; trained; travel-tired; trembling; tremendous; trim; tubby; tubular; tumbling; twiggy; twiglike; twirling; twisted; twisting; twitching; typical; ugly; ultra-feminine; ultra-slow; unattractive; unbathed; unbelievable; unbending; unclothed; unconscious; uncoordinated; uncorrupted; underexercised; underfed; undersized; underweight; undeveloped; undisciplined; undressed; ungainly; unhealthy;

unidentifiable; unidentified; uniform; uniformed; unique; unknown; unlovely; unmistakable; unmoving; unpleasant; unremarkable; unresponsive; unruly; unseen; unsensuous; unstable; unsteady; untanned; untouched; untrained; unusual; unwashed; unwieldy; unwilling; unworthy; unyielding; upper; upright; upside-down; used-up; useless; vampiric; vast; veal-white; vegetative; veiled; velvety; vertical; vigorous; vile; virgin; virginal; virile; visible; voluminous; voluptuous; vulnerable; waiting; warm; washed; wasted; waxy; weak; weakened; weary; wee; weightless; weighty; well-built; well-developed; well-maintained; well-muscled; well-nourished; well-proportioned; well-rested; well-shaped; well-toned; well-trimmed; wet; whalelike; whippet-thin; white; whole; wide; wild; willing; willowy; wind-whipped; wiry; wise; withered; wizened; womanly; wonderful; wondrous; wooden; work-wracked; worn-out; worst; worthless; worthy; wounded; wrapped; wrapped-up; wrecked; wretched; wriggling; wriggly; writhing; yielding; young; youthful.

Verbs and Phrasal Verbs in Alphabetical Order

A - C

abandoned; absorbed; accepted; acclimated; accompanied by; accustomed to; ached; ached all over; ached because of; ached from; ached with; acquainted with; acquired; acquired in; acted; acted on; acted upon; adapted; adapted to; added; adjusted; adjusted to; administered by; adopted; adorned with; affected by; afflicted by; agreed with; aimed at; aimed for; airlifted to; aligned with; allowed; alternated between; angled forward; angled toward; annoyed; anointed with; answered; appealed; appealed to; appeared; approached; arced; arced away; arced up; arched; arched back; arched backward; arched toward; arched up; arched upward; arose; arose from; arrived; arrived at; arrived in; assumed; assumed by; attached; attached to; attacked; attempted; attempted to; attracted; attuned; attuned to; awakened; awakened in; balanced; bared; barreled into; bashed; bashed into; bathed; bathed in; battered; beaded; beaded with; beat; beating; became; began; began to; begged for; behaved; belied; believed; belonged; belonged to; bent; bent at; bent back; bent down; bent forward; bent over; bent to; betrayed; bisected by; blanketed; bled; blighted with; blocked; bludgeoned; blushed; bobbed; boiled; boiled beneath; boiled inside; bore; bounced; bounced back; bounced off; bounced on; bounced up; bounced with; bound; bound by; bound together; bowed; braced; braced against; braced for; breathed; breathed in; breathed out; breezed past; bristled; bristled with; broke; broke out; broke through; brought back; brought from; brought in; brought into; brought near; brought to; bruised; bruised from; brushed; brushed against; brushed down; bucked; bucked in; bucked with; buckled; buckled with; built for; built like; built up; bulged; bulged beneath; bulged in; bulged with; bumped; bumped against; bumped into; bunched; bunched up; bundled; bundled in; buried; buried at; buried beneath; buried in; buried under; burned from; burned out; burned with; burned/burnt; burned with; burrowed; burrowed into; burst; burst with; butchered; buzzed; buzzed with; called for; called out; calmed; came back; came close; came closer; came down; came forward; came in; came into; came out; came to; came together; came up; camouflaged; camouflaged by; canted; canted forward; cared; cared for; careened; careened off; carried; carried away; carried by; carried in; carried off; carried on; carried out; carved; cast; cast out; catapulted; catapulted forward; catapulted off; caught; caught in; caught inside; caught on; caught up; caused; caused by; caved in; ceased; changed; charged with; chased; checked; chilled; chilled with; choked; choked on; chomped on; circled; clad in; claimed; clenched; clenched against; clenched tight; clenched with; climbed; climbed out; closed; closed against; closed in; closed in on; clothed; clothed in; clothed with; clung to; coated; coated in; coated with; coaxed; cocked; coiled; coiled into; coiled up; collapsed; collapsed from; collapsed in; collapsed to; collided; collided with; colored; combined with; comforted; commanded to; committed to; communicated; compared; compared to; compared with; compensated for; complained; composed of; comprised of; concealed; concealed in; conceded; concentrated; concentrated on; concerned; conjoined with; connected; connected to; connected with; considered; consisted of; constituted; consumed; consumed by; contained; continued; continued to; contorted; contorted in; contorted into; contracted; contracted in; contracted with; contrasted with; controlled; controlled by; converged; converged with; conveyed; convulsed; convulsed in; convulsed uncontrollably; convulsed with; cooked in; cooled; cooled under; counted on; covered; covered by; covered in; covered with; crackled; crackled with; cradled; cradled in; cramped; cramped up; crashed; crashed against; crashed down; crashed into; craved; crawled; creaked; creased at; created; cremated; cried; cried for; cried out; crossed; crossed over; crouched; crouched beside; crouched down; crowded; crowded around; crumbled; crumbled into; crumpled; crumpled on; crumpled over; crunched; crunched up; crushed; crusted; cuddled; cuddled up to; cupped; cupped in; cured; curled; curled around; curled back; curled in; curled into; curled like; curled on; curled over; curled under; curled up; curved; curved around; curved into; curved like; curved to; curved toward; cushioned; cut; cut down; cut in; cut into; cut off; cut up.

D - G

danced; dancing; dangled; dangled below; dangled from; dangled on; dangled out; dangled over; darkened; dealt with; decayed; decided; decided to; declared; declined; decorated; decorated with; defaced; defined by; defines; deflated; delighted; delighted in; demanded; denied; depended on; depended upon; deposited in; depressed; deprived of; derived from; descended; descended on; described; described by; described in; designed for; desired; destroyed; destroyed by; deteriorated; determined; determined to; developed; devoted; devoured; dictated; died; differed; differed from; differed in; digested; diminished; dimpled; dipped; dipped below; disappeared; disappeared behind; disappeared beneath; disappeared in; disappeared into; disappeared through; disappointed; disassociated with; discovered; discovered by; discovered in; disfigured; disfigured by; disguised; disintegrated; dismembered; disobeyed; displayed; disposed of; dissected; dissolved; dissolved in; divided; divided by;

23

divided into; dominated by; donated; doubled over; doused in; dragged; dragged in; dragged into; dragged through; drained; drained of; draped across; draped in; draped over; drenched; drenched in; dressed; dressed in; drew forward; drew inwards; drew out; drew up; dried; dried up; drifted; drifted away; drifted past; drifted toward; dripped; drooped; dropped; dropped from; dropped into; dropped on; dropped to; drove; dug up; dumped; dumped behind; dumped by; dwarfed; dwarfed by; eased; eaten away; eaten by; echoed; eclipsed; elected for; elected to; eluded; emanated from; embalmed; embarrassed; embedded in; emblazoned on; embraced; emerged; emerged from; emitted; emphasized; emphasized by; employed; emptied; emptied of; enabled; enacted; encased in; enclosed; enclosed by; enclosed in; encountered; endowed with; endured; enfolded in; engaged in; engulfed in; enjoyed; enlarged; enriched; enriched by; enslaved; entered; entitled to; entombed; entombed in; entrusted with; entwined; entwined with; enveloped; enveloped in; enwrapped in; equipped with; erect; erupted; erupted from; erupted in; erupted with; executed; exercised; exerted; exerted on; exhausted; exhausted by; exhausted with; exhibited; exhumed; existed; expanded; expected; expelled; experienced; expired; exploded; exploded into; exploded with; exposed; expressed; extended; exuded; faced; faced down; faced up; faded; faded into; faded out; failed; failed to; faltered; fascinated; fatigued; feasted; featured; fed; fed on; fell; fell across; fell apart; fell away; fell awkwardly; fell back; fell beneath; fell down; fell forward; fell from; fell hard; fell in; fell into; fell limply; fell on; fell out; fell over; fell still; fell to; fell under; felt; felt around; felt better; felt close; felt like; festered; filled; filled out; filled up; filled with; filtered; filtered out; firmed; firmed up; fit; fit for; fit into; fitted; fitted for; fitted with; fixed; fixed on; fizzed; fizzled out; flailed; flared; flared out; flashed; flashed by; flattened; flattened against; flattened by; flattened on; flattened out; fled; flew; flew across; flew backward; flew out; flew over; flew through; flexed; flexed underneath; flickered; flinched; flinched inward; flipped; flipped over; floated; floated down; floated downstream; floated near; floated past; floated through; floated to; floated up; flopped; flopped around; flopped back; flopped down; flopped into; flopped over; flowed; flowed with; flung; flung back; flung backward; flung forward; flung into; flung like; flung out; flushed; flushed with; folded; folded down; folded in; folded into; folded over; folded protectively; folded together; folded up; followed; forged; forgot; formed; fought; fought off; found; found at; found by; found in; found on; fractured; framed; framed by; freed from; froze; froze in; functioned; functioned at; furled up; fused to; gained; gasped; gasped for; gathered; gave; gave off; gave out; gave up; generated; gestured; glazed with; gleamed; gleamed with; glided; glinted; glinted in; glistened; glistened in; glistened with; glittered; glittered in; glowed; glowed from; glowed with; grabbed; graced; graced with; grasped; greeted; grew; grew increasingly; grew more; grew still; gripped; gushed; gyrated.

H - Q

hammered; hammered against; harbored; hardened; hardened by; hardened to; harmed; hauled; headed; headed for; headed to; headed toward; healed; heaped on; heaped with; heated; heaved; heaved with; held; held back; held down; held in; held together; held up; helped; helped with; hesitated; hid; hid away; hid beneath; hid by; highlighted; hit; hoisted; honed; honed by; honed from; hopped; housed; hovered; hovered over; huddled; huddled together; hugged; hunched; hunched down; hunched forward; hunched over; hunched up; hung; hung above; hung from; hurt; hurt from; hurtled; hurtled down; hurtled toward; identified; identified from; ignited; ignored; illuminated; illuminated by; immersed in; impacted; impeded; impelled by; impinged on; implied; impregnated with; included; increased; increased in; indicated; inflicted; inflicted upon; inserted into; insisted; insisted on; intended to; intensified; interacted with; interfered with; interred; interred in; intertwined; intertwined with; invited; involved; issued; itched; jammed; jarred; jarred against; jerked; jerked backward; jerked forward; jerked upright; jerked with; jiggled; jogged; joined; joined together; jolted; jolted from; jostled; jounced; juiced; jumped; jumped about; jumped from; jumped on; jumped with; jutted; jutted forward; kept; kicked; kissed; knelt; knew; knocked; knocked aside; knotted; knotted with; laced with; lacked; lagged; laid; laid across; laid along; laid in; laid on; laid out; laid upon; landed; landed heavily; landed on; languished; lashed; launched; leaned; leaned backward; leaned forward; leaned into; leaned on; leaned out; leaned over; leaned toward; leapt; leapt out; learned; led; led by; left; left behind; lengthened; lessened; let out; let up; levered; levered off; levitated; levitated above; lifted; lifted from; lifted up; lightened; liked; lined up; lit up; lived; lived to; loaded with; located in; locked up; lolled; lolled toward; longed for; looked; looked like; loomed; loosened; lost; loved; lowered; lowered into; lugged; lurched; lurched forward; lurked; made for; made of; maimed; maintained; managed; marched; marched on; marched past; marked; marked by; marked with; matched; measured; melted; melted against; melted away; melted into; merged; merged with; met; metabolized; might; mimed; mingled with; missed; mixed with; molded; molded into; molded to; morphed; morphed from; mounted; moved; moved away; moved back; moved by; moved close; moved forward; moved from; moved in; moved inside; moved into; moved like; moved off; moved on; moved through; moved to; moved toward; moved with; nailed into; nailed to; narrowed; needed; nestled; nestled against; nodded; normalized; noted; noticed; nourished; numbed; nuzzled; nuzzled up; obeyed; obscured; obscured by; obtained; occupied; occupied with; offered; oiled; opened; opened up; operated; opposed; ought; outfitted in; outlined; outlined against; outlined by; overcame; overflowed with; overtook; overwhelmed; packed; packed in; packed into; pained; painted; painted with; paralyzed; paralyzed with; parted; participated in; partook in; partook of; passed; passed away; passed down; passed through; peeked out; penetrated; perched; perched on; performed; perfumed; perished; persevered; persisted; perspired; persuaded; picked up; pierced; pierced by; pierced with; pinned; pinned to; pinned under; pitched; pitched about; pitched forward; pivoted; pivoted around; pivoted away; placed; placed at; placed in; placed on; placed upon; placed within; plastered with; played; pleated with; plowed through; plummeted; plummeted out; plunged; plunged down; plunged into; pocked; pocked with; pointed; pointed down;

poised; poised almost; poked; poked out; popped; popped out; positioned; possessed; possessed by; possessed of; prepared; prepared by; prepared for; preprogrammed for; presented; preserved; preserved in; presided over; pressed; pressed against; pressed into; pressed to; pressed up; pressed up against; pressed up to; prevented; prickled; prickled from; proceeded; proclaimed; produced; produced by; progressed; projected; prompted; propelled; propelled forward; propped up; protected; protected by; protested; protruded; protruded from; proved; provided; provided for; provided with; puffed up; pulled; pulled against; pulled down; pulled up; pulsated; pulsated with; pulsed; pulsed like; pummeled; pumped; punched; punished; purged; purged of; purpled; pushed; pushed back; pushed into; pushed through; put down; put in; put into; put on; quaked; quaked beneath; quaked in; quaked with; quickened; quieted; quit; quivered; quivered with.

R - S

raced; raced to; racked; racked by; racked with; radiated; radiated out; railed; railed against; railed at; raised; raised by; raised from; ran; ran through; rang; rang like; rang with; ravaged by; reabsorbed; reached; reacted; reacted to; reacted when; reacted with; readjusted; readjusted to; reappeared; reawakened; rebelled; rebelled against; rebounded; rebounded off; recalled; recalled with; received; recognized; recoiled; recoiled at; recovered; recovered from; reduced to; reeked; reeked like; reeked of; reeled; reeled backward; reflected; refused; refused to; regained; registered; regretted; rejected; relaxed; relaxed into; relaxed on; relaxed when; released; relied on; remained; remained still; remained upright; remembered; reminded; removed; removed by; removed from; rendered; repelled; repelled by; replaced; replaced by; replaced with; replenished; replenished by; replied; reported; represented; required; resembled; resisted; responded; responded by; responded to; responded with; rested; rested in; rested on; restricted; resumed; retained; retracted; retreated; retreated backward; retreated into; returned; returned to; revealed; reverted; reverted to; revolved; rewarded; reworked; ricocheted; ricocheted down; riddled with; ripened; ripened into; ripped apart; rippled; rippled like; rippled with; rivaled; riveted; robbed of; rocked; rocked against; rocked back; rocked forward; rode; rode in; rode on; roiled; rolled; rolled around; rolled down; rolled forward; rolled into; rolled off; rolled out; rolled over; rose; rose from; rose up; rotated; rotated to; rotted; rotted away; roused; roused by; ruled; rumbled; ruptured; rushed; rushed forward; rushed towards; rustled; rustled in; sagged; sagged against; sagged back; sagged forward; sailed; sailed down; sailed through; sailed up; sank; sank back; sank down; sank from; sank into; sat; sat up; sat upright; satisfied; scarred; scarred from; scooped up; scraped; scraped across; scraped against; scraped along; scraped up; screamed; screamed for; screwed up; sculpted; searched; seemed; seized up; selected for; sensed; sent; separated; separated from; served; served as; served up; set; set down; set in; set off; set out; settled; settled down; settled into; severed; severed from; shaped; shaped like; shared with; shattered; sheathed; sheathed in; shedded; sheened with; sheltered; shielded; shielded from; shifted; shifted beneath; shifted under;

shifted upward; shimmered; shimmered like; shivered; shivered with; shocked; shocked into; shone; shone beneath; shone like; shone with; shook; shook against; shook all over; shook when; shook with; shot back; shot forward; shot up; shot upward; shouted; shouted wordlessly; shoved; shoved backward; showed; showed through; showed up; shrank; shredded; shredded by; shriveled; shriveled up; shuddered; shuddered against; shuddered with; shuffled; shuffled forward; shut down; shut off; shut out; signaled; silhouetted against; silhouetted by; situated; situated at; situated in; skated; skated across; skewered; skidded; skidded across; skimmed; skimmed along; slackened; slackened against; slammed; slammed against; slammed back; slammed into; slanted; slanted over; slapped; slept; sliced; sliced up; sliced with; slid; slid across; slid along; slid down; slid into; slid sideways; slipped; slipped from; slipped into; slipped off; slipped onto; slipped through; slipped under; slithered; slithered across; slouched; slouched into; slowed; slowed down; slumped; slumped across; slumped against; slumped down; slumped forward; slumped over; slung over; smashed; smashed into; smashed through; smeared; smeared with; smelled; smelled of; smoked; smoothed over; smothered; snapped; snapped around; snapped to; snuggled; soaked; soaked in; soared; soared upward; softened; somersaulted; sought; sounded; sounded like; spasmed; spent; splashed; splayed; split apart; spoke of; spooned; sported; spouted; sprang; sprang to; sprawled; sprawled across; sprawled against; sprawled beside; sprawled out; spread; spread out; spread over; spun; spun around; spun toward; squatted; squeezed; squirmed; stabilized; staggered; staggered down; staggered forward; stained with; stalked; started; started out; started to; startled; starved; stayed; steadied; steamed; steeled; steeled for; steeped in; stepped; stepped out; stiffened; stilled; stirred; stood; stood in; stood out; stood straight; stood up; stood upright; stooped; stopped; stowed; straddled; straightened; strained; strained against; strained with; strapped to; streaked with; streamed past; stressed; stretched; stretched across; stretched alongside; stretched on; stretched out; stripped; strode; stroked; struck; struggled; struggled for; struggled with; stuck in; stuck out; stuck to; stuffed; stuffed into; stuffed with; stumbled; stumped; stung; stunk; stunk up; subjected to; submerged; submitted; succeeded in; succumbed; succumbed to; suffered; suggested; supplied; supported; supported by; supported on; surfaced; surfaced from; surfed; surged; surged toward; surged with; surprised; surrendered; surrounded; surrounded by; survived; suspended; suspended above; suspended by; suspended from; suspended in; swaddled in; swam; swamped with; swathed in; swayed; swayed back; swayed in; swayed to; swayed with; sweat; swelled; swelled up; swelled with; swept past; swung; swung from; symbolized.

T - Y

tackled; tangled; tangled in; tanned; tapered; tapered to; tattooed; teased; tended to; tended toward; tensed; tensed beneath; tensed up; tensed with; testified to; thawed; thickened; thickened with; thrashed; thrashed around; threw; threw back; threw forward; threw off; threw onto; threw sideways; thrilled; thrilled at; throbbed; throbbed against; throbbed for; throbbed to; throbbed with; thrust;

thudded; thudded onto; thumped; thumped into; thunked; thunked off; tickled; tied; tied down; tied up; tied with; tightened; tightened with; tilted; tilted at; tilted forward; tilted into; tilted up; tingled; tingled all over; tingled from; tingled with; tipped; tipped forward; tipped sideways; tired; tired of; tobogganed down; told; toned; took; took on; took over; took up; toppled; toppled back; toppled backwards; toppled onto; toppled out; toppled over; toppled sideways; toppled to; tore apart; tormented; tossed; tossed beneath; tossed into; touched; traced; trailed; trained; transformed; transformed into; trapped; trapped beneath; trapped inside; trapped underneath; traveled; traveled downstream; treated; treated with; trembled; trembled in; trembled with; tried to; triggered; trimmed; tripped; tripped on; troubled; tucked into; tumbled; tumbled down; tumbled downward; tumbled from; tumbled out; tumbled past; tumbled through; turned; turned away; turned into; turned over; turned sideways; turned to; turned toward; twirled; twisted; twisted sideways; twisted toward; twitched; unbalanced; uncoiled; underwent; unfolded; unhinged; united; united with; unrolled; upstaged; urged; used; used for; used to; used up; vanished; vanished in; vanished into; vanished under; varied; varied in; vaulted; vaulted off; vibrated; vibrated like; vibrated with; violated; waddled; waddled down; wagged; waited; waited for; waited on; wanted; warmed; warmed to; warned; washed; washed ashore; washed down; washed in; washed into; washed up; washed with; wasted away; wavered; weakened; weakened by; wearied; weaved; weaved through; wedged against; wedged between; wedged in; weighed; weighed down; weighted with; welcomed; went out; went still; went through; went under; went up; wet; wet with; whipped; whipped against; whipped around; whirled; wiggled; willed; willed to; winded; withered; wobbled; woke; woke up; wore; wore out; worked; worked against; worked in; worried; wound through; wound up; wove; wracked; wracked by; wracked with; wrapped; wrapped around; wrapped in; wrapped up; wrapped with; wrecked; wrecked with; wrenched; wriggled; wriggled from; writhed; yearned; yearned for; yearned to; yielded; yielded to.

Noun Phrases

A - I

ability of the body; abnormality of the body; abuse of the body; acceptance of the body; action(s) of the body; activities of the body; acts of the body; adaptation of the body; adjustment of the body; adornment of the body; affection of the body; affliction(s) of the body; age of the body; agency of the body; agility of the body; agitation of the body; agony of the body; aid of the body; ailments of the body; alignment of the body; alteration of the body; amount of body; anatomy of the body; angle of the body; appearance of the body; appendages of the body; appetites of the body; area(s) of the body; arrangement of the body; arteries of the body; articulation of the body; ashes of the body; aspect(s) of the body; atoms of the body; attraction of the body; attributes of the body; awareness of the body; axis of the body; back of the body; balance of the body; base of the body; beauty of the body; birth of the body; bits of the body; blood of the body; bones of the body; borders of the body; boundaries of the body; breadth of the body; breakdown of the body; building of the body; bulk of the body; burden of the body; burial of the body; by-product of the body; capacity of the body; care of the body; carriage of the body; cavities of the body; cells of the body; center of the body; changes of the body; character of the body; characteristics of the body; chemistry of the body; circulation of the body; circumference of the body; cleanliness of the body; cleansing of the body; clothing of the body; coldness of the body; collapse of the body; color of the body; comfort of the body; command of the body; comparison of the body; complexity of the body; components of the body; composition of the body; compression of the body; concealment of the body; concentration of the body; conception of the body; condition of the body; configuration of the body; consciousness of the body; consecration of the body; consent of the body; consideration of the body; constituents of the body; constitution of the body; construction of the body; contact of the body; contents of the body; contortion(s) of the body; contour(s) of the body; contraction(s) of the body; control of the body; coordination of the body; core of the body; corners of the body; corruption of the body; creation of the body; cremation of the body; crudeness of the body; cultivation of the body; cure of the body; curvature of the body; curve(s) of the body; death of the body; decay of the body; decomposition of the body; decoration of the body; defects of the body; defenses of the body; deformation of the body; deformity of the body; degradation of the body; dehydration of the body; delights of the body; demands of the body; denial of the body; density of the body; dependence of the body; depletion of the body; depths of the body; description of the body; design of the body; desire(s) of the body; destruction of the body; details of the body; deterioration of the body; development of the body; diameter of the body; dimension(s) of the body; direction of the body; disability of the body; disappearance of the body; discipline of the body; discomfort of the body; discovery of the body; disease(s) of the body; disintegration of the body; dismemberment of the body; disorder(s) of the body; display of the body; disposal of the body; dissection of the body; economy of the body; edge(s) of the body; edification of the body; effect(s) of the body; efficiency of the body; effort(s) of the body; elasticity of the body; electricity of the body; elements of the body; elevation of the body; elongation of the body; emaciation of the body; emotion(s) of the body; endowments of the body; energy of the body; entropy of the body; equilibrium of the body; essence of the body; evaluation of the body; evolution of the body; examination of the body; excavation of the body; excellence of the body; excretions of the body; exercise of the body; exertion of the body; exhaustion of the body; exhumation of the body; existence of the body; expansion of the body; experience(s) of the body; exposure of the body; expression of the body; extension(s) of the body; extent of the body; extremities of the body; eyes of the body; face of the body; faculties of the body; failure of the body; fate of the body; fatigue of the body; feature(s) of the body; feebleness of body; feeding of the body; feel of the body; feelings of the body; feet of the body; fibers of the body; figure of the body;

firmness of body; fitness of body; flesh of the body; flexibility of the body; fluids of the body; folds of the body; food of the body; force of the body; form of the body; formation of the body; foundation of the body; fracture(s) of the body; fragment(s) of the body; frailty of the body; frame of the body; freedom of the body; front of the body; fullness of body; function(s) of the body; garment of the body; geometry of the body; gesture(s) of the body; glands of the body; glimpse of the body; glorification of the body; grace of the body; gravity of the body; growth of the body; gyration of the body; habits of the body; hair of the body; hairs of the body; half of the body; hands of the body; happiness of the body; hardiness of body; hardness of the body; harmony of the body; hatred of the body; head of the body; healing of the body; health of the body; heart of the body; heat of the body; heaviness of the body; height of the body; hunger of the body; identification of the body; identity of the body; illness of the body; ills of the body; image of the body; immortality of the body; imperfections of the body; importance of the body; impotence of the body; impulses of the body; impurities of the body; inability of the body; inactivity of the body; inclinations of the body; independence of the body; inertia of the body; infection of the body; infirmity of the body; inflammation of the body; influence of the body; inside of the body; inspection of the body; instincts of the body; integrity of the body; intelligence of the body; interaction of the body; involvement of the body; issues of the body.

J - Z

jerk of the body; joints of the body; juices of the body; kind of body; labor(s) of the body; language of the body; layers of the body; leanness of the body; length of the body; level of the body; life of the body; lifting of the body; ligaments of the body; lightness of the body; limberness of body; limbs of the body; limitations of the body; limits of the body; line(s) of the body; liquids of the body; litheness of the body; location of the body; loss of the body; lurch of the body; lust of the body; maintenance of the body; majority of the body; maladies of the body; manipulation of the body; margins of the body; mastery of the body; material of the body; materiality of the body; materials of the body; matters of the body; meal of the body; measure of the body; measurement(s) of the body; mechanics of the body; mechanisms of the body; memories of the body; metabolism of the body; middle of the body; midline of the body; mind of the body; modesty of the body; modification(s) of the body; moisture of the body; molecules of the body; momentum of the body; mortality of the body; motion(s) of the body; mouth of the body; movement(s) of the body; muscles of the body; musculature of the body; mutilation of the body; nature of the body; necessities of the body; needs of the body; neglect of the body; nerves of the body; nourishment of the body; nuances of the body; nutrition of the body; objectification of the body; observation of the body; odor of the body; oneness of body; openings of the body; operation(s) of the body; organ(s) of the body; organisms of the body; orientation of the body; orifices of the body; origin of the body; ornaments of the body; outline(s) of the body; pain(s) of the body; pangs of the body; paralysis of the body; part(s) of the body; passions of the body;

passivity of the body; penetration of the body; perceptions of the body; perfection of the body; performance of the body; physicality of the body; physiology of the body; piece(s) of the body; placement of the body; planes of the body; pleasure(s) of the body; points of the body; poise of the body; pores of the body; portion(s) of the body; position of the body; positioning of the body; possession of the body; posture of the body; pounding of the body; power of the body; practices of the body; preparation of the body; presence of the body; presentation of the body; preservation of the body; pressure of the body; principles of the body; problem(s) of the body; processes of the body; product(s) of the body; proportions of the body; protection of the body; proteins of the body; punishment of the body; purification of the body; purity of the body; qualities of the body; reaction(s) of the body; recesses of the body; recovery of the body; reddening of the body; regions of the body; regulation of the body; rejection of the body; relationship of the body; relaxation of the body; release of the body; relief of the body; remainder of the body; removal of the body; representations of the body; requirements of the body; reserves of the body; resistance of the body; resources of the body; respect of the body; response(s) of the body; rest of the body; restlessness of the body; resurrection of the body; rhythm(s) of the body; rigidity of the body; rising of the body; rites of the body; ritual of the body; robustness of the body; rotation of the body; rotundity of the body; rupture of the body; sacrifice of the body; safety of the body; salvation of the body; sanctification of the body; sanctity of the body; scent of the body; scrutiny of the body; search of the body; secretions of the body; secrets of the body; section(s) of the body; segment(s) of the body; sensation(s) of the body; senses of the body; sensibility of the body; serenity of the body; shadow of the body; shape of the body; sheen of the body; sickness of the body; side(s) of the body; sight of the body; sinews of the body; sins of the body; size of the body; skeleton of the body; skin of the body; slumber of the body; smell of the body; softness of the body; solidity of the body; sort of body; soul of the body; sounds of the body; speed of the body; spirit of the body; stability of the body; state of the body; stature of the body; stiffness of the body; stillness of the body; stimulation of the body; straining of the body; strength of the body; structure of the body; study of the body; substances of the body; surface(s) of the body; surrender of the body; survival of the body; suspension of the body; sustenance of the body; swing of the body; symmetry of the body; system of the body; taste of the body; techniques of the body; temper of the body; temperament of the body; temperature of the body; temple of the body; temptation of the body; tension of the body; termination of the body; texture(s) of the body; thickness of the body; thinness of the body; thrill of the body; thud of the body; thump of the body; tissues of the body; tone of the body; torment of the body; torture of the body; traces of the body; training of the body; traits of the body; tranquility of the body; transcendence of the body; transformation of the body; transport of the body; treatment of the body; troubles of the body; trunk of the body; twist of the body; type of body; underside of the body; undulations of the body; uneasiness of the body; union of the body; unit of the body; unity of the body; veins of the body; velocity of the body; vessel of the body; vibration(s) of the body; view of the body; vigor of the body; violation of the body; virtue of the body; vision of the body; vitality of the body; voice of the body; volume of the body; vulnerability of the body; wall of the body; warmth of the body; water of the body; weakness of the body; weariness of the body; weight of the body; welfare of the body; whiff of the body; wholeness of body; width of the body; wisdom of the body; work of the body; workings of the body; worship of the body; wounds of the body; zones of the body.

USAGE EXAMPLES

Her *lithe body arched backward* before springing back into an upright position.

The shabby-looking girl's *body was pallid and reed-thin.*

His *hulking body looked like* something out of a comic book.

The police *discovered* Jane's *decomposing body* buried in a shallow grave behind her barn.

Gary's *muscular body glinted in* the blue moonlight.

5

BOTTOM / BUTT

Adjectives in Alphabetical Order

aching; aging; ample; ancient; artificial; average; bad; bare; beautiful; beefy; bent-over; best; better; big; black; black-polyester-clad; blood-crusted; blue; blue-black; bony; bouncing; broad; brown; bruised; bulbous; bulging; burned; chapped; clean; cold; common; cool; crushed; curved; curvy; cute; damp; dark; dense; diapered; dirty; dried; drum-tight; dry; enormous; entire; excellent; extensive; fair; fake; fallen; false; fat; fifty-six-year-old; fine; fine-looking; firm; firm-looking; fit; flabby; flat; flattened; flattish; flexible; foul; frozen; full; funky; furry; generous; ghostly; giant; good; great; hairy; hard; heart-shaped; heated; heavy; high; hot; huge; incredible; indented; inner; irregular; large; lazy; leaky; little; lovely; low; low-hanging; lower; lush; mammoth; massive; middle-aged; minimum; miniskirted; minuscule; moderate; moist; mud-soiled; muddy; muscular; mushy; mythical; naked; narrow; natural; nice; nominal; non-existent; normal; obvious; old; oozy; open; ordinary; otherwise-smooth; outer; oversized; padded; painted; pale; pantied; pear-shaped; perfect; perky; pert; pinchable; pink; plain; plump; poor; prodigious; puffy; quivering; rancorous; red; regular; rigid; ripe; rising; rosy; rotten; rough; round; rounded; rugged; rumpled; sandy; scalded; scandalous; scraped; scratched; sensitive; shaky; shapely; shimmering; shiny; significant; skinny; slick; slight; slim; slimy; slippery; sloping; smacked; small; smoldering; smooth; soft; soggy; solid; sopping wet; sore; special; spongy; square; squashed; stable; stained; standard; steadfast; steady; striking; strong; submerged; sweaty; sweet; taut; teenage; terrible; thick; thin; tight; tiny; too-white; touched; treacherous; tremendous; typical; ugly; ultimate; uneven; unfortunate; upturned; usual; vast; visible; voluptuous; waddling; warm; wet; white; whole; wide; wobbly; wounded; wiggling.

Verbs and Phrasal Verbs in Alphabetical Order

accentuated; accentuated by; allowed; appeared; approached; attached to; backed out; ballooned; became; began; belonged to; bent; blew; bore; bounced; bounced off; bracketed by; bristled; bristled with; broke wind; brought up; brushed; bucked; bucked back; built up; bumped; bunked; buried; burned; caked with; caked in; came out; came down; came up; carried; cast; caught; caused; cleaned; climbed; climbed up; closed; clung to; composed of; connected; connected with; considered; consisted of; contained; continued; covered; covered by; covered with; crept up; crossed; cut; dampened; dangled; depressed; depressed into; disappeared; dragged; dressed; drew up; dropped; dropped down; drove; dumped; emerged; examined; exposed; extended; faced; farted; fell; felt; filled out; filled with; fit; fitted with; fixed; flashed; flecked with; floated; flooded with; flowed; formed; found; framed; framed by; gave off; got close; gleamed; gleamed with; glinted; grated against; grew; gyrated; hauled; headed; held; helped; hissed; hit; humped; hung; hung out; hurt; hurt from; inched up; increased; indicated; insulated; jabbed; jammed; jammed in; jutted; jutted out; kept; kicked; knocked; laid on; left; left with; let; lifted; lifted off; lined; lined with; looked; mounted; moved; needed; opened; parked; parked in; passed; pasted to; paved; perched; perched on; pierced with; pinched; placed; planted; planted in; played with; poked; poured; presented; pressed; prevented; produced; propped on; protruded; protruded from; proved; provided; pushed; pushed into; raised; raised in; ran; reached; reached down; reamed; reamed out; received; registered; remained; removed from; represented; required; rested; rested in; rested on; rippled; rippled with; rode; rode up; rolled; rolled over; rolled onto; rose; rounded out; rubbed; sagged; sagged down; sank; scraped; scratched; scratched at; seemed; set; settled; settled into; shaped like; shone; shook; shook when; showed; slicked; slid; slid out; sloped; smacked; snapped; sniffed; soaked; soaked in; farted; spiked up; squeezed; squeezed into; squirmed; squirmed against; stared at; stirred; stood; stopped; struggled; stuck to; stuck out; stuck up; suffered; supported; surrounded by; suspended; swayed; swayed in; swelled; swelled out; swung; swung down; swooshed; swooshed about; swung around; tapped; tended to; thumped; thumped against; took; tore through; touched; traced; traveled up; turned; used to; waited; waited on; woke up; walked by; wanted; warmed; watched; waved; wore; weighed; welded to; welded together; went up; went down; whipped; wiggled; wiggled when; worked.

Noun Phrases

angle of the bottom/butt; appearance of the bottom/butt; area of the bottom/butt; back of the bottom/butt; base of the bottom/butt; breadth of the bottom/butt; center of the bottom/butt; character of the bottom/butt; cheek(s) of the bottom/butt; circumference of the bottom/butt; cleft of the bottom/butt; color of the bottom/butt; condition of the bottom/butt; contour(s) of the bottom/butt; corner of the bottom/butt; crack of the bottom/butt; curvature of the bottom/butt; curve(s) of the bottom/butt; depression of the bottom/butt; depth of the bottom/butt; diameter of the bottom/butt; dimensions of the bottom/butt; edge(s) of the bottom/butt; elevation of the bottom/butt; form of the bottom/butt; formation of the bottom/butt; fullness of the bottom/butt; globes of the bottom/butt; half of the bottom/butt; height of the bottom/butt; hold of the bottom/butt; imprint of the bottom/butt; irregularities of the bottom/butt; length of the bottom/butt; level of the bottom/butt; line(s) of the bottom/butt; motion of the bottom/butt; movement of the bottom/butt; muck of the bottom/butt; nature of the bottom/butt; pain of the bottom/butt; part of the bottom/butt; piece of the bottom/butt; portion of the bottom/butt; position of the bottom/butt; profile of the bottom/butt; proportion of the bottom/butt; rest of the bottom/butt; section of the bottom/butt; side(s) of the bottom/butt; sight of the bottom/butt; size of the bottom/butt; skin of the bottom/butt; slope of the bottom/butt; surface of the bottom/butt; thickness of the bottom/butt; top of the bottom/butt; underside of the bottom/butt; unevenness of the bottom/butt; view of the bottom/butt; waggle of the bottom/butt; weight of the bottom/butt; width of the bottom/butt.

USAGE EXAMPLES

Her classmates laughed as Amanda's *ample bottom struggled to squeeze into* her chair.

They all *slid on their butts* as soon as their feet hit the ice.

Ken *smacked my bottom* playfully outside the boss's office.

When she looked down she noticed that Roger had left an *imprint of his huge bottom* in the sand.

My 3-year-old son *exposed his muddy butt* to the little girl next door.

6
CHEEK(S)

Adjectives in Alphabetical Order

A - M

abused; acne-scarred; aged; ample; angled; angry; animated; apricot-like; ashen; ashy; baby-doll; baby-pink; babyish; baggy; ballooned; bare; bearded; beardless; beautiful; beet-red; big; black; blackened; blanched; blank; bleached; bleak; bleeding; blessed; blistered; bloated; bloodied; bloodstained; bloody; blotchy; blue; bluish; blushing; bold; bonny; bony; boyish; brazen; bright; brilliant; bristled; bristly; broad; bronzed; brown; bruised; bulging; burned / burnt; burning; bursting; busy; cadaverous; calm; careworn; carmine; caved-in; cavernous; charming; cheerful; cherubic; childhood-rounded; childish; chiseled; chubby; cinnamon-brown; cinnamon-colored; clean; clean-shaven; clear; close-shaven; cloudy; coarse; cold; collapsed; colorless; colossal; comely; concave; cool; copper-colored; corpse-like; courtly; craggy; creamy; creased; crimson; crumpled; curved; dainty; damp; dark; delicate; delicious; dewy; dimpled; dirty; domed; doughy; downy; drooping; dry; dusky; dusty; elevated; emaciated; ever-blushing; exposed; fair; fat; fatty; feminine; fever-hollowed; fevered; feverish; fiery; flabby; flaccid; flaming; flat; fleshless; fleshy; florid; floury; flushed; fragrant; freckled; freezing; fresh; frigid; frozen; full; furrowed; fuzzy; gaunt; gentle; ghostly; ginger; girlish; glabrous; glassy; glowing; gray; gray-stubbled; great; grimy; grinning; grizzled; haggard; hairless; hairy; half-shaven; happy; hard; healed; healthy; heated; heavy; hectic; high; high-boned; hoary; hollow; hot; huge; humid; hungry; icy; immense; inflamed; inflated; jolly; jovial; jowly; languid; large; lean; leathered; leathery; leering; left; lilac-scented; little; lively; livid; lovely; lumpy; made-up; maiden; manly; maroon; masculine; massive; meager; milky; misshapen; modest; moist; moon-shaped; motherly; mottled; mournful; muddy; muscleless.

N - Y

narrow; noble; numb; old; olive; olive-skinned; once-ruddy; opposite; other; oval; oversize; padded; painted; pale; pallid; palpitant; papery; passion-red; pasty; peachy; perfect; perfumed; pierced; pinched; pink; pink-flushed; pink-tinged; pinkish; pitted; plump; pocked; pockmarked; polished; pouchy; powder-stippled; powdered; powdery; pretty; prominent; proud; pudgy; puffed; puffed-out; puffed-up; puffing; puffy; purple; purple-scarred; quivering; radiant; radishy; rage-darkened; rain-wet; ravaged; raw; red; red-veined; reddened; reddening; reddish; reddish-purple; rich; right; rose-colored; roseate; roseless; rosy; rosy-red; rotund; rouged; rough; round; rounded; roundish; rubbery; rubicund; ruddled; ruddy; rugged; sad; sagging; salient; sallow; salty; sandy;

sanguine; satiny; scarified; scarlet; scarred; scented; scratched; scratchy; sculpted; sea-drenched; seamed; shaggy; shapely; sharp; shaved; shaven; sheer; shining; shiny; shrunken; sickly; silky; slack; slapped; sleep-flushed; small; smiling; smooth; smooth-shaven; smudged; sodden; soft; sorrowful; splotchy; spotted; spray-wet; stained; starved; stinging; stretched; stubble-covered; stubbled; stubbly; sucked-in; sullen; summer-stained; sun-kissed; sun-stained; sunburned / sunburnt; sunken; sunny; super-sized; supple; swarthy; sweaty; sweet; swelling; swollen; tanned; tartar; taut; tawny; tear-crusted; tear-dampened; tear-stained; tear-streaked; tear-wet; tearful; teary; tender; thick; thin; thoughtful; tingling; tinted; tiny; tired; tissue-paper; tropic; twitching; unblemished; unblushing; unhealthy; unkissed; unpainted; unpowdered; unshaven; unwrinkled; upper; varicose; veined; velvety; virgin; wan; waning; warm; watery; waxen; waxy; weather-beaten; weathered; weeping; well-shaved; well-tanned; wet; whiskered; white; whole; wide; wilting; wind-chapped; wind-reddened; windblown; windburned; withered; wizened; woolly; wrinkled; young; youthful.

Verbs and Phrasal Verbs in Alphabetical Order

A - L

accentuated; accentuated by; ached; ached from; added; added to; adorned; alighted; appeared; attested; balanced; balanced on; ballooned; ballooned out; bandaged; bathed; bathed in; became creased; became flushed; belied; bestowed by; betrayed; bit; blanched; blanched of; blazed; bleached; bleached of; blended; blew out; bloomed; bloomed with; blushed; bore; bounced; branded with; brightened; brightened by; brightened with; bristled; bruised; brushed; brushed against; bulged; bulged out; bunched; burned; captured; cast; caught; caused; caved; caved in; changed; chapped by; clashed with; cleaned; collapsed; colored; contrasted; covered; covered by/with; cracked; cradled; cradled in; creased; crimsoned; crinkled; crushed; cupped; curved; curved in; cut; dampened; dappled with; darkened; deepened; deflated; depicted; descended; dimpled; discolored; discolored by; disguised by; dotted with; drained; drained of; dripped onto; drooped; dropped; dug into; dyed (color); eased; emphasized; enlivened; exploded with; faded; fell; felt; felt pinched; filled out; filled with; flamed; flamed with; flapped; flared; flashed; flattened; flecked with; flexed; flicked; flicked up; flooded with; flushed; flushed with; folded in; framed; freckled; furrowed; gleamed; gleamed against; glistened; glittered; glowed; grew; grew wan; grizzled with; heated; heightened; held; hit; hollowed; hung; hung down; hurt; imprinted with; inflamed; inflated; inflated with; intensified; jerked back; jiggled; jumped; kindled; kissed; laid against; laid on; landed on; laughed; leaned against; leaned on; lifted; lightened; lit up / lighted up; looked; looked drawn; lost their color.

marked with; mashed; mashed against; melted away; melted into; moved; moved in; nestled; offered; overwhelmed; painted; painted with; paled; paled with; pillowed in; pinched; pinked; pinkened; pitted with; planted on; played with; plumped; plumped up; popped; popped in and out; possessed; pressed; pressed against; pressed into; protruded; puffed; puffed out; puffed up; pulsated; pulsed; pulsed with; pushed; pushed against; quivered; raised; raised in; reclined; recovered; reddened; reflected; relaxed; remained; removed from; replenished; reposed; resembled; rested; rested against; rested on; retained; revived; rippled; rippled in; rivaled; rose; rose up; rose with; rouged; rounded; rubbed; sagged; sank; scraped; scratched; scrubbed; scrunched; seamed; shadowed by; shimmered; shone; showed; slapped; slid; slid across; sloped; slumped; smarted; smashed against; smashed into; smeared; smeared with; smiled; smudged; smudged with; softened; spasmed; splotched with; spread; spread with; stained; stained with; stirred; stood out; strained; streaked; streaked with; stretched; struck; stuck to; studded with; stuffed; stung; sucked in; suffused with; sunk; sweated; swelled; swept; swept in; tensed; testified to; thinned; thinned with; tightened; tinged; tinged with; tingled; touched; trembled; trembled with; turned; twisted; twitched; vibrated; waned; warmed; warmed by; warmed from; warmed with; were too; were tore; wet; wet against; wet with; widened; widened in a smile; wobbled.

Noun Phrases

ball of the cheek(s); blush of the cheek(s); bones of the cheek(s); center of the cheek(s); color of the cheek(s); contour(s) of the cheek(s); curve of the cheek(s); dip of the cheek(s); edge of the cheek(s); flesh of the cheek(s); folds of the cheek(s); furrows of the cheek(s); glow of the cheek(s); hollows of the cheek(s); line(s) of the cheek(s); lining of the cheek(s); outline(s) of the cheek(s); pair of cheeks; pallor of the cheek(s); plane(s) of the cheek(s); prominence of the cheek(s); redness of the cheek(s); rise of the cheek(s); side(s) of the cheek(s); sinking in of the cheek(s); skin of the cheek(s); slope of the cheek(s); stroke of the cheek; surface of the cheek(s); thickness of the cheek(s); tightening of the cheek(s).

USAGE EXAMPLES

Her father's *jowly cheeks ballooned out* whenever he ate mashed potatoes.

Georgina softly *rubbed* the newborn's *cherubic cheeks*.

Her *cheeks lost their color* at the sight of her wedding dress lying there in tatters.

The boy's *cheeks crimsoned* at the sound of his name being called out.

The words made Lily's *freckled cheeks flush scarlet*.

7

CHEST

Adjectives in Alphabetical Order

A - L

aching; adequate; afflicted; amazing; ample; angular; armored; athletic; atypical; average; bad; bare; bared; barrel-like; barreled; battered; bear-like; bearish; beaten; beautiful; beefy; best; big; bird-thin; black; bleeding; blond; blood-caked; blood-soaked; bloodstained; bloody; bony; brawny; brazen; bristling; bristly; broad; broadening; bronzed; brown; bruised; budding; buff; bulging; bulky; bull-like; burly; burned; burning; buxom; carved; chiseled; chubby; clean; clear; cold; confident; constricted; cool; creamy; crushed; curly; damp; dark; decent; deep; defined; deformed; delicate; developed; developing; diminutive; distended; distinct; elongated; emaciated; enormous; expanded; expansive; exposed; extensive; fair; fake; famous; fat; fatty; feeble; feminine; fine; firm; flabby; flat; flattened; fleshy; fragile; frail; freckled; frightening; frozen; full; generous; glistening; glowing; good; gray-haired; great; grizzled; hair-covered; hair-roughened; hairless; hairy; handsome; hard; haughty; healthy; heavy; high; horrible; hot; huge; immature; immense; impressive; incredible; inflated; inner; jutting; laboring; large; lean; leathery; little; lordly; lovely; lower.

M - Y

magnificent; mammoth; manly; marked; masculine; massive; matted; meager; mighty; miraculous; modest; motionless; moving; much-too-muscled; muscled; muscular; naked; narrow; nice; noble; outer; oversized; painful; pale; pallid; penetrating; pillowy; pink; plain; plump; portly; powerful; pretty; prodigious; prominent; protruding; proud; puffed; puny; rasping; resonant; respectable; revealing; rigid; rippling; robust; rock-hard; rounded; sagging; saggy; scabbed; scabby; scrawny; sculpted; sculptured; shaggy; shapeless; shapely; shaved; shiny; shriveled; shrunken; significant; sinewy; skeletal; skinny; sleek; slender; slick; slight; slippery; small; small-ribbed; smooth; soaking; sodden; soft; solid; sopping; sore; splendid; stiff; still; stoic; stout; straining; streamlined; strong; stunning; substantial; sunken; swarthy; sweating; sweaty; swelling; swollen; tall; tan; tanned; terrible; thick; thin; thumping; tight; tiny; titanic; tough; towering; unmarked; unmoving; unremarkable; unwavering; unyielding; upper; vast; vigorous; voluminous; voluptuous; warm; waxed; weak; well-built; well-defined; well-muscled; well-proportioned; well-tanned; wet; wheezy; white; white-haired; wide; wonderful; wondrous; young.

Verbs and Phrasal Verbs in Alphabetical Order

A - M

accompanied; accompanied by; ached; ached from; ached with; acquired; adorned with; alleviated; appeared; arose; ballooned; bandaged; bared; bared to; barreled; barreled outward; beaded with; beat; became; began; bellowed; belonged; bled; blew out; blocked; blushed; boomed; bothered; bounced; bounced against; breathed; brimmed; brimmed with; brushed; bulged; burned; burned with; came out; carved; caught; caused; clenched; clogged; clutched; collapsed; collapsed beneath; compressed; compressed between; consisted of; constricted; constricted with; continued; contracted; covered; covered by; covered with; crossed; crushed; cut; dangled; darkened; darkened with; decorated with; deflated; demanded; displayed; divided by; dominated; drew; dripped; dropped; eased; enlarged; exhaled; expanded; exploded; exposed; faced; fell; felt; filled with; flashed; flattened; floated; flowed; fluttered; followed; forced; formed; found; froze; glistened; glittered; glowed; got tight; grew; grew tight; gripped; hammered; hardened; heaved; heaved against; heaved out; held; hid; highlighted; hit; huffed; hugged; hummed; hung; hurt; increased; indicated; inflated; itched; jumped; jutted out; labored; labored under; laden with; laid; laughed; leaped / leapt; lessened; lifted; lined with; loosened; marked; marked by; marred by; matted with; moved.

P - W

pierced; poked; poked out; presented; pressed; pressed against; pressed to; prickled; prickled with; proved; provided; puffed; puffed out; puffed up; pushed; pushed forward; pushed out; pushed up; quaked; quavered; quivered; raised; rattled; reached; relaxed; remained; reminded; resembled; rested on; revealed; reverberated; ripped; rippled; rippled with; rose; rose up; rubbed; rubbed against; sagged; sank; sat; scraped against; seized up; seized with; shifted; shone; shook; shot out; showed; shrank; shuddered; slammed; slammed into; slashed; sliced; slid; slid over; snapped forward; soaked with; sounded; spilled out; sported; sprang; spread; spread out; sprung out; squeezed; stabbed; stood; stood out; stopped; strained; strained against; strained with; strapped to; struck; stuck out; suggested; supported; swathed in; sweated; swelled; swelled with; threatened; throbbed; throbbed with; thrust forward; thrust out; tickled; tightened; tightened with; touched; traveled down; trembled; trembled beneath; turned; uncovered; unveiled; vibrated; went tight; wet; whirred; whistled; whistled with; widened; wore; wounded; wrapped in.

Noun Phrases

apex of the chest; appearance of the chest; area of chest; bones of the chest; bottom of the chest; breadth of the chest; bulk of the chest; center of the chest; compression of the chest; constriction of the chest; contraction of the chest;

curve(s) of the chest; development of the chest; enlargement of the chest; expanse of chest; expansion of the chest; exploration of the chest; extent of the chest; fall of the chest; form of the chest; indrawing of the chest; infection of the chest; inflammation of the chest; inflation of the chest; line of the chest; measurement of the chest; middle of the chest; midline of the chest; motion of the chest; movement of the chest; muscles of the chest; musculature of the chest; pain in the chest; palpation of the chest; part of the chest; pressure of the chest; region of the chest; rigidity of the chest; section of the chest; shape of the chest; size of the chest; skin of the chest; slab of chest; soreness of the chest; spasm of the chest; stiffness of the chest; strength of the chest; structure of the chest; surface of the chest; thickness of the chest; tightness of the chest; top of the chest; vibration of the chest; weight of the chest; width of the chest.

USAGE EXAMPLES

Her *buxom chest bounced* as she bounded up the stairs.

Derek *heaved* his arms and *bulging chest*, helping them secure the rope.

Her *chest constricted* at the thought of what lay ahead.

His *toned chest expanded*, taking in a lungful of much needed oxygen.

The man *held her tightly against* his *powerfully built chest*.

8
CHIN

Adjectives in Alphabetical Order

A - L

aggressive; ample; angular; arrogant; awful; baby-smooth; bare; beard-darkened; beard-stubbled; bearded; beardless; beautiful; bepimpled; big; black; blood-smeared; blue; blunt; bony; bracing; brave; bristled; bristling; bristly; broad; brown; brutal; butt-shaped; childish; chiseled; chiseled-looking; chubby; classical; clean; clean-shaved; clean-shaven; cleft; cloven; confident; contemplative; curved; dainty; dark; decisive; deep; defiant; delicate; determined; diminutive; dimpled; distinct; double; downy; drooping; dropped; edged; elegant; elevated; enormous; esteemed; exposed; extra; fat; fine; firm; flabby; flat; fleshy; forceful; full; funny-looking; furry; glistening; good; graceful; gray; gray-stubbled; greased; greasy; great; grinning; gristled; grizzled; hairless; hairy; handsome; hard; heavy; hoary; incredulous; indignant; insipid; jutting; large; leathery; level; little; long; longish; lovely; lower.

M - Y

manly; massive; miniature; missing; monstrous; narrow; neat; noble; noticeable; obstinate; odd; old; orange; outstretched; oval; pale; perfect; pert; pimply; pink; plump; pocked; pointed; pointy; poor; powerful; pretty; projecting; prominent; pronounced; protruding; proud; quivering; raised; raven-black; razor-nicked; receding; recessed; rectangular; red; resolute; rolling; rough; round; rounded; royal; sagging; saggy; scarred; scratchy; scrawny; scrubby; sculpted; shallow; shapely; sharp; shaved; shaven; shiny; short; shriveled; skinny; sloping; small; smooth; soft; solid; sparsely-haired; square; square-cut; squarish; steady; stiff; stray; strong; stubble-free; stubbled; stubbly; stubbly-bearded; stubborn; stubby; sunken; swarthy; swollen; tangled; tanned; tender; thin; throbbing; thrusting; tiny; too-wide; triangular; triple; ugly; unshaved; unshaven; uplifted; upraised; upturned; vixenish; warm; weak; weathered; well-chiseled; whiskered; white; white-bristled; whole; wide; wiry; wrinkled; wrinkly; young; youthful.

Verbs and Phrasal Verbs in Alphabetical Order

A - O

added; aggravated; aggravated by; angled; angled up; appeared; balanced; bent; bent down; betrayed; bobbed; bore; bounced; bounced against; boxed; boxed out; bristled; broke; brushed; buckled; buckled in/with; bumped; buried; buried in; came down; came out; came up; chafed; compressed; countered; covered; covered by/with; cracked; cracked against; cradled; cradled in; crinkled; cupped; cupped in; cut; deepened (dimple); dimpled; dipped; dipped into; directed; disappeared; dotted with; drew attention; drifted; drifted to; dripped; dripped with; drooped; dropped; dropped to; dug into; encompassed; faced; faced up; fell; firmed up; flinched; formed; framed by; frowned; froze; glistened; grazed; grinned; held; hit; hung; hurt; inched; inched up; indicated; instructed; itched; jabbed; jerked; jutted; jutted forward; jutted out; jutted up; leaned; leaned on; lifted; lodged against; lodged on; looked; lowered; marred; marred by; moved; nestled; nodded; oozed.

P - W

peaked; perched; perched on; pitted by/with; plopped; plowed; pointed; pointed at; pointed down; pointed in; pointed to; pointed up; poked; poked at; poked out; pressed; pressed against; pressed into; pressed on; pressed to; projected; propped on; propped up; protruded; pulled; pulsed; pushed; quivered; raised; ran; reached; receded; regarded; remained; reposed; resisted; rested; rested on; resumed; retreated; rocked; rose; roughened by; rounded out; ruled; sagged; sagged below; sagged toward; sank against; sank on; sank to; scraped; scraped against; scratched; set; shaved; shook; shot out; shot up; showed; slapped; slid; snapped; snapped back; snapped up; softened; splashed; sported; sprinkled by/with; squared off; squeezed; stained; started trembling; started wobbling; stayed; stayed up; stiffened; stood out; stopped; strained; strained upward; stroked; struck; stubbled with; stuck out; sucked in; sunk; supported; supported by; surrounded by; swayed; tapped; tensed; textured by/with; thrust; thrust forward; thrust out; thrust up; tightened; tilted; tilted up; tipped; tipped forward; tipped up; touched; trembled; tucked; tucked in; turned; twitched; went up; wiped; wobbled.

Noun Phrases

absence of a chin; base of the chin; center of the chin; contour of the chin; dip of the chin; edge of the chin; elevation of the chin; end of the chin; formation of the chin; jerk of the chin; lack of a chin; length of the chin; level of the chin; line of the chin; movement of the chin; muscles of the chin; outline of the chin; part of the chin; point of the chin; position of the chin; projection of the chin; prominence of the chin; region of the chin; rise of the chin; shape of the chin; side of the chin; sight of the chin; skin of the chin; stump of a chin; tilt of the chin; tip of the chin; underside of the chin.

USAGE EXAMPLES

She rubbed her cheek against his *baby-smooth chin.*

Frances observed that he had a *broad masculine chin* that had not seen a razor for many days.

She *raised her graceful chin* defiantly.

He had a *gray-stubbled chin* that *came up* whenever he spoke in that cool calm voice of his.

Both of their *chins were dotted with* beads of sweat.

9
EAR(S)

Adjectives in Alphabetical Order

A - M

abnormal; absent; accurate; accustomed; aching; acute; aged; alert; ample; anxious; appreciative; apprehensive; aristocratic; artificial; astonished; astounded; attentive; average; awful; back-tilted; bad; bandaged; barbarous; bat-like; beautiful; bent; best; bewildered; big; bitten-off; bleeding; bloodied; bloody; blue; blunt; blunt-tipped; bobbing; boxed; boyish; brilliant; broad; brown; brownish; bruised; burned; burning; butchered; capable; captive; carved; cat-like; cauliflower; charming; chewed-off; childish; chilled; chocolate-brown; circular; classic; classical; clean; closed; clothed; cocked; cold; colored; comical; common; concave; cream-colored; credulous; critical; crooked; cropped; cultivated; cultured; cupped; curious; curly; cut; dainty; damaged; dark; deaf; deafened; decent; deep; defective; deformed; delectable; delicate; developing; diligent; dirty; discerning; discriminating; divine; dog-like; double-pierced; doubtful; dreary; dried; drooping; droopy; dropped; drowsy; dry; dull; eager; earringed; elderly; elongated; elven; emphatic; empty; enchanted; enormous; enthusiastic; envious; erect; excellent; exceptional; excited; expectant; experienced; exposed; exquisite; extraordinary; failing; fair; faithful; faultless; favorable; fawn-like; feminine; fine; flabby; flaccid; flapping; flappy; flat; flattened; fleshy; floppy; fluffy; folded; fox-like; frantic; freckled; free; freezing; friendly; frostbitten; frozen; funny; furry; fuzzy; gaping; generous; gentle; giant; gifted; gigantic; glossy; good; great; gristled; hair-pricked; hairy; half-flattened; half-folded; half-perked; handsome; hardy; harmonious; healthy; heavenly; heavy; high; hollow; hooded; hot; huge; humble; icy; idle; ignorant; immense; impartial; impatient; impeccable; impenetrable; imperfect; imperial; impervious; impressive; inattentive; incredulous; indifferent; indignant; inexperienced; inflamed; inner; innermost; innocent; inquisitive; intelligent; interested; internal; jealous; jeweled; judgmental; keen; kissable; lanky; large; lazy; leaky; leathery; left; left-hand; liberal; light-tinted; listening; little; loamed; lobeless; lone; long; longish; lopsided; lovely; lower; lowered; loyal; lukewarm; magical; magnificent; malformed; mammalian; mammoth; mangled; mangy; marvelous; masculine; massive; misshapen; missing; modest; monstrous; muffled; multi-pierced; musical; mutilated.

M - Y

naked; narrow; near-deaf; nearest; nervous; nice; nicked; nimble; noble; nonexistent; normal; nubby; numb; odd; oily; old; open; opposite; other; outer; outstanding; outward; oval; overlarge; painful; pale; parched; partial; patient;

pear-shaped; pearl-studded; pearly; peculiar; pendulous; pensive; perceptive; perfect; perforated; perky; pierced; pink; pinkish; pious; pleased; pleasing; plugged; plump; poetic; pointed; pointy; poor; prejudiced; pretty; pricked; princely; projecting; prominent; pronounced; protective; protruding; protuberant; proud; punctured; purple; quick; ragged; raked; rapt; rat-like; receptive; red; red-lined; refined; reluctant; remarkable; resistant; restless; retentive; right; right-hand; rosy; rough; round; rounded; royal; rubbery; scabby; scarred; scraggy; sculpted; sensitive; sensual; serrated; shaggy; shapeless; sharp; shell-like; shocked; short; shrinking; shriveled-up; sickly; silken; silky; silly; simian; sinful; single; sizable; slashed; slippery; slumbering; small; snoopy; soapy; sober; soft; solitary; sophisticated; sore; sparkly; splendid; split; spotted; square; squared-off; stand-out; stick-out; stiff; stone-deaf; straining; stray; stubborn; stuffed-up; subtle; superb; suspicious; sweaty; sweet; swollen; sympathetic; tall; tattered; teeny; tender; thick; thick-lobed; thin; thoughtful; throbbing; ticklish; tiny; tired; too-large; too-small; torn; trained; translucent; transparent; triangular; trollish; trusty; tufted; tuneful; twitchy; ugly; ultra-sensitive; unaccustomed; unaffected; unaided; unbelieving; uncomprehending; uncovered; uncultivated; uneducated; unenlightened; unerring; unfailing; unfortunate; ungainly; uninitiated; unlearned; unmusical; unpracticed; unprejudiced; unprotected; unreceptive; unreluctant; unsuspecting; unsympathetic; untrained; untroubled; untutored; unwilling; upper; upright; upstanding; upturned; velvety; vigilant; visible; vulnerable; wakeful; warm; warped; wary; waving; waxy; weak; weary; well-trained; wet; white; whole; whorled; wide; wide-open; willing; wonderful; worldly; wrinkled; young; youthful.

Verbs and Phrasal Verbs in Alphabetical Order

A - J

accentuated; accentuated by; ached; adapted; adjusted; adorned with; affected; affixed to; afforded; agitated; aimed at; alerted; alerted to; allowed; announced; appeared; aquiver; aquiver with; assailed by; assaulted; attached to; attuned; attuned to; awaited; banged; banged against; barked into; bashed; beheld; belonged to; bent; bent back; bent toward; betrayed; bewildered; bit; bit off; blasted; blasted with; bled; bled from; blew into; blew on; blocked; bobbed; bobbed up; boxed; bristled; brushed; brushed against; burned; buzzed; came up; captured; caught; charmed; checked; chewed on; chopped; clamped; clamped between; cleaned; cleared; clipped; closed; cocked; cocked up; colored; concealed; confounds; considered; contained; contracted; conveyed; covered; covered with; crackled; crashed against; crimsoned; cupped; cupped to; curled; curved; cut; dangled; deafened by; deceived; deemed; delighted; detected; developed; disappeared; discerned; disconnected; discovered; distinguished between; distracted by; draped over; drew back; drooped; dropped; drummed; dulled; eavesdropped; echoed in; emptied of; enabled; encrusted with; engaged; enjoyed; enticed; examined; expanded; expected; exploded in; exposed;

extended; faded; faded away; failed; fanned; fanned out; fell; felt; filled with; filtered out; fixed on; flapped; flared; flattened; flattened against; flattened by; flattened out; flicked; flipped back; flopped; flopped about; flushed; fluttered; folded; followed; found; frayed; functioned; gathered; gave out; glinted; glistened; glowed; glued to; gnawed; gnawed on; grabbed; grabbed onto; greeted; greeted by; grew; grew more; heard; held; held back; helped; hid; hinted; hinted at; hovered; hovered above; hummed; hummed with; hung; hung down; hurt; identified; imbibed with; included; indicated; interpreted; invaded; issued from; itched; jangled; jerked; jutted out.

L - W

laced with; laid against; leaned; leaped; leaped up; learned; led; lent; lifted; liked; lingered in; listened; listened for; listened to; looked; lost; loved; lowered; made; marked; mashed; masked by; missed; moved; moved back; noted; noticed; numbed; offended; opened; ornamented with; overwhelmed; paralyzed; paused; peeled back; penetrated; perceived; perked; perked forward; perked up; picked; picked up; pierced; pierced by; pinned back; piqued; placed; planted on; played with; plugged; plugged with; pointed at; pointed forward; pointed straight; poised; poked; poked out; poked through; popped; popped out; popped painfully; popped up; pounded; prepared; presented; pressed; pressed against; pricked; pricked up; probed; prompted; protested; protruded; pulled; pulled back; pulled down; quirked; quirked forward; quivered; raised; rang; rang with; rattled; reached; rebuked; received; recognized; recoiled; recoiled against; reddened; reddened with; refused; regarded; registered; rejected; rejoiced; remained; remembered; required; resembled; rested; rested against; resumed; reverberated; riled; rimmed with; rose; roused; rubbed; sagged; scratched; scrubbed; sealed; settled; settled down; shaped like; sharpened; shifted; shone; shot up; shot upright; showed; shut; signaled; slapped; sliced off; smacked; smoothed; snagged; snapped back; sprouted; started; startled; stayed; stirred; stirred with; stood out; stood up; stopped; stopped up; strained; strained against; strained for; stuck out; stuck to; stuffed with; stung; stunned; submerged; subsided; suffered; suggested; throbbed; thumped; tickled; tilted; tingled; tipped; tired; tormented; touched; trained; translated; trembled; tuned; tuned to; turned toward; twitched; uncovered; uncurled; vibrated; waited; warmed; warmed with; went back; went down; went flat; went forward; whispered into; wiggled; woke up; wrapped up.

Noun Phrases

ability of the ear(s); absence of ears; appearance of the ear(s); application of the ear(s); area of the ear(s); aspect of the ear(s); back of the ear(s); base of the ear(s); border of the ear(s); bottom of the ear(s); canal of the ear(s); cartilage of the ear(s); cavity of the ear(s); center of the ear(s); chamber of the ear(s); characteristics of the ear(s); color of the ear(s); couple of ears; curve of the ear(s); drum of the ear(s); edge of the ear(s); entrance of the ear(s); examination of the ear(s); flap of the ear(s); formation of the ear(s); form of the ear(s); function of the ear(s); hole of the ear(s); hollow of the ear(s); infection of the ear(s); inflammation of the ear(s); inside of the ear(s); length of the ear(s); lobe of the ear(s); look of the ear(s); margin of the ear(s); movement of the ear(s); orifice of the ear(s); pair of ears; part of the ear(s); passage of the ear(s); position of the ear(s); pressure of the ear(s); rim of the ear(s); ringing of the ear(s); sensitivity of the ear(s); set of ears; shape of the ear(s); side of the ear(s); size of the ear(s); skin of the ear(s); structure of the ear(s); surface of the ear(s); tip of the ear(s); treatment of the ear(s); view of the ear(s); wall of the ear(s); wax of the ear(s).

USAGE EXAMPLES

The strange-looking man had a large nose and *protruding ears*.

The language that she *heard bewildered her ears*.

As a result of being a boxer, my uncle has *cauliflower ears*.

The girl *cupped an ear to* the door, *eavesdropping* on the conversation going on in the next room.

Carol watched on as the teen *plugged her multi-pierced ears* with her fingers.

10
ELBOW(S)

Adjectives in Alphabetical Order

ample; angular; ashen; bare; beefy; bent; big; bony; broken; bruised; busted; callused; cocked; cradled; crooked; crossed; dimpled; dirty; dry; exposed; extended; fractured; free; full; good; great; hard; heavy; high; hollow; huge; injured; inner; jacketed; jutting; knobby; large; leathern; left; little; locked; long; massive; meaty; old; opposite; other; outstretched; painful; pale; patched; plaid-covered; plump; pointed; pointy; protruding; puffy; ragged; red; right; round; scrawny; sharp; shattered; short; silken; skinned; skinny; sleeved; small; soft; solid; sore; stiff; stinging; sweaty; swinging; swollen; tanned; throbbing; unwashed; velvet-clad; weak; well-clothed; white; wide; worn; wounded; wrinkled.

Verbs and Phrasal Verbs in Alphabetical Order

ached; angled; angled outward; appeared; banged; banged against; banged up; became; began; bent; bent at; bore; bore down; braced; braced against; braced for; braced on; broke; bruised; brushed; brushed against; buckled; bumped; bumped against; bumped into; burrowed into; came forward; came through; came up; caught; caused; clamped; clamped against; clamped tight; clamped to; clasped; clasped between; closed; clutched; cocked; collided; collided with; covered; cracked; cracked on; cradled; crossed; cupped; cut; dragged; dug into; elbowed; extended; felt; flapped; flexed; flopped; flopped onto; flung; flung out; flying; folded; fractured; gave out; grazed; ground; ground against; healed; held; held close; hit; hitched; hitched against; hooked; hooked around; hooked over; hovered above; hovered over; hung; hung down; hung out; hurt; jabbed; jabbed into; jostled; jostled against; jostled into; jutted; jutted out; kinked; knocked; knocked against; laid on; landed; landed on; leaned on; lifted; linked; locked; looked; massaged; moved; moved upward; nudged; opened; perched on; pinched; pinioned; placed; planted on; pointed forward; pointed out; poked; poked through; pressed; pressed into; propped against; propped on; propped up; protruded; protruded from; protruded through; pumped; pushed; pushed into; put out; raised; raised above; reached across; remained; rested on; rose; sank; sank into; scraped; scraped against; set; shook; showed; skinned; slammed; slammed into; slipped from; slipped off; smarted; smashed into; smashed on; snapped; spread out; squared; squeezed; started; stayed; steered; stood; stopped; struck; stuck; stuck out; stung; supported; supported by; swung; threatened; threw;

throbbed; thudded against; tingled; touched; tucked in; turned; twisted; wedged; wedged under; worked; wrenched; wrenched down.

Noun Phrases

angle of the elbow(s); arthritis of the elbow(s); articulation of the elbow(s); bend of the elbow(s); bit of elbow; bones of the elbow(s); brush of the elbow(s); bump of elbows; cradle of the elbow(s); crease of the elbow(s); crook of the elbow(s); dislocation of the elbow(s); edge of the elbow(s); end of the elbow(s); extension of the elbow(s); fracture of the elbow(s); hold of the elbow(s); hollow of the elbow(s); injury of the elbow(s); inside of the elbow(s); jab of the elbow(s); jerk of the elbow(s); joint of the elbow(s); lock of the elbow(s); middle of the elbow(s); motion of the elbow(s); movement of the elbow(s); muscles of the elbow(s); nudge of the elbow(s); part of the elbow(s); point of the elbow(s); position of the elbow(s); region of the elbow(s); side of the elbow(s); skin of the elbow(s); stiffness of the elbow(s); surface of the elbow(s); sway of the elbow(s); swipe of the elbow(s); thrust of the elbow(s); thud of the elbow(s); tip of the elbow(s); underside of the elbow(s).

USAGE EXAMPLES

He *clasped* one of her *bony elbows* and led her out of the hall.

He tumbled to the ground, *landing directly on his weak elbow.*

The edge of Lucy's pointy elbow banged against the doorframe.

He *struck* Frank in the face with a *stiff right elbow.*

The injury had caused his *skinned elbow to throb* relentlessly.

11
EYEBROW(S) / BROW(S)

Adjectives in Alphabetical Order

A - M

accusing; active; ample; amused; angled; angry; angular; anxious; arched; arching; aristocratic; arrow-straight; ash-pale; astonished; attractive; auburn; awful; bald; batwing; beastly; beautiful; big; black; bleached; blond / blonde; bristling; bristly; broad; brown; bunched; burly; burning; bushy; busy; caterpillar-sized; cautioning; cautious; challenging; charming; cinnamon-colored; circumflexed; clear; close; close-knit; cloudy; cold; compelling; concerned; continuous; cool; coppery; corrugated; craggy; crazy; creased; crinkled; crooked; curious; curved; cynical; dark; dark-brown; darkened; defiant; delicate; dense; determined; disapproving; disbelieving; dismissive; doubtful; down-drawn; downcast; drawn-on; drooping; dubious; dull; dyed; earnest; elegant; elevated; enormous; expectant; expressive; faint; fair; false; feathery; fervent; fevered; fierce; fine; flaxen; fluffy; fox-red; frantic; frazzled; freshly-plucked; full; furious; furrowed; furry; fuzzless; fuzzy; gentle; ginger; gingery; glamorous; gloomy; golden; golden-brown; graceful; gracious; gray; gray-black; gray-blond; graying; great; grim; grizzled; hairless; hairy; half-raised; handsome; hanging; happy; hardened; haughty; hazel; heated; heavy; hemispheric; high; high-arching; honest; honey-colored; horizontal; humorous; immense; impatient; impeccable; imperial; imperious; impressive; incredulous; indeterminate; inky; innocent; inquiring; inquisitive; intense; interested; interrogative; interrogatory; ireful; irritated; judgmental; jutting; knitted; knotted; knowing; large; left; lemon-colored; level; light; lined; little; lofty; long; lovely; low; lowered; lush; luxuriant; majestic; manicured; manly; marked; masculine; massive; matching; merciless; mighty; minute; missing; modest.

N - Y

narrow; narrowed; near-white; neat; nice; noble; nonexistent; old-man; open; overgrown; overhanging; overplucked; overwhelming; painted; painted-on; pale; pasted-on; patchy; peaked; pencil-drawn; pencil-thin; penciled; penciled-in; penciled-on; pensive; perfect; pierced; pinched; pivoting; placid; plucked; plucked-out; poetic; pointed; pointy; prominent; proud; puny; puzzled; questioning; quizzical; radiant; ragged; raised; raised-up; raven; rectangular; red; red-blond; reddish; reddish-brown; refined; right; rise-and-fall; rocky; roguish; rough; royal; ruddy; rueful; rugged; sable; sad; salon-arched; salt-and-pepper; sandy; sardonic; scanty; scar-crossed; scraggly; scruffy; scrunched; sculpted; seductive; serious; severe; shaded; shadowy; shady; shaggy; shameless; shaped; shapeless; shapely; sharp; sharpened; shaven; shining; significant; silky; silver-blond; single; sizable; skeptical; sketched-in; sketchy; slanted; slate-gray; sleek; slender; sloping; smartly-groomed; smoky; smooth; snow-white; snowy; soft; solemn; somber; sparse; squiggly; steep; stern; still-thick; stormy; straight; straw-colored; stray; streaked; strong; stubborn; substantial; suggestive; sullen; surprised; suspicious; swarthy; sweaty; tangled; tawny; tender; tentlike; thick; thin; thin-plucked; thoughtful; threadlike; tilted; tiny; triumphant; troubled; tufted; unequivocal; uneven; unevenly-arched; unhappy; unimpressed; unkempt; unplucked; unruly; unsmirched; untrimmed; upraised; upward-flaring; victorious; warlike; warm; wary; waxed; weary; well-defined; well-plucked; well-shaped; white; wide; wild; winged; wiry; wispy; wolfish; woolly; wrinkled; wry; yellow; youthful.

Verbs and Phrasal Verbs in Alphabetical Order

A - F

accentuated; adorned; angled; angled down; appeared; arced; arced across; arched; arched above; arched across; arched over; arched up; arched upward; arrowed; arrowed down/downward; ascended; beetled; beetled down; beetled together; bent; bent in; betrayed; bobbed; bobbed up; bowed; bristled; buckled; buckled together; bunched; bunched above; bunched together; bunched up; came closer together; came down; came together; came up; cast; caused; charged together; chastised; cinched; cinched together; cleared; clicked; clicked together; climbed; closed down over; closed together; clouded; cocked; cocked up; collided; collided over; combined; compressed; connected; continued; contracted; convulsed; covered; crawled; crawled toward; creased; created; crept down/downward; crept together; crept up/upward; crinkled; crowned; curled; curled up/upward; curved; curved down/downward; curved up/upward; danced; dangled over; darkened; darted; deepened; delineated; descended; dipped; disappeared; disappeared under; displayed; dived; dived together; drew back; drew closer; drew down; drew together; drifted; drifted up; drooped; dropped; dropped down; elevated; encircled; encroached on each other; entwined with each other; exhibited; faced; fell; flapped; flapped up; flared; flattened; flew apart; flew together; flew up/upward; flickered; floated above; floated up; fluttered; formed; framed; frowned; furled; furled together; furrowed.

G - W

gathered; glued together; grew; grew together; hidden behind; hiked; hiked up; hinted at; hung; inched together; inched upward; jerked; joined; journeyed; jumped; jutted; jutted out; kicked up; knitted; knitted together; knotted; knotted together; lay above; leapt; leapt up; lifted; lifted up; lofted; loomed; lowered; made; marked; masked; matched; merged; met; met above; met over; moved; narrowed; overgrew; overhung; painted; painted with; peaked; penciled; perched; pierced; pinched; pinched together; pleated; plowed downward; plowed together; plucked; plunged; plunged together; popped above; popped apart; popped over; popped up; portrayed; pressed together; pricked; protruded;

puckered; puckered up; pulled; pulled together; pushed; pushed together; quirked; quivered; raised; ran; reached; rearranged; registered; relaxed; remained; reminded; resumed; rolled; rose; rose up; rumpled; sagged; sailed up/upward; sat up; screwed; scrunched; scrunched together; set; settled; shaped; shaved; shifted; shot; shot up/upward; showed; shriveled; shrugged; singed; slammed together; slanted; slanted down; slanted up; slashed; slashed together; slid; slid up; sloped; smoothed; snapped; snapped back; snapped down; snapped together; sprang; spread; squinched; squinched together; squirmed; started; stayed; stitched together; stood; stood out; strained; stretched; stuck out; suggested; tangled; tangled together; thickened; thinned; tightened; tilted; told; took on; trembled; trimmed; turned; tweezed; twisted; twitched; twitched together; twitched up/upward; uplifted; wagged; went up; wiggled; worked; worked down; wrinkled.

Noun Phrases

angle(s) of the eyebrow(s) / brow(s); arc(s) of the eyebrow(s) / brow(s); arch(es) of the eyebrow(s) / brow(s); bar(s) of the eyebrow(s) / brow(s); black of the eyebrow(s) / brow(s); blackness of the eyebrow(s) / brow(s); bob of the eyebrow(s) / brow(s); both of the eyebrows/brows; bristling of the eyebrow(s) / brow(s); brown of the eyebrow(s) / brow(s); cant of the eyebrow(s) / brow(s); cock of the eyebrow(s) / brow(s); color of the eyebrow(s) / brow(s); contour of the eyebrow(s) / brow(s); corner(s) of the eyebrow(s) / brow(s); crease of the eyebrow(s) / brow(s); crescent(s) of the eyebrow(s) / brow(s); crest(s) of the eyebrow(s) / brow(s); crook of the eyebrow(s) / brow(s); curve of the eyebrow(s) / brow(s); darkness of the eyebrow(s) / brow(s); dip of the eyebrow(s) / brow(s); drop of the eyebrow(s) / brow(s); each of the eyebrows/brows; edge(s) of the eyebrow(s) / brow(s); elevation of the eyebrow(s) / brow(s); end(s) of the eyebrow(s) / brow(s); fall of the eyebrow(s) / brow(s); flick of the eyebrow(s) / brow(s); flicker of the eyebrow(s) / brow(s); furrow of the eyebrow(s) / brow(s); hairs of the eyebrow(s) / brow(s); heaviness of the eyebrow(s) / brow(s); height of the eyebrow(s) / brow(s); hike of the eyebrow(s) / brow(s); hitch of the eyebrow(s) / brow(s); inclination of the eyebrow(s) / brow(s); jiggle of the eyebrow(s) / brow(s); jut of the eyebrow(s) / brow(s); knit of the eyebrow(s) / brow(s); ledge of the eyebrow(s) / brow(s); length of the eyebrow(s) / brow(s); lifting of the eyebrow(s) / brow(s); lilt of the eyebrow(s) / brow(s); line(s) of the eyebrow(s) / brow(s); look of the eyebrow(s) / brow(s); lowering of the eyebrow(s) / brow(s); middle of the eyebrow(s) / brow(s); movement of the eyebrow(s) / brow(s); narrowing of the eyebrow(s) / brow(s); outline of the eyebrow(s) / brow(s); peak(s) of the eyebrow(s) / brow(s); pinch of the eyebrow(s) / brow(s); play of the eyebrow(s) / brow(s); plucking of the eyebrow(s) / brow(s); point of the eyebrow(s) / brow(s); prominence of the eyebrow(s) / brow(s); quirk of the eyebrow(s) / brow(s); raising of the eyebrow(s) / brow(s); ridge of the eyebrow(s) / brow(s); rise of the eyebrow(s) / brow(s); ruggedness of the eyebrow(s) / brow(s); scrunch of the eyebrow(s) / brow(s); sculpturing of the eyebrow(s) / brow(s); set of eyebrows/brows; shape of the eyebrow(s) / brow(s); shaping of the eyebrow(s) / brow(s); shooting of the eyebrow(s) / brow(s); shrug of the eyebrow(s) / brow(s); sight of the eyebrow(s) / brow(s); silk of the eyebrow(s) / brow(s); silkiness of the eyebrow(s) / brow(s); slanting of the eyebrow(s) / brow(s); slash(es) of the eyebrow(s) / brow(s); slope of the eyebrow(s) / brow(s); snap of the eyebrow(s) / brow(s); straightness of the eyebrow(s) / brow(s); strip(s) of the eyebrow(s) / brow(s); sweep of the eyebrow(s) / brow(s); swoop of the eyebrow(s) / brow(s); texture of the eyebrow(s) / brow(s); thatch of the eyebrow(s) / brow(s); thickness of the eyebrow(s) / brow(s); tilt of the eyebrow(s) / brow(s); tip(s) of the eyebrow(s) / brow(s); top of the eyebrow(s) / brow(s); tug of the eyebrow(s) / brow(s); twist of the eyebrow(s) / brow(s); twitch of the eyebrow(s) / brow(s); uplifting of the eyebrow(s) / brow(s); uprising of the eyebrow(s) / brow(s); upshoot of the eyebrow(s) / brow(s); upsweep of the eyebrow(s) / brow(s); volume of the eyebrow(s) / brow(s); wag of the eyebrow(s) / brow(s); waggle of the eyebrow(s) / brow(s); wiggle of the eyebrow(s) / brow(s); wing(s) of the eyebrow(s) / brow(s); wisp(s) of the eyebrow(s) / brow(s); wriggle of the eyebrow(s) / brow(s).

USAGE EXAMPLES

She *lifted an accusing eyebrow* in his direction.

Luke's *dark eyebrows lowered* questioningly.

Helen *raised her brows in* surprise at his boldness.

She had *attractive angular eyebrows* which *framed* her deep blue eyes.

He *arched an imperious brow* at her words.

12
EYELASHES / LASHES

Adjectives in Alphabetical Order

absurd; artificial; auburn; batted; beautiful; big; black; blackish; blinking; blond / blonde; bottom; brown; clustered; clustering; coated; cobwebby; curling; curly; curved; curving; dark; darkened; delicate; dense; dramatic; drooping; drowsy; elegant; enormous; fair; fake; false; feathery; feminine; fine; flickering; flittery; fluttering; fluttery; fringed; full; gold; golden; gray; healthy; heavy; inch-long; incredible; jet black; jetty; little; long; lower; lowered; lushest; luxurious; made up; mascara-coated; mascara-encrusted; mascara-heavy; mascaraless; mile-long; non-existent; painted; pale; pretty; professional; quivering; raddled; ragged; red; remaining; seductive; shaggy; short; silken; silky; smoky; soft; sparse; spidery; spiky; straight; stray; stubby; sweeping; tangled; thick; toned; upper; upswept; upward-curling; wet; white; white-blond; yellow.

Verbs and Phrasal Verbs in Alphabetical Order

added; attracted; batted; bent; blinked; brushed; brushed against; caressed; cast; closed; clotted; clotted with; clumped; clumped with; commanded; curled; drew together; drooped; fell; flapped; flicked; flickered; flickered against; floated; fluttered; fluttered against; framed; framed by; glistened; glittered; lined; lowered; mashed together; matted with; painted; rested against; rested on; rustled; shaded; shadowed; slathered; spaced; spread; stood out; straightened; stuck; stuck to; stuttered; swept; swept against; thickened with; trembled; uncurled; wet with.

Noun Phrases

agitation of the eyelashes / lashes; arc of the eyelashes / lashes; arch of the eyelashes / lashes; back of the eyelashes / lashes; barrier of the eyelashes / lashes; base of the eyelashes / lashes; batting of the eyelashes / lashes; beauty of the eyelashes / lashes; black of the eyelashes / lashes; blackness of the eyelashes / lashes; blink of the eyelashes / lashes; blur of the eyelashes / lashes; bottom of the eyelashes / lashes; brush of the eyelashes / lashes; canopy of the eyelashes / lashes; circle of the eyelashes / lashes; closeness of the eyelashes / lashes; clumps of the eyelashes / lashes; color of the eyelashes / lashes; confines of the eyelashes / lashes; corner of the eyelashes / lashes; cover of the eyelashes /

lashes; crescent of the eyelashes / lashes; curl of the eyelashes / lashes; curtain of the eyelashes / lashes; curve of the eyelashes / lashes; dampness of the eyelashes / lashes; darkness of the eyelashes / lashes; delicacy of the eyelashes / lashes; denseness of the eyelashes / lashes; density of the eyelashes / lashes; depth of the eyelashes / lashes; descent of the eyelashes / lashes; downsweep of the eyelashes / lashes; drift of the eyelashes / lashes; droop of the eyelashes / lashes; drop of the eyelashes / lashes; each of the eyelashes / lashes; edge of the eyelashes / lashes; end of the eyelashes / lashes; fall of the eyelashes / lashes; fan of the eyelashes / lashes; feathering of the eyelashes / lashes; feel of the eyelashes / lashes; femininity of the eyelashes / lashes; fineness of the eyelashes / lashes; flick of the eyelashes / lashes; flicker of the eyelashes / lashes; flutter of the eyelashes / lashes; forest of the eyelashes / lashes; frame of the eyelashes / lashes; fringe of the eyelashes / lashes; fullness of the eyelashes / lashes; glide of the eyelashes / lashes; glitter of the eyelashes / lashes; gold of the eyelashes / lashes; heaviness of the eyelashes / lashes; hedge of the eyelashes / lashes; hood of the eyelashes / lashes; kiss of the eyelashes / lashes; leap of the eyelashes / lashes; length of the eyelashes / lashes; lift of the eyelashes / lashes; line of the eyelashes / lashes; look of the eyelashes / lashes; lowering of the eyelashes / lashes; lushness of the eyelashes / lashes; luxuriance of the eyelashes / lashes; mesh of the eyelashes / lashes; movement of the eyelashes / lashes; net of the eyelashes / lashes; one of the eyelashes / lashes; points of the eyelashes / lashes; quiver of the eyelashes / lashes; raise of the eyelashes / lashes; rim of the eyelashes / lashes; rise of the eyelashes / lashes; roots of the eyelashes / lashes; screen of the eyelashes / lashes; shade of the eyelashes / lashes; shadow of the eyelashes / lashes; shape of the eyelashes / lashes; shelf of the eyelashes / lashes; shelter of the eyelashes / lashes; shield of the eyelashes / lashes; sight of the eyelashes / lashes; silk of the eyelashes / lashes; silkiness of the eyelashes / lashes; slant of the eyelashes / lashes; slide of the eyelashes / lashes; slit of the eyelashes / lashes; smokiness of the eyelashes / lashes; smudge of the eyelashes / lashes; softness of the eyelashes / lashes; sootiness of the eyelashes / lashes; spikes of the eyelashes / lashes; spikiness of the eyelashes / lashes; stiffness of the eyelashes / lashes; stirring of the eyelashes / lashes; swathe of the eyelashes / lashes; sweep of the eyelashes / lashes; swoop of the eyelashes / lashes; tangle of the eyelashes / lashes; texture of the eyelashes / lashes; thickness of the eyelashes / lashes; tickle of the eyelashes / lashes; tilt of the eyelashes / lashes; tips of the eyelashes / lashes; tops of the eyelashes / lashes; touch of the eyelashes / lashes; tremble of the eyelashes / lashes; upsweep of the eyelashes / lashes; veil of the eyelashes / lashes; waves of the eyelashes / lashes; web of the eyelashes / lashes; wedge of the eyelashes / lashes; weight of the eyelashes / lashes; wetness of the eyelashes / lashes; whisper of the eyelashes / lashes.

USAGE EXAMPLES

Dark curling lashes gave her young eyes a look of innocence.

Michelle's *feathery eyelashes fluttered* seductively.

Her *spidery eyelashes framed* her exotic black eyes.

The *inch-long false lashes brushed against* her cheeks.

A *set of black lashes shadowed* his deep-set eyes.

13
EYE(S)

Adjectives in Alphabetical Order

A - C

abashed; abnormal; absent; accurate; accusatory; accusing; accustomed; aching; acid-green; acorn-brown; acorn-colored; acorn-shaped; acrostic; acute; additional; adjusted; admiring; adoring; affectionate; afflicted; afraid; aged; ageing/aging; ageless; aggressive; aggrieved; agonized; alarmed; albino; alert; alien; all-intrusive; all-knowing; all-present; all-seeing; all-white; alluring; almond-brown; almond-colored; almond-shaped; amazed; amazing; amber; amber-brown; amber-colored; ambiguous; amiable; amnesiac; amorous; amused; anaemic; analytical; ancient; angelic; angled; angry; anguished; animalistic; animated; annoyed; anxious; apologetic; apparent; appealing; appraising; appreciative; apprehensive; appropriate; approving; aqua-blue; aqua-colored; aquamarine; aqueous; arching; arctic; ardent; arid; arresting; arrogant; artful; articulate; artificial; ash-brown; Asian; Asian-looking; Asian-shaped; assaulting; astonished; astonishing; astounded; astounding; attentive; attractive; auburn; authoritative; avaricious; average; averted; avid; awake; awakening; awe-struck; awed; awesome; awful; azure-blue; baby-blue; backward; bad; baffled; baggy; baleful; baltic; bandaged; banged-up; bar-gray; bashful; battered; battle-hardened; beady; beauteous; beautiful; bedimmed; beetle-like; befuddled; begoggled; beguiling; belligerent; beloved; bemused; benevolent; benign; berry-bright; beseeching; bespectacled; best; betraying; better; bewildered; bewitching; biased; bicolored; big; biggest; biggish; billiard-ball; binocular; bird-blue; bird-like; bitter; bituminous; bizarre; black; black-ball; black-bead; black-button; black-hole; black-lined; black-olive; black-rimmed; black-ringed; blackened; blackest; blank; blast-blinded; blasted; blazing; bleak; bleary; bleeding; blind; blind-looking; blinded; blinding; blinking; blinky; blistered; blistering; blond-lashed; blood-dashed; blood-red; blood-rimmed; blood-shrouded; blood-stained; blood-streaked; blood-threaded; bloodshot; bloodthirsty; bloody; blue; blue-beyond-blue; blue-flecked; blue-gold; blue-gray; blue-green; blue-rimmed; blue-ringed; blue-shadowed; bluest; bluewater; bluish; bluish-green; blunt; blurred; blurring; blurry; bold; bolt-black; boozy; bored; bottle-green; bottomless; boyish; brave; brazen; Brazilian-brown; breathtaking; bright; bright-blue; bright-green; bright-hazel; brightest; brilliant; broad; broad-lashed; broken; broken-hearted; bronzy; brooding; brown; brown-black; brown-blue; brown-bronze; brown-button; brown-green; brownest; bruised; bruised-looking; bugged-out; buglike; bulbous; bulging; bulgy; burned; burning; bushy; busted; busy; button-sized; cagey; calculating; calm; candid; candy-brown; candy-dark; canny; captivating; caramel-colored; carbon-black;

careful; careless; caring; carnal; carp-like; case-hardened; cast-down; cast-iron; casual; cat-colored; cat-green; cat-like; cat-sharp; cat-yellow; cataract-afflicted; cataract-clouded; cautioning; cautious; cavernous; celebratory; censorious; cerulean; cerulean-blue; chaldean; challenging; chameleon-like; changeless; charcoal-colored; charcoaled; charismatic; charming; charred; chaste; cheerful; Cherokee-dark; chestnut-brown; chestnut-colored; child-like; childish; chilly; china-blue; china-doll; Chinese; chocolate-brown; chocolate-colored; cinnamon-brown; circled; clairvoyant; clay-colored; clean; clear; clear-brown; clearest; clearing; clenched; clever; clever-looking; clinical; close; close-set; close-together; closed; closing; cloth-bound; clouded; cloudy; coal-black; coal-dark; cobalt-blue; cocked; cocoa-colored; coffee-brown; coffee-colored; cognac-colored; coked-up; cold; coldest; collective; colorful; colorless; comfortable; commanding; common; compassionate; compassionless; compelling; concerned; conditioned; confident; confused; connected; conniving; conquering; consistent; conspiratorial; constant; contagious; contemptuous; controlling; contused; cool; coolest; copper; copper-brown; copper-colored; copper-green; coppery; corky; cornflower-blue; countless; courteous; covert; covetous; coy; crafty; crazed; crazy; cream-clotted; creamy; creative; crescent-shaped; crestfallen; crimson; crinkled; crinkly; critical; crocodilian; crooked; cross-eyed; crossed; crudest; cruel; cruelest; crusted; crusty; crystal-blue; crystalline; cunning; curious; curled; curly-lashed; curved; cute; cyanotic; cyclopean; cynical.

D - G

damaged; damned; damp; damp-lashed; dangerous; dangling; dark; dark-accustomed; dark-adapted; dark-blue; dark-brown; dark-circled; dark-dilated; dark-fringed; dark-gray; dark-green; dark-rimmed; dark-ringed; dark-seeing; darkened; darkening; darkest; darkling; darting; darty; dazed; dazzled; dazzling; dead; dead-fish; dead-looking; deadened; deadly; death-cold; death-glazed; death-like; decaying; deceitful; declining; deep; deep-blue; deep-brown; deep-green; deep-sea; deep-seeing; deep-set; deep-socketed; deep-sunken; deep-turquoise; deepening; defeated; defective; defensive; deferential; defiant; definite; degenerative; deific; dejected; deliberate; delicate; delighted; demented; democratic; demonic; demure; deprived; depthless; derisive; desolate; despairing; desperate; destroyed; detached; determined; developed; dewy; different; differently-colored; dilated; diligent; dim; dimmed; dimming; direct; dirt-colored; dirty; disappearing; disappointed; disapproving; disbelieving; discerning; disconcerting; discontented; discriminating; diseased; disenchanted; disfigured; disgusted; disgusting; disillusioned; disinterested; disparaging; dispassionate; distant; distended; distinct; distinctive; distorted; distrustful; distrusting; disturbing; diversionary; divine; doe-like; dog-brown; doleful; doll-baby; doll-like; dollar-signed; dominant; dormant; dosed; doting; doubtful; dour; dove-colored; dove-gray; downcast; downslanting; downturned; downward; drab-colored; dreadful; dreading; dreaming; dreamy; dreary; drenched; dried; dried-out; drifting; drink-softened; driven; drizzly; drooping; droopy; droopy-lidded; drowned; drowning; drowsy; drunken; dry; dubious; dull; dulled; dumb; dusk-blue; dusky; dust-gray; dusty; dying; eager; earnest;

easy-going; educated; eerie; effulgent; eidetic; eighteen-year-old; elderly; electric; electric-blue; elegant; elevated; elfish/elvish; elliptical; elm-leaf; elongated; eloquent; embarrassed; emerald-green; emotionless; empathetic; empty; enameled; enchanted; enchanting; encumbered; end-of-the-day; endless; engorged; enhanced; enigmatic; enlarged; enormous; enraged; enthusiastic; entranced; entrepreneurial; envious; envying; Eurasian; evasive; even; ever-bright; ever-frightened; ever-moving; ever-present; ever-remarkable; ever-vigilant; evergreen; evil; exacting; exasperated; excellent; excitable; excited; excruciating; exhausted; exhaustion-stitched; exotic; expectant; experienced; exposed; expressionless; expressive; extinguished; extra; extra-wide; extraordinary; extruded; faceted; faded; faded-blue; faery; failing; faint; fair; faithful; fake; fallen; false; familiar; fanatical; fanciful; farsighted; fascinated; fast; fast-darkening; fastidious; fatalistic; father-figure; fatherly; fathomless; faulty; favorable; fawn; fawn-like; fear-bright; fear-filled; fear-stricken; fear-widened; fearful; fearless; fearwide; feathered; feeble; feline; female; feminine; feral; fervent; fevered; feverish; fierce; fierce-looking; fiery; filmed; filmy; filthy; fine; finest; fire-dazzled; firm; fish-black; fish-colored; fishy; flame-red; flame-reflecting; flaming; flashing; flat; flattened-looking; fleeting; flickering; flinty; flirtatious; flirty; floating; flooded; flowing; fluttering; focused; fog-colored; fog-white; fogged; foggy; foggy-looking; fond; foolish; foreign; forest-adapted; forest-green; forlorn; formal; forward-looking; frail; framed; frank; frantic; freakiest; free; freedom-crazed; frenzied; fresh; fretful; friendly; frightened; frightening; frog-like; frosty; frozen; frugal; full; functional; funny; furious; furtive; gaping; garish; gas-blue; gay; gazelle-like; gelatinous; gem-like; generous; gentle; gentleman's; ghostly; ghoulish; giant; giddy; gigantic; ginger; glacial; glad; glaring; glass-bead; glass-button; glass-green; glass-like; glassy; glaucomatous; glazed; glazed-over; gleaming; gleamy; gleeful; glimmering; glinting; glinty; glistening; glittering; glittery; globe-like; gloomy; glorious; glossy; glow-in-the-dark; glowing; goddamn; godly; goggled; goggling; goggly; gold; gold-brown; gold-flecked; gold-green; gold-hazel; gold-lashed; gold-rimmed; gold-speckled; gold-yellow; golden; golden-brown; golden-flecked; golden-yellow; goo-goo; good; good-humored; gooey; goofy; googly; gorgeous; gouged; gouged-out; graceful; gracious; grainy; grandmotherly; grape-blue; grapefruit-sized; grass-green; grateful; grave; gray; gray-black; gray-blue; gray-green; gray-violet; grayest; grayish; great; greedy; green; green-blue; green-brown; green-flecked; green-gold; green-gray; green-shadowed; green-yellow; greenest; greenish; greenish-blue; greenish-gray; greenish-yellow; grief-blurred; grief-stricken; grief-welled; grieving; grim; grinning; grit-caked; gritty; groggy; grown-woman; grudging; guarded; guileless; guilty; gullible; gummy; gunmetal; gunmetal-gray.

H - M

haggard; half-alive; half-blinded; half-closed; half-crazed; half-crazy; half-hidden; half-hooded; half-interested; half-lidded; half-open; half-opened; half-seeing; half-shaded; half-shut; hallucinating; handsome; handy; happy; harassed; hard; hardest; harsh; hasty; hate-crazed; hate-filled; hate-laden; hateful; haughty;

haunted; haunting; hawk-dark; hawk-like; hawkish; hazel; hazel-blue; hazel-brown; hazel-colored; hazel-green; hazy; healthy; heartless; heavenly; heavy; heavy-lidded; heedful; heedless; helpless; hidden; hideous; hollow; hollowed-out; homesick; honest; honey-bear; honey-brown; honey-colored; hooded; hopeful; hopeless; horrible; horrified; horror-stricken; horror-struck; horsey; hostile; hot; hot-blue; hovering; huge; human; humble; humid; humorless; humorous; humungous; hungover; hungry; hunted; hurried; hurt; hurtful; hyacinth-blue; hypnotic; hypnotized; ice-blue; ice-cold; ice-gray; ice-green; icy; icy-blue; identical; idiotic; idle; ignorant; illuminated; immaculate; immense; immobile; immortal; impartial; impassioned; impassive; impatient; impeccable; impenetrable; imperfect; imperial; imperious; imperturbable; imploring; impoverished; impressionable; impudent; inattentive; incandescent; incautious; incomparable; inconspicuous; incredible; incredulous; incurious; indifferent; indignant; indigo; indigo-colored; indiscernible; indiscreet; individual; indolent; indulgent; inexperienced; infected; inferior; infinite; inflamed; infrared; infuriated; ingenuous; inhuman; injured; ink-blue; inky; inlaid; inner; innocent; innumerable; inquiring; inquisitive; insane; insatiable; inscrutable; insinuating; insolent; insomnia-ravaged; insomniac-stained; inspired; insulated; intellectual; intelligent; intelligent-looking; intense; intent; interested; interesting; internal; interrogative; intimate; intoxicating; intriguing; intruding; intrusive; intuitive; invisible; inviting; irate; iridescent; irisless; ironic; irreducible; irrelevant; irritated; itching; itchy; jade-colored; jade-green; jaded; jaundiced; jealous; jet-black; jet-lagged; jewel-blue; jewel-green; jewel-like; jeweled; jittery; jolly; joyful; joyless; judgmental; judicious; jumping; jumpy; jungle-colored; just; just-opened; kahlua-white; keen; keenest; kind; kindest; kindly; knowing; knowledgeable; kohl; kohl-blown; kohl-darkened; kohl-lined; kohl-rimmed; lake-blue; lamb-like; lamp-lit; languid; lapis-blue; larcenous; large; lascivious; laser-beam; laser-green; laser-sharp; lashless; laughing; lavender-blue; lazy; leaden; leading; leaf-green; leaky; leering; leery; left; lemur-like; lenient; leonine; level; liberal; licorice-drop; lidded; lidless; lifeless; light; light-adjusted; light-blinded; light-blue; light-brown; light-colored; light-filled; light-gathering; light-gray; light-green; light-sensitive; lighted; lightless; lightning-blue; lime-green; lined; lineless; liquid; liquid-black; liquid-bright; liquid-onyx; liquid-violet; listless; lit-up; little; little-bitty; lively; lizard-like; lizardy; locked; lone; lonely; long; long-lashed; loose; lost; love-drowned; lovely; lovesick; loving; low; lowered; lucky; luminescent; luminous; lurid; luscious; lust-filled; lusterless; lustful; lustrous; mad; mad-dog; made-up; magic; magnificent; magnified; maintained; male; malevolent; malicious; malignant; mangled; maniacal; manic; manly; Manson-like; many-faceted; marble-like; marvelous; mascara-clotted; mascara-ringed; mascara-spiked; mascaraed/mascared; masked; massive; matching; maternal; maturing; mean; mean-spirited; meanest; meaningful; meaningless; measuring; mechanical; Mediterranean; medium-brown; medium-sized; meek; melancholy; mellow; menacing; mental; merciless; mercurochrome-colored; mermaid-green; merry; mesmerizing; metallic; meticulous; midnight-blue; midnight-satin; mild; military; milk-chocolate; milk-white; milky; milky-light; mindless; minimal; mirror-like;

mirthful; mirthless; misaligned; mischievous; mismatched; miss-nothing; missing; mist-colored; misty; mobile; mocking; modest; moist; moist-rimmed; molasses-colored; molten; monocled; monocular; monstrous; moody; moon-yellow; moony; moorish; moral; morning-glory; morose; mortal; moss-green; motionless; mournful; mouse-like; moving; mud-brown; mud-colored; muddy; muddy-brown; muddy-colored; multifaceted; multiple; murderous; murky; mutilated; mutinous; myopic; mysterious; mysterious-looking; mystic; mythical.

N - S

nacreous; nagging; naive; naked; narrow; narrow-pupiled; narrow-set; narrowed; narrowing; nasty; native; natural; nauseating; navy-blue; near; near-black; near-blind; nearsighted; neat; negligent; neighboring; nervous; neutral; new; newborn; nice; nickel-colored; night-adapted; night-shaded; nightwise; nimble; noble; nocturnal; normal; now-dark; nut-brown; nutty; obedient; oblique; oblivious; oblong; obscure; obscured; observant; observed; obsessive-compulsive; ocean-blue; odd; odd-colored; offended; official; ogling; oil-black; oil-colored; oily; oily-black; old; old-man; olive; olive-black; olive-colored; omnipresent; only; oozing; opal-colored; opalescent; opaque; open; opened; opposite; orange; orchid-colored; orchid-dark; ordinary; oriental; original; other; otherworldly; outer; outraged; oval; oval-shaped; over-made-up; overdone; overgrown; overlarge; oversized; owl-like; owlish; owly; pain-filled; pain-widened; pained; painful; painted; pale; pale-blue; palest; panic-stricken; panicked; panicky; partial; particular; passing; passion-bright; passionate; passionless; passive; patched; paternal; pathetic; patient; peaceful; peach-colored; pearl-gray; pearly; pebbly; pecan-brown; pecan-shaped; peculiar; peeled; peering; pellucid; penetrating; pensive; perceptive; perfect; perplexed; persuasive; petrified; philosophic; phony; phosphorescent; photographic; piercing; piggish; pinched; pink; pinkish; pinpoint; pistachio-green; pitch-black; pitch-dark; piteous; pitiable; pitiful; pitiless; pitying; pixelated; placid; plaintive; playful; pleading; pleady; pleasant; pleasing; plucked-out; plum-colored; poetic; polished; polite; poor; porcelain-white; porcine; possessed; powder-blue; powerful; practical; practiced; pre-teen; precious; precise; predator-like; predatory; pregnant; prejudiced; present; presuming; prettiest; pretty; primitive; probing; profane; professional; prominent; prophetic; prosecutorial; protected; protective; protestant; protruding; protuberant; proud; provocative; prune-dark; prying; psychopathic; puce-russet; puffed; puffed-up; puffy; pupilless; puppy-dog; puppy-like; pure; puritanical; purple; purple-blue; purply; purulent; pus-steeped; puss-ridden; puzzled; queer; questioning; quick; quick-darting; quick-looking; quickest; quiet; quizzical; rabid; raccoon-like; radiant; ragged; raging; rain-colored; raised; raisin-brown; raisin-like; rakish; rapacious; rapid; rapt; raptorial; rapturous; ravaged; raven; ravenous; raw; ready; reasonable; reassuring; rebellious; receding; receptive; recessed; red; red-amber; red-brown; red-flashing; red-glowing; red-lined; red-rimmed; red-veined; reddened; refined; reflected; reflective; regal; regular; relentless; relieved; religious; reluctant; remaining; remarkable; remorseless; remote; removable; reproachful; reptilian; requisite; resentful; resigned; resolute; respectable; respectful; responsible;

restless; retentive; retrospective; returning; reversed; rheum-smeared; rheumy; rheumy-red; ridiculous; right; righteous; rimmed; ripe-olive; riveting; rock-hard; rodent-like; roguish; rolled; rolling; round; rounded; roving; royal; ruby; rude; rueful; ruined; rum-colored; runny; rural; russet; rusty; sacred; sad; sad-dog; saddest; safe; sagacious; sage-green; saggy; sallow; same-shaped; sanctimonious; sand-colored; sand-filled; sandy-colored; sapphire-blue; sarcastic; sardonic; sassy; sated; saucer-sized; saucy; savage; scared; scarlet; scary; scathing; scattered; scientific; scorched; scornful; scowling; screaming; screwed-up; screwy; scrupulous; scrutinizing; sculpted; sea-blue; sea-colored; sea-glass; sea-gray; sea-green; searching; seared; searing; secretive; seedy; seething; self-conscious; self-critical; semi-Asian; sensitive; sensual; sensuous; sentient; septic; serious; serpentine; set; severe; sewn-shut; sexual; sexy; shaded; shadowed; shadowy; shallow; shamrock-green; shapely; shark-like; sharp; sharpened; sharpest; shattered; sheepish; shifting; shifty; shimmering; shining; shiny; shocked; shortsighted; shrewd; shrouded; shut; shy; siamese; sick; sidelong; sideways; sideways-facing; sightless; silent; silver; silver-blue; silver-filmed; silver-gray; silver-green; silvery; silvery-blind; silvery-blue; simian; similar; simple; sincere; sinful; single; sinister; skeptical; sketchy; skewed; skilled; skittish; sky-blue; sky-colored; skyward; slanted; slanting; slanty; slate-blue; slate-gray; sleep-bleary; sleep-blurred; sleep-deprived; sleep-drowsed; sleep-fogged; sleep-heavy; sleep-sluggish; sleep-smeared; sleeping; sleepless; sleepy; slight; slit-like; slit-pupiled; slitted; sloping; slow; slow-blinking; slumberous; sly; small; smallish; smart; smiling; smoky; smoky-blue; smoky-dark; smoldering/smouldering; smudgy; snappy; sober; sobering; soft; softening; sole; solemn; solicitous; solid; solitary; somber/sombre; somewhat-jaundiced; soothing; sore; sorrow-filled; sorrowful; sorry; soulful; soulless; soupy; sour; sovereign; spacious; sparkling; sparkly; special; speckled; spectacular; spectral; speculative; spice-brown; spicy; spiritual; splendid; spooky; spotted; sprightly; square; squeezed-shut; squinchy; squint-thin; squinting; squinty; stained; stalking; staring; stark; starlit; starry; startled; startled-looking; startling; starving; steadfast; steady; stealthy; steel-blue; steel-gray; steely; stern; sticky; still; still-innocent; still-open; still-sealed; still-sleepy; still-staring; still-stinging; still-stunned; stinging; stolid; stone-blue; stony; storm-cloud-colored; storm-gray; stormy; strained; strange; strange-staring; stricken; strict; striking; strong; stunned; stupefied; stupid; stylized; subordinated; substitute; subtle; suburban; successful; suffering; suicidal; sulfur-yellow; sulky; sullen; sultry; summer-sky; sun-scorched; sunglassed; sunken; sunlit; sunny; supercilious; superficial; superior; supportive; sure; surly; surprised; surreptitious; surviving; suspicious; suspicious-looking; swamp-leaf; sweet; swelling; swirling; swiveling; swollen; sympathetic.

T - Z

tan-colored; tartar; tawny; tawny-colored; tea-brown; tear-blinded; tear-bloated; tear-blurred; tear-brimmed; tear-filled; tear-glazed; tear-soaked; tear-stained; tear-strained; tear-streaked; tear-swollen; tear-worn; teardrop-shaped; tearful; tearless; teary; teasing; teenage; tender; tense; terrible; terrific; terrified; terror-stricken; textured; thick; thick-browed; thick-lashed; thick-lidded; thickly-lashed; thin; thirsty; thoughtful; threatening; throbbing; tight; tilted; tilting; timid; tiny; tired; tired-looking; tobacco-colored; toffee-colored; tolerant; too-big; too-blue; too-bright; too-close; too-large; too-pale; too-wide; too-wise; tormented; tortured; tough; tragic; trained; traitorous; tranquil; transfixed; translucent; transparent; tribal; troubled; trusting; trustworthy; turd-colored; turned-away; turquoise; turquoise-blue; tutored; twinkling; twinkly; twitching; two-color; ubiquitous; ugly; unabashed; unaccommodated; unaccustomed; unaffected; unaided; unarmed; unassailable; unassisted; unattached; unauthorized; unbearable; unbelieving; unblinkable; unblinking; unbloodied; unborn; uncaring; uncautious; uncertain; unchanging; unclouded; uncomfortable; uncomplicated; uncomprehending; uncompromising; unconscious; unconvinced; uncritical; undamaged; undazzled; underwater; undetectable; unearthly; uneasy; uneducated; unembarrassed; unerring; uneven; unfailing; unfathomable; unfavorable; unflinching; unfocused; unforgiving; unfortunate; unfriendly; unhappy; unimpaired; uninitiated; uninjured; uninvested; unique; unknowing; unmoving; unnatural; unnerving; unobstructed; unpatched; unpracticed; unpredictable; unprejudiced; unprotected; unreadable; unreal; unrefined; unrelenting; unrevealing; unscientific; unseeing; unseen; unsettling; unshielded; unsighted; unsleeping; unsmiling; unsophisticated; unsparing; unsuspecting; unsympathetic; untrained; untroubled; untutored; unusual; unwavering; unwilling; unwinking; up-tilted; uplifted; upper; upraised; upset; upside-down; upturned; upward-slanting; upward-turned; urgent; useful; useless; vacant; vague; valuable; vanishing; vapid; various; veiled; vein-reddened; veined; veiny; velvety; vengeful; venomous; vigilant; vigorous; vindictive; violet; violet-blue; viperous; virgin; virginal; virile; virtuous; visible; vivacious; vivid; vulgar; vulnerable; wakeful; walnut-colored; wandering; wanting; wanton; warm; wary; washed-out; wasted; watchful; watching; water-blue; water-blurred; water-colored; water-gray; waterless; watermelon-size; watery; watery-blue; watery-brown; wavering; waxen; wayward; weak; weakened; weakening; weaksighted; weary; weaselly; weathered; weed-green; weeping; weepy; weird; weird-looking; welcoming; well-spaced; well-trained; western; wet; whirling; whiskey-brown; whiskey-colored; white; white-painted; white-ringed; whiteless; whitish; whitish-blue; whole; wicked; wide; wide-awake; wide-open; wide-set; wide-spaced; widened; widening; wild; willful; willing; wilting; wily; wincing; Windex-blue; window-like; winking; wintry; wise; wise-looking; wishful; wistful; withering; witless; wobbling; woeful; wolfish; womanly; wonderful; wondering; wondrous; wonky; wooden; working; world-weary; worldly; worn; worried; worry-bright; worry-wrung; worshipful; wounded; wretched; wrinkle-framed; wrinkled; wrinkly; yearning; yellow; yellow-blue; yellow-brown; yellow-gray; yellow-green; yellowed; yellowing; yellowish; yellowish-hazel; yellowy; young; youthful; zealous.

(ADJ) Color: Black

bituminous; black; black-olive; blackest; bolt-black; carbon-black; charcoal-colored; charcoaled; charred; Cherokee-dark; coal-black; coal-dark; dark;

darkest; fish-black; inky; jet-black; liquid-black; liquid-onyx; molasses-colored; near-black; oil-black; oil-colored; oily-black; olive; olive-black; olive-colored; pitch-black; pitch-dark; raven.

(ADJ) Color: Blue
aqua-blue; aqua-colored; aquamarine; azure-blue; baby-blue; baltic; bird-blue; blue; blue-beyond-blue; blue-flecked; blue-gold; blue-gray; blue-green; bluest; bluewater; bluish; bright-blue; brown-blue; cerulean; cerulean-blue; china-blue; cobalt-blue; cornflower-blue; crystal-blue; crystalline; cyanotic; dark-blue; deep-blue; deep-sea; deep-turquoise; dusk-blue; dusky; electric-blue; faded-blue; gas-blue; grape-blue; gray-blue; hot-blue; hyacinth-blue; ice-blue; icy-blue; ink-blue; jewel-blue; lake-blue; lapis-blue; lavender-blue; light-blue; lightning-blue; midnight-blue; midnight-satin; morning-glory; navy-blue; ocean-blue; pale-blue; powder-blue; sapphire-blue; sea-blue; sea-colored; silver-blue; silvery-blue; sky-blue; sky-colored; slate-blue; smoky-blue; steel-blue; stone-blue; summer-sky; too-blue; turquoise; turquoise-blue; water-blue; water-colored; watery-blue; whitish-blue; Windex-blue.

(ADJ) Color: Brown / Amber
acorn-brown; acorn-colored; almond-brown; almond-colored; amber; amber-brown; amber-colored; ash-brown; auburn; Brazilian-brown; bronzy; brown; brown-black; brown-blue; brown-bronze; brown-button; brown-green; brownest; candy-brown; candy-dark; caramel-colored; chestnut-brown; chestnut-colored; chocolate-brown; chocolate-colored; cinnamon-brown; clay-colored; clear-brown; cocoa-colored; coffee-brown; coffee-colored; cognac-colored; copper; copper-brown; copper-colored; coppery; corky; dark-brown; deep-brown; dirt-colored; doe-like; dog-brown; fawn; fawn-like; ginger; gold; gold-brown; golden; golden-brown; honey-bear; honey-brown; honey-colored; light-brown; medium-brown; milk-chocolate; mud-brown; mud-colored; muddy-brown; muddy-colored; nut-brown; pecan-brown; prune-dark; puce-russet; raisin-brown; red-amber; red-brown; rosewood; rum-colored; russet; rusty; sand-colored; sandy-colored; spice-brown; tan-colored; tawny; tawny-colored; tea-brown; tobacco-colored; toffee-colored; turd-colored; walnut-colored; watery-brown; whiskey-brown; whiskey-colored.

(ADJ) Color: Gray
bar-gray; cast-iron; dark-gray; dove-colored; dove-gray; dust-gray; dusty; fish-colored; flinty; gray; gray-black; grayest; grayish; gunmetal; gunmetal-gray; ice-gray; light-gray; metallic; mist-colored; nickel-colored; pearl-gray; pebbly; rain-colored; sea-gray; silver; silver-gray; silvery; slate-gray; smoky; smoky-dark; steel-gray; storm-cloud-colored; storm-gray; water-gray.

(ADJ) Color: Green / Hazel
acid-green; blue-green; bluish-green; bottle-green; bright-green; bright-hazel; brown-green; cat-green; copper-green; dark-green; deep-green; elm-leaf; emerald-green; evergreen; forest-green; glass-green; gold-green; gold-hazel;

grass-green; gray-green; green; green-blue; green-brown; green-flecked; green-gold; green-gray; green-yellow; greenest; greenish; greenish-blue; greenish-gray; greenish-yellow; hazel; hazel-blue; hazel-brown; hazel-colored; hazel-green; ice-green; jade-colored; jade-green; jewel-green; laser-green; leaf-green; light-green; lime-green; mermaid-green; moss-green; orchid-colored; orchid-dark; pistachio-green; ripe-olive; sage-green; sea-glass; sea-green; shamrock-green; silver-green; swamp-leaf; weed-green.

(ADJ) Color: Violet / Indigo
gray-violet; indigo; indigo-colored; liquid-violet; opal-colored; opalescent; plum-colored; purple; purple-blue; purply; violet; violet-blue.

(ADJ) Color: White
albino; all-white; dove-colored; fog-colored; fog-white; kahlua-white; marble-like; milk-white; mist-colored; opaque; pearly; porcelain-white; tartar; white; whitish.

(ADJ) Color: Miscellaneous
drab-colored; gold-flecked; gold-yellow; golden-flecked; golden-yellow; light-colored; mercurochrome-colored; moon-yellow; odd-colored; orange; peach-colored; pink; pinkish; ruby; scarlet; sulfur-yellow; yellow; yellow-blue; yellow-brown; yellow-gray; yellow-green; yellowish; yellowish-hazel; yellowy.

Verbs and Phrasal Verbs in Alphabetical Order

A - B
abandoned; absorbed; abulge; accepted; acclimated; acclimated to; accommodated; accompanied; accused; accustomed to; ached; ached for; ached from; ached with; acknowledged; acquired; adapted; adapted for; adapted to; added; added to; adjusted; adjusted to; adored; advertised; affected; affected by; affected with; affixed; affixed to; aglint; aglitter; aimed; aimed at; aimed up; alarmed; alerted; alerted to; alight; alight with; alighted; alighted on; aligned; aligned on; aligned with; allowed; altered; alternated; alternated between; amazed; amused; analyzed; angled; angled up; angled upward; animated; animated by; animated with; announced; answered; appealed; appealed longingly; appeared; appeared at; appeared from; appeared in; appeared like; appraised; appreciated; approached; arched; arched with; argued; aroused; arranged; arranged in; ascended; ashine; ashine with; asked; asked for; assessed; associated; assumed; assured; astounded; aswirl; aswirl with; ate up; attached to; attempted; attempted to; atwinkle; averted; averted from; averted in; averted toward; avoided; awaited; awakened; awoke; backed; backed down; backed up; baited; ballooned; bandaged; banged; bared; bathed; bathed in; batted; batted at; beamed; beamed on; beamed with; became; became almost; became hard; became less; became like; became more; became round; beckoned; beckoned

for; bedewed with; began; began to; begged; begged for; begged; begged for; begot; beheld; beheld from afar; beheld in; beheld with; belied; believed; belonged; belonged to; bemoaned; bent; bent down; bent downward; bent toward; beseeched; bespoke; betrayed; bid farewell; bit; bit at; blackened; blackened at; blackened by; blackened with; blanked; blanked on; blared; blasted; blazed; blazed at; blazed beneath; blazed down; blazed like; blazed on; blazed up; blazed with; bleared; bleared by; bleared with; bled; blended; blended with; blessed; blew into; blinded; blinded by; blinded from; blinded with; blindfolded; blinked; blinked about; blinked at; blinked away; blinked back; blinked behind; blinked once; blinked open; blinked with; blipped; blipped like; blistered; blistered through; blocked by; blossomed; blossomed into; blotted out; blurred; blurred from; blurred with; bobbed; bobbed down; bobbled; boggled by; boiled; boiled with; bolted; bolted back; bordered; bordered on; bore; bore down; bore into; bore through; bounced; bounced from; bounced off; bounced on; bound; bound up; bowed; bowed down; bowed toward; bracketed by; branded; brightened; brightened at; brightened up; brightened with; brimmed over; brimmed with; broke; broke away; broke from; brooded; brooded with; brought; brought back; brought down; brought on; brought up; bruised; brushed; brushed across; brushed by; brushed over; brushed past; brushed up; brushed up and down; bubbled; bubbled with; budded; budded with; bugged; bugged at; bugged out; bugged with; bulged; bulged at; bulged from; bulged like; bulged out; bulged with; bunched; bunched up; bunged up; bunked; burbled with; buried; buried in; burned; burned at; burned beneath; burned bright(er); burned down; burned for; burned from; burned into; burned like; burned on; burned out; burned through; burned with; burrowed; burrowed into; burst; burst from; burst out; busied; buzzed; bypassed.

C - D

calculated; called; called back; called out; called up; calmed; calmed down; came around; came at; came back; came closer; came down; came in; came open; came out; came round; came to; came up; canopied by; canopied with; canvassed; capped by; captivated; captured; caressed; carried; carved into; cast; cast about; cast around; cast down; cast downward; cast on; cast to; cast toward; cast up; cast upon; cast upward; catalogued; caught; caught a glimpse; caught at; caught by; caught in; caught on; caught up; caused; caused by; cautioned; cavorted; cavorted in; ceased; centered; centered in; centered on; challenged; chanced; changed; changed again; changed from; changed into; changed when; charged with; chased; chased away; checked; checked for; chilled; chuckled; churned; circled; circled by; circled in; clamored; clamped; clamped down; clamped tight; clapped; clashed; clashed with; clawed at; cleaned; cleared; clenched; clenched in; clenched tight; clicked; climbed; climbed past; climbed up; cloaked by; cloaked with; closed; closed against; closed at; closed briefly; closed halfway; closed hard; closed in on; closed on; closed slightly; closed tightly; closed together; closed under; closed up; closed wearily; closed with; clotted; clotted with; clouded; clouded by; clouded over; clouded with; clung to; clustered; coasted; coasted down; coasted over; coated by; coated with; cocked;

cocked at; cocked on; collapsed; collapsed into; collided; collided with; colored; colored by; commanded; commenced; commiserated; communicated; compared with; compelled; compelled to; completed; composed; comprehended; compressed; compressed into; concealed; concealed behind; concealed by; concentrated; concentrated on; condemned; confirmed; confronted; confused; confused by; conjured; conjured up; connected; connected to; connected with; considered; consisted of; constricted; constricted into; consumed; consumed by; contacted with; contained; continued; continued downward; continued to; contracted; contracted visibly; contrasted; contrasted with; controlled; converged; conveyed; cooled; cooled down; corrected; corresponded with; corroborated; could; couldn`t believe; counted; counted off; coursed; coursed down; courted; covered; covered by; covered in; covered with; cowered; cowered in; cracked; cracked open; crackled; crackled with; craned; crawled; crawled over; crawled toward; crawled up; crawled with; creaked; creased; creased at; creased into; creased up; crept; crept down; crept up; cried; cried for; cried out; crimped; crimped in; crinkled; crinkled in; crinkled up; crinkled when; crinkled with; crossed; crowded; crowded in; cruised; crumpled; crunched; crunched up; crystallized; curtained by; curved; curved like; cut; cut across; cut around; cut away; cut back; cut down; cut into; cut like; cut out; cut over; cut through; cut to; daggered; daggered into; damaged; damaged in; dampened; dampened with; danced; danced about; danced across; danced around; danced in; danced to; danced up; danced with; dangled; dangled from; dared; darkened; darkened at; darkened with; darted; darted about; darted across; darted along; darted around; darted at; darted away; darted back; darted between; darted down; darted everywhere; darted from; darted in; darted into; darted nervously; darted out; darted over; darted past; darted quickly; darted sideways; darted skittishly; darted swiftly; darted through; darted to; darted toward; darted up; darted wildly; dashed; dawdled; dawdled over; daydreamed; dazed; dazzled; dazzled by; dazzled with; deadlocked; dealt; dealt with; deceived; decided; declared; declined for; deepened; deepened in; deepened with; defied; defocused; defocused for; deformed; delighted; delighted at; delighted in; demanded; denied; depended on; depressed; deprived; deprived of; descended; descended from; desired; desired to; detached; detected; detected in; determined; deviated; devoured; did a double-take; did up; died away; differed; differed from; differed in; dilate into; dilated; dimmed; dimmed in; dimmed slightly; dimmed with; dipped; dipped to; directed; directed ahead; directed at; directed in; directed inward; directed out; directed past; directed toward; directed upward; disagreed; disappeared; disappeared behind; disappeared in; disappeared into; disappointed; discerned; disclosed; discolored; discolored by; discovered; disintegrated; dislodged; displayed; dissipated; dissolved; dissolved in; dissolved to; distended; distinguished; distorted; distorted by; distorted into; distracted; distressed; dithered; dithered among; diverted; diverted from; divided; divided between; dodged; dogged; dominated; donned; dosed; dosed in; dotted; dotted on; dove; dove down; drank; drank in; dreamed; dreamed of; dredged; drew; drew back; drew down; drew in; drew onto; drew up; dried; dried out; dried up; drifted; drifted across; drifted around; drifted back; drifted down; drifted downward; drifted from; drifted in; drifted off; drifted open; drifted out; drifted over; drifted past; drifted to; drifted toward; drifted up; drifted upward; drilled; drilled into; drilled through; dripped; dripped with; drooped; drooped under; dropped; dropped away; dropped back; dropped below; dropped down; dropped from; dropped on; dropped out; dropped to; drove; drove through; drowned; drowned in; drowsed; drowsed over; drugged; drugged with; dug into; dug out; dulled; dulled by; dulled to; dulled with; dwelt; dwelt on; dwelt with; dwindled.

E - F

eased; eased into; echoed; eclipsed; edged with; edited out; elevated; elevated toward; eluded; embedded in; embraced; emerged; emerged from; emerged through; emitted; emphasized; emptied; emptied of; enabled; encircled; encircled with; encompassed; encountered; encouraged; encrusted with; endeared; ended up; endured; engaged; enhanced; enlarged; enlarged by; enlarged with; entertained; entreated; evolved; examined; exchanged; exhausted; expanded; expanded in; expanded like; expected; exploded; exploded in; exploded with; explored; exposed; expressed; extended; extended on; exuded; eyed; faced; faced down; faced forward; faced into; faced sideways; faced toward; faded; faded into; failed; failed to; faltered; fanned by; fanned out; fascinated; fascinated by; fastened on; fastened onto; fastened to; fatigued; fatigued after; feasted on; fell; fell at; fell away; fell back; fell before; fell beneath; fell down; fell from; fell on; fell out; fell to; fell under; fell with; felt; felt like; ferreted for; filled; filled up; filled with; filmed; filmed over; filmed up; filmed with; finished; fired; fired back; fired by; fitted; fixated; fixated on; fixed; fixed ahead; fixed at; fixed forward; fixed on; fixed onto; fixed straight; fixed toward; fixed upward; fixed with; fizzled; flailed; flamed; flamed with; flared; flared at; flared in; flared like; flared up; flared with; flashed; flashed across; flashed angrily; flashed around; flashed at; flashed back; flashed behind; flashed beneath; flashed from; flashed in; flashed like; flashed through; flashed to; flashed toward; flashed with; flattened; flattered by; flecked with; fled; fled to; flew; flew around; flew back; flew down; flew open; flew out; flew over; flew past; flew to; flew toward; flew up; flew wide; flicked; flicked about; flicked across; flicked around; flicked at; flicked back; flicked between; flicked down; flicked downward; flicked from; flicked into; flicked over; flicked past; flicked sideways; flicked to; flicked toward; flicked up; flickered; flickered around; flickered away; flickered back; flickered beneath; flickered between; flickered from; flickered in; flickered on; flickered out; flickered over; flickered sideways; flickered through; flickered to; flickered toward; flickered up; flickered when; flickered with; flinched; flinched hard; flinched in; flipped back; flirted; flirted with; flitted; flitted about; flitted across; flitted around; flitted at; flitted between; flitted down; flitted from; flitted over; flitted to; flitted up; floated; floated away; floated back; floated down; floated over; floated to; floated toward; floated up; floated upward; flooded; flooded in; flooded with; flowed; flowed down; flowed like; flowed with; flung; fluttered; fluttered at; fluttered back; fluttered behind; fluttered between; fluttered downward; fluttered for; fluttered halfway; fluttered in; fluttered open; fluttered sleepily; focused; focused ahead; focused at; focused forward; focused in; focused on; focused onto; focused to; focused toward; focused with; fogged; fogged up; followed; followed across; followed back; followed to; followed with; fondled; fooled; forced; foresaw; forestalled; formed; fought; fought against; found; foundered; fractured with; framed; framed by; framed in; framed under; framed with; freaked; freed; freed from; fringed by; fringed with; frosted; frosted over; froze; froze in; froze on; froze over; fumbled; fumbled over; fumed; fumed at; functioned; functioned in; furnished; fuzzed; fuzzed over.

G - K

gained; galloped; galloped over; gaped; gaped at; gaped in; gaped with; gathered; gauged; gave; gave away; gave off; gave out; gawked; gawked at; gazed; gazed around; gazed at; gazed down; gazed into; gazed off; gazed on; gazed out; gazed over; gazed straight; gazed toward; gazed up; gazed upon; gazed upward; gazed with; generated; gestured; gestured to; glanced; glanced around; glanced at; glanced away; glanced down; glanced from; glanced into; glanced on; glanced over; glanced to; glanced toward; glanced up; glanced upon; glanced upward; glanced with; glared; glared at; glared back; glared down; glared from; glared in; glared into; glared on; glared out; glared over; glared up; glared upon; glared with; glassed over; glazed; glazed from; glazed like; glazed over; glazed with; gleamed; gleamed above; gleamed across; gleamed at; gleamed behind; gleamed beneath; gleamed from; gleamed in; gleamed like; gleamed through; gleamed under; gleamed when; gleamed with; glided; glided along; glided down; glided over; glided past; glided to; glided toward; glimmered; glimmered from; glimmered in; glimmered like; glimmered with; glimpsed; glinted; glinted back; glinted behind; glinted down; glinted in; glinted like; glinted with; glistened; glistened behind; glistened in; glistened like; glistened with; glittered; glittered at; glittered beneath; glittered down; glittered in; glittered into; glittered like; glittered out; glittered through; glittered under; glittered when; glittered with; gloated; glowed; glowed in; glowed like; glowed with; glowered; glowered at; glowered down; glowered from; glowered up; glued on; glued to; glued upon; goaded; goggled; goggled with; got better; got hard(er); got to; gouged; gouged out; grabbed onto; graced by; gravitated to; gravitated towards; grazed; grazed over; greeted; grew; grew hard; grew more; grew round; grinned; grinned up; groped; groped for; guarded; guided; gushed; half-shut; half-shut against; half-shut behind; half-shut with; haloed with; halted; halted on; happened to; happened upon; hardened; hardened at; hardened from; hardened into; hated; haunted; haunted by; hazed; hazed from; hazed over; healed; heaped with; heightened by; held; held by; held for; held in; held on; helped; hesitated; hesitated for; hibernated; hid; hid behind; hid beneath; hid under; highlighted; highlighted by; highlighted in; hinted at; hit; hit on; hollowed; hollowed out; homed in on; honed; honed by; honed into; hooded; hooded in; hooked; hooked into; hooked on; hoped; hopped; hopped forward; housed; hovered; hovered above; hovered on; hovered over; humbled; humbled by; hung around; hung on; hunted; hunted among; hunted for; hurt; hurt from;

hurt like; iced over; identified; ignited; ignited by; ignited with; ignored; illuminated; illuminated by; illuminated with; imagined; impaled; implied; implored; impressed; imprinted; imprinted on; included; increased; indicated; inflamed; inflamed with; inlaid with; inquired; inserted; insinuated; insisted; insisted on; inspected; instructed; insulated; intensified; intercepted; interfered; interfered with; interpreted; inventoried; invited; involved; irritated; irritated by; itched; jabbed; jerked; jerked away; jerked back; jerked down; jerked in; jerked sideways; jerked to; jerked toward; jerked up; jittered; jittered back; joined in; jolted; jostled for; jostled with; judged; judging; jumped; jumped back; jumped from; jumped onto; jumped to; jumped toward; jumped up; jutted; jutted out; jutted to; kept; kept on; killed; kindled; kindled at; kindled in; kindled with; knew; knocked; knocked out.

L - P

lacked; laid; laid back; landed; landed on; lasered in; lasered in on; lashed; lashed up; latched; latched on; latched onto; latticed with; laughed; laughed at; leaned; leaned closer; leaned over; leapt at; leapt out; leapt to; leapt/leaped; learned; led; led by; leered; leered at; left; lent; let; leveled; leveled on; levitated; levitated toward; lidded by; lidded with; lifted; lifted at; lifted from; lifted heavenward; lifted in; lifted to; lifted toward; lifted up; lifted with; lighted; lighted like; lighted on; lighted up; lighted upon; lighted with; lightened; lightened in; lightened to; lightened up; lightened with; liked; lined; lined in; lined up; lined with; lingered; lingered for; lingered on; lingered over; lingered there; liquefy; lit; lit by; lit from; lit on; lit up; lit with; loaded with; located; locked; locked across; locked into; locked on; locked onto; locked over; locked to; locked together; locked with; lodged in; lolled; lolled back; longed for; longing; longs for; looked; looked about; looked around; looked at; looked back; looked behind; looked better; looked beyond; looked down; looked downward; looked for; looked from; looked heavenward; looked in; looked into; looked inward; looked like; looked off; looked on; looked out; looked over; looked past; looked straight; looked through; looked to; looked toward; looked up; looked upward; loomed; loosened; lost; lost in; loved; lowered; lowered in; lowered to; lowered toward; lunged; lurched; lurched toward; lurked; lusted; lusted after; maddened; maddened by; made eye contact; made out; magnified; managed; marched; marked; marked by; marred; marred by; masked; masked by; matched; materialized; materialized on; measured; melted; melted back; melted in; melted with; mesmerized; mesmerized by; met; met across; met briefly; met through; might as well; might never; migrated; migrated from; mirrored; mismatched; misplaced; misplaced in; missed; misted; misted over; misted up; misted with; mixed with; mocked; moistened; moistened with; monitored; moped; moped about; morphed; morphed from; morphed into; motioned; motioned to; motioned toward; moved; moved across; moved around; moved away; moved back; moved beneath; moved down; moved downward; moved everywhere; moved from; moved in; moved inside; moved like; moved off; moved on; moved over; moved to; moved toward; moved up; moved with; nailed; named; narrowed; narrowed at; narrowed down; narrowed in; narrowed into; narrowed on; narrowed with; needed; needed to; negotiated; negotiated for; nodded; nodded in; nodded toward; noted; noticed; numbed; numbed by; numbed with; obscured; obscured behind; obscured by; observed; occupied; offended; offended by; offered; offset by; oozed; opened; opened almost; opened at; opened enough; opened for; opened fully; opened halfway; opened in; opened into; opened on; opened onto; opened to; opened up; opened wide; opened with; operated; operated under; ornamented with; oscillated around; ought; outlined; outlined by; outlined in; overflowed with; overlaid with; overlooked; overpowered by; overwhelmed; overwhelmed by; pained; painted; painted in; painted on; painted with; paled; paled to; panicked; panned; panned around; panned back; panned down; panned like; panned up; parted; passed; passed across; passed down; passed from; passed on; passed over; patrolled; paused; paused at; paused on; pecked out; peeked; peeked around; peeked at; peeked out; peeked through; peeled; peeled at; peeled back; peeled on; peeped; peeped around; peeped from; peeped out; peeped through; peered; peered at; peered down; peered from; peered inside; peered into; peered out; peered past; peered through; peered to; peered up; penetrated; perceived; perched; perched on; perfected; performed; perked up; permitted; perused; picked; picked out; picked up; pictured; pierced; pierced into; pierced through; pinched; pinched against; pinched hard; pinched into; pinched inward; pinned; pinned on; pinned to; piqued; pitied; pivoted; placed; placed on; planted; planted on; planted upward; played; played in; played over; played with; pleaded; pleaded for; pleaded with; pleased; pled; pled with; plowed; plucked out; plunged down; plunged into; pointed; pointed at; pointed down; pointed downward; pointed in; pointed to; pointed toward; pointed up; pointed upward; pointed with; poked; poked out; pondered; pooled; pooled up; pooled with; popped at; popped back; popped open; popped out; popped up; popped wide; popped with; popped; positioned; positioned in; positioned on; possessed; pounded; pounded with; poured; poured down; practiced; praised; prayed for; preferred; prepared; prepared for; presented; presented with; presided over; pressed; pressed against; pressed to; pretended; prevented; pricked; pricked with; prickled; prickled with; pried; pried at; probed; probed for; processed; prodded; produced; promised; prompted; pronounced; protected; protected by; protested; protruded; protruded from; protruded like; protruded when; proved; provided; puckered; puffed; puffed from; puffed into; puffed up; pulled; pulled back; pulled down; pulled into; pulled out; pulsed; pulsed in; pulsed with; punched; punctuated; purged; pursued; pushed; pushed against; put out; puzzled.

Q - S

quaked; quaked with; questioned; quit; quivered; quivered in; raced; raced ahead; raced around; raced back; raced over; raced with; racked; racked toward; radiated; raged; raised; raised in; raised on; raised to; raised toward; raised up; raised upward; raked; raked across; raked over; raked through; ran; ran along; ran between; ran down; ran into; ran over; ran to; ran up; ran with; rang; ranged; ranged along; ranged down; ranged over; rattled; rattled back; reached; read; readjusted; readjusted to; reappeared; reared; reared up; reassured; recalled;

receded; receded behind; receded in; receded into; received; recessed; recessed under; recognized; recorded; recovered; recovered from; reddened; reddened by; reddened with; reflected; reflected back; reflected in; refocused; refocused on; refocused with; refused; refused to; regained; regarded; registered; reinforced; relaxed; relinquished; remained; remained in; remained on; remained wide; remembered; reminded; removed; reopened; repeated; replaced by; replied; reposed; reposed on; reposed with; reproached; required; resembled; resided; responded; responded by; rested; rested for; rested on; resumed; retained; retracted; retreated; retreated back; retreated to; returned; returned from; returned to; revealed; revealed how; reviewed; revived; revived for; ricocheted; ricocheted from; ricocheted like; ricocheted off; riddled; riddled with; rimmed; rimmed in; rimmed like; rimmed with; ringed; ringed in; ringed like; ringed with; ripped out; rivaled; riveted; riveted on; riveted to; riveted upon; roamed; roamed about; roamed around; roamed from; roamed over; roamed toward; rocketed; rocketed toward; rode; rolled; rolled about; rolled around; rolled away; rolled back; rolled beneath; rolled into; rolled off; rolled over; rolled to; rolled toward; rolled up; rolled upward; rolled with; rooted to; rose; rose to; rose up; rose upward; rose with; rotated; rotated in; rotated to; rotated upward; rounded; rounded in; rounded to; roused; roved; roved about; roved across; roved around; roved beneath; roved from; roved over; roved past; roved to; roved up; roves over; rubbed; ruined; ruined from; ruled; ruled out; rummaged; rummaged around; rung; rung out; rushed; rushed to; saddened; sagged; said; sailed; sailed to; sailed toward; sank; sank back; sank backward; sank inward; sat; sat on; satisfied with; saucered; saucered by; saved; saw; saw through; scalded; scalded with; scanned; scanned about; scanned across; scanned around; scanned down; scanned for; scanned from; scanned through; scanned up; scared; scarred by; scattered; scattered with; scolded; scooped out; scooted; scooted everywhere; scoped; scoped out; scorched; scored; scoured; scrambled; scraped; scratched; scratched out; screamed; screamed to; screamed with; screened; screwed; screwed tight; screwed to; screwed up; scrolled; scrunched; scrunched tightly; scrunched up; scrutinized; scurried; scurried about; sealed by; searched; searched around; searched for; searched out; searched over; searched through; seared; seared into; seared up; seared with; seated; seated upon; seduced; seemed; seemed to; seethed; seized; sent; sent forth; sent out; separated; separated by; serenaded; served; set; set above; set against; set at; set back; set beneath; set close; set deep; set down; set far; set forward; set hard; set in; set into; set like; set off; set on; settled; settled back; settled on; settled upon; sewed up; shaded; shaded by; shaded from; shaded in; shadowed; shadowed beneath; shadowed by; shadowed with; shamed; shaped like; shared; shared in; sharpened; sharpened by; sharpened on; sharpened with; shed; sheened; sheened with; shied; shied away; shied from; shielded; shielded against; shielded behind; shielded beneath; shielded by; shifted; shifted around; shifted at; shifted away; shifted back; shifted down; shifted from; shifted over; shifted sideways; shifted to; shifted toward; shimmered; shimmered like; shimmered with; shocked; shocked against; shone; shone above; shone at; shone back; shone beneath; shone forth; shone in; shone like; shone on; shone out; shone through; shone with; shook; shoot; shot back; shot down; shot downward; shot forth; shot out; shot over; shot past; shot to; shot toward; shot up; shot upward; shot wide; shouted; showed; showed above; showed in; showed through; shrank; shrank at; shrank back; shrank behind; shrank in; shriveled; shriveled in; shrouded; shrouded with; shut; shut against; shut down; shut hard; shut in; shut on; shut with; sidled over; sifted; sighted; signaled; signified; silenced; singled out; situated; situated at; situated in; situated on; sized up; skated; skated across; skated over; skated through; sketched; sketched in; skewed; skewed in; skewed up; skewered; skidded; skidded off; skidded over; skidded toward; skimmed; skimmed across; skimmed down; skimmed over; skimmed past; skimmed up; skipped; skipped down; skipped from; skipped over; skittered; skittered around; skittered back; skittered from; skittered sideways; skittered to; slanted; slanted down; slanted toward; slanted up; slanted with; slashed; slept; slewed; slewed away; sliced; sliced through; slickened; slickened with; slid; slid across; slid around; slid away; slid back; slid from; slid in; slid into; slid off; slid over; slid sideways; slid to; slid toward; slipped; slipped away; slipped down; slipped from; slipped into; slipped off; slipped over; slipped sideways; slipped to; slipped toward; slithered sideways; slithered; slitted; slitted against; slitted by; slitted in; slitted with; slowed; smarted; smarted from; smarted with; smiled; smiled at; smiled back; smiled down; smiled in; smiled into; smiled on; smiled out; smiled slyly; smiled up; smoked; smoldered; smoldered at; smoldered down; smoldered like; smoldered with; smudged; smudged with; snagged; snagged at; snagged on; snaked; snapped; snapped at; snapped away; snapped back; snapped from; snapped into; snapped like; snapped on; snapped open; snapped to; snapped up; snapped wide; snapped with; snatched; snatched at; snatched up; snuck a look; snuffed out; soaked; soaked in; sobered; sobered up; softened; softened in; softened to; softened with; soiled by; soothed; sought; sought for; sought in; sought only; sought out; spaced around; spaced evenly; spaced out; spaced wide; spangled with; sparked; sparked like; sparked through; sparked with; sparkled; sparkled against; sparkled anew; sparkled at; sparkled behind; sparkled beneath; sparkled in; sparkled like; sparkled over; sparkled through; sparkled under; sparkled underneath; sparkled when; sparkled with; spat a look; speared; speared straight; spent; spewed; spied; spiked; spiked by; spiked with; spilled; spilled down; spilled on; spilled over; spiraled; splintered; splintered with; split; splodged with; spoiled; spoke; spoke of; spoke to; spoked with; sported; spotted; sprang; sprang open; sprang to; sprang up; sprawled across; sprawled over; spread; spread equally; spun; spun about; spun around; spun back; spun down; spun to; spun up; squeezed; squeezed closed; squeezed shut; squeezed tight; squinched; squinched against; squinched tight; squinted; squinted against; squinted at; squinted behind; squinted down; squinted from; squinted in; squinted into; squinted up; squirmed; squirmed with; stabbed; stabbed at; staggered; stalked; stalked through; stalked toward; stared; stared ahead; stared at; stared away; stared back; stared beneath; stared beyond; stared down; stared for; stared into; stared off; stared out; stared over; stared past; stared through; stared toward; stared up; stared with; started; started to; started toward; started with; startled; startled by; stated; stayed; stayed down; stayed hard; stayed level; stayed on; stayed with; steadied; steadied on; steered to; stiffened; stifled; stilled; stole a glance; stole a look; stole to; stoned; stood; stood before; stood out; stood still; stood straight; stopped; stopped at; stopped on; stopped still; strained; strained at; strained in; strained into; strained on; strained through; strained up; strayed; strayed across; strayed around; strayed for; strayed from; strayed off; strayed over; strayed seaward; strayed to; strayed toward; strayed up; streaked across; streaked with; streamed; streamed from; streamed with; strengthened; stretched; stretched out; stretched to; stretches over; stroked; strolled; strolled to; struck; struck out; struggled; struggled for; struggled to; struggled up; struggled with; stuck; stuck in; stuck on; stuck out; stuck to; studied; stumbled; stumbled over; stung; stung when; stung with; stunned; stunned with; sucked in; suffered; suffered from; suffused with; suggested; summed up; summoned; sung; surged; surged past; surged with; surprised; surrendered; surrendered to; surrounded; surrounded by; surrounded with; surveyed; suspended; suspended in; swallowed; swallowed up; swam; swam back; swam in; swam into; swam like; swam over; swam toward; swam when; swam with; swarmed; swarmed with; swelled; swelled up; swelled with; swept; swept across; swept along; swept around; swept back; swept over; swept past; swept through; swept to; swept towards; swept up; swerved; swerved down; swerved downward; swerved up; swerved upward; swirled; swirled with; switched; switched back; switched from; switched to; swiveled; swiveled around; swiveled from; swiveled in; swiveled on; swiveled to; swiveled toward; swooped; swooped down; swooped in; swung; swung away; swung back; swung between; swung from; swung over; swung to; swung toward.

T - Z

talked for; targeted; teared; teared at; teared from; teared over; teared up; teased; teased open; telegraphed; telescoped; telescoped outward; tended to; tensed; terrified; tested; testified; testified to; thickened; thickened with; thinned; thirsted; thirsted for; thought; thrashed; threaded with; threatened; threw daggers; throbbed; throbbed from; thrust; thrust back; thrust out; ticked; ticked back; tied; tied to; tightened; tightened around; tightened at; tightened down; tightened in; tightened on; tilted; tilted down; tilted heavenward; tilted in; tilted to; tilted toward; tilted up; timed; tinged with; tingled; tinted; tinted with; tipped; tipped up; tired; told; told of; tolled; tolled back; took; took after; took in; took on; took to; took up; tore at; tore out; tormented; touched; touched with; toured; traced; traced along; traced down; traced out; traced up; traced with; tracked; tracked across; tracked after; tracked down; tracked over; trailed; trailed after; trailed away; trailed over; trailed upward; trained; trained away; trained behind; trained down; trained downward; trained forward; trained in; trained on; trained straight; trained up; trained upon; transfixed; transfixed by; transfixed like; transfixed on; transfixed upon; transformed; transformed into; transmitted; trapped; trapped beneath; traveled; traveled across; traveled along; traveled around; traveled back; traveled down; traveled downward; traveled from; traveled over; traveled to; traveled up; traveled upward; traversed; trawled; treated; treated with; trembled; trembled with; tried to; tripped; tripped on;

troubled; trusted; tuned; tuned to; turned; turned aside; turned at; turned away; turned back; turned backward; turned down; turned downward; turned forward; turned from; turned heavenward; turned in; turned inward; turned on; turned onto; turned to; turned toward; turned up; turned upon; turned upward; turned with; twinkled; twinkled above; twinkled at; twinkled behind; twinkled beneath; twinkled in; twinkled like; twinkled under; twinkled up; twinkled when; twinkled with; twitched; twitched at; twitched behind; twitched from; twitched like; unblinked; unclouded; undercast with; underlined; underlined by; underscored; understood; undressed; undulated; unfocused; unglued; united; united with; unlocked; unlocked from; unmoved; unnerved; uplifted; uplifted at; uplifted in; upset; urged; used; vanished; varied; veered; veered away; veered in; veiled; veined with; ventured; ventured to; vibrated; vibrated with; visualized; waited; waited for; waited in; waited until; walked; walked up; wandered; wandered about; wandered above; wandered across; wandered ahead; wandered around; wandered away; wandered back; wandered beyond; wandered down; wandered from; wandered in; wandered off; wandered over; wandered past; wandered sideways; wandered skyward; wandered through; wandered to; wandered toward; wandered up; wandered when; wandered with; wanted; warbled; warmed to; warmed up; warned; warped; warred; warred with; washed; washed away; washed over; watched; watched as; watched closely; watched for; watched from; watched in; watched over; watered; watered at; watered from; watered in; watered up; watered with; wavered; wavered for; wavered in; wavered over; weakened; wearied; wearied with; weigh; weighed; weighed in on; welcomed; welled; welled up; welled with; went after; went around; went away; went back; went dead; went down; went everywhere; went from; went hard; went in; went over; went past; went still; went straight; went to; went up; wept; wept behind; were taken aback; wet; wet from; wet with; whipped across; whirled; whirled about; whirled with; widened; widened in; widened with; wiggled; winced; winced when; winked; winked at; withdrew; witnessed; wobbled; wobbled back; woke; woke up; wore; wore a look of; wore out; worked; worried; worried at; wounded by; wrenched up; wrestled with; wrinkled; wrinkled with; writhed in; yawed; yearned; yearned after; yielded; zeroed in; zeroed in on; zipped; zipped back; zoomed; zoomed in; zoomed in on.

Noun Phrases

A - G

ability of the eye(s); abnormalities of the eye(s); absence of the eye(s); accuracy of the eye(s); action of the eye(s); activity of the eye(s); acuity of the eye(s); adaptation of the eye(s); adjustment of the eye(s); affliction of the eye(s); aid of the eye(s); alignment of the eye(s); amusement of the eye(s); anatomy of the eye(s); angle of the eye(s); anticipation of the eye(s); appearance of the eye(s); apple of the eye; application of the eye(s); area of the eye(s); aspect of the eye(s); assistance of the eye(s); assortment of eyes; attention of the eye(s); authority of the eye(s); avoidance of the eye(s); axis of the eye(s); ball of the eye(s); base of the eye(s); beauty of the eye(s); behavior of the eye(s); bit of eye; blindness of the eye(s); blink of the eye(s); blurriness of the eye(s); body of the eye(s); border of the eye(s); breadth of the eye(s); brightness of the eye(s); brilliance of the eye(s); brilliancy of the eye(s); brown of the eye(s); capabilities of the eye(s); capacity of the eye(s); capillaries of the eye(s); care of the eye(s); caress of eyes; cataract of the eye(s); cavity of the eye(s); center of the eye(s); character of the eye(s); characteristics of the eye(s); circle of the eye(s); circumference of the eye(s); clearness of the eye(s); closeup of the eye(s); closing of the eye(s); closure of the eye(s); cluster of eyes; color of the eye(s); comparison of the eye(s); condition of the eye(s); conformation of the eye(s); congestion of the eye(s); contact of the eye(s); contraction of the eye(s); control of the eye(s); convergence of the eye(s); coordination of the eye(s); core of the eye(s); cornea of the eye(s); corner of the eye(s); couple of eyes; covering of the eye(s); crookedness of the eye(s); curvature of the eye(s); curve of the eye(s); deception of the eye(s); defect of the eye(s); degeneration of the eye(s); delicacy of the eye(s); delight of the eye(s); depression of the eye(s); depth(s) of the eye(s); description of the eye(s); desire of the eye(s); development of the eye(s); deviation of the eye(s); diameter of the eye(s); dimensions of the eye(s); dimness of the eye(s); direction of the eye(s); disease of the eye(s); disorder of the eye(s); distance of the eye(s); divergence of the eye(s); drop of the eye(s); dryness of the eye(s); edge(s) of the eye(s); effect of the eye(s); efficiency of the eye(s); effort of the eye(s); elements of the eye(s); elevation of the eye(s); emptiness of the eye(s); end of the eye(s); enlargement of the eye(s); evasion of the eye(s); examination of the eye(s); experience of the eye(s); exposure of the eye(s); expression of the eye(s); extension of the eye(s); faculty of the eye(s); failure of the eye(s); fascination of the eye(s); fatigue of the eye(s); features of the eye(s); fire of the eye(s); fixation of the eye(s); flash of the eye(s); flicker of the eye(s); flinch of the eye(s); fluid of the eye(s); focus of the eye(s); form of the eye(s); function of the eye(s); gaze of the eye(s); glance of the eye(s); glare of the eye(s); gleam of the eye(s); glint of the eye(s); glitter of the eye(s); globe of the eye(s)); gratification of the eye(s); group of eyes.

H - Y

hardness of the eye(s); health of the eye(s); heart of the eye(s); heaviness of the eye(s); hollows of the eye(s); humor of the eye(s); illumination of the eye(s); imperfections of the eye(s); impressions of the eye(s); inability of the eye(s); infection of the eye(s); inflammation of the eye(s); influence of the eye(s); injuries of the eye(s); innocence of the eye(s); inspection of the eye(s); integrity of the eye(s); interior of the eye(s); involvement of the eye(s); iris of the eye(s); irritation of the eye(s); judgment of the eye(s); keenness of eye; kind of eyes; language of the eye(s); leer of the eye(s); lens(es) of the eye(s); level of the eye(s); lid(s) of the eye(s); lift of the eye(s); line(s) of the eye(s); loss of the eye(s); lust of the eye(s); luster of the eye(s); meeting of the eye(s); moisture of the eye(s); motion of the eye(s); movement of the eye(s); muscle(s) of the eye(s); myriads of eyes; narrowing of the eye(s); nature of the eye(s); nerves of the eye(s); number of eyes; observation of the eye(s); on account of the eye(s);

optics of the eye(s); orb(s) of the eye(s); outline of the eye(s); pain of the eye(s); pair(s) of eyes; part of the eye(s); perception of the eye(s); perfection of the eye(s); periphery of the eye(s); physiology of the eye(s); pigment of the eye(s); play of the eye(s); pleasure of the eye(s); point of the eye(s); pools of eyes; position of the eye(s); power of the eye(s); precision of the eye(s); presence of the eye(s); prevalence of eyes; prickle of the eye(s); pride of the eye(s); prominence of the eye(s); protection of the eye(s); protrusion of the eye(s); pupil(s) of the eye(s); quality of the eye(s); quickness of the eye(s); range of the eye(s); reach of the eye(s); reaction of the eye(s); redness of the eye(s); refraction of the eye(s); region of the eye(s); removal of the eye(s); resolution of the eye(s); response of the eye(s); rest of the eye(s); retina of the eye(s); rim of the eye(s); ring of the eye(s); roll of the eye(s); roomful of eyes; rotation of the eye(s); row(s) of eyes; satisfaction of the eye(s); score of eyes; scorn of the eye(s); sea of eyes; search of eyes; sensations of the eye(s); sense of the eye(s); sensibility of the eye(s); sensitivity of the eye(s); series of eyes; set(s) of eyes; shape of the eye(s); sharpness of the eye(s); shifting of the eye(s); side(s) of the eye(s); sight of the eye(s); size of the eye(s); slant of the eye(s); sleepiness of the eye(s); slits of eyes; smallness of the eye(s); smile of the eye(s); socket(s) of the eye(s); soreness of the eye(s); sort of eyes; sparkle of the eye(s); speed of the eye(s); squint of the eye(s); steadiness of the eye(s); straining of the eye(s); sweep of the eye(s); tension of the eye(s); training of the eye(s); treatment of the eye(s); trick of the eye(s); twinkle of the eye(s); type of eyes; use of the eye(s); vacancy of the eye(s); vacuity of the eye(s); vanity of the eye(s); velocity of the eye(s); view of the eye(s); vision of the eye(s); wall of eyes; warmth of the eye(s); water of the eye(s); weakness of the eye(s); white(s) of the eye(s); widening of the eye(s); width of the eye(s); window(s) of the eye(s); wink of the eye(s); yellowness of the eye(s).

USAGE EXAMPLES

But it was Vivian's *brilliant blue eyes* that had always captivated him.

She *averted her eyes* for a brief moment, sensing something in this stranger's gaze that left her feeling uneasy.

His *cold menacing eyes pierced* her very soul.

Carly *cast her eyes downward*, unable to speak.

The sunlight bounced off her *emerald-green eyes*, making them *appear even more luminous*.

14
FACE

Adjectives in Alphabetical Order

A - D

absurd; academic; acceptable; acne-covered; acne-scarred; acned; addled; adjacent; administrative; adorable; adoring; adult; affectionate; afflicted; African; age-creased; age-ravaged; aged; ageing/aging; ageless; aggravated; aghast; agitated; agonized; agreeable; alabaster-white; alarmed; alert; alien; all-American; all-business; almond-colored; already-pale; altered; amazed; amazing; amber; American; amiable; amorphous; ample; amused; ancient; angelic; angelic-looking; angled; Anglo-Saxon; angry; anguished; angular; animated; annoyed; anonymous; antagonistic; antique; anxious; ape-like; apologetic; apoplectic; appalled; apparent; appealing; apple-cheeked; apple-shaped; appraising; approachable; appropriate; approving; apricot-colored; Arab; arid; aristocratic; armored; arresting; arrogant; ascetic; asexual; ash-whitened; ashed; ashen; ashy; Asian; asleep; astonished; astonishing; asymmetrical; atrocious; attentive; attractive; austere; average; averted; awe-struck; awesome; awful; baby-doll; bad; badgered; baffled; bald; ball-shaped; bandaged; banged-up; barbarian; bare; barren; battered; beaked; beaky; beaming; bearable; beard-stubbled; beard-stubbly; bearded; beardless; beaten; beatific; beauteous; beautiful; beefy; beer-bloated; beet-red; befuddled; beguiling; bellicose; beloved; bemused; benevolent; benign; benignant; bent-over; bespectacled; best; bestial; betrayed; bewhiskered; bewildered; big; big-toothed; bilious; birdlike; bite-swollen; bitter; black; black-and-white; black-bearded; black-dyed; black-skinned; black-stubbled; blackened; blanched; bland; blank; blasted; bleak; bleary; bleeding; blemished; blessed; blind; blindfolded; blinking; blistering; bloated; blocky; blond; blonde; blood-encrusted; blood-smeared; blood-spattered; blood-stained; blood-streaked; blood-suffused; bloodied; bloodless; bloodshot; bloody; blotched; blotchy; blubbery; blue; blue-black; blue-eyed; bluesy; bluish; blunt; blurred; blurry; blush-red; blushing; blustery; bobbing; boiled; boiled-looking; bold; bone-lean; bone-white; bony; bowed; boyish; braid-wrapped; bran-muffin; branded; brave; brazen; brick-red; bright; brightened; brilliant; bristled; bristly; broad; broad-browed; broad-jawed; broken; broken-up; bronzed; brooding; browed; brown; bruised; brutal; brutalized; brutish; bulbous; bulging; bulgy; burly; burned/brunt; burning; burnished; busted; busted-up; butchered; buzzard-like; cackling; cadaverous; calm; camera-ready; candid; capable; caramel-brown; caramel-colored; care-worn; caring; carved; Caucasian; chalk-white; chalky; changed; changing; charismatic; charming; charred; cheap; cheerful; cheery; cherubic; chestnut-brown; child-like; childish; childlike; chilled; china-doll; Chinese;

chinless; chiseled; chiseled-looking; chubby; chumpy; chunky; cinematic; circular; classic; classical; clay-colored; clean; clean-cut; clean-shaven; clear; clear-eyed; clenched; clever; close-shaven; closed-up; clouded; cloudy; clove-brown; clownish; clumsy; coal-black; coarse; coarse-skinned; cockeyed; coffee-dark; coffined; cold; cold-eyed; collective; colored; colorless; comatose; comely; comic; comical; commanding; common; compassionate; compelling; complete; complex; complexioned; complicated; composed; concealed; concentrated; concerned; condescending; confident; confused; congested; conscious; contemplative; contented; contentious; contorted; contradictory; conventional; cool; cooling; copper-colored; copper-hued; coppery; cordial; corpse-pale; corpulent; cosmetic-enhanced; cosmetic-free; countless; covered; cracked; crafty; craggy; crazed; crazy; cream-colored; cream-smooth; cream-white; creased; creasy; crimson; crimsoned; crinkly; critical; crocodilian; crooked; cross-eyed; cruel; crumpled; crumpling; crushed; crusted; cultivated; cunning; curious; curly; curved; cute; cutest; cynical; damaged; damn; damned; damp; dampened; dampish; dappled; dark; dark-bronze; dark-grimed; dark-skinned; darkened; darkish; dazzling; dead; deadly; dear; death-mask; death-slackened; decay-ravaged; decayed; decaying; deceitful; decent; decorated; deep; deep-brown; deep-eyed; deeply-lined; defeated; defiant; defiled; deflatable; deformed; dejected; delicate; delicate-featured; delighted; demented; demonic; demure; despairing; desperate; despondent; destroyed; determined; devastated; dewy; diabolic; different; dignified; dim; diminutive; dimming; dimpled; direct; dirt-smudged; dirt-stained; dirt-streaked; dirty; disappointed; disapproving; disbelieving; discernible; discolored; discontented; disdainful; disembodied; disfigured; disgruntled; disgusted; disheveled; dishonest; disillusioned; disinterested; dismal; dismissible; dismissive; dispassionate; disreputable; dissatisfied; distant; distinct; distinctive; distinguished; distorted; distracting; distraught; distressed; ditzy; divine; dogmatic; doleful; doll-like; dough-ball; doughy; dour; downbent; downcast; downlooking; downturned; downy; drab; drained; dramatic; dreadful; dreaming; dreamy; drenched; dried; dried-up; drifting; drink-reddened; driven; droll; drooping; droopy; drowsy; drunken; dry; dubious; dull; dumb; dumbfounded; dun-colored; dusky; dusky-toned; dust-grimed; dust-streaked; dusty; dying.

E - L
eager; earnest; earth-colored; easy-going; ecstatic; egg-shaped; eggshell-pale; eighty-year-old; elderly; elegant; elfish; elongated; eloquent; elven; emaciated; embarrassed; embittered; emotional; emotionless; emptied; empty; enchanting; endearing; energetic; English; enhanced; enigmatic; enormous; enraged; enraptured; enthusiastic; enthusiastic-looking; entire; entranced; ethereal; European; evasive; even-featured; ever-cheerful; everyday; evil; exaggerated; exalted; exasperated; excellent; excited; exhausted; exotic; expectant; exposed; expressionless; expressive; exquisite; extraordinary; facial-hair-free; faded; fair; fair-tinted; fake; fallen; false; familial; familiar; familiar-looking; famished; famous; fancy; fanged; farm-boy; fascinated; fascinating; fastidious; fat; fat-creased; fatigued; fattish; fearful; fearless; fearsome; featureless; female;

feminine; feral; ferocious; ferret-like; ferrety; fetal; fetching; fever-flushed; fevered; feverish; fiendish; fierce; fiery; filthy; filthy-bearded; fine; fine-boned; fine-featured; fire-shadowed; firm; firm-jawed; fish-like; fishbelly-white; flabbergasted; flabby; flaccid; flaming; flashlit; flat; flat-nosed; flattened; flawed; flawless; fleshy; flickering; flinty; flirtatious; floating; florid; flush-mottled; flushed; flushed-red; foggy; foolish; forbidding; foreign; forgettable; forlorn; formal; formidable; formless; forthright; forward-sloping; foul; fox-like; foxy; fractured; fragile; frank; freakish; freckled; fresh; fresh-scrubbed; freshly-powdered; fretful; friendly; frightened; frightening; frightful; frog-like; frosty; frowning; frowsy; frozen; frustrated; full; full-moon; fuming; funny; fur-framed; furious; furred; furrowed; furry; fury-contorted; fury-darkened; fuzzy; gagging; gangstery; gaping; gaunt; gay; geisha-white; genderless; general; generic; generous; genial; gentle; gentleman's; geriatric; ghastly; ghost-like; ghost-pale; ghostly; giant; gingerbread-brown; girl-pretty; girlish; glad; glaring; glassy; glassy-eyed; gleaming; glimmering; glistening; glittering; gloomy; glorious; glossy; glowering; glowing; glum; gnarled; goddamn; godlike; godly; goggled; gold-skinned; golden; golden-eyed; good; good-humored; good-looking; good-natured; goofy; goofy-looking; goose-egg-shaped; gorgeous; gorilla-like; gory; gothic; graceless; gracious; grainy; grand; grandmotherly; granite-like; grave; gray; gray-bearded; gray-fringed; gray-white; graying; grayish; greased; greasy; great; greed-glowing; Greek; green; green-eyed; green-lit; greenish; grief-ravaged; grief-scarred; grief-stricken; grief-torn; grieving; grim; grimacing; grime-streaked; grimy; grinning; grizzled; groaning; grossed-out; grotesque; grouchy; grubby; gruesome; gruff; grumpy; guileless; guilt-ridden; guilty; haggard; hair-covered; hairless; hairy; half-blind; half-childish; half-concerned; half-hidden; half-lit; half-obscured; half-paralyzed; half-ruined; half-shadowed; half-turned; half-womanly; hand-painted; handsome; happy; hard; hard-lined; hard-looking; hardened; harmless; harsh; hate-filled; hateful; haughty; haunted; haunting; hawk-like; hawkish; healthy; heart-shaped; heat-flushed; heated; heavenly; heavily-bandaged; heavily-lined; heavy; hellish; helmeted; hidden; hideous; high; high-boned; high-browed; high-cheekboned; high-cheeked; high-held; hollow; holy; homely; honest; honey-colored; hooded; hook-nosed; hopeful; hopeless; hopped-up; horizontal; horrible; horrid; horrific; horrified; horror-stricken; horse-like; horsey; hostile; hot; hot-skinned; hovering; huge; human; humane; humanoid; humorless; humorous; hungry; hurt; hyper-intense; ice-blue; icy; identical; ignorant; ill; imagined; immature; immense; immobile; immovable; immutable; impassioned; impassive; impatient; impenetrable; imperfect; imperious; impersonal; imperturbable; impish; implacable; important; imposing; impossible; impressed; impressive; improved; impudent; inanimate; inbred; inclined; inconsolable; incredible; incredulous; Indian; Indian-looking; indifferent; indignant; indiscernible; indistinct; individual; indulgent-looking; inert; inexpressive; infantile; inflamed; inflated; ingenuous; inhuman; injured; inner; innocent; innocent-looking; inquisitive; insane; inscrutable; insipid; intellectual; intelligent; intense; intent; interested; interesting; internal; intimidating; intolerant; intricate; intriguing; invisible; inviting; irascible; ironic; irritated; Islamic; Italian; itchy; Japanese; jaundiced; jaunty; jealous; Jewish;

jolly; jovial; jowled; jowly; joyful; joyless; joyous; judgmental; keen; keen-eyed; kind; kindly; kindly-looking; knife-scarred; lacerated; laid-back; lamp-lit; large; large-boned; large-eyed; Latin; laughing; lean; leathered; leathery; leering; lewd; lifeless; light; light-brown; lighted; likeable/likable; lined; listening; little; little-boy; little-girl; lively; liver-spotted; livid; local; locked; lonesome; long; long-absent; long-jawed; long-nosed; longish; looking; looming; loose; lopsided; lost; lovable; lovely; loving; lower; lowered; lugubrious; lukewarm; luminous; lumpish; lumpy.

M - Y
mad; made-up; magnetic; magnificent; majestic; makeup-free; makeupless; male; malevolent; malformed; mangled; manlike; manly; mannequin-like; mannish; many-chinned; marble-like; marked; marred; marvelous; mascara-stained; masculine; mask-like; masked; massive; maternal; matte-white; mature; maturing; mean; meaty; meek; melancholy; melted; memorable; merciless; mere; merry; messy; middle-aged; mild; military; miserable; mocking; modest; moist; monstrous; moon-shaped; moonlit; morose; mortal; motherly; motionless; mottled; mournful; muddy; multi-chinned; mustachioed; mutilated; mysterious; naked; narrow; nasty; natural; negative; nervous; neutral; new; nice; nineteen-year-old; no-nonsense; noble; normal; nut-brown; odd; official; old; older; olive; olive-colored; once-pretty; open; opposite; optimistic; orange; ordinary; oriental; original; other; outer; outraged; oval; oval-shaped; overheated; owlish; pained; painted; painted-on; pale; pallid; panic-stricken; panicked; panting; paper-white; paralyzed; particular; passing; passionate; passive; pasty; patched; pathetic; peaceful; peaky; peculiar; pensive; perfect; perky; perplexed; perspiring; petulant; pimpled; pimply; pinched; pink; pinkish; piquant; pissed-off; piteous; pitiful; pitted; placid; plain; pleading; pleasant; pleased; pleasing; plump; pocked; pockmarked; pointed; pointless; pointy; poor; positive; pouchy; pouting; pouty; powdered; powerful; poxy; present; pretty; prim; private; professional; projected; proud; public; puckered; puckish; pudgy; puffy; pugnacious; pure; purple; purple-red; puzzled; queer; questioning; quick; quiet; radiant; rapt; rat-like; ravaged; real; reassuring; recognizable; red; red-cheeked; red-flushed; reddened; reddening; reddish; refined; reflected; regal; regular; relaxed; remarkable; remembered; remote; reproachful; reptilian; repulsive; resolute; ridiculous; rigid; robust; roguish; rosy; rouged; rough; round; rounded; roundish; royal; rubicund; ruddy; rueful; rugged; ruined; rumpled; sacred; sad; sagging; saintly; sallow; sardonic; satisfied; savage; scared; scarf-wrapped; scarlet; scarred; scary; scorched; scornful; scowling; scratched; scrawny; screaming; screwed-up; scrubbed; scruffy; scrunched-up; sculpted; sculptured; seared; secret; sensible; sensitive; sensual; serene; serious; severe; sexy; shadowed; shadowy; shaggy; shallow; shaped; sharp; sharp-boned; sharp-featured; sharpening; shattered; shaven; sheepish; shining; shiny; shocked; shrewd; shriveled; shrunken; shy; sickly; sightless; silent; silly; simian; similar; simple; single; sinister; skeletal; skeptical; skinny; skull-like; slack; slanted; slashed; sleeping; sleepless; sleepy; slender; slick; slight; slim; sloping; sloppy; sly; small; smart; smashed; smeared; smiling; smirking; smooth; smudged;

smug; snarling; snub-nosed; soaked; sober; sober-visaged; sociable; social; sodden; soft; soft-featured; softening; soiled; solemn; solicitous; solid; somber/sombre; somewhat-harried; soot-coated; soot-stained; sooted; sooty; sorrowful; sour; Soviet; spacious; spade-shaped; Spanish; sparkling; special; speckled; spectacled; spit-strewn; splendid; splotchy; spongy; spotty; square; square-jawed; squarish; squashed; squashed-in; squat; squinty; squirrel-like; stained; staring; stark; starlit; startled; steadfast; steady; steak-red; steel-blue; stern; sticky; stiff; stiffened; stiffening; still; still-animated; still-hairless; still-handsome; still-lathered; still-unsmiling; stinging; stinking; stinky; stoic; stolid; stony; straight; straight-nosed; strained; straining; strange; strangled; streaked; streaming; stressed-out; stretched; stricken; striking; striped; strong; strong-boned; strong-nosed; struggling; stubbled; stubbly; stubborn; studious; stuffed; stunned; stunning; stupefied; stupid; sturdy; sublime; sucking; suffering; suffused; sugar-brown; sulky; sullen; sun-baked; sun-battered; sun-bitten; sun-bronzed; sun-browned; sun-darkened; sun-dried; sun-kissed; sun-leathered; sun-lined; sun-reddened; sun-warmed; sun-washed; sun-weathered; sunbeaten; sunburned/sunburnt; sunburnished; sunglassed; sunken; sunken-cheeked; sunny; suntanned; supercilious; surly; surprised; surprising; surrealistic; suspicious; swarthy; sweat-beaded; sweat-covered; sweat-dewed; sweat-glistening; sweat-soaked; sweat-stained; sweat-streaked; sweating; sweaty; sweet; swelling; swollen; swollen-up; symmetrical; sympathetic; synthetic; syrupy; tan; tanned; tattooed; taut; tawny; tear-bloated; tear-blotched; tear-covered; tear-drenched; tear-ravaged; tear-smudged; tear-stained; tear-streaked; tear-streamed; tear-swollen; tearful; tearing; tearless; teary; teenage; teenaged; tender; tense; tension-drawn; terrible; terrified; terrifying; terror-stricken; terrorized; thick; thickened; thicker; thin; thinned; thinner; thoughtful; thoughtful-looking; threatening; tight; tight-jawed; tight-lipped; tightened; tilted; time-widened; timeworn; timid; tinted; tiny; tired; tired-looking; toad-like; too-handsome; too-old; too-pretty; too-round; too-tan; too-thin; too-young; toothless; toothy; tormented; tortured; total; tough; tough-guy; traditional; tragic; traitorous; trancelike; tranquil; travel-weary; trembling; tremendous; triangular; tribal; triumphant; tropical; troubled; troubling; true; trusting; trustworthy; truthful; turbulent; turnip-colored; twisted; twitching; typical; ugly; unacceptable; unadorned; unbandaged; unblemished; unburned; uncertain; unchanged; unchanging; uncomprehending; uncompromising; unconscious; unctuous; undistinguished; undulating; unearthly; uneasy; uneven; unfamiliar; unfeeling; unflappable; unforgettable; unfriendly; ungainly; unguarded; unhandsome; unhappy; unharried; unimpressed; unkempt; unknown; unlined; unmade-up; unmarked; unmistakable; unmoved; unpampered; unpleasant; unprotected; unreadable; unreal; unrecognizable; unremarkable; unresponding; unseeing; unseen; unsexy; unshaved; unshaven; unsmiling; unspectacled; unsuspecting; untamable; untamed; untroubled; untrustworthy; unveiled; unwashed; unwrinkled; unyielding; up-peering; uplifted; upper; upraised; upside-down; upturned; useless; usual; v-shaped; vacant; vacuous; vague; vanishing; vapid; various; vast; vee-shaped; veiled; veined; venerable; vibrant; vibrating; Vietnamese; violent; virginal; visible; visored; vitreous; vivid; vomiting;

voracious; vulgar; vulnerable; waiting; wan; war-painted; warm; wart-ridden; warty; wary; washed; washed-out; wasted; watery; wax-yellow; waxen; waxy; weak; weak-featured; weary; weasel-like; weather-beaten; weather-browned; weather-roughened; weathered; wee; weeping; weird; welcoming; well-articulated; well-bred; well-fed; well-groomed; well-known; well-loved; well-made; well-remembered; well-scrubbed; well-shaven; well-structured; well-worn; welted; Western; wet; whiskered; whiskerless; whiskey-shattered; white; white-bearded; white-maned; white-painted; whitened; whitewashed; whitish; whole; wholesome; wicked; wide; wide-boned; wide-cheekboned; wide-eyed; wild; wild-eyed; wincing; wind-abraded; wind-burned; wind-cracked; wind-pink; wind-reddened; wind-worn; windswept; winking; winning; winsome; wintry; wise; wispy; wistful; withered; withering; wizened; woeful; wolfish; womanly; wonderful; wooden; work-sweated; working; working-class; working-man; world-weary; wormy; worn; worried; worry-fraught; wounded; wrathful; wrecked; wretched; wrinkled; wry; yearning; yellow; yellowed; yellowish; young; young-looking; young-woman; youthful.

Verbs and Phrasal Verbs in Alphabetical Order

A - C

accented; accented by; accentuated; accompanied by; accused; accustomed to; ached; acknowledged; acquired; added; added to; addressed; adopted; adorned; adorned with; affected; afforded; affronted; aged; aged with; aimed; aimed at; aimed straight; aimed up; alarmed; alerted; alerted by; alight; alight with; allowed; altered; ambled by; amused; angled; angled away; angled into; angled toward; angled with; animated; announced; answered; appalled; appeared; appeared above; appeared again; appeared against; appeared amid; appeared around; appeared at; appeared before; appeared behind; appeared beside; appeared between; appeared from; appeared in; appeared more; appeared next to; appeared on; appeared out; appeared outside; appeared over; appeared through; appeared to; approached; arose; arranged; arranged in; arranged into; arrested; arrived; arrived at; ascended; asked; assaulted; associated; associated with; assumed; assured; astonished; attached to; attempted to; attested; attested to; attracted; averted; averted from; awaited; backed; backed into; bandaged; banded; banded with; based on; bashed; bashed in; bathed; bathed in; bathed with; battered; battered from; beaded; beaded with; beamed; beamed at; beamed like; beamed on; beamed upon; beamed with; beat; beat with; became; bedewed; bedewed with; befitted; began; began to; begged for; begrimed; begrimed with; beheld; belied; belied by; belonged; belonged on; belonged to; bent; bent back; bent close; bent down; bent downward; bent forward; bent on; bent over; bent toward; beset; beset with; besmeared; besmeared with; bespoke; bestowed; betrayed; bisected; bisected by; blackened; blackened with; blanched; blanched in; blanched to; blanched with; blanked; blanked in; blasted; blazed; blazed from; blazed into; blazed with; bleached; bleached of; bled; bled from; blended; blended together; blew off; blew on; blew up; blinked; blistered; bloated;

blocked; bloodied; bloodied with; bloomed; blossomed; blossomed into; blossomed with; blotched; blotched with; blowing; blued; blued by; blurred; blurred beyond; blurred from; blurred in; blushed; blushed in; blushed with; boasted; bobbed; bobbed at; bobbed up; bore; bore down; bored; born of; bounced; bound; bound up; bounded; bowed; bowed down; bowled over; braced; braced for; branded; branded with; breathed; brightened; brightened at; brightened by; brightened in; brightened into; brightened like; brightened to; brightened up; brightened with; brimmed with; broadened; broadened into; broke down; broke into; broke out; broke through; brought; brought back; brought down; brought forward; brought on; brought to; brought up; brought with; bruised; bruised from; bruised on; brushed; brushed against; buckled; buckled in; built for; bulged; bulged like; bunched; bunched in; bunched inside; bunched into; bunched up; buried; buried against; buried beneath; buried in; buried on; buried under; burned at; burned like; burned with; burned/burnt; burrowed; burrowed deep; burrowed into; burst; burst into; burst like; burst through; burst with; caked in; caked with; called; called forth; called to; came back; came before; came between; came closer; came down; came in; came into; came nearer; came out; came to; came together; came up; camouflaged; capped with; captivated; captivated by; captured; captured in; caressed; carried; carved from; carved in; carved into; carved on; carved out; cast; cast down; cast downward; cast forward; caught; caught by; caught in; caused; caused by; caved; caved in; caved into; centered; centered on; chafed; challenged; changed; changed at; changed beneath; changed from; changed in; changed into; changed to; changed toward; changed with; charged; charged with; checked; chewed; chewed up; chimed off; chiseled; chopped; cinched; cinched up; cinched with; circled; circled in; clarified; clawed; cleaned; cleaned off; cleaned up; cleared; cleared into; cleared up; cleared with; clenched; clenched in; clenched into; clenched up; climbed; cloaked; cloaked in; closed; closed down; closed in; closed off; closed up; clothed; clouded; clouded at; clouded for; clouded over; clouded up; clouded with; coalesced; coated with; cocked; cocked against; collapsed; collapsed in; collapsed into; collected; collided; collided with; colored; colored a; colored like; colored with; combined; combined with; commenced; communicated; compared to; compared with; compelled; competed for; competed with; completed; composed; composed of; composed to; concealed; concealed between; concealed by; concealed in; concealed under; concentrated; concentrated on; condensed; confessed; confirmed; confronted; confused; connected; connected with; considered; consisted of; constricted; constricted toward; constricted with; contacted; contained; contemplated; continued; contorted; contorted at; contorted by; contorted in; contorted into; contorted with; contracted; contracted in; contracted into; contracted with; contrasted with; contributed; contributed to; controlled; conveyed; convinced; convulsed with; cooked in; corresponded; could; coupled with; covered; covered by; covered in; covered over; covered up; covered with; cracked; cracked in; cracked into; crackled; crackled under; cradled; cradled against; cradled in; cradled inside; crammed into; cramped; crashed; crashed down; crashed into; creaked; creased; creased by; creased from; creased in; creased into; creased like; creased up; creased with; created; crept; crept toward; crept up; crested; cried; cried out; crimped; crimped in; crimsoned; crimsoned over; crimsoned with; cringed; crinkled; crinkled in; crinkled into; crinkled like; crinkled up; crinkled with; crisscrossed; crisscrossed by; crisscrossed with; crossed; crossed in; crowded; crowned; crowned by; crowned with; crumbled; crumbled into; crumbled to; crumbled with; crumpled; crumpled for; crumpled from; crumpled in; crumpled into; crumpled up; crumpled with; crunched; crunched between; crunched into; crunched up; crushed; crushed by; crushed into; cupped; cupped between; cupped by; cupped in; curdled; curdled with; cured; curled; curled into; curled up; curled with; cut; cut by; cut in; cut into; cut off; cut on; cut through; cycled through.

D - H

damaged; danced; danced in; danced on; danced through; danced to; dangled; dappled with; dared; darkened; darkened at; darkened behind; darkened by; darkened further; darkened in; darkened to; darkened with; darted; darted up; dashed; dashed through; daubed with; dazzled; dazzled with; decided; declared; decorated; decorated with; deepened; deepened from; deepened in; deepened into; deepened to; deepened with; deflated; deformed; delighted; demanded; denoted; depended on; depicted; deposited on; descended; descended in; descended to; described; described by; designed; designed by; determined; developed; died of; died out; differed; differed from; differentiated by; dilated; dimmed; dimmed with; dimpled; dimpled from; dimpled with; dipped; directed; directed at; directed towards; disappeared; disappeared back; disappeared for; disappeared from; disappeared in; disappeared inside; disappeared into; disappointed; disbelieved; disclosed; discolored; discolored on; disconcerted; discouraged; disfigured; disfigured by; disfigured with; disguised; disguised by; disgusted; displayed; dissected; dissected by; dissolved; dissolved in; dissolved into; dissuaded; distended; distinguished; distinguished by; distorted; distorted against; distorted behind; distorted by; distorted in; distorted into; distorted on; distorted with; distressed; disturbed; divided; divided by; divided into; dominated; dominated by; dragged in; drained; drained away; drained of; drained to; drank; drank in; drawing; drawn; drawn by; drawn in; drawn into; drawn on; drawn tight; drawn to; drawn together; drawn with; dreamed; drenched; drenched in; dressed in; drew closer; drew in; drew into; drew tight; drew up; dried; dried up; drifted; drifted across; drifted down; drifted in; drifted into; dripped; dripped with; drooped; drooped in; drooped into; drooped on; drooped when; drooped with; dropped; dropped into; dropped to; dropped toward; dropped upon; dropped when; drove; drove away; drowned; drowned in; dug into; dusted with; earned; eased; eased into; eased out; echoed; emblazoned; emblazoned on; embodied; emerged; emerged from; emitted; emphasized; emptied for; emptied of; encircled by; encouraged; encrusted; ended in; ended up; engraved; engulfed; engulfed by; enlarged; enlarged by; enlivened; enlivened by; entered; enveloped; enveloped in; erased; erect; erupted; erupted from; erupted in; erupted into; etched; etched in; etched with; evaporated; evoked; examined; exasperated; excelled; excited; exhausted; exhibited;

expanded; expanded into; exploded; exploded in; exploded into; exploded out; exploded with; exposed; exposed to; expressed; extended; exuded; eyed; faced; faded; faded away; faded from; faded in; faded into; faded to; failed to; faltered; fascinated; fastened; fastened on; fell; fell apart; fell at; fell back; fell down; fell flat; fell for; fell forward; fell in; fell into; fell like; fell when; felt; felt like; felt tight; fidgeted; filled; filled for; filled out; filled up; filled with; filmed; filmed with; finished; fit; fit into; fixed; fixed by; fixed in; fixed into; fixed on; fixed straight; fixed with; flagged; flagged with; flamed; flamed at; flamed with; flared; flared in; flared like; flared up; flashed; flashed across; flashed against; flashed in; flashed into; flashed like; flashed off; flashed on; flashed through; flashed with; flattened; flattened against; flattened into; flattened out; flattened to; flattered; flecked; flecked with; fled; flew back; flew forward; flicked; flicked onto; flickered; flickered across; flickered from; flickered in; flickered with; flinched; flinched at; flitted; flitted between; floated; floated above; floated across; floated before; floated between; floated down; floated in; floated inside; floated like; floated near; floated out; floated there; floated through; floated toward; floated up; flooded; flooded like; flooded with; flopped; flowed; flowed in; flushed; flushed at; flushed in; flushed with; fluttered; focused; focused into; focused on; focused with; folded; folded in; folded into; folded on; followed; fooled; forbade; forced; forced up; forgot; formed; formed into; forsaken by; fought; fought over; found; framed; framed by; framed in; framed inside; framed on; framed with; freckled; frightened; frowned; frowned in; froze; froze at; froze in; froze up; froze when; froze with; fumed; furrowed; furrowed by; furrowed with; gagged; gained; gained back; gasped; gasped for; gathered; gathered in; gave; gave away; gazed; gazed at; gazed back; gazed down; gazed out; gazed up; gentled; glanced; glanced at; glared; glared at; glared down; gleamed; gleamed behind; gleamed in; gleamed like; gleamed with; glimmered; glimmered with; glimpsed; glinted; glinted in; glistened; glistened in; glistened like; glistened with; glittered; glowed; glowed at; glowed in; glowed like; glowed under; glowed with; glowered; glowered at; glued to; got closer; got hard; got tight; gouged; grabbed; graced; graced by; graced with; gratified; greeted; grew; grew closer; grew deeper; grew long; grew more; grew still; grew tight; grimaced; grimaced at; grimaced in; grimed with; grinned; grinned at; grinned down; grinned in; grinned over; grinned through; grinned up; grinned with; gripped; gripped at; gripped by; gripped in; groaned; grooved with; ground; ground into; grunted; guarded; guarded by; happened; harbored; hardened; hardened against; hardened at; hardened in; hardened into; hardened with; haunted; headed; headed off; headed through; healed; heated; heated by; heated from; heated up; heated with; held; held out; held up; helped; helped by; hesitated; hid; hid behind; hid in; highlighted; highlighted by; hinted at; hit; hollowed; hollowed with; horrified; housed; hovered; hovered above; hovered close; hovered in; hovered over; howled; hung; hung before; hung down; hung over; hungered; hungered for; hungered from; hurt; hurt from; hurt with.

I - P

ignited; ignited with; illuminated; illuminated by; illuminated with; immersed in; immortalized; immortalized on; implied; imploded; imploded like; implored; impressed; imprinted; imprinted with; imprisoned; imprisoned in; incensed; incensed at; included; increased; indicated; infuriated; inherited; inquired; inserted; inset; inset with; insinuated; inspired; intensified; interested; intersected; intrigued; intruded; invaded; involved; irritated; itched; jammed; jammed against; jerked; jerked back; jerked in; jerked sideways; jerked to; jerked up; jerked with; jiggled; jiggled with; joined; joined to; jolted; jounced; jounced with; jumped; jumped out; jumped to; jutted; jutted forward; jutted out; keeled over; kindled; kindled from; kindled like; kindled with; kissed; knew; knocked; knotted; knotted in; knotted up; knotted with; lacked; laid; lapsed; lapsed back; lapsed into; lathered; lathered up; laughed; laughed at; launched into; leached; leaked; leaned; leaned closer; leaned forward; leaned in; leaned over; leaned toward; leaped out; leaped/leapt; leathered; leathered by; led; leered; leered at; leered from; leered into; left; left in; lengthened; let; lifted; lifted at; lifted in; lifted into; lifted off; lifted to; lifted toward; lifted up; lifted with; lighted; lighted by; lighted up; lightened; lightened at; lightened up; lightened with; lined; lined by; lined from; lined like; lined with; lingered; lingered for; lingered with; lit; lit at; lit by; lit from; lit like; lit up; lit with; lived; lived in; located; locked; locked in; locked into; lodged in; lolled; lolled against; looked; looked a; looked at; looked back; looked down; looked hard; looked in; looked into; looked like; looked more; looked on; looked out; looked over; looked still; looked to; looked up; loomed; loomed above; loomed before; loomed down; loomed from; loomed over; loomed up; loosened; loosened toward; loosened up; lost; lost in; lowered; lowered into; lowered to; lunged; lunged down; made for; made up; maintained; managed; mangled; mangled beyond; marked; marked by; marked with; marred; marred by; mashed; mashed against; mashed into; masked; masked by; masked in; matched; materialized; materialized at; materialized in; materialized on; matured; mauled by; meant for; melded with; melted; melted away; melted in; melted into; melted with; merged; merged with; mesmerized; met; met by; metamorphosized; metamorphosized into; migrated; migrated to; mimicked; mirrored; mirrored back; mirrored in; mirrored off; missed; mocked; modeled / modelled; morphed; morphed into; mounted on; moved; moved between; moved close(r); moved down; moved into; moved over; moved through; moved up; muffled; muffled by; muffled in; mushed; mushed in; mustached; muttered; muttered behind; narrowed; narrowed to; needed; nestled in; nodded; nodded down; nodded to; nodded up; nosed; noticed; nuzzled; nuzzled in; nuzzled into; obliterated; obscured; obscured by; obscured in; occupied; offered; offered up; opened; opened in; opened into; opened to; opened up; opened with; opposed; oriented; oriented in; ornamented; ornamented with; ought to; outlined; outlined in; outshone; overhung by; overlaid with; overlooked; overshadowed by; overspread with; pained; pained in; painted; painted by; painted in; painted like; painted on; painted with; paled; paled over; paled to; paled under; paled when; paled with; panicked; panned over; paralyzed; paralyzed in; paralyzed on; paralyzed with; passed; passed by;

passed in; passed through; pasted; pasted against; patched; patched up; patched with; paused; paused for; pecked; peeked; peeked out; peeked through; peeled; peeled back; peeped from; peeped in; peeped like; peeped out; peered; peered around; peered at; peered back; peered down; peered from; peered in; peered into; peered out; peered over; peered through; peered up; peered with; pelted; pelted by; peppered with; perched on; performed; perplexed; persisted; perspired; perspired in; perspired with; picked out; picked up; pierced; pierced like; pierced out; pinched; pinched by; pinched into; pinched with; pinked; pinked with; pinkened; pitched forward; pitted; pitted against; pitted by; pitted from; pitted like; pitted with; placed; planted; planted in; plastered; plastered across; plastered on; plastered with; played; pleaded; pleaded with; pleased; plunged; plunged to; plunged toward; pocked with; pockmarked; pockmarked by; pockmarked with; pointed; pointed at; pointed down; pointed in; pointed straight; pointed through; pointed to; pointed toward; pointed upward; poked; poked around; poked in; poked into; poked out; poked over; poked through; poked up; polished; pontificated; pontificated about; pooled; pooled up; popped; popped into; popped out; popped over; popped through; popped up; portrayed; posed; posed for; possessed; possessed of; pounded; pounded with; powdered; prayed; prepared; presented; presented by; preserved; pressed; pressed against; pressed back; pressed close; pressed down; pressed forward; pressed into; pressed sideways; pressed through; pressed tight; pressed to; pressed up; pressed within; pretended; prevailed; prevented; prickled; prickled against; prickled up; primed; printed on; proclaimed; produced; produced by; projected; projected on; projected onto; promised; pronounced; propelled; propelled forward; propelled toward; propped; propped on; propped up; protected; protected by; protruded; protruded from; protruded through; proved; provided; provoked; puckered; puckered in; puckered into; puckered like; puckered up; puckered with; puffed; puffed up; pulled; pulled away; pulled back; pulled down; pulled downward; pulled in; pulled into; pulled together; pulped; pulsated; pulsed; pulsed with; punched; punched in; punctuated by; purpled; pursed; pursed in; pursed up; pursed with; pursued; pushed; pushed against; pushed down; pushed forward; pushed into; put on; puzzled.

Q - S

questioned; quirked; quirked into; quivered; quivered with; radiated; raised; raised for; raised from; raised in; raised off; raised to; raised towards; raked; raked down; rambled; rambled past; ran; ran straight; ran through; ran together; ran toward; ran with; rapped; ravaged; ravaged by; ravaged with; reached; reached for; reached up; read; readied; reappeared; reappeared in; reappeared on; reappeared overhead; reared up; rearranged; rearranged into; reassumed; reassured; recalled; recaptured; receded; receded into; received; reclined; reclined against; recognized; recognized among; recoiled; recoiled from; recoiled in; recoiled with; reconstructed; recorded; recovered; reddened; reddened at; reddened by; reddened from; reddened in; reddened under; reddened with; reduced in; reflected; reflected against; reflected back; reflected by; reflected in; reflected off; reflected on; reflushed; refused; regained;

regarded; registered; relaxed; relaxed for; relaxed from; relaxed in; relaxed into; relaxed with; released; relieved; remained; remained in; remained so; remained still; remembered; reminded; removed from; rendered; renewed; repeated; repelled; replaced; represented; required; resembled; reshaped; resigned; resisted; resolved; responded; responded with; rested; rested against; rested in; rested on; restored; resumed; retained; retreated; returned; returned to; revealed; reveled in; reverted; reverted to; revisited; revived; riddled with; riled up; rimmed with; ringed by; ringed with; ripened; ripened to; rippled; rippled in; rippled into; rippled with; rivaled; rode up; rolled; rolled into; rolled through; rose; rose above; rose from; rose in; rose off; rose out; rose toward; rose up; rotated; rounded; rubbed; rubbed in; ruined; rushed; rushed toward; rushed up; saddened; saddened by; sagged; sagged with; said; said back; said otherwise; said so; sandwiched; sandwiched between; sang; sang out; sank; sank back; sank below; sank in; sank into; sat; sat down; sat in; sat next to; sat on; satisfied; sauntered past; saved; saw; scalded; scalded by; scanned; scanned over; scared; scarred; scarred by; scarred from; scarred with; scorched; scorched with; scowled; scowled at; scowled with; scraped; scraped against; scratched; scratched against; screamed; screamed with; screened behind; screened by; screwed; screwed in; screwed into; screwed up; scrubbed; scrubbed off; scrunched; scrunched in; scrunched into; scrunched up; scrunched with; scrutinized; searched; seduced; seemed; seized; seized by; seized up; sent; separated; served; set; set against; set hard; set in; set into; set off; set on; set onto; set toward; set with; settled; settled back; settled into; shaded; shaded by; shaded in; shaded under; shadowed; shadowed by; shadowed in; shadowed with; shaped by; shaped in; shaped into; shaped like; sharpened; sharpened by; sharpened in; sharpened into; sharpened with; shattered into; shaved; sheered; sheltered; sheltered by; shielded; shielded by; shielded from; shifted; shifted back; shifted from; shifted into; shifted to; shivered; shivered with; shocked; shocked by; shone; shone forth; shone from; shone in; shone like; shone out; shone upon; shone with; shook; shot out; shouted; shoved; showed; showed above; showed at; showed through; showed under; shriveled / shrivelled; shriveled into; shriveled like; shrouded; shrouded by; shrouded in; shuddered; shut down; shut tight; shut up; sighed; signified; silenced; silhouetted; silhouetted behind; simulated; skimmed; slackened; slackened in; slackened with; slammed; slammed against; slammed into; slanted; slanted in; slapped; slapped by; slashed; slept; sliced; slid; slid away; slid beneath; slid down; slid into; slid past; slipped; slipped by; slipped into; slipped over; sloped down; smacked; smacked against; smarted; smashed; smashed against; smashed into; smashed through; smeared; smeared in; smeared with; smelled; smelled like; smiled; smiled at; smiled back; smiled down; smiled from; smiled out; smiled up; smiled when; smoked; smoothed; smoothed away; smoothed into; smoothed out; smoothed to; smothered; smothered in; smothered into; smudged; smudged with; snapped; snapped back; snapped into; snarled; sneered; soaked in; soaked with; soared; sobered; softened; softened at; softened by; softened for; softened in; softened into; softened up; softened with; solidified; soured; soured at; soured with; sparked; sparkled; sparkled with; spasmed; spasmed in; spasmed

91

into; spasmed with; spattered with; spilled out; splashed; splashed with; splintered into; split; split in; split into; split with; splotched with; spoiled; spoke; spoke for; spoke of; spoke to; spoke up; spotted with; sprang; sprang into; sprang to; sprang up; spread across; spread into; spread out; spread over; sprouted; spun; spun away; spun into; spun out; squashed; squashed into; squashed up; squeezed; squeezed into; squeezed up; squinched; squinched up; squinted; squinted against; squinted in; squinted up; squished; squished against; stained; stained by; stained in; stained with; stamped; stamped by; stamped on; stamped with; stared; stared at; stared back; stared down; stared out; stared up; started; started to; startled; stayed; stayed in; stayed with; steadied; stepped from; stepped out; stiffened; stiffened for; stiffened in; stiffened into; stiffened with; stilled; stippled with; stirred; stood; stood at; stood before; stood between; stood by; stood for; stood out; stood up; stopped; straightened; strained; strained in; strained toward; strained under; strained with; streaked by; streaked with; streamed in; streamed with; stretched; stretched back; stretched in; stretched into; stretched tight; stretched up; stretched with; strickened; striped with; stripped of; struck; struck at; struck with; struggled to; struggled with; stubbled; stuck out; stuck to; stuck up; studded with; studied; stuffed; stuffed with; stung; stung from; stunned; submerged; submerged in; sucked in; suffocated; suffocated in; suffused; suffused with; suggested; sulked; sunburned; superimposed; superimposed on; superimposed over; supported; supported by; supported in; surfaced; surfaced with; surmounted by; surpassed; surprised; surrendered; surrounded; surrounded by; surrounded with; suspended; suspended above; suspended between; suspended over; swam; swam in; swam into; swam up; swarmed; swarmed out; swathed in; swayed; sweat; swelled; swelled from; swelled in; swelled into; swelled up; swelled with; swept across; swept by; swiveled; swiveled toward; swooned; swooned with; swooped; swooped toward; swung back; swung from; swung into; swung toward.

T - Z

talked; tanned; tapered; tapered in; tasted; tasted like; tattooed; taxed; teared up; teased; teetered; teetered over; telegraphed; tempered; tempered by; tended to; tensed; tensed from; tensed with; terrified; thawed; thought; threatened; threw back; threw into; threw up; throbbed; throbbed with; thrust; thrust against; thrust close; thrust forward; thrust into; thrust out; thrust through; thrust toward; tickled; tickled against; tickled at; tied up; tightened; tightened at; tightened for; tightened inside; tightened into; tightened with; tilted; tilted away; tilted back; tilted down; tilted forward; tilted slightly; tilted to; tilted toward; tilted up; tilted upward; tinged; tinged with; tingled; tingled from; tingled like; tipped; tipped back; tipped down; tipped to; tipped up; told; told of; took; took on; took up; topped by; topped off; topped with; tore into; tormented; touched; touched off; touched with; toughened; toughened by; towered; towered over; tracked; tracked with; trained; trained on; trained to; transfixed; transfixed by; transfixed with; transformed; transformed by; transformed into; transformed with; trapped; trapped in; traveled; trembled; tried; troubled; tucked in; tucked into; tugged at; turned; turned around; turned away; turned back; turned backward; turned down;

turned downward; turned earthward; turned from; turned hard; turned heavenward; turned in; turned into; turned on; turned out; turned over; turned sideways; turned skyward; turned to; turned toward; turned up; turned upon; turned upward; twisted; twisted away; twisted by; twisted closer; twisted from; twisted in; twisted into; twisted to; twisted under; twisted up; twisted with; twitched; twitched with; unclenched; uncovered; underwent; undid; unmade; unmasked; unveiled; unwound; uplifted; uplifted to; uptilted; uptilted to; used for; used to; vacillated; vacillated between; vanished; vanished beneath; vanished for; vanished into; vanished like; varied; veiled; veiled in; verged on; vibrated; visited; waited; waited at; waited for; walked; walked beside; walked over; walked toward; walked up; wanted; warmed; warmed to; warmed toward; warmed under; warmed up; warned; washed; washed away; washed in; washed with; wasted; wasted away; watched; watched over; wavered; wavered behind; wavered between; wavered in; weakened; weathered; weathered by; weathered from; weathered with; weaved; wedged; wedged in; welled up; welled with; went; went away; went down; went from; went hard; went in; went into; went out; went still; went straight; went through; went tight; went to; went up; wet; wet against; wet with; whipped; whipped by; whispered; whitened; whitened by; whitened with; whizzed by; widened; widened into; wiggled; wilted; wilted into; winced; winced up; winced with; winked; wiped; wiped out; withered; withered with; witnessed; wizened; wizened by; wobbled; woke; woke up; wondered; worked; worked against; worked in; worked with; worried; worried for; wound up; wracked; wracked with; wrapped; wrapped in; wrapped up; wreathed; wreathed in; wreathed with; wrenched; wrenched into; wrenched with; wrinkled; wrinkled by; wrinkled in; wrinkled like; wrinkled up; wrinkled with; writhed; writhed in; yelled; yellowed; yellowed by; yellowed from; yellowed like; yielded; zipped; zipped tight.

Noun Phrases

abnormalities of the face; absence of a face; acne on the face; action of the face; air of the face; alteration of the face; anatomy of the face; angle of the face; appearance of the face; area of the face; aspect of the face; asymmetry of the face; base of the face; beauty of the face; blueness of the face; blur of faces; bones of the face; bottom of the face; brazenness of the face; breadth of the face; brightness of the face; capillaries of the face; capturing of the face; cavities of the face; center of the face; changes of the face; character of the face; characteristics of the face; charm of the face; close-up of the face; color of the face; complexion of the face; composure of the face; concealment of the face; condition of the face; confusion on the face; contemplation of the face; contortion of the face; contour(s) of the face; contraction of the face; corner of the face; curvature of the face; curve(s) of the face; deformity of the face; depth of the face; description of the face; detail(s) of the face; diameter of the face; dignity of the face; dimensions of the face; direction of the face; discoloration of the face; disfigurement of the face; distance of the face; distortion of the face;

eczema of the face; edge(s) of the face; effect of the face; elements of the face; elevation of the face; elongation of the face; end of the face; enlargement of the face; epiphany of the face; eruption of the face; examination of the face; expanse of the face; exposure of the face; expression(s) of the face; expressiveness of the face; eyes of the face; fairness of the face; fear on the face; features of the face; feelings of the face; flatness of the face; flesh of the face; flushing of the face; form of the face; formation of the face; freshness of the face; glimpse of the face; glory of the face; gravity of the face; growth of the face; hair(s) on the face; half of the face; heat of the face; height of the face; hue of the face; illumination of the face; image of the face; impression of the face; inclination of the face; infection of the face; inflammation of the face; injuries of the face; inspection of the face; involvement of the face; kind of face; lacerations of the face; language of the face; largeness of the face; length of the face; lesions of the face; level of the face; likeness of the face; lines of the face; lividity of the face; loss of face; loveliness of the face; majesty of the face; majority of the face; manner of the face; markings of the face; mask of the face; measurements of the face; motion(s) of the face; movement(s) of the face; muscles of the face; musculature of the face; mystery of the face; name of the face; nature of the face; nerves of the face; neutrality of the face; nose of the face; number of faces; numbness of the face; on account of the face; orientation of the face; outline(s) of the face; oval of the face; owner of the face; pair of faces; paleness of the face; pallor of the face; paralysis of the face; part(s) of the face; patch of face; photograph of the face; picture of the face; piece of face; pigmentation of the face; planes of the face; point of the face; portion of the face; position of the face; power of the face; presence of the face; presentation of the face; profile of the face; projection of the face; proportion of the face; protection of the face; puffiness of the face; question on the face; radiance of the face; recognition of the face; recollection of the face; red of face; redness of (the) face; reflection of the face; region of the face; remainder of the face; remembrance of the face; resemblance of the face; resignation of the face; rest of the face; rotation of the face; roundness of the face; section of the face; sensation of the face; series of faces; set of faces; shadow(s) of the face; shame of the face; shape of the face; side(s) of the face; sight of the face; size of the face; skeleton of the face; skin of the face; slope of the face; solemnity of the face; sort of face; spasm of the face; state of the face; stimulation of the face; strength of the face; stretching of the face; structure of the face; study of the face; surface of the face; sweat of the face; sweetness of the face; swelling of the face; symmetry of the face; tint of the face; tone of the face; top of the face; transformation of the face; treatment of the face; twitchings of the face; type of face; variety of faces; veins of the face; view of the face; vision of the face; whiteness of the face; width of the face; wounds of the face; wrinkles of the face.

USAGE EXAMPLES

The baby's *adorable face grinned up* at her.

His *angular face held an amused expression.*

Her *face clouded with* concern.

Mark's *tanned face shone with* sweat.

The man's *enigmatic face angled toward* the sky.

15
FOOT / FEET

Adjectives in Alphabetical Order

A - F

1st; 2nd; abnormal; absent; abused; aching; advancing; adventurous; afflicted; aged; agile; agonizing; aimless; alternating; angled; angular; apelike; approaching; arched; aristocratic; armored; arthritic; artificial; ashy; autonomous; available; average; baggy-skinned; ballet-slippered; bandaged; bare; bared; battered; beautiful; best; better; big; birdlike; black; black-booted; black-shoed; blackened; blanketed; bleeding; blistered; blood-covered; bloody; blue; blue-socked; blue-toed; blue-veined; bluish; bold; bony; booming; boot-clad; booted; bootless; bound; brave; brazen; bright; broad; broken; brown; bruised; brutal; bunioned; burning; busy; calloused; careful; careless; caught; cautious; charging; chasing; child-size(d); childish; chilled; chilly; chubby; clammy; clamped; clattering; clawed; clawlike; clean; cloven; clovened; clubbed; clumsy; cold; colored; colorless; cool; coppery; correct; countless; cracked; cramped; crashing; crazy; crimson; crippled; crooked; crossed; crushing; crusty; curious; curled; curved; cut; cute; dainty; damn; damp; dangling; dapper; daring; dark; dead; decisive; declining; dedicated; deformed; deft; delicate; descending; desperate; detached; dirt-encrusted; dirty; disciplined; diseased; disembodied; distant; distinct; distorted; divine; doubtful; drunken; dry; drying; dumb; dusty; eager; earthy; efficient; elderly; elegant; elevated; elongated; enormous; enthusiastic; entire; entwined; escaping; excellent; expectant; experienced; exposed; extended; fair; fair-size; fake; false; faltering; far; fast; fast-moving; fat; fearful; feeble; female; feminine; fidgety; filthy; fine; firm; fisted-up; five-toed; flailing; flapping; flat; fleeing; fleshy; flip-flopped; floating; floppy; flying; fore; foul; free; freezing; front; frostbitten; frozen; full; fumbling; furry; fuzzy-slippered.

G - Q

galloping; gangrened; gangrenous; gargantuan; giant; gigantic; goddamn; goddamned; goddess-like; gold-sandaled; golden; good; grasping; gray; great; green; grimy; grotesque; grubby; gruesome; gym-shoed; hairless; hairy; halting; handsome; happy; hard; hard-pounding; hasty; healthy; heat-swollen; heavenly; heavy; heavy-booted; heedless; hesitant; hidden; hide-booted; high; high-arched; high-heeled; hobbled; homely; hooved; hostile; hot; huge; hurrying; hurt; icy; identifiable; idle; immediate; immense; impatient; individual; infected; inflamed; inflated; initial; injured; inner; inside; irregular; itchy; jutting; kicking; knobby; lacerated; lame; large; lazy; leaden; leading; leaping; leather-clad; leather-soled; leathern; leathery; left; lethal; light; light-hued; limp; lingering;

little; loafer-clad; loafered; long; long-booted; loose-sandaled; lordly; loud; lovely; lower; maimed; male; mammoth; manacled; mangled; manicured; marching; masculine; mashed; massive; meaty; mechanical; medium-size; mere; merry; mighty; mismatched; misshapen; missing; mobile; moccasined; monstrous; moving; mud-laden; mud-spattered; mud-stained; muddy; muffled; multiple; multitudinous; mummified; muscular; nailless; naked; narrow; nasty; nearest; nervous; nice; Nike-clad; nimble; noble; noiseless; normal-sized; numb; numbed; numerous; nylon-stockinged; nyloned; odd; offending; old; old-woman; opposite; ordinary; other; outer; outstretched; oversize; padded; painful; pale; pale-pink; pampered; panicked; paper-white; partial; passing; pasty; pattering; peculiar; pedicured; penny-loafered; perfect; pink; plain; planted; plastered; pleasant; plump; poetic; pointed; poised; poor; powerful; precarious; preceding; precious; pretty; previous; primal; princely; printless; probing; prodding; prosthetic; protruding; proud; pudgy; purposeful; quick; quiet.

R - Y
raised; rapid; ready; rear; red; reeking; regular; reluctant; remaining; restless; retreating; rhythmic; right; rigid; rollerbladed; rooted; rosy; rotten; rotting; rough; royal; rubber-soled; rugged; running; rushing; sandal-clad; sandaled / sandalled; sandy; scabby; scaly; scarred; scented; scrawny; scuffing; scuffling; scurrying; searching; seasoned; sensitive; servile; set; severed; sexy; shackled; shaky; shapely; sharp-taloned; shell-pink; shifting; shoed; shoeless; short; shriveled; shrunken; silent; silk-slippered; silk-socked; silken; single; skeletal; skidding; skilled; skinny; slapping; slender; sliding; slight; slim; slipper-clad; slippered; slippery; slow; sly; small; smelly; smooth; sneaker-clad; sneakered; snow-white; snowy; soaking; sock-clad; socked; sockless; soft; soft-slippered; soiled; soled; solitary; sore; soundless; speedy; spike-heeled; splayed; sprained; sprightly; square; stable; staggering; stained; stamped; stampeding; stamping; stationary; steadfast; steady; steadying; stealthy; sticky; stiff; stiffening; stinky; stocking-clad; stockinged; stockingless; stomping; stout; striding; strong; stubborn; stubby; stubby-toed; stumbling; stupid; sturdy; substantial; sun-brown; supple; sure; swaying; sweaty; swelling; swift; swinging; swollen; taloned; tan; tangled; tanned; tape-wrapped; tender; tentative; thawing; thick; thin; throbbing; thundering; thunderous; tied; timid; tiny; tired; tireless; toe-tapping; toeless; tough; trampling; trapped; trembling; twisted; twitching; ugly; unbound; unburned; uncertain; unclean; uncomfortable; uncovered; ungainly; unhurried; uninjured; unseen; unsteady; unwary; unwashed; unwearied; uplifted; upper; upturned; veined; veiny; visible; vulgar; wandering; warm; water-softened; waxy-white; wayward; weak; weary; webbed; wet; white; white-sandaled; white-sneakered; white-socked; whole; wide; wobbly; wounded; wrinkled; wrong; young; youthful.

Verbs and Phrasal Verbs in Alphabetical Order

A - F

accustomed to; ached; ached from; ached with; acted; adapted; advanced; advanced upon; affected; alerted; allowed; allowed for; alternated; amputated; anchored; anchored to; anchored under; angled; angled inward; angled outward; appeared; appeared through; applied to; approached; arched; arose; arrived; assaulted; attached to; attacked; backed toward; balanced on; bandaged; banged; banged against; bared; bathed; bathed in; beat; beat against; became; began; beguiled; belonged to; bent; betrayed; bled; blistered; blocked; blurred; bobbed; bolted; bore; bothered; bounced; bound; bound together; bound with; bowed; braced; braced against; branded; branded with; bristled; bristled with; broadened; broke; broke through; brought down; brought up; bruised; brushed against; brushed away; bumped; bumped against; bumped into; bundled in; buried; buried in; buried under; burned; burned from; burst into; caked in; calloused; came down; came through; came up; carried; catapulted; caught; caught against; caught between; caught in; caught under; ceased; chained; chained to; charged; chased; chilled; chopped off; clamped onto; clattered; clattered down; clawed; cleaned; clicked; climbed; clipped; clomped; clopped; closed onto; clung; clutched; clutched at; confined; connected; connected with; contained; continued; continued on; continued up; contracted; contracted into; covered; covered by; covered in; covered with; cracked; crammed into; cramped; creaked; creaked across; created; crept; crossed; crowded; crunched; crunched across; crunched on; crunched over; crushed; crusted with; curled; curled up; cushioned; cut; cut off; dabbed; dampened; danced; dangled; dangled above; dangled down; dangled over; dashed; dashed past; descended; dipped; dirtied; disappeared; disappeared beneath; discovered; dispersed; displayed; disrupted; disturbed; dragged; dragged across; dragged along; dragged behind; dragged on; dragged through; dressed; drew up; dried; drifted; drilled; dropped; drummed against; dug; dug into; eased; eased down; echoed; elevated; emerged; encased in; enclosed; enclosed in; encountered; encouraged; engaged; enjoyed; entangled; entered; entwined; escaped; evoked; examined; exposed; extended; faced; faced down; faced up; faded; failed to; faltered; fanned out; fastened to; fell; fell away; fell into; fell on; fell through; felt; fettered; fiddled with; filled with; fit; fit inside; fit into; fixed; flailed; flanked; flanked by; flapped; flapped against; flashed; flattened; fled; flew out; flew up; flexed; flickered; flipped; floated; flopped; floundered; fluttered; folded together; followed; followed by; forced; forced back; formed; fought; found; freed; froze; fumbled.

G - R

gained; galloped; gathered; gave out; gleamed; glided; glided over; got closer; grabbed; grasped; grasped at; grated; grated on; grazed; gripped; groped; groped for; ground; hammered; hammered into; hammered through; hardened; hardened under; healed; held; held on; held up; helped; hesitated; hid; hiked; hiked up; hit; hit against; hobbled; hooked; hooked around; hopped; hopped onto; hovered; hovered over; hung; hung down; hung off; hung over; hurried; hurried over; hurried toward; hurt; hurtled toward; immersed in; impacted; imprisoned by; inched toward; inclined; inclined outward; increased; indicated; inscribed;

inserted; inserted in; insisted; itched; jabbed; jammed; jammed against; jammed in; jerked; joined together; jostled; jumped; jutted out; kicked; kicked against; kicked in; kicked out; kicked up; killed; kissed; knocked; knocked against; laced; laced in; lagged; laid; landed; landed in; landed on; lashed; launched off; leaned against; leapt / leaped; led; left; left up; lifted; lifted off; lifted up; limped; limped across; lined; lined up; linked; lodged in; loitered; looked; looped around; lost; lowered; lowered into; managed to; maneuvered; manipulated; marched; marched out; marked; marred; mashed; massaged; matched; materialized; measured; merged; merged into; met; mingled with; missed; mixed; mounted; moved; moved across; moved up; numbed; numbed by; occupied; offended; oozed; opened; opened up; oriented; outgrew; paced; padded; padded over; paddled; pained; painted; paraded; passed; passed over; passed through; patrolled; pattered; paused; pawed; pawed at; peeked out; peeped out; perched on; performed; perspired; pierced; pierced by; pinned; placed in; placed on; planted; planted against; played; plodded; plodded through; plonked into; plopped; plopped into; plunged in; plunged into; plunged through; pointed down; pointed heavenward; pointed outward; pointed to; pointed toward; pointed up; poised; poised atop; poised on; poised over; poked; poked out; poked through; popped out; posed; positioned; possessed by; pounded; pounded across; presented; pressed; pressed against; pressed together; pricked; prickled; prickled with; prodded; produced; projected out; propelled; propped against; propped up; protected; protected by; protruded; protruded from; proved; provided; pulled; pulled through; pulled up; pummeled; pumped; punched; punched through; pursued; pushed; pushed against; pushed forward; pushed off; pushed through; put forward; put in; put into; put on; quickened; quivered; raced; raced past; radiated from; raised; raked; ran; rang; rattled; reached; reached down; reached out; reappeared; reared; reared up; reattached; receded; received; recoiled; recoiled from; refused; refused to; registered; relaxed; relaxed on; remained; removed; removed from; required; resembled; responded; rested; rested in; rested on; retreated; returned; revealed; roasted; rocked; rocked on; rolled up; rooted to; rose; rubbed; rummaged; rushed; rushed toward; rustled.

S - Y

sailed; sank; sank back; sank into; sat; scampered; scampered away; scrabbled; scrambled; scraped; scraped against; scraped at; scraped on; scraped up; scratched; scratched against; scuffed; scuffed across; scuffled; scurried; searched for; secured; separated; set; set against; set down; settled; settled on; severed; shackled; shifted; shocked; shone; shot forward; shot out; shot up; shoved; showed; shrunk back; shuffled; shuffled across; shuffled over; sizzled; skidded; skidded across; skimmed; skimmed over; skipped; skipped across; skittered; slammed; slammed down; slammed into; slapped across; slapped against; slapped down; slashed; sliced; slid; slid across; slid down; slid off; slid on; slid over; slid toward; slipped; slipped into; slipped off; slipped on; slipped out; slipped underneath; slippered; sloshed; sloshed in; slowed; smacked; smacked against; smacked down; smashed; smashed down; smashed into; smashed through; smelled; smelled like; snagged; snagged by; snagged on; snapped out; snapped up; sneaked / snuck; soaked; soaked in; sought; sought out; sounded; spaced; spanned; spasmed; spat up; speared; speared by; sped; spilled over; splashed; splashed in; splattered with; splayed; sprang; sprawled; sprayed; spread; spread apart; spread out; spread wide; sputtered; squared; squared to; squared with; squeaked; squeaked on; squeezed; squeezed into; squelched; squelched in; squelched through; squirmed; squirmed inside; squished; squished in; staggered; stalked; stamped; stank; started; stayed; steamed; stepped; stepped backward; stepped closer; stepped down; stepped forward; stepped in; stepped into; stepped on; stepped out; stepped over; stirred; stomped; stomped down; stomped in; stomped on; stomped out; stomped up; stood; stood before; stood in; stood on; stood out; stood up; stood upon; stopped; stormed; straightened; straightened out; strapped; strapped down; strapped to; strayed; strengthened; stretched; stretched across; stretched out; strode; strode across; stroked; strolled; struck; struck against; stuck; stuck in; stuck inside; stuck into; stuck out; stuck to; stuffed into; stumbled; stumbled against; stumbled on; stung; stung with; stuttered; stuttered on; submerged; succeeded at; sucked out; suffered; suggested; sunk; sunk in; sunk into; supported; supported by; surrounded; surrounded by; suspended; suspended above; suspended in; suspended off; suspended over; swam; swam up; swarmed; swathed in; sweat; swelled; swelled up; swept; swept away; swept by; swept through; swished through; swung around; swung back; swung beneath; swung freely; swung off; synchronized; tangled; tangled in; tangled together; tangled up; tangled with; tapped; tapped against; tapped in time; tapped on; tapped to; teetered; teetered on; tended to; thrashed; threatened; threw down; threw up; throbbed; thrust; thrust forward; thrust into; thrust out; thudded; thudded against; thudded on; thumped; thumped against; thumped down; thumped on; thundered; tickled; tickled with; tied; tied around; tied together; tied up; tied with; tilted; tilted up; tingled; tipped; tipped downward; tired; toasted; toed; tossed about; touched; touched down; towered over; traced; tracked; trailed; trailed behind; trailed off; trampled; trampled on; trapped; trapped in; trapped under; traveled / travelled; travelled by; traversed; trekked; trembled; tried; tripped; trod; trod on; tromped; trotted; trudged; trudged forward; tucked back; tucked behind; tucked beneath; tucked in; tucked into; tucked under; tucked underneath; tucked up; tugged; tugged on; tumbled; tumbled into; turned; turned backwards; turned in; turned inward; turned left; turned on; turned outward; turned to; turned towards; turned up; twisted; twisted in; twisted up; twitched; twitched back; twitched beneath; twitched with; unbalanced; uncovered; underwent; unhooked; uplifted; upraised; urged; used; vanished; vibrated; vibrated with; vied for; waggled; waited; waiting; walked; walked across; walked by; walked down; walked in; walked on; walked over; walked sideways; walked through; walked toward; walked up; wandered; wandered down; wanted; warmed; warmed by; washed; washed in; watered with; waved; wedged; wedged between; wedged into; wedged under; weighed; wet; whitened; wiggled; wiped; withdrew; wobbled; wore; worked; wounded; wrapped in; wrapped up; writhed; yanked.

absence of feet; amputation of the foot; anatomy of the feet; angle of the foot; appearance of the feet; arch of the foot; area of the foot; army of feet; arrangement of the feet; balls of the feet; base of the feet; beauty of the feet; body of the foot; bone of the foot; bottoms of the feet; breadth of the foot; center of the foot; character of the feet; circumference of the foot; clamoring of feet; clamor of feet; clatter of feet; claws of the feet; coldness of the feet; commotion of feet; condition of the feet; contact of the foot; contraction of the feet; control of the foot; coordinates of the foot; corner of the foot; couple of feet; crackle of feet; crowd of feet; crunch of feet; crush of feet; dance of the feet; depression of the foot; descent of the foot; diameter of the foot; digits of the feet; direction of the feet; dislocation of the foot; drumming of feet; dust of the feet; edge of the foot; elevation of the feet; exposure of the feet; extension of the foot; extremities of the feet; fastness of foot; fleetness of foot; flesh of the foot; force of feet; form of the feet; frenzy of feet; gangrene of the feet; hair of the feet; heels of the feet; height of the foot; impact of feet; impressions of the feet; imprints of the feet; infection of the feet; inflammation of the feet; injuries of the foot; injury of the foot; joints of the feet; kick of the feet; kind of feet; length of the feet; lift of the feet; lightness of foot; line of feet; loss of the foot; lot of feet; marks of the feet; masses of feet; mobility of the foot; motion of the feet; movement of the feet; moving of the feet; multitude of feet; muscles of the feet; musculature of the foot; nails of the feet; nimbleness of foot; noise of feet; numbers of feet; outline of the foot; pair of feet; part of the feet; pattering of feet; patter of feet; perspiration of the feet; phalanges of the foot; position of the feet; posture of the feet; pounding of feet; power of the foot; pressure of the feet; print of the feet; quickness of foot; restlessness of foot; rest of the foot; rhythm of feet; rotation of the foot; row of feet; rush of feet; rustle of feet; scent of the foot; scores of feet; scuffing of feet; scuffle of feet; scuffling of feet; scurry of feet; series of feet; set of feet; shape of the feet; shuffle of feet; shuffling of feet; side of the feet; size of the feet; skin of the feet; slide of feet; slip of the foot; smell of feet; sole of the foot; sound of feet; speed of foot; splashing of feet; spring of the foot; stampede of feet; stamp of the foot; state of the feet; steps of the feet; stomping of feet; strength of the foot; sureness of foot; swiftness of foot; swish of feet; tangle of feet; tapping of feet; thickness of the foot; thrust of feet; thud of feet; thump of feet; thunder of feet; tips of the feet; toes of the feet; top of the feet; track of feet; trampling of feet; turn of the foot; twist of the foot; ulcer of the foot; underside of the foot; vein of the foot; velocity of feet; washing of feet; weakness of the foot; width of the foot; withdrawal of the foot; wounds of the feet.

USAGE EXAMPLES

She heard the sound of *advancing feet approaching* from the right.

A set of boot-clad feet raced past them.

Nick gingerly removed his shoe to reveal a *frost-bitten foot*.

He loved the pale skin of her *goddess-like feet*.

A *broad foot kicked up* sand, blinding him.

16
FINGER(S)

Adjectives in Alphabetical Order

A - F

absent; abused; accusative; accusatory; accusing; aching; active; additional; adept; adjacent; adorable; age-spotted; aged; agile; agitated; amputated; angry; anxious; apprehensive; arched; aristocratic; armed; artful; arthritic; articulated; artificial; artistic; ashy; assaulting; audacious; awkward; babyish; bad; bandaged; bare; battered; beaten; beautiful; beckoning; beefy; bejeweled / bejewelled; bent; best; big; big-knuckled; bite-sized; black; black-gloved; black-nailed; black-stained; black-tipped; blackened; bleeding; blimpy; blistered; bloated; blood-dripping; blood-smeared; blood-soaked; bloodied; bloodless; bloodstained; bloody; blotchy; blubbery; blue; blue-edged; blue-veined; bluish; blunt; blunt-edged; blunt-tipped; boiling; bony; bored; branchlike; bright; brilliant; brisk; brittle; broad; broken; bronzed; brooding; brown; brownish; bruised; brusque; burned / burnt; burning; busy; callused; capable; careful; careless; caressing; cautionary; cautioning; cautious; century-old; chalky; chapped; charming; chastising; childish; childlike; chilling; chilly; chubby; chunky; cigar-like; clammy; clasped; claw-like; clawed; clawing; clay-caked; clay-covered; clean; clenched; clever; closed; clumsy; coarse; cold; colored; colorful; common; conscious; convulsive; cool; corpselike; correcting; corresponding; countless; crafty; cramped; cramping; crawling; cream-colored; creamy; crimson; crimson-tipped; crippled; crooked; crossed; cruel; cunning; cupped; curious; curled; curled-up; curved; cut; cylindrical; dainty; damaged; damp; dangerous; dark; deadly; dear; decaying; deformed; deft; delicate; derisive; desiccated; desperate; dewy; dexterous; diffident; dimpled; dirt-black; dirt-covered; dirt-smudged; dirty; dirty-nailed; disapproving; disciplinary; disdainful; diseased; disgusted; disgusting; disintegrating; dismembered; dismissing; distended; distinct; distorted; distraught; disturbing; divine; double-jointed; dramatic; dried-up; droopy; dry; dumpy; dusty; eager; effeminate; electrified; elegant; elongated; eloquent; emaciated; emphatic; enchanting; enormous; entire; entwined; erratic; ethereal; excellent; excited; exposed; expressive; exquisite; extended; extra; fair; fake; false; faltering; familiar; fast; fastidious; fat; favorite; feeble; female; feminine; feminine-looking; feverish; fickle; fierce; filthy; fine; firm; fleshless; fleshy; flexible; floating; floppy; flour-dusted; floury; fluent; fluttering; fluttery; foamy; folded; forbidding; foreign; foremost; fourth; fractured; fragile; frail; frantic; free; freezing; frenzied; fresh-scrubbed; friendly; frightened; frigid; frost-burned; frostbitten; frosty; frothy; frozen; full; fumbling; funky; furtive.

G - R

gaunt; gentle; ghastly; ghostly; giant; glittering; gloved; gloveless; glowing; glue-parched; gnarled; gnawed-off; goddess-like; good; gooey; gory; gouty; graceful; grasping; grateful; gray; grazing; grease-blacked; grease-stained; greasy; great; greedy; green-stained; grimy; gripping; groping; grubby; guiding; guitar-calloused; hairy; hairy-backed; hairy-knuckled; half-frozen; half-numb; half-submerged; half-warmed; hard; hardened; hasty; heavenly; heavy; heavy-knuckled; helpless; hesitant; hidden; hooked; hopeless; horny; hot; huge; human; human-like; hungry; hurt; hushing; ice-cold; icing-covered; icy; identifying; idle; illuminating; immaculate; impatient; imperious; impudent; inconsiderate; indignant; individual; industrious; inexperienced; infected; injured; ink-stained; inky; inner; inquiring; inquisitive; insinuating; insistent; interlocked; interlocking; intermediate; intertwined; intertwining; intruding; investigative; iron-hard; itchy; jeweled / jewelled; jittery; joined; knitted; knobby; knotted; knotty; lacerated; lame; large; large-knuckled; latex-gloved; latexed; lax; lazy; leaden; leaf-stained; lean; leather-gloved; leathered; leathery; lecturing; lifeless; light; limber; limp; lingering; linked; listless; lithe; little; lively; liver-spotted; livid; lone; long; long-nailed; loose; lopped-off; lost; lovely; loving; lower; lubricated; lumpy; lumpy-knuckled; magic; magical; male; mangled; manicured; manly; masculine; mashed; massive; matchstick-thin; maternal; meager; mean; meaty; mechanical; menacing; metallic; middle; milk-wet; milky; mischievous; misshapen; missing; mittened; mocking; moist; moistened; monolithic; monstrous; monumental; motherly; motionless; moving; mud-caked; muddied; muddy; multiple; murderous; muscle-bound; muscular; mushy; mutilated; mystic; nail-bitten; nailless; nailpolished; naked; narrow; neat; neighboring; nervous; nice; nicotine-stained; niggling; nimble; normal; nubby; numb; numerous; offending; oily; old; olive; once-powerful; once-slender; oozing; open; opposable; orange; ordinary; other; outer; outraged; outspread; outstretched; overlapping; oversized; painful; painted; pale; pallid; panicking; paper-white; paralyzed; parted; passive; pensive; perfect; persistent; perspiring; petite; phantom; piano-playing; pink; pink-nailed; pink-tipped; plain; playful; pliant; plucking; plump; pointed; pointing; pointy; pointy-nailed; powdery; powerful; practiced; precious; precise; pretty; pricked; principal; probing; prodding; professional; prophetic; protruding; psychic; pudgy; puffed-up; puffy; pulsing; quavering; quick; quivering; radiant; raised; rapid; ready; red; red-nailed; red-painted; red-stained; red-tipped; reddened; refined; relaxed; relentless; reluctant; remaining; remorseless; reproachful; restless; rheumatic; rigid; ring; ring-free; ringed; ringless; robotic; rock-hard; roguish; rolling; ropelike; rose-tipped; roseate; rosy; rotted; rough; roughened; rounded; royal; rubbery; ruddy; rude; rugged; rust-colored; ruthless.

S - Y

saliva-coated; sallow; salty; sandy; sausage-like; sausage-thick; scalded; scaly; scarlet; scarred; scorched; scornful; scraping; scrawny; scrubbed; sculpted; sensitive; seventy-year-old; severed; shadowy; shaky; shapely; sharp; shifting; shimmering; shining; shiny; short; shriveled; shushing; significant; silencing;

silent; simple; sinewy; single; skeletal; skilled; skillful; skinned; skinny; slack; slate-gray; sleeping; sleepy; slender; sliced; slick; slight; slim; slimy; slippery; slow; sly; small; smelly; smoking; smooth; snaking; snaky; sneaky; snotty; snowy; soap-smelling; soapy; soft; soiled; solemn; solitary; sooty; sordid; sore; spatula-shaped; spidery; spiky; spindly; splayed; splinted; split; sprawled; spreading; square; square-nailed; square-tipped; stained; stamping; steady; steel-gloved; steely; steely-strong; stern; sticklike; sticky; stiff; stiffened; stiffening; stifling; still; stinging; stinky; stolid; stony; stout; straggly; straight; stringy; strong; stubborn; stubby; stumpy; stunted; sturdy; succulent; suggestive; sunburned / sunburnt; sunlit; supple; sure; sweating; sweaty; sweet; sweet-smelling; swelling; swift; swollen; synthetic; talented; talon-like; talon-tipped; taloned; talonlike; tanned; taped; taped-up; tapered; tapering; tattooed; taut; teasing; tempering; ten-year-old; tenacious; tender; tense; tentative; tepid; terrible; thick; thick-gloved; thick-knuckled; thick-skinned; thieving; thievish; thimbled; thin; thin-jointed; thoughtful; threatening; throbbing; thrusting; tickling; tight; timid; tingling; tiny; tired; tobacco-stained; tough-looking; trembling; tremulous; triumphant; twig-like; twiggy; twisted; twisting; twitching; twitchy; ugly; unaccustomed; unadorned; unaided; unbelieving; uncallused; uncertain; unclean; unconscious; uncouth; uncurling; unerring; unfamiliar; ungloved; unharmed; unhurt; uninvited; unmoving; unpracticed; unseen; unskilled; unsteady; unwashed; unwearied; unwilling; upper; upraised; upturned; upward-pointing; useful; useless; veined; vertical; visible; wagging; wandering; warm; wavering; waving; waxen; weak; weary; weathered; webbed; wedding-band; wee; well-manicured; wet; white; white-hot; white-knuckled; white-nailed; whitened; whole; wicked-looking; wide; wiggling; wild; willing; willowy; wily; wiry; wise; wispy; withered; wizened; womanish; work-gnarled; work-hardened; work-roughened; worn; worried; worst; wounded; wrapped; wriggling; wriggly; wrinkled; wrinkly; young.

Verbs and Phrasal Verbs in Alphabetical Order

A - D

abated; abraded; abstained from; accomplished; ached; ached for; ached from; acknowledged; acted; added; adjusted; affected; aimed at; aimed toward; alighted; alighted on; amputated; angled; anticipated; appeared; applied; arched; arranged; assessed; attached; avoided; backed away; balled up; bandaged; bared; beat; beat against; became; beckoned; began; belonged to; bent; bent backward; bit; bit into; blanched; bleached; bled; blew off; blew on; blistered; bloated; blurred; bobbed; bore; bounced; bound; bound by; bound with; broke; broke through; brought up; brushed; brushed across; brushed against; brushed along; brushed back; brushed over; brushed up; bumped; bumped against; bunched; bunched into; buried; buried in; burned; burned by; burned from; burned with; burrowed into; burst through; busied themselves; bypassed; caked with; came down; came out; came up; caressed; carried; caught; caught between; caught in;

caught on; caused; ceased; changed; chattered against; checked; chewed; chilled by; choked; chopped; chopped off; cinched; circled; clamped; clamped around; clamped down; clamped onto; clapped; clasped; clasped around; clasped together; clawed; clawed against; clawed around; clawed at; cleaned; cleared; clenched; clenched around; clenched in; clenched into; clenched together; clicked; climbed down; climbed up; clipped; closed; closed around; closed on; closed over; clung to; clutched; clutched around; clutched at; clutched into; cocked; coiled; coiled around; colored; combed; combed through; compressed; compressed on; connected with; contained; continued; continued down; continued up; contorted; contracted; contracted against; contracted over; convulsed; corresponded; corresponded to; counted; covered; covered in; covered with; cracked; cramped; cramped from; craved; crawled; crawled up; crept; crept across; crept down; crept up; crimped; crippled; crossed; crowded; crumbled; crunched; crushed; cupped; curled; curled against; curled around; curled together; curved; curved around; curved outward; cut; cut off; dabbed; dabbed at; dabbed in; dampened; dampened with; danced; danced across; danced on; danced over; dangled; darted; darted across; darted from; darted into; darted over; darted toward; dawdled; decorated with; delved into; dented; depressed; descended; detached; detected; developed; dialed; dipped; dipped in; dipped inside; dipped into; directed; dirtied; disappeared; disappeared into; discolored by; discovered; displayed; dotted with; dove; dove into; dragged; dragged against; draped; dressed; drew; drew back; drew on; dried; drifted; drifted across; drifted down; drifted over; drifted toward; drilled; dripped; dripped with; dropped; dropped down; dropped onto; drove; drowned in; drummed; drummed on; dry on; dug; dug against; dug at; dug beneath; dug in; dug into; dug up.

E - M

eased back; eased up; echoed; edged across; edged down; edged up; embedded in; embraced; emerged; employed; encircled; enclosed; encountered; ended in; engaged; ensured; entered; entwined; entwined in; entwined with; erupted; etched; exchanged; expanded; explored; explored between; explored further; exposed; extended; extended toward; faced; faded; faded from; failed to; faltered; faltered on; faltered over; fanned; fanned out; fascinated; fascinated by; fashioned; fastened; feathered; fell; fell off; fell on; fell still; felt; felt against; felt as if; felt for; felt like; felt so; fiddled; fiddled with; fidgeted; fidgeted for; fidgeted with; filled; filled with; fingered; fisted; fit; fit into; fixed; flapped; flared; flared out; flashed; flashed over; flashed through; flew across; flew back; flew over; flew through; flew toward; flew up; flexed; flexed around; flexed on; flicked; flicked across; flicked against; flicked away; flinched; flinched away; flipped; flitted; floated; floated toward; flourished; flung; flurried; fluttered; fluttered over; folded; followed; fondled; forced; formed; fought; fought through; found; framed; freed; freed from; froze; froze at; froze on; fumbled; fumbled about; fumbled around; fumbled at; fumbled for; fumbled in; fumbled through; fumbled with; fused together; fussed with; gained; gathered; gave; gestured; glided along; glided over; glistened; glued; glued to; gouged; grabbed;

grappled; grappled with; grasped; grazed; grazed across; grazed over; grew; grinded; gripped; groped; groped for; guided; hammered; handled; hardened; healed; held; held out; held together; held up; hesitated; hit; hooked; hooked on; hovered; hovered over; hugged; hung; hung down; hurried; hurt; ignored; inched closer; inched toward; indicated; inserted; inserted in; inserted into; inserted through; instructed; interfered; interfered with; interlinked; interlocked; interrogated; intertwined; introduced; invaded; invited; irritated; irritated by; itched; itched for; jabbed; jabbed at; jammed; jerked; jerked against; jerked up; jittered; jittered across; joined; joined together; jumped; jutted; jutted out; kissed; kneaded; knitted; knotted; laced; lacked; laid; laid across; laid on; laid out; landed on; latched onto; leafed through; learned; left; let; levitated; licked; lifted; lifted away; lifted from; lifted toward; lingered on; lingered over; lingered under; linked; located; locked; locked around; locked together; longed for; longed to; looked; looked like; looped; loosened; loosened around; lost; lowered; lurked; made; maintained; maneuvered; manipulated; marked; mashed; massaged; measured; messed; met; mimed; mimicked; mingled; moistened; moistened with; molded; moved; moved across; moved against; moved along; moved between; moved down; moved over; moved through; moved to; moved toward; moved up; moved with.

N - R

navigated; needed; nibbled; nibbled at; nicked; nipped; nudged; numbed; numbered; nursed; obeyed; occupied; offered; oozed; opened; opposed; outlined; overlapped; painted; pantomimed; parted; passed; passed over; passed through; patted; paused; paused at; paused on; pawed; pawed through; pecked; peeled; penetrated; perched; perched above; performed; persisted; picked; picked at; picked out; picked through; pierced; pierced through; pincered; pinched; pinched together; pinned; placed; placed in; placed on; placed over; planted; played; played along; played over; played with; pleated; plied; plodded; plucked; plucked at; plugged; plugged up; plunged; plunged into; pocketed; pointed; pointed at; pointed down; pointed out; pointed outward; pointed skyward; pointed straight; pointed to; pointed toward; pointed up; poised; poised above; poised against; poised like; poised on; poised over; poked; poked at; poked through; popped; popped out; possessed; pounded; prepared; presented; pressed; pressed against; pressed between; pressed down; pressed in; pressed into; pressed on; pressed together; pricked; pried; pried at; probed; probed for; prodded; produced; projected; promised; propped up; protected; protected by; protruded; protruded from; provided; pulled; pulled apart; pulled at; pulled back; punched; punched out; punched through; punctured; pushed; pushed against; pushed aside; pushed at; pushed down; pushed into; pushed through; put together; quivered; raced across; raced over; rained down; raised; raised against; raised from; raised to; raked; raked across; raked down; raked over; raked up; ran; ran along; ran down; ran over; rapped; rapped against; rattled; reached; reached across; reached around; reached down; reached for; reached in; reached into; reached out; reached over; reached toward; reached up; reappeared; received; reconnected; recovered; reentered; refused; reignited; relaxed; relaxed on; released; remained; reminded; removed; removed from; required; rested; rested against; rested in; rested inside; rested on; rested over; resumed; retained; retracted; retreated; returned; revealed; riffled; ripped; rippled; rippled across; rippled over; roamed; roamed over; rolled; rolled into; rose; roughened; roused; roved; roved across; rubbed; rubbed against; rubbed at; rubbed behind; ruffled; rummaged; rummaged around.

S - Z

sank; sank into; sat; scattered; scented with; scooped; scooped up; scorched; scrabbled; scrabbled at; scraped; scraped against; scraped along; scratched; scratched against; scratched at; scratched behind; scudded; scudded against; scurried; scurried around; scuttled; searched; searched for; seized; sensed; sent; separated; served; set; settled; settled on; settled once; severed; shadowed; shaped; shaped like; shifted; shifted on; shifted to; shocked; shone; shook; shook beneath; shot off; shot up; shoved; shoved into; showed; shriveled; shut; sifted through; signaled; signed; skated; skated along; skimmed; skimmed over; skipped; skittered; skittered along; skittered over; slackened; slammed; slapped; slashed; sliced; sliced away; sliced by; sliced off; sliced through; slid; slid across; slid along; slid beneath; slid between; slid down; slid inside; slid into; slid off; slid on; slid onto; slid over; slid through; slid to; slid up; slipped; slipped along; slipped behind; slipped beneath; slipped between; slipped down; slipped inside; slipped into; slipped off; slipped on; slipped over; slipped through; slowed; slowed down; smashed; smashed into; smeared; smeared with; smelled; smelled of; smoothed; smoothed over; smudged; smudged with; snagged; snagged on; snaked; snaked over; snapped; snapped at; snapped off; snared; snared by; snatched; sneaked / snuck; sought; sought out; sparkled; sparkled with; spasmed; speared; speared into; speared through; sped; sped over; spidered; spidered through; spilled through; splayed; splayed across; splayed on; splayed out; splayed over; split; sported; spread; spread against; spread apart; spread around; spread out; spread over; spread wide; squared; squeezed; squeezed together; stabbed; stabbed at; stained with; started; stayed; steadied; steered; stiffened; stilled; stirred; stood; stopped; stopped against; stopped at; stopped by; stopped in; stopped on; straightened; strained; strained against; strained apart; strangled; strayed; strengthened; stretched; stretched out; stretched toward; stroked; struck; struggled; struggled with; strummed; strummed over; strung; stuck; stuck between; stuck in; stuck on; stuck together; stuck up; stumbled; stumbled across; stumbled along; stung; stunk; sucked; suggested; summoned; supplied; supported; surged; surrounded; swam; swam down; swam inside; sweat; swelled; swept; swept through; swirled; switched on; swiveled / swivelled; tangled; tangled in; tangled together; tantalized; tapped; tapped against; tapped at; tapped on; teased; tended; tensed; tensed around; tensed on; tested; threaded; threaded through; threatened; thrilled; throbbed; thrummed; thrust; thrust into; thrust up; tickled; tied; tied up; tightened; tightened around; tightened on; tingled; tingled against; took; tore; tore at; tore away; tore out; tore through; touched; toyed with; traced; traced across; traced around; traced down; traced over; traced up; trailed; trailed across; trailed along;

trailed down; trailed over; trapped; trapped in; traveled down; traveled / travelled; traveled up; traversed; trembled; trembled against; trembled around; trembled on; trembled over; trembled with; tremored; tried; tucked; tugged; tugged at; tunneled; tunneled between; tunneled through; turned; turned inward; turned to; twirled; twirled around; twisted; twisted around; twisted inside; twisted together; twitched; twitched with; typed; unclenched; uncrumpled; uncurled; undid; undressed; unfastened; unfolded; unfurled; unhooked; united; unlaced; unraveled / unravelled; unsnagged; unthreaded; untied; uplifted; upraised; used; vanished; vibrated; vibrated beneath; vied for; wagged; waggled; waited; walked; walked up; wandered; wandered across; wandered along; wandered over; wanted; warmed; warmed against; waved; wavered; weaved; weaved through; wedged; wedged in; wedged into; wet; whirled; whirled through; wielded; wiggled; wiped; withdrew; wore; worked; worked at; worked on; worked over; wormed; wound; wound around; wove; wrapped; wrapped around; wrestled; wriggled; wriggled around; wrinkled; writhed; writhed in; wrote; yanked; yearned; zipped.

Noun Phrases

absence of fingers; action of the finger(s); activity of the finger(s); aid of the finger(s); amount of fingers; amputation of the finger(s); appearance of the finger(s); arthritis of the finger(s); articulations of the finger(s); axis of the finger(s); back(s) of the finger(s); ball(s) of the finger(s); base of the finger(s); bone(s) of the finger(s); brush of fingers; bunch of fingers; caress of the finger(s); collection of fingers; contact of the finger(s); contraction of the finger(s); control of the finger(s); couple of fingers; curl of the finger(s); dance of the finger(s); dexterity of finger(s); direction of the finger(s); display of fingers; edge of the finger(s); end(s) of the finger(s); extension of the finger(s); fist of fingers; flexibility of the finger(s); flexing of fingers; flick of the finger(s); flip of the finger(s); flutter of fingers; fracture(s) of the finger(s); function of the finger(s); gangrene of the finger(s); grasp of fingers; grip of the finger(s); hook of the finger(s); impression of the finger(s); infection of the finger(s); insertion of the finger(s); itch of the finger(s); joint(s) of the finger(s); knuckle(s) of the finger(s); length of the finger(s); loss of the finger(s); mark(s) of the finger(s); middle of the finger(s); mobility of the finger(s); motion of the finger(s); movement of the finger(s); muscles of the finger(s); nail(s) of the finger(s); nerves of the finger(s); nimbleness of finger; number of fingers; numbness of the finger(s); pair of fingers; part of the finger(s); placement of the finger(s); pointing of the finger; position of the finger(s); power of the finger(s); press of the finger(s); pressure of the finger(s); removal of the finger(s); rest of the fingers; sensation of fingers; separation of the finger(s); series of fingers; set of fingers; shake of the finger; shape of the finger(s); side(s) of the finger(s); size of the finger(s); skin of the finger(s); slap of fingers; slip of the finger; snap of the finger(s); snapping of fingers; sound of fingers; stiffness of the finger(s); surface of the finger(s); sweep of the fingers; tangle of fingers; tapping of fingers; tendons of the finger(s); thickness of the finger(s); tip(s) of the finger(s); top(s) of the finger(s); touch of fingers; trail of the finger(s); tremor of the finger(s); twiddling of fingers; twist of the finger(s); withdrawal of the finger(s).

USAGE EXAMPLES

She *pointed an accusatory finger at* him from the witness stand.

He *washed his blood-soaked fingers* in the bathroom sink.

Ben's *broken finger ached.*

He has *callused fingers* from playing guitar.

James took her *pale delicate fingers* in his hand and led her to the dance floor.

17
FOREARM(S)

Adjectives in Alphabetical Order

bandaged; bangled; bare; bared; big; black; bleeding; bloody; broken; bronzed; bruised; bulging; burly; calloused; clawed; corded; creamy; dark; dirty; entire; exposed; extended; fat; firm; fleshy; giant; greasy; grimy; hairless; hairy; hefty; huge; inner; large; lateral; leathery; left; little; liver-spotted; long; lower; magnificent; mammoth; massive; meager; meaty; mechanical; metallic; missing; muscled; muscular; naked; opposite; other; outer; outstretched; oversized; pale; pink; plaster-encased; powerful; prosthetic; protruding; raised; right; ropey; scarred; scratched; shapely; short; sinewy; skeletal; slender; slight; slippery; small; smooth; solid; spindly; stringy; strong; stubby; stumpy; sturdy; suntanned; sweaty; tanned; tattooed; taut; thick; thin; tiny; toned; tree-like; twisted; unguarded; upper; upraised; vein-covered; veiny; weather-darkened; well-muscled; white; whole; wiry; young.

Verbs and Phrasal Verbs in Alphabetical Order

ached; appeared; bandaged; bared; bent; braced; brushed; bunched; burst out; came up; chopped; covered; covered with; cramped; crisscrossed; crossed; crossed over; cut; dangled; drifted; exposed; extended; fell; felt; flattened; flew out; flew up; flexed; flinched; folded; folded across; folded over; fought off; gleamed; gleamed with; glowed; grazed; grew tense; held; hit; hurt; jammed against; jammed into; knocked; lengthened; lifted; looked; placed; pressed; pressed against; propped; propped on; pushed; quivered; raised; rested; rested on; rose; saluted; sat; sat on; shaded; shattered; shattered by; shaved; shielded; showed; showed beneath; slammed; slammed against; slanted; slanted into; slung; slung across; smudged with; stood; stood out; stood up; strained; struck; struck against; stung; suggested; supported; swelled; swelled beneath; swelled with; tensed; thickened; tightened; tingled; tired; touched; trembled; turned; twisted; twitched; worked; wrapped.

Noun Phrases

amputation of the forearm(s); bones of the forearm(s); center of the forearm(s); extension of the forearm(s); fracture of the forearm(s); length of the forearm(s); line of the forearm(s); movement of the forearm(s); muscles of the forearm(s);

position of the forearm(s); rotation of the forearm(s); side of the forearm(s); skin of the forearm(s); surface of the forearm(s); top of the forearm(s); veins of the forearm(s); weight of the forearm(s).

USAGE EXAMPLES

His *strong muscular forearms bulged* as he lifted the cabinet.

Kevin had *greasy forearms* from working on the car all day.

The old woman *folded her veiny forearms across* her chest.

He rolled up his sleeves, *exposing his well-muscled forearms*.

A *long forearm flew out*, knocking her on her back.

18
FOREHEAD

Adjectives in Alphabetical Order

A - M

aching; adorable; ample; angry; anguished; animated; anxious; arched; ardent; austere; baby-smooth; babyish; bald; balding; bandaged; bare; barren; bashful; battered; beaded; beautiful; beetled; big; blank; bleak; bleeding; blood-caked; bloody; blunt; bold; bonny; bony; boyish; branded; brazen; breezy; bright; broad; bronzed; brown; bruised; bulbous; bulging; bumpy; burned / burnt; burning; busy; candid; capacious; careworn; changeless; cheerful; childish; chiseled; clammy; classic; clean; clear; cloudy; cloven; cold; commanding; concave; concerned; confident; conscious; contemptuous; convex; cool; corrugated; craggy; creamy; creased; crinkled; crosshatched; crushed; cunning; curious; curved; curving; cut; dainty; damp; dangerous; dark; darkened; dauntless; dazzling; deep; deepening; dejected; delicate; dented; depressed; dewy; diabolic; dirty; discontented; disdainful; disorderly; distinctive; domed; domelike; double; doubtful; downcast; dreadful; dreary; drooping; dry; dull; dusky; dusty; earnest; elegant; elevated; elongated; enormous; expansive; exposed; expressive; extended; fair; fearful; fearless; fevered; feverish; fierce; fine; flaming; flat; flawless; flushed; forbidding; formidable; frank; freckled; frosty; frown-lined; frozen; full; furled; furrowed; gathered; generous; genial; gentle; giant; girlish; glistening; gloomy; glossy; glowing; graceful; grand; grave; greasy; great; Grecian; grim; haggard; handsome; hard; hardened; haughty; heated; heavenly; heavy; heroic; high; hot; huge; icy; immense; imperial; imperious; impudent; incredulous; indignant; ingenuous; innocent; intimidating; joyless; joyous; jutting; kingly; knightly; knitted; knotted; languid; large; leathery; lined; lineless; lively; liverspotted; livid; lofty; long; lordly; lovely; lower; lowered; lowslanted; luminous; lumpy; magisterial; magnificent; majestic; manly; marble-smooth; marked; massive; meek; menacing; mighty; mild; milky; modest; moist; moody; motionless; mottled; mournful; mysterious.

N - Y

Narrow; Neanderthal-like; noble; obstinate; oily; old; olive; orbed; overgrown; overhanging; oversized; pale; pallid; pensive; perfect; perspiration-beaded; perspiring; pierced; pimpled; pinched; pink; placid; pleasant; plump; poetic; polished; ponderous; powdered; powerful; precipitous; pretty; princely; prominent; pronounced; protruding; protuberant; proud; puzzled; questioning; radiant; raised; red; refulgent; regal; resolute; retreating; revealing; ridged; rigid; rocky; rotund; rough; round; rounded; royal; ruddy; rugged; russet; sad; sallow; savage; scarred; scorched; scornful; scraggly; scrunched; scrunched-up;

seamless; serene; serious; severe; shaded; shadowed; shadowy; sharp; shining; shiny; short; silken; skeptical; sketchy; slashing; slick; slight; slim; slimy; sloped; sloping; small; smooth; sober; soft; solemn; solitary; somber; speckled; spherical; split; spotted; square; stately; steadfast; steady; steep; stern; sticky; still-damp; stony; stormy; straight; strong; stubborn; studious; sullen; sultry; sunburned / sunburnt; suntanned; supercilious; surly; suspicious; swarthy; sweat-beaded; sweat-drenched; sweat-glistening; sweat-moistened; sweat-streaked; sweating; sweaty; sweeping; swollen; tall; tan; tanned; tawny; tempestuous; tender; tenebrous; tense; terrible; thick; thickened; thin; thoughtful; throbbing; tight; tightening; time-heightened; timid; tired; too-high; too-prominent; towering; tranquil; tremendous; tremulous; triangular; troubled; ugly; unabashed; unblushing; unclouded; uncontrolled; uncreased; undaunted; unembarrassed; unfurrowed; unkind; unlined; unruffled; untroubled; unwizened; unwrinkled; upper; upturned; vacant; vast; vaulted; veiled; veined; venerable; victorious; virgin; wandering; warlike; warm; waxen; waxy; weary; well-sculpted; wet; white; whole; wide; withered; wizened; worried; wrinkle-free; wrinkled; wry; young; youthful.

Verbs and Phrasal Verbs in Alphabetical Order

A - L

ached; adorned with; appeared; arched; arched in; bandaged; banged; banged against; bathed; bathed in; beaded; beaded with; beamed; beat; belied; bent; betrayed; bled; bled from; blushed; bobbed; bobbed up; bonked; bore; bound; bound in; bound with; bowed; braced; braced against; branded; branded with; broke out; brooded; bruised; brushed; buckled; bulged; bumped; bunched; burned; came together; cast; caught; chafed; cleared; cleared up; clenched; climbed; closed together; clouded; coated with; cocked; cocked in; collapsed; collapsed into; collided with; colored; composed; connected with; continued; contracted; covered; covered in; covered with; cracked; cracked on; creased; crimsoned; crinkled; crisscrossed with; crowned by; crowned with; crumpled; dampened; darkened; deepened; descended; dominated; dotted with; drew forward; drew together; dried; dripped; dripped with; drooped; dropped; eased; elevated; embraced; encircled; encircled by; encircled with; etched into; evaporated; expanded; exposed; extended; fell; fevered; flared; flexed; flicked; flicked upward; flushed; folded; framed; freckled; frowned; furrowed; gathered; gleamed; glinted; glistened; glittered; glowed; grew deeper; hardened; hid; hinted; hit; hung; hung over; hurt; increased; indicated; knitted; knotted; leaned against; lifted; lightened; lined; lined from; lined with; looked confused; loomed; lost; lowered.

M - W

marked; marked by; marked with; marred; marred by; moistened; moved down; moved up; obscured by; overhung; overlooked; painted; peeked through; pinched; pressed; pressed against; projected; protruded; pulled up; pulsed;

punctuated by; pursed; quirked; quirked upward; quivered; raced down; radiated; raised; ran across; receded; reddened; reflected; relaxed; remained; replaced; rested; rested on; retreated; revealed; rolled; rose; rose up; rounded; rumpled; sank; scrunched; scrunched in; scrunched up; seamed; seared; set in; shone; shot up; showed; signaled; sketched upward; slammed; slammed into; slanted; sloped; sloped back; slumped; slumped against; smoothed; softened; split; sported; sprouted; stayed; stiffened; stood; stood out; stooped; straightened; streaked with; streamed with; stretched; struck; suggested; swelled; thickened; throbbed; thrust; thrust out; thudded against; tightened; tilted; tilted up; tipped; tipped toward; told; topped; topped by; touched; trembled; trembled against; turned; twisted; twitched; twitched upward; unbound; uncovered; unfolded; uplifted; waned; went up; wet; wiped; wore; worked; wrapped; wrapped in; wreathed with; wrinkled.

Noun Phrases

angle of the forehead; area of the forehead; base of the forehead; breadth of the forehead; center of the forehead; curve of the forehead; edge of the forehead; expanse of forehead; furrows of the brow/forehead; hair of the forehead; height of the forehead; length of the forehead; lines of the forehead; lowness of the forehead; middle of the forehead; midline of the forehead; outline of the forehead; part of the forehead; plane of the forehead; prominence of the forehead; ridge of the forehead; shape of the forehead; side of the forehead; skin of the forehead; slope of the forehead; spread of the forehead; stretch of forehead; strip of forehead; veins of the forehead; width of the forehead; wrinkles of the brow/forehead.

USAGE EXAMPLES

Her *pensive forehead betrayed* her true feelings.

His *solemn forehead cleared* when she spoke the words he'd imagined would never come.

Looking across at her with her brother, Jack's *forehead knitted* in confusion.

Her *anxious forehead signaled* that she was about to break out in hysterics.

The nurse's *waxy bulbous forehead wrinkled* slightly when she spotted them entering a restricted area.

19

HAIR

Adjectives in Alphabetical Order

A - D

abdominal; abominable; absent; absurd; abundant; acorn-colored; adequate; afrolike; aging; albino; almost-to-the-shoulder; amazing; amber; amber-colored; amber-streaked; ambrosial; ample; angelic; apricot; apricot-colored; army-short; ash-blonde / ash-blond; ash-brown; ash-colored; ash-gray; ashen; ashen-blonde; ashy; astonishing; attractive; auburn; auburn-red; auburny; autumn-grass; average; awful; baby-fine; back-long; bad; bad-smelling; balding; banana-yellow; barbered; barbie-doll; bark-brown; basic; beaded; beauteous; beautiful; bedraggled; beet-colored; beige; beribboned; best; best-dressed; big; billowing; billowy; black; black-brown; blackish; bleach-blonde / bleach-blond; bleach-fried; bleached; bleached-blonde / bleached-blond; bleached-out; bleached-streaked; blond-and-gray; blond-brown; blond-gray; blond-white; blonde / blond; blondish; blondish-brown; blood-red; blossom-colored; blow-dried; blowsy / blowzy; blue; blue-black; blue-gray / blue-grey; blue-tinged; blue-tinted; bluish; blunt; blunt-cut; bobbed; bobby-pinned; body; bonny; boot-black; bottle-blonde / bottle-blond; bouffant; bouncing; bouncy; bound-up; bountiful; bowl-cut; boy-short; boyish; braided; branching; brass-colored; brassy; bread-brown; breeze-tousled; breezy; brick-red; bright; bright-red; brilliant; brindle-colored; brindled; bristling; bristly; brittle; broad; bronze-colored; bronzed; bronzish; bronzy; brown; brown-blond; brownish; brownish-black; brownish-blond; brownish-gray; brownish-red; brown-streaked; brunette; brunette-colored; brush-cut; brushed; brylcreemed; bunched; bunned-up; burgundy; burnished; burnt-sienna; bushy; butch; butter-colored; buttered; buttery; buzz-cut; Byronic; camel-colored; canary-colored; caramel-colored; careless; carmine; carrot-colored; carrot-orange; carrot-red; carroty; cascading; casual; catastrophic; center-parted; chalk-white; champagne-blond; chemical-red; chestnut; chestnut-brown; chestnut-colored; chestnut-red; chestnut-tinted; chic; childish; chin-length; chocolate-brown; choppy; cider-colored; cinder-gray; cinereous; clairol-red; clammy; classical; clean; clean-smelling; clipped; close-cropped; close-cut; closely-cropped; cloudlike; clumped; clumpy; coal-black; coal-colored; coarse; cocoa-brown; coffee-brown; coffee-colored; coffee-dark; coiffed; coiffured; coiled; coiling; cold; collar-length; colored; colorful; colorless; comb-over; combed; combed-over; comely; comical; common; conservative; considerable; contemporary; conventional; convict-style; cool; copious; copper; copper-blond; copper-colored; copper-gray; copper-orange; copper-penny; copper-red; coppery; coppery-brown; coppery-red; corn-colored; corn-rowed; corn-tassel; cornrow-braided; cotton-candy; cotton-white; cottony;

crazy; crazy-ass; crazy-mop; creative; crew-cut; crimped; crimson; crinkle-permed; crinkled; crinkly; crisp; cropped; crow-black; crumpled; curled; curly; currant-colored; cut; cute; dainty; damaged; damp; dampened; dandelion-fluff; dandelion-white; dangerous; dank; dark; dark-as-midnight; dark-blonde / dark-blond; dark-brown; dark-fire; dark-red; dark-straw; darkened; darkish; darkly-golden; dazzling; decorative; deep-auburn; deep-black; deep-red; delicate; delightful; dense; dewy; dirt-brown; dirt-colored; dirty; dirty-blonde / dirty-blond; dirty-brownish; disarrayed; disastrous; discolored; disheveled; dishwater-blonde / dishwater-blond; disobedient; disordered; disorderly; distinctive; distinguished; doe-brown; dome-like; down-like; downy; drab; draggled; dramatic; dreadful; dreadlocked; dreamy; drenched; dried; dripping-wet; drooping; dropped; drowned; dry; dull; dull-colored; dung-colored; dusky; dust-colored; dust-white; dusty; dyed; dyed-black; dyed-blond; dyed-brown; dyed-red.

E - M

ebony; eccentric; eggplant-colored; elaborate; electric; electric-blue; electrified; elegant; elevated; elongated; enchanting; endless; enormous; espresso-colored; excellent; excessive; executive-gray; exotic; expensive; exposed; exquisite; extensive; extraordinary; extravagant; extreme; exuberant; fabulous; facial; faded; fair; fairish; fake; fallen; falling; false; fancy; fantastic; fashionable; fawn-colored; feathered; feathery; feminine; fiery; fiery-red; filmy; filthy; fine; fire-red; flamboyant; flame-colored; flame-like; flame-red; flaming; flat; flat-top; flattened; flaxen; floating; floppy; floral; flourishing; flowered; flowery; flowing; fluffed; fluffy; fly-away / flyaway; flying; foaming; fog-dampened; foolish; foolish-looking; formal; forties-style; fox-colored; fox-red; foxy; fragile; fragrant; frail; frayed; free; french-braid; french-braided; freshly-washed; fried; frightening; frightful; frilly; fringed; frizz-free; frizzed; frizzed-out; frizzed-up; frizzled; frizzy; frost-blonde; frost-coated; frosted; frosty; frowsy / frowzy; full; funky; funny; fuzzy; garish; garlanded; garnet-colored; gay; gelled; gentle; ghost-blonde; ghostly; giant; gilded; gilt-edged; ginger; ginger-ale; ginger-colored; gingerish; gingery; gingery-gray; girlish; girly; glamorous; gleaming; glistening; glistening-black; glittering; glorious; glossy; glowing; gold; gold-blonde; gold-bright; gold-pink; gold-red; golden; golden-blond; golden-brown; golden-red; good-smelling; gorgeous; graceful; grand; grassy; gray; gray-and-yellow; gray-black; gray-blonde / gray-blond; gray-brown; gray-flecked; gray-streaked; gray-white; graying; graying-blond; graying-yellow; grayish; grayish-brown; grayish-white; grease-caked; greased; greased-back; greased-down; greasy; greasy-looking; great; grimy; grizzled; groovy; gross; grotesque; hairsprayed; handsome; hanging; hatless; hay-colored; hazel; healthy-looking; heavenly; henna-red; hideous; highlighted; hip-length; honey-blonde / honey-blond; honey-brown; honey-colored; honeyed; hopeless; horrible; horrid; hot; huge; humidity-curled; hypnotic; ice-blonde; icy; immaculate; impeccable; inch-long; incredible; indigo; ink-black; inky; intricate; invisible; irksome; iron-gray; irritating; itchy; jet-black; jeweled / jewelled; jojoba-scented; just-cut; just-washed; kinked; kinky; knotted; knotty;

lackluster; lacquer-black; lamb's-wool; lanky; large; lavish; layered; lazy; lead-gray; lemon-yellow; lengthy; lice-infested; licorice-black; lifeless; light; light-blonde; light-brown; light-colored; light-streaked; lightened; lightish; lilac; limp; linty; listless; lively; long; long-black; long-flowing; longish; loose; loose-curled; loose-hanging; loosened; lopsided; lousy; lovely; luminous; luscious; lush; lusterless; lustful; lustrous; luxuriant; luxurious; magical; magnetic; magnificent; mahogany-colored; maiden; manageable; mangled; mangy; manicured; manly; marcelled; marmalade-colored; maroon; marvelous; masculine; massive; matted; mature; mauve; medium; medium-brown; medium-length; mercurochrome-orange; messed-up; messy; metallic; midnight-black; midnight-blue; midnight-brown; midnight-dark; military-short; milk-weed-pale; milk-white; misty; mocha-colored; mohawked; moist; monkish; moon-colored; moon-silvered; moon-white; moonlit; moppish; moppy; mostly-gray; mouse-brown; mouse-colored; moussed; mousy; mousy-brown; mud-brown; mud-caked; mud-colored; muddied; muddy; multi-colored; mushroom-colored; musky; mussed; mussed-up; mussy.

N - R

nasal; natural; natural-blonde; near-black; near-perfect; near-white; nearly-white; neat; neatly-combed; new; new-cut; newly-red; newly-wet; nice; night-black; noble; Nordic; not-too-clean; nut-brown; nut-colored; oak-brown; oak-colored; oaky; obsidian-colored; obstinate; odd; odd-colored; odd-looking; odorous; offensive; oil-black; oiled; oily; oily-dark; old-fashioned; olive; once-blond; once-brown; once-dark; once-glorious; once-long; once-red; once-sandy; once-yellow; opulent; orange; orange-brown; orange-colored; orange-dyed; orange-red; orderly; ordinary; organic; ornamental; ornate; outrageous; outspread; outstanding; over-moussed; overdyed; overgrown; overhanging; overlying; overturned; padded; pageboyed; pale; pale-blonde / pale-blond; pale-brown; pallid; pampered; parted; patchy; peach-colored; pearl-white; penny-bright; penny-colored; pepper-gray; peppered; peppery; perfect; perfectly-coiffed; perfumed; periwinkle-blue; permed; peroxide-blonde; peroxided; pewter-colored; picturesque; pigmented; pigtailed; piled-up; pink; pink-gold; pink-streaked; pink-striped; pinkish; pinky-red; pinned-up; pitch-black; pitch-dark; pitchy; pixie-cut; pixie-short; pixie-style; plain; plaited; plastered; platinum-blonde; platinum-colored; plentiful; plum-colored; Pocahontas-looking; poetic; pointed; pointy; pomade; pomaded; pompadoured; pony-tailed / ponytailed; poofy; poppy-colored; poppy-red; poufy; powdered; pretty; pretty-yellow; prickly; prim; prison-cropped; prominent; pubic; puffed; puffed-out; puffed-up; puffy; pumpkin-colored; punk-red; pure-silver; pure-white; purple; purple-tinted; purple-tipped; purplish; purplish-black; radiant; ragged; raggedy; rain-slicked; rain-soaked; rain-wet; rainbowy; raspberry-purple; ratted; ratty; raven; raven-black; raven-blue; raven-dark; razor-cut; receding; reckless; red; red-black; red-blonde / red-blond; red-brown; red-dyed; red-frizzed; red-gold; red-golden; red-yellow; reddish; reddish-blonde / reddish-blond; reddish-brown; reddish-dyed; reddish-orange; refined; regal; relaxed; remaining; remarkable; repulsive; respectable; resplendent; retouched; retreating; retro; ribboned; rich;

ridiculous; rigid; ringleted; rinsed; rinso-white; riotous; rock-god; rock-n-roll; rock-star; ropy; rose-gold; rosy; rough; royal; rubber-black; ruddy; ruffled; rugged; ruined; rumpled; russet; russet-colored; rust-colored; rust-red; rusty; rusty-brown; rusty-looking; rusty-red.

S

sable; salt-and-pepper; salt-bleached; salt-matted; salt-stained; salt-stiffened; salty; salty-gray; sand-caked; sand-coated; sand-colored; sandy; sandy-blonde / sandy-blond; sandy-brown; sandy-colored; satiny; satisfactory; saturated; savage; scanty; scarlet; scattered; scented; scissor-cut; scorching; scraggly; scraggy; scraped-back; scrappy; scruffy; sculpted; serpentine; sexy; shabby; shaded; shaggy; shampoo-smelling; shampooed; sharp; shaven; sherry-colored; shimmering; shining; shiny; shitty; shocky; short; short-barbered; short-clipped; short-cropped; short-cut; short-trimmed; shortish; shoulder-length; side-parted; silk; silken; silky; silky-smooth; silly; silver; silver-and-white; silver-black; silver-blonde / silver-blond; silver-frosted; silver-gray; silver-platinum; silver-shot; silver-streaked; silver-threaded; silver-tipped; silver-white; silvered; silvering; silvery; silvery-blonde / silvery-blond; silvery-white; silvery-yellow; slate-colored; sleek; sleep-flattened; sleep-matted; sleep-tangled; sleep-tousled; sleety; slept-on; slick; slicked; slicked-back; slicked-down; slippery; sloppy; smart; smelly; smoke-colored; smoky; smooth; smooth-as-silk; smooth-combed; snakelike; snaky; snow-and-rust; snow-cold; snow-colored; snow-white; snowy; soaked; soaking; soap-smelling; soapy; sodden; soft; soiled; soot-streaked; sooty; sophisticated; sopping; sopping-wet; sour-smelling; sparkling; sparkly; sparse; spectacular; spiked; spiky; spiraled; sprayed; springy; spun-gold; squalid; square; square-cut; squiggly; stale; stand-up; starched; staticky; steam-slick; steel-gray; steel-wool; steely; steely-gray; stick-straight; sticky; sticky-looking; stiff; stiff-looking; still-blond; still-damaged; still-damp; still-grimy; still-thick; stinky; stony; stormy; stout; straggly; straight; straightened; strange; straw-blonde / straw-blond; straw-colored; straw-like; straw-tinted; straw-white; straw-yellow; strawberry-blonde / strawberry-blond; strawy; stray; straying; streaked; streaked-blond; streaky; striking; stringy; striped; strong; stubbly; stubborn; stunning; stupid; styled; stylish; sultry; sun-bleached; sun-blonde; sun-choked; sun-filled; sun-raked; sun-streaked; sun-whitened; sunburned; sunkissed; sunlit; sunny; sunshiny; sunsilked; superb; superfluous; surfer-blond; swarthy; sweat-damp; sweat-dampened; sweat-glued; sweat-matted; sweat-slick; sweat-soaked; sweaty; sweeping; sweet-smelling; swept-up; swingy; swirling; swirly-curly.

T - Y

taffy; taffy-blond; taffy-brown; taffy-colored; tall; tamed; tan; tangled; tar-black; tar-colored; tarred; Tarzan-style; tattered; tawny; tea-colored; teak-colored; teased; teased-up; tempestuous; terrible; terrific; textured; thatched; thatchy; thick; thin; thinning; thinnish; thread-like; tidy; tight; tight-coiled; tight-curled; tight-curly; tightly-curled; tinted; tired; tiresome; titanium-blue; titian; toast-brown; toast-colored; too-long; too-thick; topmost; tortoise-shell; tough; toupee-shaped; tousled; tow-colored; tow-yellow; towering; traditional; trailing; trashy-looking; trendy; tressed; tri-colored; trim; trimmed; troublesome; tubular; tufted; tufty; tumbled; tumbling; tumultuous; turquoise; twelve-dollar; twisted; two-colored; two-tone; ugly; unadorned; unattractive; unbarbered; unblanched; unbound; unbraided; unbrushed; unclean; uncoiffed; uncoiled; uncombable; uncombed; unconfined; uncontrollable; uncovered; uncropped; uncut; underarm; undisciplined; undone; undulant; undulating; undyed; uneven; unfashionable; unfixed; unfortunate; ungroomed; unhealthy; unique; unkempt; unloosened; unmanageable; unnatural; unpermed; unpinned; unplaited; unpredictable; unrestrained; unruly; unshaven; unsightly; unstraightened; unstyled; untamable; untamed; untended; untidy; untrained; untreated; untressed; untrimmed; unusual; unwashed; upright; upscale; upstanding; upturned; useless; usual; vanishing; varnished; varying; veiled; velvety; vibrant; Victorian; violet; visible; vital; vivid; voluminous; vomit-speckled; waist-length; waist-long; walnut-colored; wan; wanton; warm; washed; washed-out; water-heavy; watery; waving; wavy; waxed; waxen; waxy; wayward; weak; weary; weedy; weird; weird-looking; well-coiffed; well-groomed; well-oiled; well-trimmed; wet; wheat-blonde / wheat-blond; wheat-colored; wheat-stalk; wheaten; wheaty; white; white-blonde / white-blond; white-gold; white-streaked; whitened; whitish; wide; wiglike; wild; wild-looking; wind-mussed; wind-tangled; wind-tossed; windblown / wind-blown; windswept; windy; wine-red; wiry; wispy; wispy-white; witch-like; witchy; womanly; wonderful; wondrous; woollen / woolen; woolly / wooly; woven; wretched; wrung-out; yellow; yellow-blonde / yellow-blond; yellow-dyed; yellow-gray; yellow-red; yellow-white; yellow-yarn; yellowish; yellowish-white; youthful.

(ADJ) Color: Black

black; black-brown; blackish; boot-black; coal-black; coal-colored; crow-black; dark; dark-as-midnight; darkened; darkish; deep-black; dusky; dyed-black; ebony; glistening-black; ink-black; inky; jet-black; lacquer-black; licorice-black; long-black; midnight-black; midnight-dark; near-black; night-black; obsidian-colored; oil-black; oily-dark; olive; pitch-black; pitch-dark; pitchy; raven; raven-black; raven-dark; rubber-black; sable; sooty; swarthy; tar-black; tar-colored; tarred.

(ADJ) Color: Blonde / Blond

ash-blonde / ash-blond; ashen-blonde; banana-yellow; barbie-doll; beige; bleach-blonde / bleach-blond; bleached; bleached-blonde / bleached-blond; bleached-out; bleached-streaked; blond-and-gray; blond-brown; blond-gray; blond-white; blonde / blond; blondish; blondish-brown; bottle-blonde / bottle-blond; butter-colored; buttered; buttery; camel-colored; canary-colored; caramel-colored; champagne-blond; cider-colored; copper-blond; corn-colored; dark-blonde / dark-blond; dark-straw; darkly-golden; dirty-blonde / dirty-blond; dishwater-blonde / dishwater-blond; dyed-blond; fair; fairish; flaxen; frost-blonde; ghost-blonde; gilded; gilt-edged; gold; gold-blonde; gold-bright; golden; golden-blond; hay-colored; honey-blonde / honey-blond; honey-colored;

honeyed; ice-blonde; lemon-yellow; light; light-blonde; light-colored; light-streaked; lightened; lightish; natural-blonde; Nordic; pale; pale-blonde / pale-blond; peroxide-blonde; peroxided; platinum-blonde; platinum-colored; pretty-yellow; rose-gold; salt-bleached; sand-colored; sandy; sandy-blonde / sandy-blond; sandy-colored; spun-gold; still-blond; straw-blonde / straw-blond; straw-colored; straw-like; straw-tinted; straw-white; straw-yellow; strawberry-blonde / strawberry-blond; strawy; streaked; streaked-blond; streaky; sun-bleached; sun-blonde; sun-streaked; sun-whitened; surfer-blond; taffy-blond; tawny; tow-colored; tow-yellow; wheat-blonde / wheat-blond; wheat-colored; wheat-stalk; wheaten; wheaty; white-blonde / white-blond; white-gold; yellow; yellow-blonde / yellow-blond; yellow-dyed; yellow-white; yellow-yarn; yellowish; yellowish-white.

(ADJ) Color: Blue
blue; blue-black; blue-gray / blue-grey; blue-tinged; blue-tinted; bluish; electric-blue; indigo; midnight-blue; periwinkle-blue; raven-blue; titanium-blue.

(ADJ) Color: Brown
acorn-colored; ash-brown; auburn; auburny; bark-brown; blondish-brown; bread-brown; brindle-colored; bronze-colored; bronzed; bronzish; bronzy; brown; brown-blond; brown-streaked; brownish; brownish-black; brownish-blond; brownish-gray; brownish-red; brunette; brunette-colored; burgundy; burnt-sienna; chestnut; chestnut-brown; chestnut-colored; chestnut-tinted; chocolate-brown; cocoa-brown; coffee-brown; coffee-colored; coffee-dark; coppery-brown; dark-brown; deep-auburn; dirt-brown; dirt-colored; dirty-brownish; doe-brown; dung-colored; dyed-brown; espresso-colored; fawn-colored; golden-brown; hazel; honey-brown; light-brown; mahogany-colored; medium-brown; midnight-brown; mocha-colored; mouse-brown; mouse-colored; mousy; mousy-brown; mud-brown; mud-colored; nut-brown; nut-colored; oak-brown; oak-colored; oaky; pale-brown; russet; russet-colored; rusty-brown; sandy-brown; taffy; taffy-brown; taffy-colored; tan; tea-colored; teak-colored; titian; toast-brown; toast-colored; walnut-colored.

(ADJ) Color: Gray
ash-colored; ash-gray; ashen; ashy; blond-and-gray; blond-gray; blue-gray / blue-grey; brindled; cinder-gray; cinereous; copper-gray; dust-colored; executive-gray; gingery-gray; gray; gray-and-yellow; gray-black; gray-blonde / gray-blond; gray-brown; gray-flecked; gray-streaked; gray-white; graying; graying-blond; graying-yellow; grayish; grayish-brown; grayish-white; grizzled; iron-gray; lead-gray; mature; metallic; misty; moon-colored; moon-silvered; mostly-gray; patchy; pepper-gray; peppered; peppery; pewter-colored; pure-silver; salt-and-pepper; salt-matted; salt-stained; salty; salty-gray; silver; silver-and-white; silver-black; silver-blonde / silver-blond; silver-frosted; silver-gray; silver-platinum; silver-shot; silver-streaked; silver-threaded; silver-tipped; silver-white; silvered; silvering; silvery; silvery-blonde / silvery-blond; silvery-

white; silvery-yellow; slate-colored; smoke-colored; smoky; steel-gray; steel-wool; steely; steely-gray; stony; streaky; yellow-gray.

(ADJ) Color: Purple

beet-colored; blossom-colored; currant-colored; eggplant-colored; lilac; mauve; plum-colored; purple; purple-tinted; purple-tipped; purplish; purplish-black; raspberry-purple; violet.

(ADJ) Color: Red / Orange

amber; amber-colored; amber-streaked; apricot; apricot-colored; auburn-red; autumn-grass; blood-red; brass-colored; brassy; brick-red; bright-red; burgundy; burnt-sienna; carmine; carrot-colored; carrot-orange; carrot-red; carroty; chemical-red; chestnut-red; clairol-red; copper; copper-colored; copper-orange; copper-penny; copper-red; coppery; coppery-red; crimson; dark-fire; dark-red; deep-red; dyed-red; fiery; fiery-red; fire-red; flame-colored; flame-like; flame-red; flaming; fox-colored; fox-red; garnet-colored; ginger; ginger-ale; ginger-colored; gingerish; gingery; gold-red; golden-red; henna-red; marmalade-colored; maroon; mercurochrome-orange; newly-red; orange; orange-brown; orange-colored; orange-dyed; orange-red; peach-colored; penny-bright; penny-colored; poppy-colored; poppy-red; pumpkin-colored; punk-red; red; red-black; red-blonde / red-blond; red-brown; red-dyed; red-frizzed; red-gold; red-golden; red-yellow; reddish; reddish-blonde / reddish-blond; reddish-brown; reddish-dyed; reddish-orange; rosy; ruddy; rust-colored; rust-red; rusty; rusty-looking; rusty-red; scarlet; sherry-colored; wine-red; yellow-red.

(ADJ) Color: White

albino; chalk-white; cotton-white; dandelion-white; dust-white; ghostly; gray-white; milk-weed-pale; milk-white; moon-white; mushroom-colored; near-white; nearly-white; pearl-white; pure-white; rinso-white; silver-white; silvery-white; snow-colored; snow-white; snowy; white; white-streaked; whitened; whitish; wispy-white.

(ADJ) Color: Miscellaneous

colored; colorful; colorless; discolored; dull-colored; dyed; faded; gold-pink; multi-colored; odd-colored; once-blond; once-brown; once-dark; once-red; once-sandy; once-yellow; pink; pink-gold; pink-streaked; pink-striped; pinkish; pinky-red; rainbowy; snow-and-rust; tinted; tri-colored; turquoise; two-colored; two-tone.

Verbs and Phrasal Verbs in Alphabetical Order

A - D

absorbed; accentuated; accosted; accumulated; ached; achieved; acquired; acted; added; adhered; adjusted; adorned; affected; alight; allowed; alternated; ambled;

anchored; appeared; approached; arched; arranged; arranged in; arranged with; ate; attached; baked; baked under; banded; banged; bannered; bannered behind; barbered; battened; beat; became; began; begged; begged for; behaved; belied; belonged; bent; betrayed; billowed; billowed behind; billowed in; blackened; blasted; blazed; bleached; blended; blessed; blew; blinded; blocked; blossomed; blued; blustered; bobbed; bore; bounced; bound; braided; branched; brightened; brimmed; bristled; broke; brought; browned; brushed; bunched; bundled; burned; burnished; burst forth; bushed; buzzed off; caked with; capped; captured; caressed; carried; cascaded; caught; changed; chewed; choked on; chopped; cinched; circled; clapped; clashed; cleaned; cleared; clipped; closed; clotted; clouded; clumped; clung; clutched; coated; coaxed; coiffed; coiled; collected; colored; combed; compared; competed; completed; complimented; concealed; confined; contained; continued; contrasted; contributed; controlled; conveyed; corkscrewed; coupled; covered; cracked; crammed; crashed; crawled; created; crept; crested; crinkled; cropped; crossed; crowned; crushed; crusted; curled; curved; cushioned; cut; danced; dangled; darkened; darted; dashed with; dazzled; declared; decorated; deepened; defied; delivered; denoted; dented; descended; destined; detached; dewed; did up; dipped; disappeared; disarranged; discolored; disheveled; disordered; displayed; distracted; divided; dotted with; dragged; draped; drawn; drenched; dressed; drew back; drew down; drew up; dribbled; dried; drifted; dripped; drooped; dropped; drove; drowned; ducked; dulled; dusted; dyed.

E - Q

edged; electrified; embodied; emerged; emphasized; encased; encircled; encompassed; encroached; ended up; enhanced; entangled; entered; entranced; erased; erupted; escaped; exaggerated; expanded; exploded; exposed; expressed; extended; faced; faded; failed; fanned; fantailed; fascinated; fashioned; fastened; feathered; fell; felt; filled; fingered; finished; fitted; fixed; flagged; flamed; flapped; flared; flashed; flattened; flattered; flayed; flecked; flew; flicked; flickered; flipped; flipped back; flipped over; flitted; floated; flopped; flounced; flowed; fluffed; flung; fluttered; folded; followed; forced; formed; fought with; found; framed; frayed; frazzled; freed; fretted; frizzed; frizzled; froze; furled; fuzzed; garnished; garnished with; gathered; gleamed; gleaned; glided; glimmered; glinted; glistened; glittered; glowed; glued; gooped; grabbed; graced; grasped; grayed; grazed; greased; greeted; grew; gripped; groped; gushed from; gushed out of; gushed over; hacked; haloed; heaped; held; herded; hid; highlighted; hit; hooked; hovered; hugged; hung; hurt; ignited; indicated; inherited from; intertwined; intruded; irritated; itched; jetted; jiggled; jolted; jumbled; jumped; jutted; kept; kissed; knocked; knotted; laced; lacked; lacquered; laid; landed; lapped; lashed; lasted; layered; leaked; leaped; left; levitated; licked; lifted; lightened; lined; lit; looked; loomed; looped; loosened; lopped; lost; made; marcelled; marked; mashed; massed; matched; matted; measured; melted; messed; met; mingled; missed; mixed; mounted; moussed; moved; mowed; mushroomed; mussed; nagged; needed; netted; nuzzled; obscured; occupied; oiled; opened; outlined; outshone; packed; paled; parted;

passed; pasted; peeked; peeled; peppered; perched; perched atop; permeated; permed; peroxided; picked; piled; pinned; placed; plaited; plastered; played at; played with; pleaded with; plucked; plummeted; plunged; pointed; poked; pomaded; pooled; popped; possessed; poured; pressed; pricked; prickled; probed; protected; protruded; proved; provided; puddled; puffed; pulled; punctuated by; punctuated with; pushed; pushed at; queued; quivered.

R - Z

radiated; rained down; raised; raked; rambled; ran; ranged; reached; reappeared; receded; reduced; reeked; reeled in; reflected; refused; reined in; relaxed; released; remained; reminded; removed; required; resembled; resented; resisted; rested; restored; restrained; restyled; retained; retied; retreated; returned; revealed; reveals; rioted; ripped at; ripped from; ripped out; rippled; robbed; roiled; rolled; roped; rose; roughed; rubbed; ruffled; ruined; rumpled; rung; rushed; rustled; sailed; sampled; sank; sat; savaged by; scalded; scattered; scissored; scooped; scorched; scraped; scratched; screamed; screwed; secured; separated; served; serviced; set; settled; shaded; shadowed; shampooed; shaped; shaved; sheared; shellacked; shielded; shifted; shimmered; shivered; shocked; shone; shook; shot; shouted; shoved; showed; shrouded; sifted through; silvered; singed; skewed; skinned back; skirted; skittered across; sleeked; sleeked back; slept on; sliced; slicked; slicked back; slid; slipped; slithered; sluiced; smacked; smelled; smoldered; smoothed; snagged; snaked; snapped; snatched; soaked; softened; sparkled; spidered; spiked; spilled; spiraled; splashed; splayed; spoiled; sported; sprang; sprawled; sprayed; spread; sprinkled; sprouted; sprung; spun; squeezed; stacked; stained; stank; stayed; steeped; stiffened; stirred; stood; stopped; straggled; straightened; strained; strayed; streaked; streamed; stretched; strewn / strewed; stringed; stroked; struck; struggled; struggled with; stuck; stuffed; stunned; styled; sucked; suggested; suited; surrounded; swarmed; swathed; swayed; swept; swiped; swirled; swished; swoops; swung; tailed; tamed; tangled; tapered; tasseled; teased; telegraphed; tended; testified; thickened; thinned; thrashed; threaded; threatened; threw; tickled; tidied; tied; tinged; tingled; tinted; told; took; topped; tore; tossed; tossed back; touched; tousled; toweled; towered; traced; trailed; trapped; traveled; trembled; tried; triggered; trimmed; tucked; tugged; tumbled; turbaned; turned; tussled; twined; twirled; twisted; unbound; uncurled; undid; undulated; unfurled; untied; urged; vanished; varied; veiled; ventured; vibrated; wadded; wafted; warmed; washed; waved; wavered; weaved; weighed; wet; whipped; whirled; whitened; whorled; willed; wilted; wore; wound; wrapped; wreathed; wrenched; wriggled; writhed; yanked; zigzagged.

Noun Phrases

absence of hair; abundance of hair; amount of hair; appearance of hair; arrangement of hair; assortment of hair; band(s) of hair; barbs of hair; beauty of hair; beehive of hair; bit(s) of hair; blaze of hair; block of hair; blur of hair; bolt of hair; border of hair; bow of hair; braid(s) of hair; brush of hair; bunch(es) of hair; bundle(s) of hair; bun of hair; burst of hair; bush(es) of hair; cap of hair; cascade(s) of hair; catch of hair; chunk(s) of hair; circle of hair; cloud(s) of hair; clump(s) of hair; cluster(s) of hair; coil(s) of hair; collection of hair; color of hair; coronet of hair; covering of hair; crest of hair; crop(s) of hair; crown of hair; curl(s) of hair; curtain(s) of hair; cyclone of hair; density of hair; direction of hair; display of hair; drape of hair; dusting of hair; ends of hair; excess of hair; exuberance of hair; fall(s) of hair; fan of hair; feathers of hair; feeling of hair; fineness of hair; fingers of hair; fistful of hair; flag of hair; flail of hair; flame(s) of hair; flares of hair; fleck(s) of hair; flick(s) of hair; flip of hair; flop of hair; flow of hair; fluff of hair; fold(s) of hair; forelock of hair; forest of hair; formation(s) of hair; form(s) of hair; fragment(s) of hair; frame of hair; fringe of hair; frizz of hair; fuzz of hair; garlands of hair; halo of hair; handful(s) of hair; hank(s) of hair; head of hair; heap(s) of hair; hunk of hair; knob of hair; knot(s) of hair; lack of hair; layer(s) of hair; length of hair; lick(s) of hair; line(s) of hair; load(s) of hair; locket(s) of hair; lock(s) of hair; loop(s) of hair; loss of hair; lot of hair; lump(s) of hair; lushness of hair; luxuriance of hair; mane of hair; mass(es) of hair; mat(s) of hair; mesh of hair; mess of hair; mop of hair; mound(s) of hair; mountain(s) of hair; muss of hair; nest of hair; overgrowth of hair; particle of hair; patch(es) of hair; piece(s) of hair; pile(s) of hair; plait(s) of hair; plume of hair; portion(s) of hair; profusion of hair; puff(s) of hair; quality of hair; quantity of hair; rash of hair; ribbons of hair; ringlet(s) of hair; ring of hair; ripples of hair; rivers of hair; rivulets of hair; roots of hair; rope(s) of hair; row(s) of hair; ruff of hair; sample(s) of hair; scalp of hair; scattering of hair; scent of hair; scrap(s) of hair; section(s) of hair; shaft(s) of hair; shank of hair; sheet(s) of hair; shock(s) of hair; shower of hair; sidelocks of hair; silkiness of hair; slick of hair; smear of hair; smell of hair; snakes of hair; spike(s) of hair; spot of hair; spray of hair; stink of hair; storm of hair; straggle of hair; strand(s) of hair; streak(s) of hair; stream(s) of hair; stretch of hair; string(s) of hair; strip of hair; surface of hair; swath(s) of hair; sweep of hair; swirl(s) of hair; tail(s) of hair; tangle(s) of hair; tendril(s) of hair; texture of hair; thatch(es) of hair; thicket(s) of hair; thickness of hair; thread(s) of hair; tiara of hair; tongue of hair; ton(s) of hair; topknot of hair; torrent of hair; tousle of hair; tower of hair; trail of hair; tress(es) of hair; tuft(s) of hair; tumble of hair; tumult of hair; twirl(s) of hair; twist of hair; veil of hair; vestige of hair; vine of hair; wad(s) of hair; waterfall(s) of hair; wave(s) of hair; wealth of hair; web of hair; wedge of hair; weight of hair; whisper of hair; whorl(s) of hair; wig of hair; wing(s) of hair; wires of hair; wisp(s) of hair; wreath(s) of hair.

USAGE EXAMPLES

Her *dark auburn hair fluttered behind* her as the horse rode steadily toward the cottage.

He had *a crop of blond hair* and radiant green eyes.

125

Her *long silky hair trailed across* his face as she leaned over him.

The *curly red hair was tied up* in a neat little bun.

Tyson *caught a lock of her hair and twirled it around* his finger.

20
HAND(S)

Adjectives in Alphabetical Order

A - E

able; abraded; absent; accurate; aching; acknowledging; active; additional; admiring; admonitory; adoring; advancing; affectionate; affirming; afflicted; age-mottled; age-spotted; aged; ageing / aging; ageless; agile; agitated; agonized; all-too-familiar; almighty; amazing; ambidextrous; amputated; ancient; angelic; angry; angular; anointed; anonymous; answering; anxious; apprehensive; apt; armed; armored; arresting; arthritic; arthritis-knotted; articulated; artificial; artistic; ashen; ashy; astonishing; astounded; atrophied; attacking; attentive; attenuate; attractive; authoritative; autocratic; avenging; average; avid; awful; awkward; baby-powdered; back-slanting; bad; baggy-fleshed; balanced; balled; balled-up; bandage-wrapped; bandaged; bar-gripping; barbarous; barbell-calloused; bare; bared; battered; bearlike; beaten; beautiful; beckoning; beefy; beet-red; beige; beige-gloved; bejeweled; beloved; beneficent; benign; bent; beseeching; best; bestial; betraying; better; bewildered; big; big-knuckled; biggest; bilious; bird-like; black; black-fingered; black-gloved; black-mittened; black-nailed; blackened; bleeding; blessed; blistered; blistering; bloated; blocky; blood-caked; blood-drenched; blood-slick; blood-smeared; blood-soaked; blood-stained; bloodied; bloody; blotched; blue; blue-knuckled; blue-veined; bluish; blunt-fingered; blurred; bold; bone-crushing; bone-hard; bone-white; bony; bound; bound-at-the-wrist; bounteous; bountiful; bourbon-colored; bowl-shaped; boyish; braceleted; branch-like; brawny; brazen; bright; brittle; broad; broken; broken-fingered; bronzed; brotherly; brown; brown-spotted; browned; bruised; brutal; brutalizing; brutish; bulky; bumbling; buoyant; burly; burn-scarred; burned / burnt; burning; burrowing; busted; busted-knuckle; busted-up; busy; busying; butch; buzzing; cadaverous; callous; calloused; calm; calming; capable; capable-looking; captive; caramel-colored; carefree; careful; careless; caressing; caring; casual; cautionary; cautioning; cautious; chained; chalk-white; chalky; chapped; charitable; charred; cherubic; chicken-like; child-like; childish; chilled; chilly; chubby; chunky; civil; clammy; clamped; clamping; clapping; clasped; clasping; claw-like; clawed; clawing; clay-encrusted; clean; clenched; clever; clinging; clinical; close; closed; closest; clumsy; clutched; clutching; coarse; coarse-skinned; cold; collective; colored; comforting; commanding; common; communicative; compact; compassionate; competent; complacent; concealed; concerned; conciliatory; confident; conflicted; confounded; conquering; considerable; consoling; cool; cool-fingered; corresponding; corrupt; corrupted; cotton-gloved; countless; courteous; covert; crab-like; cradling; craggy; cramped; crawling; creamy; creased; creasy;

creative; creepy; crimson; crinkled; crippled; crippled-looking; crooked; crossed; cruddy; crude; cruel; crumpled; crushed; crushing; cuffed; cumbersome; cunning; cupped; cupping; curious; curled; curled-up; cursed; cut; dagger-throwing; dainty; damaged; damn(ed); damp; dangerous; dangling; dappled; daring; dark; dark-nailed; dark-stained; darting; deadly-looking; dear; decisive; defensive; defiant; deformed; deft; deftest; deliberate; delicate; delighted; demure; descending; desiccated; despairing; desperate; destructive; detached; determined; developing; devilish; dexterous; different; diligent; diminutive; dimpled; direct; dirt-caked; dirt-encrusted; dirtied; dirty; dirty-fingernailed; dirty-nailed; discreet; disembodied; disfigured; disgusted; disinterested; dismayed; dismembered; dismissing; dismissive; disobedient; dispirited; dissenting; dissolving; distant; distinct; distinguished; distracted; diverse; divine; docile; dominant; doubting; doughy; dramatic; dried; drink-free; dripping-wet; driven; dropped; drunken; dry; dual; dumb; dusty; eager; earth-stained; easy; ebony-skinned; eccentric; educated; eerie-looking; efficient; elaborate; elegant; elevated; eloquent; emaciated; eminent; emotional; emphatic; empowered; emptied; empty; encouraging; encroaching; endless; energetic; enormous; enraged; entire; entwined; equal; equivocating; errant; estranged; evil; exaggerated; exasperated; excellent; excessive; exhausted; expansive; experienced; explicit; exposed; expressive; exquisite; extended; extra; exuberant; eye-shielding.

F - M
facile; faint; fair; fairest; faithful; fake; fallen; false; faltering; familiar; famished; famous; fancy; fast; fat; fatal; fatherly; fatigue-numbed; favorable; fearful; fearless; featureless; feeble; female; feminine; fettered; fevered; feverish; fickle; fidgeting; fidgety; field-toughened; fierce; fiery; filthy; final; fine; fine-boned; fine-looking; finest; fingerless; fingertip-tapping; firm; fish-like; fishy; fisted; fitful; five-fingered; flabby; flaccid; flailing; flat; flattened; flawless; fleeting; flesh-and-blood; fleshless; fleshy; flexible; flexing; flimsy; flippant; floating; floppy; flour-covered; floured; floury; flowing; fluent; fluttering; fluttery; flying; foamy; folded; folding; fond; forbidding; forceful; foreign; forlorn; formal; fossilized; foul; four-fingered; fractured; fragile; frail; frank; frantic; freckled; free; freed; freed-up; freezing; frenzied; fresh; freshly-bleeding; fretful; fretting; friendly; frightened; frightening; frigid; frost-reddened; frostbitten; frozen; full; fumbling; functional; furious; furred; furry; furtive; garden-gloved; gashed; gaunt; generous; gentle; gentlemanly; germy; gesturing; ghastly; ghostly; giant; gifted; gigantic; ginormous; girlish; glad; gleaming; glistening; glittering; gloved; gloveless; glow-in-the-dark; glowing; gnarled; goddamn(ed); godlike; godly; gold-tipped; golden; good; graceful; gracious; grand; grappling; grasping; grateful; gray; gray-black; grease-stained; greasy; great; greedy; green-gloved; grimy; gripping; grisly; groping; grubby; guiding; guilty; gullible; haggard; hairless; hairy; hairy-knuckled; half-hearted; half-opened; half-rotted; halting; ham-fisted; ham-handed; hammy; handcuffed; handsome; hanging; haphazard; happy; hard; hard-callused; hard-knuckled; hardworking; harsh; hasty; haughty; haunted; healed; healing; healthy; heated;

heavenly; heavy; held; held-out; helpful; helpless; henna-decorated; hennaed; hesitant; hidden; high; holy; honest; hooked; hopeful; horny; horrified; hostile; hot; hovering; huge; hulking; humanoid; humongous; hungry; hurried; hurt; hypnotic; ice-bitten; ice-cold; icy; identical; idle; ignorant; imaginary; imagined; immaculate; immediate; immense; impartial; impatient; imperfect; imperial; imperious; impetuous; impious; imploring; incapable; incessant; incompetent; incredible; indifferent; indiscriminate; indomitable; industrious; ineffectual; inept; inert; inexperienced; inexpert; infamous; infected; infectious; inferior; inhuman; injured; ink-smudged; ink-stained; inky; innocent; innumerable; inquisitive; insinuating; insistent; intelligent; interesting; interlaced; interlocked; intertwined; intimidating; invisible; involuntary; iron-strong; isolated; itchy; itty-bitty; ivory-white; jabbing; jerky; jet-black; jewel-studded; jeweled; jittery; joined; joyful; jumpy; just; just-washed; kindly; knife-holding; knob-knuckled; knobby; knobby-knuckled; knot-knuckled; knotted; knotty; knowing; knowledgeable; laborious; lace-covered; lace-cuffed; lace-gloved; lacerated; lacy; ladylike; languid; large; large-knuckled; largest; latex-gloved; latte-colored; lavish; lawless; lawyerly; lazy; lean; learned; leather-clad; leather-covered; leather-gloved; leather-mittened; leathery; lecherous; left; lengthy; lenient; leprous; lethal; lethal-looking; leveled; liberal; life-giving; lifeless; light; lightning-fast; lily-white; limp; limp-wristed; linked; listless; literal; little; little-girl; liver-spotted; locked; lone; lonesome; long; long-boned; long-fingered; long-nailed; looping; loose; loosened; lopped-off; lost; lotion-slick; lousy; lovely; loving; lower; lucky; luminescent; luminous; lumpish; lumpy; lunging; luxurious; mad; magic; magic-fingered; magical; magnetic; maimed; majestic; male; malevolent; malicious; mangled; manicured; manly; mannish; many-fingered; marked; marred; masculine; massive; masterful; masterly; maternal; mature; mean; meaty; mediocre; menacing; merciful; merciless; mere; mesmeric; messed-up; metallic; meticulous; middle-aged; mighty; milk-white; milky; miniature; minute; mischievous; miserable; mismatched; misshapen; missing; mitted; mitten-covered; mittened; mobile; moist; mollifying; molten; mosquito-bitten; motionless; mottled; moving; mud-encrusted; muddied; muddy; muffiny; multi-digited; multi-fingered; multiple; mummified; murderous; muscular; mute; mutilated; mysterious.

N - S

nail-bitten; nailed; nailless; naked; narrow; narrow-boned; nasty; native; near; near-invisible; nearest; neat; necessary; nefarious; negative; negligent; nerve-sweaty; nerveless; nervous; new; nice; nicked; nicked-up; nicotine-stained; nimble; no-nonsense; noble; noisy; non-gloved; nonchalant; nondominant; none-too-gentle; normal; normal-nailed; not-very-clean; note-taking; nourished; now-healed; now-naked; now-rigid; numb; numbed; numerous; nut-colored; obedient; obsessive; obvious; odd; offended; offending; offered; official; oil-smeared; oil-stained; oiled; oily; old; old-woman; olive; olive-skinned; only; oozing; open; opened; opposite; oppressive; orange; orange-brown; ordinary; original; other; otherworldly; out-stretched; outer; outflung; outlined; outreached; outspread; outstretched; overlapping; oversize(d); pacifying;

padded; painful; paint-covered; paint-stained; painted; pale; pale-pink; pallid; palm-down; palsied; panicked; papery; papery-skinned; paralyzed; parched; parchment-like; partial; passing; passionate; passive; paternal; paternalistic; patient; paw-like; pawed; peculiar; penitent; penless; pensive; peremptory; perfect; perfumed; persistent; perspiring; perverse; petite; petting; phenomenal; phony; pierced; pinched; pink; pink-faced; pink-nailed; pink-tipped; pitiless; placating; plain; plastic-covered; plastic-gloved; playful; pleading; pleasant; plump; pocketed; pocking; podgy; pointing; poised; poor; possessed; possessive; powdery; powerful; powerful-looking; practiced; pragmatic; precarious; precious; precise; preferred; pretty; princely; probing; professional; proffered; proprietary; prosthetic; protecting; protective; prying; pudgy; puffy; pungent; puny; puppet-like; pure; purple; purple-gloved; purple-nailed; purple-stained; purposeful; pushing; putty-colored; puzzled; quailing; questioning; quick; quiet; quieting; quivering; quivery; radiant; rag-swathed; raised; random; randy; rapacious; rapid; raw; rawboned; reaching; ready; reassuring; rebellious; receiving; red; red-knuckled; red-nailed; red-smeared; red-tipped; reddened; reed-like; reflected; regal; regular; rejected; released; relentless; reliable; reluctant; remaining; remarkable; remorseless; restless; restrained; restraining; reverential; rhythmic; ridiculous; right; rigid; ring-sparkling; ringed; ringless; robotic; rosy; rotten; rotting; rough; rough-skinned; roughened; roving; royal; rubber-coated; rubber-gloved; rubbery; ruddy; rude; rugged; ruined; runty; rushing; ruthless; sacred; sacrilegious; safe; sallow; saluting; sandy; sane; sarcastic; satiny; sausage-fingered; savage; scabby; scalded; scaled; scaly; scanty; scared; scarred; scorched; scoured; scraped; scraped-raw; scratched; scrawny; scrubbed; scrunched-up; sealed; searching; secret; self-conscious; self-deprecatory; self-indulgent; semi-clean; sensational; sensitive; sensuous; serene; severe; severed; sexy; shadowed; shaggy; shaken; shaky; shapely; sharp; sharp-edged; sharp-nailed; shattered; shielding; shifting; shimmering; shiny; shivering; shivery; short-fingered; shriveled; shriveled-up; shrunken; shy; significant; silent; silt-stained; simian; simple; simultaneous; sinewy; sinful; singed; single; singular; sinister; six-fingered; sizable; skeletal; skeptical; skilled; skillful; skinned; skinny; slack; slanted; slapping; sleepy; sleeve-hidden; slender; slick; slight; slim; slim-fingered; slimy; slippery; slobbery; sloping; slow; sludge-slicked; small; small-boned; small-fingered; smart; smashed; smeared; smooth; snaky; snow-white; snowy; soaked; soap-covered; soap-slicked; soapy; soft; soiled; sole; solid; solid-feeling; solitary; soothing; sooty; sore; sorry; spare; special; speckled; spider-like; spidery; spindly; splayed; splinted; splotched; spotted; spotty; sprawling; spreading; square-fingered; squat; stable; stained; standard; startled; steady; steadying; steaming; steel-gloved; sterile; stern; sticky; stiff; stiffened; stifling; still; still-curled; still-gloved; still-shaking; still-shaky; still-sticky; still-wet; stinging; stinking; stitched; stony; stout; straight; strange; strangling; stray; streaked; street-worn; strict; striped; strong; strong-looking; struggling; stubborn; stubby; stunned; stunted; stupid; sturdy; stylish; stylized; submerged; substantial; subtle; sudden; suede-gloved; sun-bleached; sun-browned; sun-kissed; sun-stained; sunburned; suntanned; superb; supple;

suppliant; supporting; sure; surgical; swaddled; swaying; sweat-wet; sweating; sweaty; sweeping; sweet; sweet-scented; swift; swollen; sympathetic; synthetic.

T - Y

tainted; take-charge; talented; talon-like; talon-nailed; taloned; tan; tan-brown; tangled; tanned; taped; taped-up; tattooed; taunting; taut; tear-stained; teasing; teenaged; teensy; tender; tense; tentative; terrible; thawing; thick; thick-fingered; thick-gloved; thick-knuckled; thick-skinned; thin; thin-boned; thin-gloved; thoughtful; threatening; three-fingered; thrilling; throbbing; thrusting; thumbless; tied; tight-gloved; tightening; timid; tingling; tiny; tired; tireless; tobacco-stained; tomato-stained; too-heavy; too-long; too-small; too-thick; touching; tough; towel-dried; trailing; trained; traitorous; trapped; trembling; tremendous; tremulous; triumphant; trusting; twisted; twitching; ugly; unbandaged; unbeatable; unbound; uncallused; uncertain; unchained; unchanging; unclasped; unclean; unclenched; unconcerned; unconscious; uncovered; undeniable; undifferentiated; undiscovered; unencumbered; unenthusiastic; unerring; unfamiliar; unfeeling; unflinching; unfortunate; unfriendly; ungenerous; ungloved; unhurt; unidentified; uniformed; unimaginable; uninjured; unkind; unknown; unloving; unoccupied; unpracticed; unprepared; unprotected; unready; unresisting; unresponding; unresponsive; unscrupulous; unseen; unskillful; unskilled; unsteady; unstoppable; unsubtle; unsure; unsuspecting; untied; untrained; unusual; unwanted; unwashed; unwelcome; unwilling; unworthy; uplifted; upper; upraised; upstretched; upturned; useful; useless; utilitarian; vacant; valiant; vanishing; vaporous; varicose; various; vast; veiled; veined; veiny; velvety; vengeful; venomous; vertical; victorious; vigorous; violent; virgin; visible; vital; vulgar; waferish; waiting; wandering; warm; warm-blooded; warty; wary; washed; water-sodden; water-swollen; waving; waxen; waxy; wayward; weak; weaker; weaponless; weary; weather-hardened; weather-roughened; weathered; webbed; wee; weightless; weird; welcoming; well-deserved; well-kept; well-known; well-manicured; well-meaning; well-shaped; well-tended; well-used; well-washed; wet; wet-with-blood; whipped; white; white-gloved; white-knuckled; white-powdered; white-sheathed; whole; wicked; wide; wide-palmed; widespread; wifely; wild; willful; willing; wilted; wind-chapped; windburned; winning; winter-kissed; wiry; wise; wispy; witchy; withered; wizened; wobbly; womanish-looking; womanly; wonder-working; wonderful; wool-gloved; woolen; work-calloused; work-hardened; work-reddened; work-roughened; work-scarred; work-weary; work-worn; working; workman-like; worn; worried; worthy; wounded; wrapped; wriggling; wrinkled; wrinkly; wrong; yellow; yellow-gloved; yellowed; young; youthful; youthful-looking.

Verbs and Phrasal Verbs in Alphabetical Order

A - C

abandoned; absorbed; accentuated; accepted; accompanied by; accustomed to; ached; ached from; ached like; ached when; acted; acted as; activated; added; added to; adjusted; administered; adorned with; advanced; affected; affixed; affixed on; afforded; aged; aggravated; aggravated by; aided; aimed; aimed at; aimed downward; aimed for; alerted; alighted; alighted on; aligned; aligned over; aligned with; allowed; allowed for; amazed; amazed at; anchored; appealed; appealed to; appeared; appeared at; appeared between; appeared from; appeared in; appeared on; appeared out; appeared outside; appeared over; appeared through; applauded; applied; apprised; apprised of; approached; arced; arced backward; arched; armed; arose; arose from; arranged; arranged across; arrived; arrowed; arrowed past; asked; asked for; assembled; assisted; associated with; atrophied; attached; attached to; attacked; attempted; awaited; awakened; awakened to; axed; backed away; backed off; balanced; balled; balled in; balled into; balled under; balled up; bandaged; banged; banged against; banged into; banged on; banged up; bashed; bathed; bathed in; batted; battered ?; beat; beat against; beat at; beat on; became; beckoned; began to; belied; belonged to; bent; bent down; bent up; bestowed; bestowed upon; betrayed; bit into; blackened; blasted; blasted into; blasted up; blazed; blazed over; blazed with; bled; bled from; blistered; blistered up; blocked; blocked out; bloodied; blossomed; blossomed into; blotted out; blurred; blurred out; blurred with; bobbed; bolstered; bore; bore down; bore out; bounced; bounced off; bound; bound around; bound at; bound behind; bound by; bound for; bound in; bound to; bound together; bound up; bound with; braced; braced above; braced against; braced on; branched out; brandished; braved; brimmed with; bristled; bristled with; broke; broke into; broke out; broke through; brought down; brought out; brought to; brought together; brought up; bruised; brushed; brushed across; brushed against; brushed at; brushed back; brushed over; brushed up; bubbled upward; buffed; buffeted; built; bulged; bulged out; bumped; bumped against; bumped into; bunched; bunched inside; bunched into; bunched up; bundled into; bundled up; buried; buried beneath; buried in; buried under; burned / burnt; burned from; burned in; burned on; burned through; burned with; burnished; burrowed; burrowed around; burrowed into; burrowed through; burst through; burst up; busied; busted; busted up; caked with; called for; calloused; calmed; came about; came apart; came around; came away; came back; came down; came forth; came forward; came from; came in; came into; came near; came out; came over; came through; came to; came together; came toward; came up; came upon; capped; capped over; captured; caressed; carried; carved; carved up; cast; caught; caught at; caught for; caught in; caught on; caught within; caused; caused by; ceased; censored; chaffed; chalked; challenged; changed; changed to; chapped; charred; charted; chased; checked; checked for; choked; chopped; chopped at; chopped off; chose; chucked; churned; circled; circled around; claimed; clambered; clamored; clamped; clamped across; clamped around; clamped between; clamped down; clamped hard; clamped in; clamped on; clamped onto; clamped over; clamped to; clamped together; clamped under; clapped; clapped against; clapped in; clapped over; clapped to; clasped; clasped about; clasped above; clasped across; clasped against; clasped around; clasped at; clasped behind; clasped beneath; clasped between; clasped for; clasped in; clasped into; clasped on; clasped over; clasped to; clasped together; clasped under; clasped underneath; clasped upon; clattered; clawed; clawed across; clawed around; clawed at; clawed back; clawed for; clawed in; clawed into; clawed up; cleaned; cleaned out; cleared; cleared up; clenched; clenched about; clenched against; clenched around; clenched behind; clenched beneath; clenched in; clenched into; clenched on; clenched over; clenched to; clenched together; clenched with; climbed; climbed up; clinched; clipped; closed; closed about; closed against; closed around; closed in; closed into; closed on; closed over; closed up; clothed by; clung to; clutched; clutched about; clutched around; clutched at; clutched in; clutched over; clutched through; clutched to; coached; coasted; coasted along; coated; coated over; coated with; cocked; cocked back; coerced; coiled; coiled around; coiled in; coiled into; collapsed; collapsed to; collected; collided; collided with; colored; combated; combed; comforted; committed; compared to; compared with; completed; complied; complied with; concealed; concealed behind; conducted; confirmed; confronted; confronted by; connected; connected to; connected with; consisted of; constrained; consumed; contained; continued; contracted; contracted on; contrasted with; controlled; converged; converged on; conveyed; convulsed; convulsed on; convulsed when; cooled; cooled off; cooled on; cooperated; coped; coped with; corrected; counted; covered; covered by; covered in; covered up; covered with; cracked; cracked against; crackled; crackled with; cradled; cradled against; cradled in; crammed; cramped; cramped from; cramped with; cranked; crashed; crashed against; crashed into; crawled; crawled across; crawled past; crawled to; crawled underneath; crawled up; created; crept; crept back; crept down; crept forward; crept into; crept out; crept to; crept toward; crept up; cried out for; crisscrossed; crossed; crossed above; crossed behind; crossed below; crossed in; crossed on; crossed over; crossed under; crowded; crowded around; cruised; cruised through; crumpled; crumpled with; crushed; crusted with; cuffed; cuffed behind; cuffed by; cuffed in; cuffed to; cuffed together; cupped; cupped above; cupped against; cupped around; cupped at; cupped behind; cupped beneath; cupped in; cupped on; cupped over; cupped to; cupped together; cupped under; cured by; curled; curled about; curled against; curled around; curled at; curled back; curled in; curled inside; curled into; curled on; curled over; curled to; curled under; curled up; curved; curved around; curved backward; curved beneath; curved into; curved on; curved over; curved up; cushioned; cut; cut across; cut away; cut from; cut into; cut off; cut out; cut through.

D - G

dampened; dampened with; danced; danced around; danced between; danced in; danced on; danced over; dangled; dangled above; dangled across; dangled before; dangled between; dangled from; dangled over; dared to; darted; darted about; darted across; darted behind; darted for; darted forward; darted in; darted into; darted out; darted over; darted past; darted to; darted toward; darted under; darted up; darts into; darts out; darts to; dealt out; dealt with; decided; decorated;

decorated with; deepened; deepened into; defaced; deflated; delivered; delved down; delved in; delved into; demanded; dematerialized; denied; depended on; deposited; depressed on; descended; descended from; descended on; descended onto; descended to; descended toward; desired; detained; developed; dialed; differed from; dipped; dipped below; dipped in; dipped inside; dipped into; dipped toward; dipped under; directed; dirtied; dirtied in; dirtied with; disappeared; disappeared behind; disappeared inside; disappeared into; disappeared under; disappeared within; discarded; discharged; discovered; dismissed; disobeyed; displayed; dissolved; dissolved into; distracted by; dove; dove for; dove into; downed; dragged; dragged in; dragged over; draped; draped across; draped in; draped on; draped over; dressed; drew; drew around; drew aside; drew away; drew back; drew down; drew in; drew into; drew on; drew out; drew to; drew together; drew up; dried; drifted; drifted across; drifted away; drifted down; drifted onto; drifted out; drifted over; drifted to; drifted upward; dripped; dripped with; drooped; drooped against; dropped; dropped away; dropped back; dropped below; dropped down; dropped from; dropped in; dropped into; dropped on; dropped onto; dropped to; drove; drove up; drummed; drummed on; dug; dug at; dug in; dug into; dug out; dwarfed; dwindled; dwindled into; dyed with; eased; eased down; eased past; eased up; echoed; embraced; emerged; emerged from; emerged with; employed; employed at; employed by; employed in; employed on; emptied; encased; encased in; encircled; enclosed; enclosed in; encompassed; encountered; encumbered; encumbered with; ended at; ended in; ended up; enfolded; engaged; engaged in; engulfed; enhanced; enjoyed; ensnared; entered; entered into; entwined; entwined in; entwined with; enveloped; erased; erupted; erupted from; escaped; etched; etched in; examined; exchanged; exerted; expanded; experienced; exploded; exploded against; exploded out; explored; explored beneath; explored down; explored inside; explored under; exposed; extended; extended against; extended forward; extended from; extended on; extended over; extended past; extended to; extended toward; extinguished; extracted; extruded; faced; faced down; faced up; faded; faded from; faded to; failed; failed to; faltered; fanned; fascinated by; fastened; fastened behind; fastened on; fastened over; fastened to; feathered; featured; fed; fell; fell apart; fell away; fell back; fell by; fell down; fell from; fell into; fell on; fell to; fell together; fell upon; felt; felt along; felt for; felt in; fiddled; fiddled with; fidgeted; fidgeted over; fidgeted with; filled; filled with; fingered; finished; fired; fisted; fit; fit for; fit into; fitted; fixed; fixed on; fixed to; flailed; flailed around; flailed in; flailed out; flaked; flamed; flanked; flapped; flapped around; flapped out; flared; flared at; flashed; flashed downward; flashed forward; flashed from; flashed in; flashed out; flashed to; flashed toward; flashed up; flattened; flattened against; flaunted; flecked with; flew; flew across; flew apart; flew forward; flew from; flew in; flew into; flew out; flew over; flew through; flew to; flew toward; flew up; flexed; flexed on; flexed with; flicked; flicked from; flickered; flickered on; flickered over; flickered toward; flinched; flipped; flirted; flirted on; flirted with; flitted; flitted across; flitted back; floated; floated across; floated back; floated down; floated in; floated into; floated up; flocked; flocked above; flocked below; flopped;

flopped out; floundered; floundered on; flourished; flowed; flowed across; flowed into; flowed over; flowed past; flowered; flung; flung across; flung into; flung out; flung up; flushed; flushed with; fluttered; fluttered about; fluttered across; fluttered around; fluttered over; fluttered to; fluttered toward; fluttered up; focused on; folded; folded above; folded across; folded around; folded at; folded behind; folded between; folded in; folded into; folded on; folded over; folded to; folded together; folded under; followed; fondled; forced; forged; forgot; forked; formed; fought; fought back; fought for; fought off; fought under; fought with; found; framed; freed; freed from; fretted; fretted with; frisked; froze; froze above; froze in; froze on; froze over; froze with; fumbled; fumbled about; fumbled along; fumbled around; fumbled for; fumbled in; fumbled on; fumbled over; fumbled with; fussed; fussed on; fussed with; gained; gathered; gathered up; gave; gave away; gave out; gentrified; gesticulated; gestured; gestured toward; glanced; glanced across; glanced up; gleamed; glided; glided across; glided against; glided along; glided down; glided into; glided over; glided past; glided to; glided towards; glided under; glided up; glimmered; glimmered in; glinted; glinted in; glistened; glistened in; gloved; glowed; glowed in; glued; glued to; gouged; gouged at; grabbed; grabbed at; grabbed for; granted; grappled; grappled with; grasped; grasped at; grasped between; grasped by; grasped in; grasped onto; grated; gravitated to; gravitated toward; grazed; grazed across; grazed against; grew; grew still; grew tired; grew weak; gripped; gripped around; gripped at; gripped between; gripped by; gripped in; gripped together; groped; groped at; groped between; groped for; groped forward; groped into; groped under; ground; grounded; grouped; grouped together; guessed; guided; guided by; guided to.

H - P

halfraised; halted; hammered; handcuffed; handcuffed behind; handcuffed together; handed; handled; happened to; hauled; hauled back; hauled on; headed; headed away; headed for; headed toward; healed; hefted; held; held above; held across; held against; held aloft; held at; held away; held back; held backward; held before; held behind; held beneath; held by; held in; held on; held onto; held out; held over; held to; held together; held under; held up; helped; helped out; hesitated; hesitated above; hesitated over; hid; hid behind; hid beneath; hid by; hid in; hid under; highlighted; hindered; hit; hitched; hoisted; hooked; hooked in; hooked into; hooked out; hooked over; hooped; hooped around; hoped; hovered; hovered above; hovered around; hovered near; hovered on; hovered over; hugged; hugged around; hung; hung between; hung down; hung from; hung in; hung out; hungered; hungered for; hurled; hurt; hurt from; idled; imbued with; immersed in; imprisoned; inched; inched across; inched along; inched between; inched closer; inched down; inched from; inched inside; inched out; inched toward; inched up; increased; indicated; induced; ingrained with; injured; injured from; inserted; inspected; interlaced; interlaced across; interlaced behind; interlocked; interposed; interpreted; intertwined; intertwined behind; intertwined in; introduced; intruded; intruded into; ironed; issued; issued from; issued out; itched; itched for; itched to; itched with; jabbed; jabbed for;

jabbed past; jammed; jammed down; jammed in; jammed into; jammed together; jammed under; jerked; jerked across; jerked away; jerked back; jerked down; jerked out; jerked to; jerked up; jerked with; jiggled; jittered; joined; joined at; joined behind; joined in; joined on; joined over; joined together; jolted; juggled; jumped; jumped back; jumped through; jumped to; jumped up; jutted; jutted out; jutted up; kept on; kept up; killed; kissed by; kneaded; knew; knitted; knitted together; knocked; knocked against; knotted; knotted at; knotted behind; knotted in; knotted into; knotted over; knotted together; knotted up; knotted with; knuckled; labored; laced; laced across; laced around; laced behind; laced over; laced together; laced with; lacked; laden with; laid; laid across; laid along; laid atop; laid in; laid on; laid out; laid to; laid upon; landed; landed flush; landed hard; landed in; landed on; lapped; lapped past; lapsed; lapsed back; lashed; lashed out; latched; latched onto; latched to; lay; lay across; lay against; lay along; lay at; lay atop; lay in; lay next to; lay on; lay still; lay upon; layered with; leaned; leaned against; leaned back; leaned down; leaned on; leaned over; leaned upon; leaped / leapt; leaped forward; leaped out; leaped to; leaped up; leapfrogged; leapfrogged over; learned; led; led with; left; let; leveled out; levitated; lifted; lifted away; lifted from; lifted heavenward; lifted into; lifted off; lifted to; lifted toward; lifted up; liked; limped; lined; lined out; lined up; lingered; lingered against; lingered at; lingered for; lingered in; lingered on; lingered over; lingered upon; linked; linked around; linked behind; linked in; linked on; linked over; loaded; loaded with; lobbed; locked; locked about; locked against; locked around; locked behind; locked in; locked inside; locked on; locked onto; locked over; locked together; lolled; looked; loomed; looped; looped through; loosened; loosened around; loosened on; lopped off; lost; lost in; loved; lowered; lowered to; lunged; lunged at; lunged down; lunged out; lurched; lurched forward; made for; maintained; managed; managed with; manipulated; mapped; marked; marred by; married to; mashed; masked; massaged; masturbated; matched; materialized; materialized out; measured; merged; merged with; messed with; met; met with; milked; mimed; minded; missed; mocked; molded; molded to; motioned; moved; moved about; moved across; moved along; moved around; moved away; moved back; moved by; moved closer; moved down; moved for; moved forward; moved from; moved in; moved inside; moved into; moved off; moved on; moved over; moved through; moved to; moved toward; moved up; moved with; mucked with; muffled; mushroomed; nailed; nailed to; navigated; neared; needed; nicked; nudged; numbed; nursed; obeyed; occasioned; occupied; occupied in; occupied with; offended; offered; oiled; oozed; opened; opened at; opened in; opened on; opened to; opened toward; opened wide; operated; outlined; outshone; overlapped; paid; paid by; painted; painted on; painted with; palmed; pantomimed; parked; parked at; parked on; parried; parted; passed; passed by; passed into; passed over; passed through; patted; patted around; paused; paused between; paused in; paused on; pawed; pawed at; peeked out; peeled away; penetrated; peppered with; perched; perched on; performed; perfumed with; persuaded; picked; picked at; picked through; picked up; pierced; piled; piled up; pillowed; pillowed behind; pinched; pinched between; pinioned; pinned;

pinned to; pinned up; pitched; placed; placed at; placed behind; placed in; placed on; placed over; placed together; placed under; placed upon; plagued; planted; planted in; planted on; planted squarely on; plastered; plastered across; played; played across; played around; played on; played out; played with; pleaded; plucked; plucked at; plucked away; plunged; plunged down; plunged in; plunged into; plunged under; pocketed; pointed; pointed at; pointed down; pointed in; pointed out; pointed skyward; pointed straight; pointed to; pointed toward; pointed up; poised; poised above; poised across; poised against; poised for; poised in; poised on; poised over; poised to; poked; poked forward; poked into; poked out; poked through; polished; popped out; popped up; posed; positioned; positioned above; positioned at; positioned over; possessed; pounced; pounced on; pounded; pounded on; poured; powdered; powdered with; practiced; prayed; preferred; prepared; prepared for; presented; pressed; pressed against; pressed between; pressed down; pressed flush; pressed in; pressed into; pressed onto; pressed together; pressed under; pressed up; pressed up against; pressed upon; pressured; prevented; prickled; prickled with; pried; pried open; probed; probed further; probed in; probed within; proceeded; produced; proffered; promised; propelled; propped against; propped behind; propped on; propped up; protected; protected by; protected with; protested; protruded; protruded from; proved; provided; prowled; pulled; pulled apart; pulled at; pulled away; pulled back; pulled down; pulled from; pulled on; pulled open; pulled out; pulled up; pumped; pumped up; punched; punched out; punched through; purified; pushed; pushed against; pushed aside; pushed at; pushed back; pushed between; pushed down; pushed forward; pushed from; pushed into; pushed on; pushed through; pushed up; put; put around; put out; put together; put up.

Q - S

quaked; quaked with; quieted; quieted down; quit; quivered; quivered in; quivered on; quivered with; raced; raced across; raced along; raced over; raced through; radiated; raged; rained down on; raised; raised above; raised against; raised in; raised into; raised over; raised to; raised toward; raised up; raised with; raked; raked against; raked through; rallied; rammed; rammed into; ran; ran along; ran down; ran over; ran through; ran to; ran toward; ran up; rang; rapped; rapped at; rapped on; reabsorbed; reabsorbed into; reached; reached across; reached around; reached back; reached beneath; reached between; reached down; reached for; reached from; reached in; reached into; reached out; reached past; reached through; reached to; reached toward; reached under; reached underneath; reached up; realized; reappeared; reassured; receded; received; reclasped; recoiled; recoiled from; recovered; reddened; reduced to; reeked; reeked of; reentered; refilled; reflected; reflected in; refused; refused to; regained; regarded; relaxed; relaxed at; relaxed on; released; remained; remained around; remained at; remained in; remained on; remained still; remained up; remembered; removed; removed from; rended / rent; repaired; replaced; reposed on; represented; required; required for; rescued; resembled; resented; resisted; rested; rested against; rested beside; rested between; rested for; rested in; rested near; rested on; rested over; rested together; rested upon; restored; restrained;

resumed; retied; retracted; retreated; retreated in; retreated to; retrieved; returned; returned to; revealed; rifled; rifled through; rinsed; ripped; ripped apart; ripped from; ripped open; ripped out; ripped up; rippled; rippled through; rippled with; roamed; roamed downward; roamed inside; roamed over; rocketed; rocketed into; rocketed out; rolled; rolled away; rose; rose above; rose from; rose to; rose up; rotated; rotted off; roughened up; rounded; rounded out; roved; roved over; roved under; rubbed; rubbed across; rubbed against; rubbed at; rubbed away; rubbed together; ruffled; rummaged; rummaged around; rummaged in; rummaged through; rushed; rushed for; rushed over; rushed to; rushed up; rustled; rustled in; sagged; sagged onto; sanded; sandpapered; sank; sank into; sat; sat in; sat on; saved; saw to; scampered; scampered over; scanned; scarred; scarred by; scarred from; scarred with; scattered; scooped; scooped beneath; scooped up; scorched; scorched up; scoured; scrabbled; scrabbled at; scrabbled for; scrambled; scrambled around; scrambled for; scrambled through; scraped; scraped against; scraped along; scraped over; scratched; scratched at; scratched on; screamed for; screwed; screwed into; scribbled; scrubbed; scrunched; scrunched in; sculpted; scuttled; scuttled on; searched; searched for; searched in; searched out; searched through; secured; seized; seized on; seized upon; selected; sensed; sent; separated; separated from; served; served up; set; set at; set down; set in; set off; set out; set up; settled; settled at; settled into; settled on; settled onto; settled over; severed; severed at; shackled; shaded; shaped; shaped into; shaped like; shared; sharpened; shattered; sheathed; sheathed in; shepherded; shielded; shifted; shifted on; shifted to; shivered; shone; shone like; shooed; shook; shook from; shook in; shook when; shook with; shot back; shot forward; shot from; shot into; shot off; shot out; shot over; shot straight; shot through; shot to; shot toward; shot up; shoved; shoved against; shoved aside; shoved down; shoved into; shoveled; shoveled in; showed; showered; shrank away; shrank back; shredded; shriveled; shrugged off; shuffled; shut; sifted; sifted through; signaled; signed; signified; silhouetted; silhouetted against; singed; situated on; sized up; sizzled; skated across; skated down; skated over; sketched; skidded; skidded on; skimmed; skimmed over; skipped; skipped along; skittered; skittered across; skittered on; slammed; slammed against; slammed down; slammed down on; slammed forward; slammed into; slammed on; slapped; slapped against; slapped away; slapped down; slapped on; slapped together; slapped up; slashed; slashed across; slashed toward; sliced; sliced through; slid; slid across; slid along; slid around; slid back; slid beneath; slid between; slid down; slid from; slid inside; slid into; slid off; slid on; slid out; slid over; slid to; slid toward; slid under; slid up; slipped; slipped against; slipped along; slipped around; slipped away; slipped back; slipped below; slipped beneath; slipped between; slipped down; slipped from; slipped inside; slipped into; slipped off; slipped on; slipped onto; slipped out; slipped through; slipped to; slithered; slithered behind; slithered into; slithered out; slopped on; slopped through; sloshed; slowed; slowed over; slumped; smacked; smacked across; smacked against; smacked on; smacked together; smarted; smarted under; smashed; smashed against; smashed into; smashed on; smashed over; smashed through; smeared; smeared with; smelled;

smelled like; smelled of; smoothed; smoothed across; smoothed down; smoothed out; smoothed over; smothered; smothered in; smudged; snaked; snaked around; snaked between; snaked down; snaked into; snaked out; snaked through; snapped; snapped behind; snapped down; snapped forward; snapped off; snapped out; snapped to; snapped up; snatched; snatched at; sneaked; sneaked / snuck; sneaked back; sneaked beneath; sneaked up; soaked; soaked on; soaped; soiled; soothed; sorted; sorted through; sought; sought out; sounded; spanned; sparked; sparked with; spasmed; sped; sped across; spelled out; spilled; splashed; splashed into; splashed through; splayed; splayed above; splayed across; splayed behind; splayed on; splayed out; splayed over; spoke of; sponged; sported; sprang; sprang to; sprang up; sprayed; spread; spread across; spread at; spread on; spread out; spread over; spun; spun backward; squared; squared on; squeezed; squeezed by; squeezed down; squinted; squinted up; squirmed; squirmed beneath; stabbed; stabbed at; stabbed out; stained; stained with; stalked; stamped; stamped down; started; started for; started to; startled; stayed; stayed between; stayed inside; stayed on; steadied; steadied at; steadied by; steadied on; steepled; steepled in; steepled on; steepled together; steepled under; steered; steered toward; stiffened; stifled; stilled; stilled in; stilled on; stirred; stirred with; stitched; stitched together; stole; stole into; stole lower; stole out; stole over; stole toward; stomped; stood; stood out; stood upright; stopped; stopped above; stopped at; stopped in; stopped on; stored; stored up; stormed; straddled; straightened; strained; strained against; strained at; strained forward; strained out of; strangled; strapped; strapped behind; strapped to; strayed; strayed downward; strayed for; strayed from; strayed near; strayed to; strayed toward; strayed under; strayed up; streaked; streaked down; strengthened; strengthened by; stretched; stretched above; stretched behind; stretched forth; stretched forward; stretched into; stretched out; stretched outward; stretched over; stretched through; stretched to; stretched toward; stretched up; stripped; strived; stroked; stroked at; stroked back; stroked upward; struck; struck down; struck off; struck out; struggled; struggled against; struggled in; struggled out of; struggled with; stuck; stuck in; stuck inside; stuck into; stuck onto; stuck out; stuck to; studied; stuffed; stuffed between; stuffed in; stuffed into; stuffed under; stumbled; stumbled on; stung; stung by; stung from; stung with; stunk; stunk of; stuttered; submerged; submerged in; subsided; succeeded; succeeded in; suffered; suffused with; suggested; suited; summoned; supported; supported by; supported on; surged; surged forward; surged from; surged toward; surprised; surrendered; surrounded; surrounded by; suspended; suspended by; suspended in; suspended over; swaddled; swaddled in; swallowed; swallowed by; swallowed up; swam; swam toward; swathed; swathed in; swayed; sweat; sweat through; swelled; swelled up; sweltered; sweltered with; swept; swept across; swept around; swept aside; swept away; swept down; swept forward; swept in; swept over; swept past; swept through; swept up; swiped; swirled; switched; switched off; switched on; swiveled; swiveled on; swooped; swooped across; swooped down; swooped into; swooped out; swooped toward; swung; swung around; swung at; swung back; swung forward; swung in; swung up; swung upward; symbolized.

T - Z

tailed; tailed on; tailored; tangled; tangled in; tangled with; tanned; taped; taped behind; taped in; taped to; taped together; tapered; tapped; tapped against; tapped on; tapped out; tarred; tarred up; teased; teased at; tended to; tensed; tensed around; tensed on; thrashed; threatened; threw; threw across; threw around; threw open; threw out; threw over; throbbed; throbbed in; throbbed with; thrust; thrust behind; thrust between; thrust down; thrust forward; thrust in; thrust inside; thrust into; thrust out; thrust through; thrust toward; thrust up; thumbed; thumped onto; thumped over; tickled; tickled over; tidied; tied; tied above; tied around; tied at; tied back; tied behind; tied by; tied in; tied overhead; tied to; tied together; tied up; tied with; tightened; tightened about; tightened around; tightened further; tightened in; tightened into; tightened on; tightened over; tightened with; tilted; tilted toward; tingled; tingled with; tinted; tipped with; tired; took; took off; took on; took over; took up; tooled; toppled; toppled sideways; tore; tore at; tore away; tore from; tore off; tore open; tore through; tossed; touched; toured; tousled; towed; toyed with; traced; traced over; trailed; trailed down; trailed downward; trailed into; trailed onto; trailed out; trailed over; trailed to; trained; transferred; transformed; transformed into; transmitted; trapped; trapped in; trapped under; traveled; traveled along; traveled down; traveled over; traveled to; traveled up; treated; trembled; trembled above; trembled against; trembled at; trembled between; trembled for; trembled in; trembled on; trembled over; trembled under; trembled when; trembled with; trespassed; tried; tripped over; tripped up; trusted; tucked; tucked against; tucked away; tucked behind; tucked beneath; tucked between; tucked in; tucked inside; tucked into; tucked under; tucked up; tugged; tugged at; tugged on; tumbled; tumbled down; turned; turned around; turned back; turned into; turned inward; turned off; turned out; turned outward; turned over; turned to; turned toward; turned up; tweaked; twiddled; twined; twined around; twined through; twined together; twinged; twirled; twirled around; twisted; twisted around; twisted in; twisted into; twisted on; twisted tight; twisted together; twitched; twitched at; twitched in; twitched on; twitched toward; typed; unbuttoned; uncaught; unclasped; unclenched; unclutched; uncovered; undid; unfolded; unglued; unloaded; unpacked; unrolled; unscrewed; unslung; unsnapped; untied; unwound; unwrapped; unzipped; upflung; upflung in; uplifted; uplifted in; uplifted toward; upraised; upraised in; upraised to; upthrust; urged; urged forward; urged toward; used; used for; used in; used to; ushered; vanished; vanished into; vaporized; vibrated; vibrated from; vibrated with; vised; vised on; vised onto; visited; visored; visored over; volunteered; wagged; waited; waited for; walked; walked down; walked over; walked up; wandered; wandered across; wandered between; wandered into; wandered over; wandered to; wandered up; wanted; warded off; warmed; warmed against; warmed beneath; warmed by; warmed on; warmed under; washed; washed in; washed with; waved; waved above; waved around; waved at; waved back; waved for; waved from; waved in; waved over; waved through; waved to; waved toward; wavered; weakened; weaved; wedged; wedged against; wedged between; wedged into;

wedged up; weeded; weighed; weighted down; welded together; went; went around; went at; went atop; went back; went down; went for; went from; went in; went inside; went into; went on; went out; went over; went past; went right; went stiff; went straight; went through; went to; went together; went toward; went under; went up; went wooden; wet; wet from; wet in; wet with; whacked; whacked at; whipped; whipped around; whipped back; whipped from; whipped out; whipped toward; whipped up; whirled; whirled across; whirred; whirred up; whisked; whispered of; whitened; widened; wielded; wiggled; wiggled back; willed to; windmilled; wiped; wiped across; wiped at; wiped away; wished; withdrew; withdrew from; withdrew into; withered; withstood; wobbled; woke; woke up; won; wore; worked; worked at; worked in; worked on; worked over; worked together; wormed; wormed under; worried; wound; wound around; wound up; wove; wove in; wove together; wrapped; wrapped about; wrapped around; wrapped in; wrapped tight; wrecked; wrenched; wrenched at; wrestled; wrestled with; writhed; writhed like; writhed under; wrote; wrote on; wrung; wrung together; yanked; yanked out; yanked up; yearned for; yearned to; yielded; zipped.

Noun Phrases

A - I

absence of hands; abundance of hands; acceptance of the hand; accompaniment of hands; accuracy of the hand(s); action(s) of the hand(s); activity of the hand(s); affliction(s) of the hand(s); age of the hand(s); aid of the hand(s); amount of hands; amputation of the hand(s); anatomy of the hand(s); angle of the hand(s); appearance of the hand(s); application of the hand(s); approach of the hand(s); arc of the hand(s); area(s) of the hand(s); arthritis of the hand(s); aspect of the hand(s); assistance of the hand(s); atrophy of the hand(s); attitude of the hand(s); awe of the hand(s); axis of the hand(s); back of the hand(s); backside of the hand(s); ball of the hand(s); band of the hand(s); base of the hand(s); beauty of the hand(s); beginning of the hand(s); bestowal of the hand(s); binding of the hand(s); blur of hands; boldness of the hand(s); bones of the hand(s); border of the hand(s); bottom of the hand(s); breadth of the hand(s); brush of the hand(s); bulge of the hand(s); bunch of hands; burden of hands; calluses of the hand(s); capacity of the hand(s); care of the hand(s); caress of the hand(s); center of the hand(s); certainty of the hand(s); chain of hands; change of hands; character of the hand(s); characteristics of the hand(s); chorus of hands; circle of hands; clamminess of the hand(s); clap of the hand(s); clasp(ing) of the hand(s); cleanliness of the hand(s); cleansing of the hand(s); clench(ing) of the hand(s); close-up of the hand(s); clumsiness of the hand(s); cluster of hands; coldness of the hand(s); collection of hand(s); color of the hand(s); combination of hands; command of the hand(s); comparison of the hands; competition of hands; compression of the hand(s); condition of the hand(s); confusion of hands; connection of the hand(s); consideration of the hand(s); contact of the hand(s); contraction of the hand(s); control of the hand(s);

coolness of the hand(s); coordination of the hand(s); couple of hands; creases of the hand(s); cup of the hand(s); curve of the hand(s); dance of the hand(s); darkness of the hand(s); deformity of the hand(s); deftness of the hand(s); delicacy of the hand(s); demand of the hand(s); dexterity of the hand(s); digits of the hand(s); dip of the hand(s); direction of the hand(s); discipline of the hand(s); disinfection of the hand(s); disposition of the hand(s); distribution of hands; drawback of the hand(s); eczema of the hand(s); edge of the hand(s); effect of the hand(s); efficiency of the hand(s); elevation of the hand(s); embrace of the hand(s); employment of the hand(s); enclosure of the hand(s); end of the hand(s); endowment(s) of the hand(s); energy of the hand(s); examination of the hand(s); excess of hands; exercise of the hand(s); experience of the hand(s); exposure of the hand(s); expression of the hand(s); extension of the hand(s); extremities of the hand(s); face of the hand(s); features of the hand(s); feebleness of the hand(s); feel of the hand(s); feeling of the hand(s); fidgeting of the hand(s); finger(s) of the hand(s); fingertip(s) of the hand(s); firmness of the hand(s); flash of the hand(s); flat(s) of the hand(s); flesh of the hand(s); flick of the hand(s); fling of the hand(s); flip of the hand(s); flourish of the hand(s); flurry of hands; flutter of the hand(s); force of the hand(s); forefinger of the hand(s); forest of hands; form of the hand(s); fracture(s) of the hand(s); freedom of the hand(s); friction of the hand(s); front of the hand(s); function of the hand(s); gesture(s) of the hand(s); gift of the hand(s); grab of the hand(s); grace of the hand(s); grasp of the hand(s); grasping of hands; grip of the hand(s); group of hands; guidance of the hand(s); hack of the hand(s); heaps of hands; heat of the hand(s); heel(s) of the hand(s); height of the hand(s); hold of the hand(s); holding of hands; identity of the hand(s); idleness of the hand(s); image of the hand(s); imitation of the hand(s); impression of the hand(s); imprint of the hand(s); impulse of the hand(s); indication of the hand(s); infection of the hand(s); influence of the hand(s); injury of the hand(s); insertion of the hand(s); inside(s) of the hand(s); inspection of the hand(s); intention of the hand(s); intervention of the hand(s); involvement of the hand(s).

J - W

jerk of the hand(s); joining of the hand(s); joint of the hand(s); kind of hands; kiss of the hand; knowledge of the hand(s); knuckles of the hand(s); labor of the hand(s); lack of hands; language of the hand(s); laying-on of hands; length of the hand(s); lesions of the hand(s); level of the hand(s); lifting of the hand(s); lightness of the hand(s); line(s) of the hand(s); location of the hand(s); loss of the hand(s); lot of hands; magic of the hand(s); majesty of the hand(s); majority of the hands; mark(s) of the hand(s); mastery of the hand(s); memory of the hand(s); middle of the hand(s); mixture of hands; mobility of the hand(s); moisture of the hand(s); motion(s) of the hand(s); movement(s) of the hand(s); multiplicity of hands; multitude of hands; muscles of the hand(s); musculature of the hand(s); mutilation of the hand(s); myriad of hands; nails of the hand(s); nature of the hand(s); nimbleness of the hand(s); number of hands; numbness of the hand(s); ocean of hands; opening-out of the hand(s); openness of the hand(s); orientation of the hand(s); osteoarthritis of the hand(s); outline of the hand(s); owner of the hand(s); pair of hands; palm(s) of the hand(s); paralysis of the hand(s); part(s) of the hand(s); pat of the hand(s); patter of hands; patting of the hand(s); perfection of the hand(s); perspiration of the hand(s); placement of the hand(s); placing of the hand(s); plane of the hand(s); point of the hand(s); poise of the hand(s); portion of the hand(s); position of the hand(s); possession of the hand(s); posture of the hand(s); pounding of hands; power of the hand(s); practice of the hand(s); praying of hands; precision of the hand(s); presence of the hand(s); press of the hand(s); pressure of the hand(s); progress of the hand(s); proportion of the hand(s); protection of the hand(s); quality of the hand(s); quantity of hands; quickness of the hand(s); raising of the hand(s); range of hands; rapidity of the hand(s); reach of the hand(s); readiness of the hand(s); readjustment of the hand(s); reassurance of the hand(s); recognition of the hand(s); redness of the hand(s); reflex of the hand(s); refusal of the hand(s); region of the hand(s); rejection of the hand(s); remainder of the hand(s); removal of the hand(s); rest of the hand(s); revolution of the hand(s); rotation of the hand(s); rows of hands; rub of the hand(s); rush of hands; rustle of hands; scarcity of hands; scoop of the hand(s); score(s) of hands; sea of hands; sensation of the hand(s); sense of the hand(s); series of hands; set(s) of hands; severing of the hand(s); shadow(s) of the hand(s); shakiness of the hand(s); shaking of the hand(s); shape of the hand(s); shift of the hand(s); shortage of hands; show of the hand(s); side(s) of the hand(s); sight of the hand(s); signal(s) of the hand(s); similarity of the hand(s); size of the hand(s); skeleton of the hand(s); skill of the hand(s); skin of the hand(s); slap of the hand(s); slash of the hand(s); slip of the hand(s); smack of the hand(s); smell of the hand(s); sort of hands; sound of the hand(s); span of the hand(s); spasm of the hand(s); speed of the hand(s); spread of the hand(s); squeeze of the hand(s); stack of hands; state of the hand(s); steadiness of the hand(s); stiffness of the hand(s); strength of the hand(s); stroke of the hand(s); supply of hands; sureness of the hand(s); surface of the hand(s); swarm of hands; sway of the hand(s); sweat of the hand(s); sweep of the hand(s); swipe of the hand(s); swivel of the hand(s); temperature of the hand(s); tendons of the hand(s); thought of the hand(s); throbbing of the hand(s); throes of hands; thumb of the hand(s); thunder of hands; tilt of the hand(s); tip(s) of the hand(s); tissue of the hand(s); top(s) of the hand(s); touch of the hand(s); treatment of the hand(s); trembling of the hand(s); tremor of the hand(s); tug of the hand(s); turn of the hand(s); twist of the hand(s); twitch of the hand(s); type of hands; underside of the hand(s); union of hands; unsteadiness of the hand(s); use of the hand(s); usefulness of the hand(s); variety of hands; vaulting of the hand(s); veins of the hand(s); vibrations of the hand(s); view of the hand(s); vision of the hand(s); wall of hands; warmth of the hand(s); washing of the hand(s); wave of the hand(s); waves of hands; weakness of the hand(s); weight of the hand(s); whirlwind of hands; whiteness of the hand(s); width of the hand(s); wipe of the hand(s); withdrawal of the hand(s); workings of the hand(s); wound(s) of the hand(s); wringing of the hand(s); wrist of the hand(s).

USAGE EXAMPLES

She *waved a frantic hand* in the air, hoping a lifeguard would see her.

He *placed his frozen hands* in front of the fire.

A *deft hand brushed across* her face and down the back of her neck.

Gillian's *free hand clutched at* a dangling branch, but missed.

The intruder *muffled* the boy's cries with a *gloved hand*.

21
HEART

Adjectives in Alphabetical Order

A - L

abandoned; abnormal; abundant; accelerated; accelerating; aching; active; adolescent; adoring; adrenaline-soaked; affectionate; aging / ageing; agitated; ailing; ambitious; amiable; amorous; ample; angry; anguished; anxious; apprehensive; arctic; ardent; arid; aristocratic; arrhythmic; artificial; artistic; artless; aspiring; bad; banging; barbarous; barren; battered; beautiful; beloved; benevolent; bereaved; besotted; betraying; bewildered; big; bitter; black; blackest; blameless; bleak; bleeding; blessed; blighted; blind; blithe; bloodless; bloody; boiling; bold; boundless; bounteous; bountiful; boyish; brave; bravest; bright; broken; brooding; brotherly; bruised; bud-like; bud-sized; budding; buoyant; burdened; buried; burned / burnt; burning; bursting; busted; busy; callous; calm; cankered; capacious; capricious; captive; carefree; careful; careless; caring; carnal; cautious; changed; changing; chaotic; charitable; chaste; chastened; cheating; cheerful; childish; childlike; chilled; chivalrous; clattering; clear; clotted; cold; coldest; collective; compassionate; compatible; complete; complex; concealed; confident; congenial; congenital; congestive; connected; conquered; conscious; considerable; contented; contracting; contrite; convulsing; cool; cooling; corrupt; courageous; covetous; cowardly; cracked; craven; crazy; crimson; crippled; crowded; cruel; cynical; damaged; damn; damned; dangerous; daring; dark; darkened; darkest; darling; dastardly; dauntless; dead; deadly; dear; dearest; deceitful; decent; deep; deepest; defective; degenerative; degraded; dejected; delicate; delighted; depraved; depressed; desolate; despairing; desperate; despondent; devoted; disappointed; discontented; diseased; disloyal; disobedient; disordered; distant; distressed; divided; divine; docile; doting; doubtful; dull; dutiful; dying; eager; earnest; effeminate; elderly; electric; electronic; elevated; elongated; elusive; embittered; emotion-charged; emotional; empty; enduring; enlarged; enlightened; enormous; enthusiastic; entire; envious; errant; erratic; eternal; ever-changing; evil; excellent; excited; expectant; exploding; exposed; exultant; failing; faint; fainting; fair; faithful; faithless; fake; false; faltering; fast; fast-beating; fatherly; fatty; faulty; fearful; fearless; feeble; feminine; ferocious; fervent; fervid; fevered; feverish; fibrillating; fickle; fierce; fiery; filial; fine; flaming; floating; fluttery; fond; foolish; forgiving; forlorn; forty-year-old; foul; fractured; fragile; frail; frank; frantic; fraught; free; freed; frenzied; friendly; frightened; frozen; full; functional; furious; gallant; galloping; galumphing; game; gaunt; gay; generous; genial; gentle; gentleman's; gentlemanly; gentlest; genuine; giant; gifted; gigantic; girlish; glad; gladsome; gloomy; glorious; glowing;

goddamned; godly; golden; good; good-natured; graceless; gracious; grateful; gray; great; greatest; greedy; grieving; growing; grudging; guileless; guiltless; guilty; gyrating; handsome; happy; hard; hardened; hardest; hardy; haughty; haunted; healthy; heathen; heavenly; heaviest; heavy; heedless; heroic; hidden; hideous; high; hollow; holy; homely; homesick; homicidal; honest; honorable; hopeful; hopeless; hospitable; hot; hot-blooded; huge; human; humane; humble; hungry; hypertensive; hypertrophied; hysterical; icy; idle; ignorant; ill; immense; immoral; impassioned; impatient; impenitent; imperfect; impetuous; impoverished; impressionable; impulsive; impure; incipient; inconstant; incorruptible; increasing; independent; indifferent; indignant; individual; indomitable; inexperienced; infinite; inflexible; ingenuous; inner; innermost; innocent; inscrutable; insensible; intact; intractable; intrepid; irregular; irritable; isolated; jack-hammering; jaded; jagged; jealous; joyful; joyless; joyous; keen; kind; kindest; kindly; kindred; kingly; knightly; laboring; laden; languid; large; largest; lazy; leaden; life-hardened; light; lightest; lightsome; little; little-girl; live; living; lofty; lone; loneliest; lonely; long-awaited; long-dead; long-overdue; lost; loveless; lovelorn; lovely; loving; lowly; loyal; lush; lustful; lusty.

M - Y

macho; mad; magnanimous; magnificent; maiden; malicious; malignant; mammalian; mangled; manly; masculine; massive; maternal; maximal; maximum; mean; meek; megalomaniacal; merciful; merry; middle-aged; mighty; mild; minor; minuscule; miserable; misfiring; misshapen; missing; misunderstood; moderate; modest; molten; monstrous; moral; mortal; motherly; motionless; mournful; muffled; musical; naked; nasty; naughty; nervous; neurotic; neutral; new; newborn; noble; noblest; normal; nutty; obdurate; obedient; obstinate; old; ordinary; original; outgoing; outraged; overburdened; overflowing; oversized; overturned; overworked; pained; painful; pale; pallid; palpitating; panicked; parched; passionate; paternal; patriotic; pea-sized; peaceful; pensive; perfect; perverse; perverted; pesky; philanthropic; pierced; pink; pink-and-red; pious; piteous; pitiful; pitiless; plain; plum-colored; poetic; polluted; ponderous; poor; powerful; precious; prideful; primitive; princely; pristine; profound; prophetic; prosthetic; proud; proudest; pulmonary; pulpy; pulseless; pulsing; pure; purest; puzzled; questioning; quick; quickening; quiet; quivering; rabbiting; racing; radiant; raging; ramshackle; rancorous; rapid; rapt; ravaged; ravenous; raw; ready; rebellious; reborn; receptive; reclaimed; red; red-hot; regular; relentless; reluctant; remarkable; remote; renewed; repentant; repetitive; resolute; responsive; restless; revengeful; reverent; rheumatic; righteous; rigid; ripe; riveted; rock-hard; rocky; romantic; rotten; rotting; rough; roving; royal; ruby-red; rude; rugged; runaway; running; ruptured; ruthless; sacred; sad; saddest; saintly; sanguine; savage; scarlet; scarred; screaming; secret; selfish; selfless; senile; senseless; sensible; sensitive; sensual; sentimental; serious; severe; shaky; shallow; sharded; shattered; shrunken; shuddering; sick; sickened; sickening; sickly; significant; silent; silly; simple; simplest; simultaneous; sincere; sincerest; sinful; sinless; sleepy; slight; slow; slow-beating; slowing; sluggish; small; soft; softest; solid; solitary; sore; sorest;

sorrowful; sorrowing; sorry; speeding; spinsterly; spiraling; spiritual; spiteful; squeezed; stable; stammering; starved; steadfast; steady; steely; stern; sternest; still; still-beating; still-raw; stirring; stolen; stomping; stoned; stoniest; stony; stopped; storming; stormy; stout; stoutest; strengthened; stressed-out; stricken; strong; strongest; struck; struggling; stubborn; stunted; stupid; sturdy; stuttering; suffering; sullen; suppressed; surging; susceptible; suspended; suspicious; sweet; sweetest; swelling; swirling; swollen; sympathetic; teenage; tender; tenderest; terrible; terrified; thankful; thankless; thirsty; thoughtful; thoughtless; thrilling; throbbing; thrumming; thudding; thumping; thundering; timid; timorous; tiny; tired; torpid; tough; traitorous; tranquil; transfixed; transplanted; treacherous; trembling; tremulous; troubled; true; truest; trustful; tumultuous; twisted; twittering; tyrannous; unanxious; unbelieving; unbreakable; unbroken; uncomforted; uncorrupted; undaunted; undesired; undeveloped; undiagnosed; uneasy; unfeeling; unforgiving; unfulfilled; ungrateful; unguarded; unhappy; unholy; unmoving; unquiet; unready; unrelenting; unruly; unsatisfied; unselfish; unshaken; unsound; unstable; unsteady; unsuspecting; untamed; unthwarted; untried; untroubled; untutored; unwilling; unworthy; unyielding; vacant; valiant; vast; vengeful; vicious; vile; violent; virgin; virtuous; visible; vital; volcanic; vulgar; vulnerable; waiting; wanton; warlike; warm; warmest; wayward; weak; weakened; weakening; weary; whirling; whole; wicked; wide; widening; widowed; wild; willing; wintry; wise; wisest; wobbly; woeful; womanly; wonderful; worldly; worn; worried; worsening; worst; worthless; worthy; wounded; wrecked; wretched; yearning; yellow; young; youthful; zealous.

Verbs and Phrasal Verbs in Alphabetical Order

A - C

abhorred; accelerated; accompanied by; ached; ached at; ached for; ached from; ached in; ached when; ached with; ached within; acknowledged; acquiesced; acted; admitted; adored; affected by; affected with; agreed; agreed with; alarmed by; alienated from; allowed; altered; answered; anticipated; appeared; approved; approved of; arose; arose from; arrested; arrested by; ashamed of; asked; aspired; assailed; associated with; assured; attached; attached to; attacked; attempted; attuned; awakened; awoke; bade; balked; balked at; ballooned; banged; banged against; banged around; banged in; basked in; battered; beat; beat against; beat at; beat audibly; beat beneath; beat faster; beat for; beat from; beat harder; beat in; beat into; beat loudly; beat on; beat quicker; beat quickly; beat rapidly; beat steadily; beat strongly; beat through; beat under; beat when; beat with; beat within; began to; begged; beguiled; beheld; believed; believed in; belonged to; bestowed; betrayed; blackened; blasted; blasted from; blazed; blazed in; bled; bled at; bled for; bled in; bled with; bled within; blocked by; bloomed; bobbed; boiled; boiled with; bolted; boomed; boomed in; bore; bothered; bounced; bound; bound at; bound for; bound up; bound with; bounded; bounded at; bounded for; bounded in; bounded with; bounded within; brightened; brimmed; brimmed at; brimmed over; brimmed with; broke; broke apart; broke down; broke for; broke into; broke with; brought on; brought to; brought up; bruised; bruised by; brushed; bucked; built; bulged; bulged inside; bumped; bumped around; buoyed; buoyed with; burdened; burdened by; burdened with; buried; buried in; burned; burned for; burned from; burned in; burned with; burned within; burst; burst forth; burst in; burst into; burst out; burst through; burst with; busted; called; called on; called out; calmed; calmed down; came apart; careened; carried; cast off; caught; caught in; caught upon; caused; caused by; caved; caved in; ceased; changed; charged with; chattered; cheered; cheered by; cheered for; chilled; choked; choked off; churned; churned over; clattered; clenched; clenched at; clenched for; clenched in; clenched up; clenched with; clicked; closed to; clung to; clutched; clutched at; committed to; compared with; composed; composed of; compressed; compressed in; conceived; condemned; confessed; confused; congealed; connected with; consented; considered; consisted of; constricted; constricted at; constricted with; consumed; consumed by; consumed with; contained; continued; continued on; contracted; contracted at; contracted in; contracted with; conveyed; convulsed; convulsed at; cooled; corresponded; counted on; cracked; cramped; cramped at; cramped up; cramped with; crapped out; crashed; crashed against; crashed into; craved; craved for; created; created by; cried; cried in; cried out; crumpled; crunched; crunched with; crushed; crushed by; curdled; cursed; cushioned; cut in half; cut out; cut through.

D - I

danced; danced around; danced at; danced in; danced with; danced within; dared; darkened; dazed; deceived; decided; declared; deepened; defected; deleted; demanded; denied; dented; departed from; depended on; deplored; descended; desired; despised; destroyed; detached; detonated; detonated with; developed; devoted; dictated; died; died away; died out; died within; differed from; dilated; dilated with; dipped; directed; disappeared; disdained; disengaged; displayed; disposed; dissolved; distrusted; disturbed; dived / dove; divided; divided between; divided in; divided into; doubled over; dragged; drew back; drew into; dried up; drifted; drifted down; drooped; dropped; dropped down; dropped from; dropped in; dropped into; dropped to; dropped with; drove against; drove around; drove through; drummed; drummed in; dwelt on; dwindled; eased; echoed; elated; embraced; emerged; emerged into; employed; emptied; emptied of; enabled; encircled by; enclosed; enclosed in; encrusted; encrusted with; ended up; endured; engaged; engaged in; engraved; enjoyed; enlarged; enshrined; entered into; enveloped in; estranged from; etched on; exalted; exclaimed; expanded; expanded at; expanded in; expanded with; experienced; exploded; exploded inside; explored; exposed; expressed; exulted; exulted in; failed; failed within; fainted; fainted within; fashioned from; fed; fell; felt; fibrillated; filled; filled up; filled with; fired; fit; fixed; fixed in; fixed on; fixed upon; flailed; flailed around; flailed in; flamed; flamed in; flapped; flared; flared against; flashed through; flattened; flattened out; flew; flew back; flickered; flickered in; flipped; flipped against; flipped in; flipped over; floated; flooded; flooded at; flooded with; flopped; flopped in; floundered; flowed;

flowed out; flowed over; flowed with; flushed; fluttered; fluttered at; fluttered in; fluttered up; fluttered with; followed; forced; foreboded; foretold; forgave; forgot; formed; found; found in; fractured; freed from; froze; froze at; froze in; froze when; fueled by; fulfilled; functioned; fused; galloped; galvanized; gathered; gave; gave in; gave out; gave up; gladdened; glimpsed; glimpsed through; glowed; glowed at; glowed with; glowed within; gnawed; gnawed with; grabbed; grew; grew more; grew quicker; grew still; grieved; grieved for; grieved over; grimaced; groaned; groaned within; gushed; gushed in; gushed with; gyrated; hammered; hammered against; hammered at; hammered in; hammered inside; hammered with; handled; hankered after; harbored; hardened; hardened further; hardened to; hardened toward; hardened with; healed; heard; heaved; heaved beneath; heaved in; heaved with; held; held onto; hesitated; hiccupped; hiccupped with; hid; hit; hit hard; hitched; hoped; hopped; hung; hung above; hung at; hungered for; hurt; hurt for; hurt from; iced over; imbued with; impelled; imploded; implored; impressed; impressed with; imprisoned; imprisoned within; increased; increased in; induced by; inflamed; informed; inspired; inspired by; intended for; invaded; invested; invested in; issued.

J - Q

jackhammered; jackhammered in; jammed; jerked; jerked in; joined; joined in; joined with; jolted; jolted from; jolted in; jolted into; jolted up; jostled; jostled in; jumped; jumped at; jumped for; jumped in; jumped inside; jumped into; jumped out; jumped up; jumped when; jumped with; jumpstarted; jumpstarted by; kept; kept on; kicked; kicked against; kicked in; kicked into; kicked up; killed; kindled; kindled at; kindled with; knew; knocked; knocked against; knotted; knotted up; labored; labored in; labored with; lagged; lagged behind; laid on; lamented; laughed; laughed within; lay in; leaked; leaped / leapt; leaped at; leaped for; leaped in; leaped inside; leaped into; leaped to; leaped toward; leaped up; leaped when; leaped with; leaped within; led; left; let; lied; lifted; lifted at; lifted by; lifted up; lifted with; lightened; lightened at; lightened by; lightened in; lightened of; liked; listened; lived for; loaded with; locked; locked with; lodged in; longed for; loosened; lost; lost in; loved; lowered; lunged; lunged toward; lurched; lurched at; lurched up; lurched within; made for; made from; made of; made up; married to; massaged; matched; measured; measured out; melted; melted at; melted away; melted in; melted into; melted with; melted within; met; mingled with; misfired; misled; missed; moaned; moaned out; mocked; mocked by; monitored; mourned; mourned for; moved; moved by; moved in; moved with; murmured; needed; noticed; nudged; obeyed; occupied; occupied by; occupied with; occurred in; offered; omitted; opened; opened at; opened by; opened to; opened up; opened wide; opposed; oppressed; oscillated; oscillated between; ought to; outpaced; overcharged with; overflowed; overflowed in; overflowed toward; overflowed with; overwhelmed with; owned by; palpitated; palpitated at; palpitated in; palpitated with; panted; panted after; panted for; panted with; parted; partook of; passed through; pasted on; patched; pattered; pattered in; paused; peeked out; penetrated; penetrated by; penetrated with; perceived; performed; perfused with; picked up; pierced; pierced by;

pierced through; pierced with; pinched; pinched at; pinched with; pinged; pinged in; pinned; pinned under; pitched; pitched up; placed; placed in; played; played about; pleaded for; plucked out; plummeted; plummeted down; plummeted to; plummeted with; plunged; popped; popped up; possessed; possessed by; possessed of; possessed with; pounded; pounded against; pounded at; pounded away; pounded in; pounded out; pounded under; pounded with; poured forth; poured out; prayed; prayed for; preferred; prepared; prepared for; presented; pressed against; prevailed; proceeded to; produced; prompted; provided; puffed up; pulled out; pulled toward; pulsated; pulsated in; pulsed; pulsed against; pulsed beneath; pulsed in; pummeled; pummeled against; pumped; pumped faster; pumped with; punched against; purred; pushed; pushed against; quailed; quailed at; quailed with; quailed within; quaked; quaked with; quickened; quickened at; quickened when; quickened whenever; quickened with; quieted; quit; quivered; quivered with.

R - S

raced; raced at; raced from; raced in; raced toward; raced whenever; raced with; racked with; raised; rammed into; ran ahead; ran away; ran over; rang; rapped; rapped against; rattled; rattled beneath; reached; reached for; reached out; read; rebelled; rebelled against; recalled; received; recognized; recoiled; recoiled at; recoiled from; recoiled in; recoiled with; recovered; recovered enough; recovered from; reflected; reflected on; refrained from; refused; regained; rejected; rejoiced; rejoiced at; rejoiced in; related; relaxed; relented; relieved; relieved from; relieved of; remained; remained in; remained with; remembered; remembered how; removed; removed from; rended / rent; rendered; renewed; repeated; repined; replaced; replenished with; replied; reposed; reproached; required; resembled; reserved for; resided; resigned; resisted; resolved; responded; responded to; responded with; restarted; rested; restored; resumed; retained; returned; revealed; reveled in; reverberated; reverberated against; reverberated in; revived; revolted; revolted against; revolted at; revolted from; revved; revved up; ricocheted; ricocheted against; ricocheted around; ripped out; rippled; roared; rocked; rolled; rose; rose above; rose against; rose at; rose in; rose to; rose up; rose with; rose within; rotted; rushed; rushed at; rushed in; rushed up; rushed with; saddened; saddened by; sagged; said; sang; sang with; sang within; sank; sank at; sank deeper; sank down; sank for; sank further; sank in; sank into; sank on; sank to; sank under; sank when; sank with; sank within; sat; sat up; satisfied; satisfied with; saved; saw; scared; scooped; scooped from; scored; scudded; scudded into; searched; secured; seized; seized up; seized with; sensed; sent; sent into; sent up; set; set in; set on; set with; settled; settled back; settled down; shattered; shifted; shifted into; shivered; shivered with; shone; shone in; shone through; shook; shook in; shook with; shot into; shot up; shouted; shouted for; showed; shrank; shrank from; shrank in; shrank to; shrank within; shrieked; shrieked in; shriveled; shriveled under; shuddered; shuddered in; shut; shut down; shut to; shut up; sickened; sickened at; sickened with; sickened within; sighed; sighed for; sizzled; sizzled with; skimmed; skimmed over; skipped; skipped a beat; skipped at; skipped when; skipped with; skittered;

skittered in; skittered into; slammed; slammed against; slammed at; slammed into; slapped; slapped against; slept; slept on; slid through; slowed; slowed down; smacked against; snapped in half; snuffed out; soared; soared at; soared with; sobbed; sobbed for; softened; softened at; softened by; softened toward; softened with; sought; sounded; spasmed; sped; sped up; spilled over; split; split in half; spoke; spoke out; sponged up; sprang up; spread in; sprinkled from; spun; sputtered; sputtered along; sputtered back; squeezed; squeezed at; squeezed in; squeezed tight; squeezed with; stalled; stalled for; stalled in; stammered; started; started again; started up; stayed; stayed with; steadied; steeled against; steeped in; stepped up; stiffened; stilled; stirred; stirred at; stirred by; stirred with; stirred within; stood; stood still; stood up; stopped; stopped altogether; stopped at; stopped for; stopped from; strained; strained against; strangled; strangled by; strengthened; strove; struck by; struggled; strung on; stuck; stuck fast; stumbled; stuttered; stuttered with; subdued; submitted; subsided; succumbed; succumbed to; suffered; suggested; surged; surged at; surged with; surmounted by; surrounded by; survived; suspended in; sustained; swayed; swelled; swelled at; swelled from; swelled in; swelled up; swelled with; swelled within; swirled with; swooned; swooped; swooped into; swung open; symbolized; sympathized with.

T - Y

talked; taped to; tapped; tattooed on; taught; teased; teased out; tended to; terrified; thanked; thawed; thickened; thought of; thrashed; threatened; thrilled; thrilled at; thrilled with; throbbed; throbbed at; throbbed for; throbbed in; throbbed on; throbbed with; thrummed; thrummed with; thudded; thudded against; thudded in; thudded with; thudded within; thumped; thumped against; thumped below; thumped from; thumped in; thumped irregularly; thumped loud; thumped through; thumped when; thumped wildly; thumped with; thundered; thundered at; thundered in; thundered inside; thwacked; thwacked against; ticked; tightened; tightened with; tingled; told; took to; tore; tore out; touched; touched by; touched with; transfixed; transfixed by; transfixed with; transformed; transplanted; trapped; trapped in; trembled; trembled at; trembled for; trembled in; trembled with; trembled within; tried; trilled; tripped up; triumphed; trotted; troubled; trusted; tugged at; tumbled; tumbled over; turned; turned against; turned away; turned back; turned from; turned in; turned into; turned over; turned to; turned upside down; turned with; turned within; twisted; twisted at; twisted in; twisted inside; twisted whenever; unclenched; understood; underwent; unfolded; unfurled; united; united with; uplifted; urged; used to; uttered; varied; vibrated; wadded up; wailed; waited; wandered; wanted; wanted out; warmed; warmed at; warmed by; warmed to; warmed toward; warmed with; warred with; watched; wavered; weakened; weaned from; wedged in; weighed down; weighed on; welcomed; welled; welled up; welled with; went out; went still; went up; wept; wept for; wheezed; whined; whinnied; whispered; widened; willed; wished; wished for; wobbled; woke; woke up; won; won out; wore out; worked; worked up; wound down; wound up; wounded; wounded by; wrapped in; wrenched; wrenched in; wrenched out; wrung; wrung by; wrung with;

yearned; yearned after; yearned for; yearned toward; yearned with; yearned within; yielded.

Noun Phrases

A – D

ability of the heart; abnormality of the heart; absence of the heart; abundance of the heart; acceleration of the heart; account of the heart; ache of the heart; actions of the heart; activation of the heart; activity of the heart; acuteness of the heart; adultery of the heart; advice of the heart; affair(s) of the heart; affection(s) of the heart; affliction of the heart; agitation of the heart; agony of the heart; alienation of the heart; allegiance of the heart; ambition of the heart; amount of heart; anatomy of the heart; aneurysm of the heart; anger of the heart; anguish of the heart; anomalies of the heart; anxiety of the heart; apex of the heart; apparatus of the heart; appearance of the heart; area of the heart; arrest of the heart; arrogance of the heart; arteries of the heart; aspect of the heart; aspiration(s) of the heart; assessment of the heart; atrophy of the heart; attachment of the heart; attack of the heart; attitude of the heart; attraction(s) of the heart; avenues of the heart; awareness of the heart; axis of the heart; back of the heart; badness of the heart; bang of the heart; base of the heart; baseness of heart; basis of the heart; beat of the heart; beating(s) of the heart; beauty of the heart; bedrock of the heart; beep of the heart; behavior of the heart; belief of the heart; benevolence of the heart; benignity of the heart; bias of the heart; bigness of heart; bit of heart; bitterness of the heart; blackness of the heart; blindness of the heart; blood of the heart; boldness of heart; bond of the heart; booming of the heart; border of the heart; bottom of the heart; brave of heart; bravery of heart; breaking of the heart; breath of heart; brokenness of the heart; bulk of the heart; bumping of the heart; buoyancy of the heart; burden of the heart; business of the heart; callousness of heart; calmness of heart; capacity of the heart; captivation of the heart; care of the heart; carelessness of heart; cavern(s) of the heart; cavities of the heart; celibacy of the heart; center of the heart; certainty of the heart; cessation of the heart; chambers of the heart; change of heart; channels of the heart; character of the heart; charity of the heart; charmer of the heart; chastity of heart; check of the heart; cheerfulness of heart; choice of the heart; chunk of the heart; cleansing of the heart; clearness of heart; coarseness of heart; coldness of heart; color of the heart; comedies of the heart; comfort of the heart; communion of the heart; complaint of the heart; complications of heart; compression of the heart; concerns of the heart; condition of the heart; confidence of the heart; confusion of the heart; congestion of the heart; conquest of the heart; consecration of the heart; consent of the heart; consequences of the heart; constancy of the heart; constriction of the heart; contentment of the heart; contraction of the heart; contrition of the heart; control of the heart; conversation(s) of the heart; conviction(s) of the heart; core of the heart; corner of the heart; correspondence of the heart; corridors of the heart; corruption of the heart; courage of the heart; cowardice of heart; crack of the heart; cravings of the heart; cruelty of heart; cry of the heart; cultivation of the heart; darkness of the heart; darling of the heart; deadness of heart; dearness of heart; death of the heart; debility of the heart; deceitfulness of the heart; dedication of the heart; defect(s) of the heart; deficiency of heart; degeneration of the heart; degree of heart; dejection of the heart; delicacy of the heart; delight of the heart; demands of the heart; depravity of the heart; depression of the heart; depth(s) of the heart; descent of the heart; desire(s) of the heart; desolation of the heart; despair of the heart; development of the heart; devotedness of the heart; devotion of the heart; diagnosis of the heart; diameter of the heart; dimensions of the heart; dimness of heart; discovery of the heart; disease(s) of the heart; disorder(s) of the heart; disposition of the heart; disquietude of the heart; disruption of the heart; distress of the heart; disturbance(s) of the heart; door of the heart; dream of the heart; drum of the heart; drumbeat of the heart; drumming of the heart; drunkenness of heart; dryness of heart; duty of the heart.

E - N

earnestness of the heart; ease of the heart; echo of the heart; edge(s) of the heart; effects of the heart; efficiency of the heart; effort of the heart; elation of the heart; elevation of the heart; eloquence of the heart; emancipation of the heart; embarrassment of the heart; emotion(s) of the heart; emptiness of heart; endeavor(s) of the heart; energy of the heart; engagement of the heart; enlargement of the heart; enthusiasm of the heart; errors of the heart; evaluation of the heart; evils of the heart; exacerbation of the heart; exaltation of the heart; examination of the heart; excellency of heart; excitability of the heart; excitation of the heart; excitement of the heart; exhaustion of the heart; expansion of the heart; experience(s) of the heart; expiring of the heart; exposure of the heart; expression(s) of the heart; extremity of the heart; exultation of the heart; failings of the heart; failure of the heart; faint(ness) of heart; faith of the heart; faithfulness of heart; falseness of heart; faults of the heart; fear of the heart; features of the heart; feebleness of heart; feelings of the heart; fervor of the heart; fever of the heart; fire of the heart; firmness of heart; flutter of the heart; flutterings of the heart; folly of the heart; force of the heart; form of the heart; frankness of heart; freedom of the heart; freshness of the heart; friend of the heart; fullness of the heart; function of the heart; fury of the heart; gaiety of the heart; gates of the heart; generosity of the heart; genius of the heart; gentleness of the heart; giddiness of heart; gifts of the heart; gladness of heart; glory of the heart; glow of the heart; goodness of the heart; gratitude of the heart; greatness of the heart; grief of the heart; growth of the heart; habit(s) of the heart; half of the heart; hammer of the heart; hammering of the heart; happiness of the heart; hardening of the heart; hardness of the heart; harmony of the heart; hatred of the heart; haughtiness of the heart; health of the heart; heart of hearts; heat of the heart; heaviness of the heart; hold of the heart; hollowness of the heart; homage of the heart; home of the heart; honesty of the heart; honor of the heart; house of the heart; hum of the heart; humanity of the heart; humbleness of heart; humiliation of the heart; humility of the heart; hunger of the heart; hypertrophy of the heart; idea(s) of the heart; idol of the heart; illumination of the heart;

image(s) of the heart; imagination of the heart; impact of the heart; importance of the heart; improvement of the heart; impulse(s) of the heart; impurity of the heart; inability of the heart; inclination(s) of the heart; indication(s) of the heart; indignation of the heart; infection of the heart; infidelity of the heart; infiltration of the heart; inflammation of the heart; influence of the heart; inhibition(s) of the heart; innocence of the heart; innocency of the heart; inquietude of heart; insensibility of heart; inside of the heart; inspiration of the heart; instinct(s) of the heart; insulation of the heart; integrity of the heart; intelligence of the heart; intensity of the heart; intention(s) of the heart; interest(s) of the heart; intuition(s) of the heart; invasion of the heart; involvement of the heart; irregularities of the heart; irritability of the heart; isolation of the heart; issues of the heart; journey of the heart; joy(s) of the heart; joyfulness of heart; joyousness of heart; judgment of the heart; keeper of the heart; keys of the heart; kind of heart; kindliness of the heart; kindness of the heart; knocking of the heart; knot(s) of the heart; knowledge of the heart; labor of the heart; lack of heart; language of the heart; largeness of the heart; layers of the heart; leap of the heart; levity of the heart; liberality of heart; liberty of the heart; lightness of heart; location of the heart; loftiness of heart; logic of the heart; loneliness of heart; longings of the heart; loss of heart; lot of heart; love of the heart; lowliness of heart; lowness of heart; loyalty of the heart; lurch of the heart; lust of the heart; madness of the heart; magnanimity of the heart; malevolence of the heart; malice of the heart; manipulation of the heart; massage of the heart; master of the heart; matters of the heart; meanness of heart; measure of heart; mechanism of the heart; meditation(s) of the heart; meekness of heart; melody of the heart; melting of the heart; memory of the heart; men of heart; merit of the heart; metabolism of the heart; mirror of the heart; misery of the heart; misgivings of the heart; mistress of the heart; modesty of heart; motions of the heart; motives of the heart; movement(s) of the heart; murmurs of the heart; muscles of the heart; music of the heart; mysteries of the heart; nature of the heart; necessity of heart; nerves of the heart; nobleness of the heart; noise of the heart; numbness of the heart.

O - Z

obedience of the heart; object(s) of the heart; offering(s) of the heart; oneness of heart; openings of the heart; openness of the heart; operation of the heart; opinion of the heart; oppression of the heart; ounce of heart; outflow of the heart; outline of the heart; outpouring(s) of the heart; overflow of heart; overflowing(s) of the heart; overheating of the heart; pace of the heart; pacemaker of the heart; pain(s) of the heart; pair of hearts; palpitation(s) of the heart; pang(s) of the heart; paralysis of the heart; partners of the heart; parts of the heart; passion(s) of the heart; pathology of the heart; peace of the heart; penitence of heart; perception of the heart; performance of the heart; perfusion of the heart; perverseness of heart; perversion of heart; perversity of heart; phantasm of the heart; phase of the heart; philanthropy of the heart; philosophy of the heart; physiology of the heart; picture of the heart; pieces of the heart; piety of the heart; pining of the heart; pit of the heart; pity of the heart; place(s) of the heart; plague of the heart; plainness of heart; pleasantry of heart; pleasure(s) of the heart; plight of the heart; poet of the heart; poetry of the heart; point of the heart; politeness of the heart; portion of heart; position of the heart; possession of the heart; pounding of the heart; poverty of heart; power(s) of the heart; prayer of the heart; preparation of the heart; preparedness of the heart; presence of the heart; pressure of the heart; prevalence of heart; pride of the heart; privacy of the heart; problems of the heart; product of the heart; prognosis of the heart; progression of the heart; projection of the heart; promise of the heart; prompting(s) of the heart; propensities of the heart; properties of the heart; prostration of the heart; protection of the heart; province of the heart; pulsations(s) of the heart; pulse(s) of the heart; pulsing of the heart; pureness of heart; purification of the heart; purity of the heart; purpose of the heart; qualities of the heart; question(s) of the heart; quickening of the heart; quietness of the heart; quietude of the heart; racing of the heart; rage of the heart; rapture of the heart; rate of the heart; reaction of the heart; readiness of the heart; reason(s) of the heart; rebellion of the heart; recesses of the heart; recovery of the heart; rectitude of the heart; red of the heart; reduction of the heart; reformation of the heart; regeneration of the heart; region(s) of the heart; regulation of the heart; relaxation of the heart; relief of the heart; reluctance of the heart; removal of the heart; renewal of the heart; repentance of the heart; replacement of the heart; representation of the heart; requirements of the heart; resistance of the heart; resolution of the heart; response of the heart; rest of the heart; restlessness of the heart; revelation of the heart; reverence of the heart; revolt of the heart; rheumatism of the heart; rhythm(s) of the heart; righteousness of the heart; romance of the heart; rupture of the heart; sacrifice of the heart; sadness of the heart; sake of the heart; sanctity of the heart; sanctuary of the heart; satisfaction of the heart; searching(s) of the heart; seat of the heart; secrecy of the heart; secrets of the heart; section of the heart; seed of the heart; segment of the heart; seizures of the heart; sensations of the heart; sense of the heart; sensibility of the heart; sensitivity of the heart; sentiment(s) of the heart; serenity of the heart; seriousness of heart; servitude of the heart; severity of the heart; shape of the heart; sickness of heart; side of the heart; signs of heart; silence of the heart; simpleness of heart; sin(s) of the heart; sincerity of the heart; singleness of the heart; sinking of the heart; situation(s) of the heart; size of the heart; slowing of the heart; slowness of heart; softness of heart; solitude of the heart; song of the heart; soreness of the heart; sorrow(s) of the heart; sound of the heart; soundness of heart; spasm(s) of the heart; spirit of the heart; spring of the heart; state of the heart; steadfastness of heart; steadiness of heart; stillness of the heart; stimulation of the heart; stirrings of the heart; stoppage of the heart; stoutness of heart; strain of the heart; strength of the heart; strings of the heart; striping of the heart; stroke of the heart; stubbornness of the heart; submission of the heart; substance of the heart; suffering(s) of the heart; sunshine of the heart; superstition(s) of the heart; suppression of the heart; surface of the heart; surgery of the heart; susceptibility of the heart; suspicion(s) of the heart; sweetness of heart; swelling(s) of the heart; symbol of the heart; sympathy of the heart; tears of the heart; temper of the heart; temperature of the heart; tempest of the heart;

temple of the heart; tempo of the heart; tendencies of the heart; tenderness of the heart; thirst of the heart; thought(s) of the heart; thrill of the heart; throbbing(s) of the heart; thrumming of the heart; thud of the heart; thumping of the heart; thundering of the heart; ticking of the heart; ticktock of the heart; ties of the heart; tranquility of the heart; transformation of the heart; treachery of the heart; treason of the heart; treasure of the heart; treatment of the heart; trembling(s) of the heart; tremor(s) of the heart; triumph of the heart; trouble(s) of the heart; truth of the heart; tumult of the heart; understanding of the heart; union of hearts; utterances of the heart; valor of the heart; values of the heart; valves of the heart; vanity of the heart; veins of the heart; venom of the heart; vessels of the heart; vexation of the heart; vices of the heart; vicinity of the heart; vigor of the heart; virtue(s) of the heart; vision(s) of the heart; voice of the heart; void of the heart; volume of the heart; wailing of the heart; wall of the heart; wandering(s) of the heart; wantonness of the heart; warming of the heart; warmness of heart; warmth of the heart; ways of the heart; weakness of the heart; wealth of heart; weariness of heart; weight of the heart; whine of the heart; whole of the heart; wholeness of heart; wickedness of the heart; willingness of the heart; window of the heart; wings of the heart; wisdom of the heart; wish of the heart; word(s) of the heart; workings of the heart; wounds of the heart; wrath of the heart; wretchedness of heart; yearning(s) of the heart; youthfulness of heart; zeal of the heart.

USAGE EXAMPLES

Her *heart skipped a beat* upon seeing him for the first time in 3 years.

His *anxious heart thrummed* hard against his rib cage.

Kylie's *heart stuttered* to life when she realized her mistake.

The girl's *huge heart overflowed with* love for the puppy.

His *bitter heart possessed* no love, only hatred, for the one they called mother.

22
HIP(S)

Adjectives in Alphabetical Order

A - N

aching; agile; ample; angular; arthritic; artificial; average; bad; bare; beautiful; big; blue-jeaned; bony; boy-thin; boyish; broad; broken; bronzed; brown; childbearing; childless; chubby; cocked; curved; curvy; denim-clad; denim-hugged; eager; elderly; endless; enormous; exaggerated; expansive; fat; fatty; female; feminine; flaccid; flat; fleshy; fractured; fragile; full; generous; girlish; gleaming; glittery; good; great; growing; grown-up; hairy; handsome; heavy; high; huge; immobile; injured; large; lascivious; lean; leather-bound; leather-clad; little; long; lovely; low; lumpy; lush; magnificent; masculine; massive; meaty; medium-sized; mighty; muscular; naked; narrow; narrow-waisted; naughty; nice; nonexistent; normal.

P - W

padded; pale; perfect; plump; plush; pointy; prominent; pronounced; pudgy; quivering; ragged; raised; rich; robed; round; rounded; seated; sensuous; shapely; sharp-boned; shattered; shiny; shrunken; skeletal; skinny; skirted; slender; slight; slim; small; smashed; smooth; soft; solid; sore; sparkly; spreading; square; squarish; stiff; still-slim; strong; sturdy; substantial; supple; swaying; swelling; swinging; swiveling; swollen; tender; thick; thin; thinning; thirty-six-inch; thrusting; tight; tiny; tired; towel-covered; trim; twitching; undefined; undulating; unspeakable; voluptuous; warm; well-rounded; white; wide; widened; widening; womanly; wonderful.

Verbs and Phrasal Verbs in Alphabetical Order

A - M

absorbed; ached; appeared; appeared even; arched; became; began; bent; bounced; bound; brushed; bucked; buckled; bulged; came around; captivated; caught; caught on; clothed; clothed by; constrained by; continued; covered; covered with; cradled; creaked; curved; curved like; danced; disappeared; disappeared behind; elevated; encircled; extended; faced; fell; felt; fitted; fixed; flared; flared out; flattened; flexed; forced; forced against; garbed in; gave out; gripped by; gyrated; hammered; heaved; held; hit; hugged; hugged by; humped; jammed; jolted; jolted forward; jutted; jutted up; knotted by; laid; leaned against; leaned on; leveled; lifted; looked; lowered; lurched; moved; moved back; moved forward.

O - W

outlined; outlined beneath; overbalanced; padded; pressed; propped up; pulsed; pumped; pushed; pushed out; raised; reached; reduced; remained; rested; rested on; rocked; rocked against; rocked back; rocked on; rolled; rose; rose up; rubbed; rushed up; seemed; settled; shaped; sharpened; shifted; shimmied; shot out; showed; slapped; slid; slid off; slimmed; slung; splashed; splashed up; sported; started; stiffened; stopped; strained; strengthened; stretched; surprised; swayed; swayed beneath; swiveled; swung; throbbed; thrust; thrust forward; thrust up; thrust upward; tilted; tilted against; touched; trembled; tucked; turned; twitched; undulated; widened; wiggled; worked.

Noun Phrases

arthritis of the hip(s); curve of the hip(s); dislocation of the hip(s); expanse of hips; extension of the hip(s); flick of the hip(s); hint of hips; kind of hips; level of the hip(s); motion of the hip(s); movement of the hip(s); pair of hips; part of the hip(s); pitch of the hip(s); position of the hip(s); region of the hip(s); rotation of the hip(s); shape of the hip(s); side of the hip(s); sway of the hip(s); swell of hips; swing of the hip(s); thrust of the hip(s); width of the hip(s).

USAGE EXAMPLES

The old man's *aching hip was throbbing* after the arduous trek.

Her *feminine hips flared out* when she bent over, sending his thoughts racing.

Wendy *rested her denim-clad hips against* the wall.

Gyrating her narrow hips, the dancer eyed her quarry a second time.

He watched her *soft pale hips* as they *swiveled* beside him.

23
KNEE(S)

Adjectives in Alphabetical Order

A - L

aching; angled; angular; aproned; armored; arthritic; artificial; awkward; bad; baggy; balky; bandaged; banged-up; bare; bared; bashed-up; battered; beefy; bent; big; black; black-hosed; bleeding; bloodied; bloody; blown; blown-out; blue; bony; bouncing; bowed; brittle; broad; broken; brown; bruised; buckled; bulging; bumpy; burgundy; busted; chronic; chubby; clean; clenched; cold; corduroyed; creaking; creaky; crippled; crooked; crossed; cursed; cute; damaged; damn; damp; dark; deficient; dimpled; dirt-stained; dirty; diseased; dislocated; doubled-up; drawn-in; drawn-up; dry; elevated; exposed; faded; fair; faltering; fat; fattish; feeble; flannel-covered; flanneled; flat; fleshy; folded; forward; fragile; freckled; free; full; giant; gimpy; gnarled; goddamn; goddamned; good; gray-trousered; grazed; hairless; hairy; half-bent; half-turned; hard; healthy; heavy; hidden; high; hind; huge; hurt; inert; infected; inflamed; injured; intact; jeaned; jutting; knobbly; knobby; knotted; lacerated; lame; large; leather-clad; left; lightning-quick; little; locked; long; loose; lower; lowered; lumpy.

M - Y

manly; massive; mechanical; middle-aged; mighty; misshapen; moist; mud-encrusted; muddy; multiple; naked; nervous; nervy; new; nice; noble; normal-looking; nubby; old; open; opposite; other; padded; painful; pajama-clad; pale; patched; patterned; pesky; pink; pitiful; pliant; plump; pointed; poor; powerful; pretty; princely; prosthetic; pudgy; quick; ragged; raised; raw; rear; rebuilt; reconstructed; red; rheumatic; rickety; right; rigid; round; rubbery; rugged; ruined; sandy; scabbed; scabby; scaly; scarred; scraped; scrawny; shaky; shattered; sheet-draped; sheeted; shiny; single; skinned; skinny; slight; small; smooth; soaked; soft; soggy; solid; sore; spheral; sprained; square; stable; sticky; stiff; stiffened; stiffening; stockinged; straight; strong; stubborn; sturdy; supple; swift; swollen; tanned; tender; thick; thin; throbbing; tight; tiny; tired; touching; tough; tremulous; troublesome; trousered; twisted; unbendable; unbowed; unstable; unsteady; untiring; unusual; updrawn; upraised; upturned; useless; vulnerable; warm; waxen; weak; weary; weeping; wet; white; whole; wide; wobbly; worn; wounded; wrenched; wrinkled; young.

Verbs and Phrasal Verbs in Alphabetical Order

A - M

ached; acted up; adjusted; aimed; aimed forward; allowed; angled; appeared; approached; arose; arranged; banged; banged against; banged together; beat; became; began; bent; bent forward; bent up; bled; blew out; bobbed; bore; bothered; bounced; bounced off; bounced up; bound; bound by; bowed; braced; braced on; broke; brought down; brought up; bruised; brushed; buckled; buckled beneath; buckled together; buckled under; buckled underneath; bulged; bulged out; bumped; bumped against; bumped up; bunched; bunched up; burned; busted; busted open; came down; came up; caught; caused; chafed; clasped; clattered; cleaned; clicked; climbed; closed; closed together; clung to; clutched; cocked; collapsed; collided; collided with; compressed; connected with; consisted of; continued; covered; covered with; cracked; cracked on; cramped; cramped up; crawled around on; crawled on; creaked; crossed; crossed over; crouched on; crumpled; crunched; crushed; curled; curled up; cut; danced; disappeared into; discovered; displayed; dissolved beneath; draped with; draping; drew up; dropped; dropped to; dug into; emerged; examined; exposed; extended; faced; failed; faltered; fell; felt; felt like; fit through; fixed; flexed; folded; folded up; forced; froze; gathered; gave out; grazed; grew; grinded; grinded together; gripped; ground; healed; held; held in; hit; hooked; hooked over; hooked up; huddled; hugged; hugged to; hugged up; hunched up; hurt; jerked; jerked up; jiggled; jumped; jumped up; jutted; jutted out; jutted up; kicked; kicked up; knocked; knocked against; knocked together; landed on; leaned against; leaned on; levered; levered up; lifted; lifted to; locked; locked beneath; locked tight; locked up; lolled; looked; loosened; marked by; matched; meditated on; merged; merged with; met; met beneath; moved; moved back; moved down; moved forward; moved up.

N - W

needed; nudged; offered; operated on; packed with; parted; patched up; peeked through; peeped out; picked; pinned; placed; placed against; planted; plastered with; pointed; pointed at; poised; poked; poked up; popped; popped back in; popped out; popped up; pressed; pressed against; pressed between; pressed to; pressed together; projected; propped on; propped up; protested; protruded; provided; pulled; pulled together; pulled up; pumped; pumped up; punched; punched through; pushed; pushed into; put up; quaked; quivered; quivered at; quivered with; raised; raised to; rammed; rammed in; rattled; rattled together; reached; received; recovered; refused; relaxed; remained; required; responded; rested; rested against; returned; rocked; rose; rubbed; sagged; sank; sank into; sat; sat beside; scabbed; scraped; scraped against; scraped over; scrubbed; scuffed; scuffed up; sent; separated; set; shifted; shook; shook with; shot into; shot up; showed; showed beneath; showed through; shut; slammed; slammed into; slid; slid apart; slid in; slid on; slipped; slipped on; slowed; snapped; snapped up; speared; spread; spread apart; stained with; started; stayed; stiffened; stiffened easily; stooped down on; stopped; straightened; strained;

strained against; strengthened; struck; stuck out; stuck up; stung; supported; sustained; swayed; swelled; swiveled; swollen; swollen to; swung; tended to; threatened; throbbed; thrust; thrust up; thudded; thudded against; tied; tightened; tired; tore; tottered; tottered beneath; tottered under; touched; trembled; trembled with; tucked in; tucked up; tugged at; turned; twinged; twinged with; twisted; twitched; vanished; walked on; weakened; wedged; wobbled; wobbled under; worked.

Noun Phrases

angle of the knee(s); arthritis of the knee(s); back of the knee(s); bend of the knee(s); bone of the knee(s); buckling of the knee(s); cap of the knee(s); cartilage of the knee(s); center of the knee(s); condition of the knee(s); contraction of the knee(s); creak of the knee(s); crook of the knee(s); curve of the knee(s); dislocation of the knee(s); edge of the knee(s); extension of the knee(s); folding of knees; fracture of the knee(s); fulcrum of the knee(s); grumbling of the knee(s); hardness of the knee(s); height of the knee(s); hollow of the knee(s); hyperextension of the knee(s); impact of the knee(s); inflammation of the knee(s); injury of the knee(s); inside of the knee(s); instability of the knee(s); joints of the knee(s); kind of knee(s); knob(s) of the knee(s); knocking of the knees; lesions of the knee(s); ligament of the knee(s); line of the knee(s); middle of the knees; motion of the knee(s); movement of the knee(s); muscles of the knee(s); pair of knees; part of the knee(s); point of the knee(s); position of the knee(s); pressure of the knee(s); region of the knee(s); rotation of the knee(s); sea of knees; set of knees; shape of the knee(s); side of the knee(s); size of the knee(s); skin of the knee(s); stability of the knee(s); state of the knee(s); stiffness of the knee(s); straightening of the knee(s); strain of the knee(s); strength of the knee(s); structure of the knee(s); surface of the knee(s); tap of the knee(s); tilt of the knee(s); tip of the knee(s); top of the knee(s); underside of the knee(s); weakness of the knee(s); wound of the knee(s).

USAGE EXAMPLES

My mother constantly whines about her *arthritic knees*.

His *weak knees buckled* under his own weight.

One-year-old Alexa *crawled on her chubby little knees* toward the door.

The kid from next door *planted his muddy knees* on the couch.

His *stiff knees were acting up* again.

24
LEG(S)

Adjectives in Alphabetical Order

A - L

absent; aching; active; additional; adjacent; afflicted; aged; ageing/aging; agile; amazing; ample; amputated; ancient; angled; aristocratic; armored; artery-lined; arthritic; artificial; ashy; astonishing; athletic; atrophied; attractive; awful; awkward; bad; baggy; bandaged; barbarous; bare; barrel-wide; battered; battle-wearied; beautiful; beefy; bent; best; best-looking; better; big; bipedal; birch-colored; bird-like; black; black-stockinged; black-tighted; black-trousered; blackened; blackish; bleeding; bloated; blonde; bloodied; bloody; blotchy; blue; blue-jean-clad; blue-jeaned; blurred; bony; booted; bound; bowed; braced; brawny; breathtaking; brier-scratched; broad; broken; bronzed; brown; bruised; bug-bitten; bulbous; bulging; bulky; burned; burning; busted; camouflaged; candy-striped; carved; chalky; childlike; chubby; chunky; clean; clothed; clubbed; clumsy; clunky; cocked; cold; colored; colossal; common; cool; corduroyed; cotton-stockinged; covered; craggy; cramped; cramping; crazy; creaky; creamy; crippled; crooked; crossed; crushed; curved; curvy; cute; cylindrical; dainty; damaged; damp; dampened; dangling; dark; dark-denimed; dark-haired; dead; decent; deformed; deft; delicate; delicious; denim-clad; denim-covered; dependable; desperate; determined; developed; diminutive; dimpled; dirty; disabled; disease-laden; diseased; disfigured; dismembered; disobedient; distant; distinct; distorted; divine; doll-like; dominant; doughy; drunken; dummy; dusty; dwarven; elegant; elephant-thick; elephantine; elevated; elongated; emaciated; encased; enchanting; endless; energetic; enormous; entangled; entire; excellent; exhausted; experienced; exposed; extended; extra; extra-long; extraordinary; faded-denimed; fair; fake; false; famous; fantastic; fast; fastest; fat; fattish; feeble; female; feminine; fickle; fierce; filthy; fine; fine-boned; finest; firm; fitful; flailing; flattened; flawless; fleshy; flexible; floating; floppy; folded; folded-up; folding; forty-seven-year-old; fractured; fragile; fragile-looking; frail; freckled; free; fresh; frozen; functional; funny; furry; fuzzy; gangly; gangrenous; gashed; gaunt; gentle; giant; gigantic; gimpy; glistening; glorious; god-like; good; gorgeous; graceful; grasshopper-like; greasy; great; grimy; growing; hairless; hairy; handsome; hard; hard-muscled; hard-working; healed; healing; healthy; heartbreaking; heavily-muscled; heavy; helpless; heronlike; high; high-heeled; hind; hobbling; honey-colored; horizontal; hot; huge; human; hurt; identical; idle; immaculate; immense; immovable; impossible; impressive; inclined; incomparable; incredible; inert; inflamed; inhuman; injured; inner; insect-like; insectile;

162

insectoid; inside; intertwined; inviting; involved; jean-clad; jeaned; jerky; jittery; jumping; jumpsuited; just-shaven; jutting; khaki-clad; kicking; knicked; knobby; knobby-kneed; knock-kneed; lacerated; lame; languid; lanky; large; lateral; lax; lazy; leaden; leading; lean; leather-clad; left; lifeless; limber; limp; limping; little; lively; locked; log-like; loggy; long; longest; longish; loose; lovely; lower; luscious.

M - Y

magnificent; male; mangled; manly; mannish; marble-white; marvelous; masculine; massive; meager; meaty; metallic; middle-aged; mighty; milk-white; miniature; misshapen; missing; monstrous; morning-stiff; moving; muddy; multi-jointed; multiple; muscled; muscular; naked; narrow; natural; nearest; nervous; never-ending; nice; nimble; nine-year-old; noiseless; normal; nubile; numb; numbed; numerous; nut-brown; nylon-clad; nylon-encased; oaken; odd; old; open; opened; opposite; ordinary; original; other; outer; outsized; outspread; outstanding; outstretched; outward-pointing; oversized; pained; painful; pale; pantyhose-clad; paper-pale; paralyzed; parted; passive; patient; pencil-thin; perfect; phony; pick-like; pillar-like; pink; pinkish; pinstriped; pipe-cleaner; pitiful; plain; planted; plastered; pleasant; pliant; plump; poor; popsicle-stick; powerful; powerful-looking; powerless; precious; pretty; prodigious; prosthetic; provocative; pudgy; puffy; pulled-up; puny; purple; quick; quivering; ragged; raised; rangy; raw; rawboned; razor-nicked; real; rear; red; red-stained; reddish; reedy; reedy-looking; regular; remaining; removable; restless; revealed; rheumatic; rickety; right; rigid; robust; rough; rubbery; running; saggy; sapped; scarlet; scarred; scorched; scraggly; scraped; scratched-up; scrawny; sculpted; sensational; sensual; serious; serviceable; severed; sexy; shackled; shaggy; shaky; shaped; shapeless; shapely; sharp; shaved-smooth; sheer; sheer-stockinged; shimmering; shiny; shivering; short; shortish; silk-clad; silk-glazed; silken; silky; simple; sinewy; single; skeletal; skinned; skinny; slacks-clad; sleek; sleeping; sleepy; slender; slight; slim; slippery; slow; small; smooth; smooth-shaven; soft; solid; sopping; sore; spangly; spastic; spiderlike; spidery; spiky; spindly; spiny; splayed; splendid; split; splotchy; spongy; spotted; sprained; sprawled; sprawling; springy; square; squashed; squat; squelchy; stabilizing; staggering; stalky; stalwart; stationary; steady; stick-thin; sticky; stiff; stiffened; stiffening; stilted; stiltlike; stilty; stockinged; stockingless; stocky; stout; straight; strained; strange; stretched; stretched-out; striding; stringy; striped; strong; stubbly; stubborn; stubby; stumpy; stunted; stupid; sturdy; substantial; succulent; summer-tanned; sun-kissed; sunbaked; sunburned/sunburnt; suntanned; superficial; superfluous; supple; supporting; swarthy; sweaty; swift; swinging; swollen; tall; tan; tangled; tanned; tapered; taut; tawny; teenage; tender; tense; tentative; terrible; terrific; thawing; thick; thick-boned; thin; throbbing; tied; tight; tilted; tiny; tired; tireless; tiring; toned; too-long; too-short; too-skinny; torn-off; tottering; trapped; tree-like; tree-sized; tree-trunk; trembling; tricky; trousered; trunk-like; tubular; tumbling; tweed-clad; tweedy; twiggy; twisted; twitching; ugly; unattractive; unbroken; uncertain; uncoordinated; uncouth; uncovered; undamaged; unending; unequal;

uneven; unfortunate; ungainly; unharmed; uninjured; unmoving; unprotected; unshaved; unshaven; unsteady; unstoppable; unsupported; unsure; unwilling; unwounded; upper; uppermost; upraised; upturned; useful; useless; varicose-veined; veined; veiny; velvet-clad; vertical; visible; walking-stick; wandlike; warm; waving; way-skinny; weak; weary; wee; weird; well-defined; well-formed; well-muscled; well-sculpted; well-shaped; well-toned; wet; white; white-stockinged; whitest; whole; wide; wiggling; wiggly; wild; wind-chapped; wire-thin; wiry; wiry-looking; withered; wobbly; womanish; wonderful; wooden; wool-covered; woolly; world-class; worn; wounded; wretched; wriggling; wrinkled; young; youthful.

Verbs and Phrasal Verbs in Alphabetical Order

A - C

absorbed; accentuated; accentuated by; accustomed to; ached; ached from; ached when; ached with; acted; activated; adapted; adapted for; added; adjusted; admired; adorned with; affected; allowed; allowed for; amazed; amazed at; amputated; amputated at; amputated below; anchored; anchored in; angled; angled in; angled over; appeared; appeared beside; appeared on; approached; approached from; arced; arced over; arose; arranged; associated with; assumed; atangle; ate up; attached to; attacked; backed down; backed up; balanced; balanced on; bandaged; banged; banged against; bared; bathed; bathed in; beamed; beat; became; began; began to; belonged; belonged to; bent; bent at; bent back; bent outward; bent sideways; bent under; bent up; betrayed; bicycled; bit off; bled; bled down; bled from; blew off; blew past; blocked; bobbed; boinged; boinged back; bolted; bolted to; bore; bothered; bounced; bounced up; bound; bound at; bound in; bound together; bound up; bound with; bowed; bowed from; bowed out; braced; braced against; braced apart; braced in; braced on; breached; broke; broke by; brought back; brought down; brought forward; brought up; bruised; bruised against; brushed; brushed against; brushed by; buckled; buckled at; buckled beneath; buckled under; buckled when; bulged; bulged with; bunched; bunched beneath; bunched up; buried; buried in; burned; burned from; burned with; busied; bustled; bustled ahead; buzzed; came against; came back; came down; came near; came out; came through; came together; came up; cared for; careened; carried; carried away; carried off; carried out; carved; cased; cast; caught; caught at; caught beneath; caught between; caught by; caught in; caught on; caught under; caught up; caused; caused by; ceased; chafed; chained to; changed; chased; chopped at; chopped off; churned; clacked against; clad in; clamped around; clanged; clanged against; clashed; clashed with; clasped; clattered; clattered against; clattered forward; clawed at; cleaned; cleaned off; cleared from; cleared to; clenched; clenched between; clicked; clicked on; climbed; closed; closed together; clothed; clothed in; clung; clung to; clutched; clutched at; cluttered; coated in; cocked; cocked out; cocked up; cocooned in; collapsed; collapsed against; collapsed beneath; collapsed under; collected; collided; collided with; compared to; complained; completed;

complied; concealed; conformed to; conjoined; connected; connected with; consisted of; contained; continued; contorted; contracted; convulsed; covered; covered by; covered in; covered up; covered with; cracked; cracked below; cradled; cradled in; crammed against; crammed into; crammed together; cramped; cramped from; craned over; crashed; crashed into; crashed through; creaked; creased; created; crept; crept up; crinkled; crinkled up; crippled; crisscrossed; crisscrossed like; crossed; crossed at; crossed behind; crossed beneath; crossed over; crossed up; crouched; crouched on; crowded together; crumpled on; crumpled under; crushed; crushed by; curled; curled around; curled beneath; curled on; curled to; curled under; curled up; cut; cut against; cut off; cut out.

D - I

dallied; danced; dangled; dangled above; dangled down; dangled from; dangled in; dangled off; dangled out; dangled over; dared to; darkened with; dashed; dashed from; decided; decorated; decorated with; defied; depended on; descended; descended to; developed; differed; dipped; dipped into; disappeared; disappeared around; disappeared behind; disappeared down; disappeared from; disappeared into; dismounted; displayed; dominated; doubled over; dragged; dragged along; draped; draped across; draped over; dressed; dressed in; drew back; drew in; drew together; drew under; drew up; drifted; drifted up; drooped; drooped at; drooped over; dropped; dropped into; dropped knee-deep; dropped onto; drove; drummed; dug into; dunked; dunked into; dwindled; eased; eased into; eased onto; elevated; elongated; emerged; emerged from; enabled; encased by; encased in; encircled; enclosed; enclosed in; encompassed; ended at; ended up; enjoyed; entangled; entangled in; entered; entwined; enveloped; enveloped in; erect with; erupted; erupted in; escaped; evoked; exaggerated; exaggerated by; excelled at; exercised; expanded; exploded; exposed; extend away; extend beyond; extended; extended to; extended toward; faced; faced inward; faced outward; faded; failed; failed to; fascinated; fastened; fastened to; fell; fell back; fell into; fell off; fell through; felt; felt better; felt like; felt trembly; fettered; fidgeted; fidgeted like; filled with; finished; fit; fitted; fixed; fixed in; flailed; flapped; flapped together; flashed; flashed by; flashed through; flattened; flew; flew about; flew backward; flew everywhere; flew in; flew out; flew skyward; flew up; flexed; flexed at; flicked out; floated; floated above; floated behind; floated on; floated out; floated straight; flopped; flopped against; flopped over; flopped sideways; flung; flung across; flung out; flung over; flung sideways; flushed; fluttered; fluttered along; folded; folded back; folded beneath; folded in; folded into; folded inward; folded under; folded underneath; folded up; followed; forced; formed; fought; fought off; found; fractured; freed; freed from; froze; furnished with; fused; fused together; gamboled; gamboled through; gathered; gathered both; gathered up; gave out; gave to; generated; girdled; gleamed; glinted; glinted in; glistened; glistened in; glistened with; glowed; glowed in; glowed with; glued to; got heavy; got sore; got tired; grated; grated on; grazed; grew; grew heavy; grew long; grew sore; grew tired; gripped; groaned; ground to a holt; guaranteed; hacked at; hacked off; happened to;

hardened; hardened by; healed; held; held beneath; held in; held out; held straight; held tight; held together; held up; helped; hid; hid by; hid in; hiked; hiked up; hinged; hit; hobbled; hobbled on; hooked; hooked around; hooked over; hovered; hovered over; huddled; huddled together; hugged; hunched; hunched over; hung; hung at; hung down; hung from; hung in; hung into; hung out; hung over; hurt; hurtled; hurtled through; immobilized; inched apart; inched together; included; increased; indicated; infested with; injured; inscribed with; inserted; inserted into; insisted; insisted on; inspected; inspired; intertwined; intertwined in; intertwined with; interwoven; interwoven under; itched.

J - R

jacked; jacked up; jackrabbited; jammed; jammed in; jammed under; jellied; jerked; jerked back; jerked sideways; jerked spasmodically; jerked with; jittered; joined; joined by; joined together; jolted; jolted back; jumped; jumped down; jumped out; jumped to; jumped up; jutted; jutted out; kept; kept on; kicked; kicked against; kicked at; kicked away; kicked back; kicked in; kicked out; kicked up; kinked up; knocked; knocked against; knotted; knotted together; labored; laced; laid; laid across; laid beneath; laid on; laid still; landed; landed in; languished; lashed; lashed out; lasted; laughed; leaned; leaned against; leaped; led; led to; led up; left; lengthened; lifted; lifted off; lifted toward; lifted up; lifted with; liked; limped; linked; linked with; loaded with; locked; locked against; locked around; locked between; locked straight; longed for; longed to; looked; loosened; loosened up; lopped off; lost; lowered; lunged; lunged forward; managed; mangled; mangled from; marched; marched forward; marched in; marked; marked with; measured; melded with; mended; merged; merged into; messed up; met; mingled; mingled with; missed; modified; mounted; moved; moved against; moved around; moved away; moved back; moved backward; moved between; moved by; moved down; moved fast; moved forward; moved in; moved through; moved under; needed; nipped at; numbed; obeyed; obscured; obscured by; offered; oiled; opened; opened to; oriented; oriented towards; ought; outlined; overlapped; paddled; pained; painted; paralyzed; parted; passed; pawed at; pedaled; peddled back; peeked; peeked out; peeped out; performed; picked up; pierced; pinched; pinched up; pinned; pinned beneath; pinned by; pinned with; pirouetted; placed; placed in; placed on; planted; planted firmly; planted in; played with; plodded; plodded into; plunged; plunged into; pointed; pointed forward; pointed in; pointed out; pointed to; pointed up; poised; poked; poked into; poked out; poked through; popped out; positioned; pounded; pounded over; pranced; pressed; pressed against; pressed to; pressed together; pressed up; prevented; prickled; prickled in; prickled with; pried open; produced; projected; propelled; propped against; propped on; propped up; propped upon; protected; protected by; protested; protruded; protruded from; proved; provided; provided with; pulled; pulled apart; pulled back; pulled down; pulled forward; pulled up; pulsed; pummeled; pumped; pumped forward; pumped hard; punctuated by; pushed; pushed against; pushed apart; pushed hard; pushed into; pushed through; pushed toward; pushed up; put in; put on; quaked; quivered; quivered in; raced; raced forward; radiated; raised;

ran; ratcheted up; rattled; rattled over; reached; reached out; reacted; reacted to; reared back; rebelled; rebelled against; rebelled at; received; recognized; reduced to; reeled; reeled around; refitted; reformed; refused; refused to; regained; remained; remembered; reminded; removed; rendered; repaired; replaced; replied; represented; required; resembled; resisted; responded; responded by; responded with; rested; rested on; rested over; resulted in; resumed; retracted; returned; revealed; revolted; ripped off; rippled; rippled down; rippled with; rocked; rocked back and forth; rocked on; rode; rolled; rolled up; rooted to; rose; rose back; rose off; rotated; rubbed; rubbed against; rubbed together.

S

sagged; sagged against; sank; sank in; sank into; sat; sat down; scabbed; scampered; scampered down; scissored; scissored under; scooted; scooted across; scorched; scrabbled; scrabbled over; scrambled; scrambled across; scraped; scraped across; scraped against; scraped over; scratched; screamed for; screamed out; screeched; screeched to a holt; scuffed; sculpted by; scurried; scurried across; scythed through; seated; seated on; secured; seemed; seized; seized up; sent; separated; served as; set; set in; set on; severed; severed at; shackled; shackled in; shaped; shattered by; shaved; sheared; sheared away; sheathed; sheathed in; shielded; shielded from; shifted; shook; shook beneath; shook like; shook under; shook with; shortened; shot down; shot out; shot up; shoved; shoved up; showcased; showcased in; showed; showed beneath; showed in; showed when; shrank; sidesaddled; signified; silhouetted; silhouetted by; skewed; skidded; skidded out; skidded sideways; skipped; slackened; slapped; slapped together; slashed; slashed through; slept; slid; slid away; slid off; slid out; slid over; slid through; slipped; slipped beneath; slipped between; slipped into; slipped on; slipped out; slipped over; sloped; sloped toward; slowed; slowed down; slumped; slung over; smarted; smarted from; smashed; smashed into; smelled; smelled like; smoothed; smoothed over; snagged; snagged by; snagged in; snagged on; snaked; snapped; snapped apart; snapped out; snipped at; soared; soared above; soared up; softened; spaced; sparked; spasmed; splashed; splashed in; splashed into; splayed; splayed beneath; splayed in; splayed on; splayed out; splayed over; split; spotted with; spraddled; sprang to; sprang up; sprawled; sprawled across; sprawled in; sprawled on; sprawled out; sprawled over; sprawled under; spread; spread apart; spread out; spread outwards; spread over; spreadeagled; sprinted; sprinted down; sprinted through; sprinted up; sprouted from; squeezed; squeezed around; squeezed tight; squeezed together; squirmed; stabbed; stained by; stared; stared back; stared straight; started; starved for; stayed; stayed in; stayed on; steadied; stepped; stepped forward; stepped into; stepped out; stepped over; stepped sideways; stepped up; stiffened; stilled; stood; stood on; stood out; stood up; stopped; straddled; straightened; straightened out; strained; strained against; strapped to; streaked; streaked across; streaked with; stretched; stretched across; stretched against; stretched apart; stretched back; stretched out; stretched toward; stretched upward; striped with; strode; strode forth; strode past; strove; struck;

struck out; struggled; stuck; stuck in; stuck into; stuck out; stuck through; stuck to; stuck together; stuck up; stuffed into; stung; stung from; suffered; suggested; supported; supported by; supported on; surged; surged forward; surged through; surged upward; surprised; surrounded; suspended; sustained; swam; swam through; swathed in; swayed; swayed back; swayed back and forth; sweat; swelled; swelled up; swirled; swished; swished back; swung; swung back; swung forward; swung freely; swung out; swung over; swung under; swung up.

T - Y

tamed; tangled; tangled in; tangled with; tanned; tanned in; tapered; tapered down; tapped; tapped against; teetered; teetered over; teetered under; tended to; tensed; testified to; thrashed; thrashed about; thrashed in; thrashed over; thrashed through; threatened to; threshed up; threw out; threw up; throbbed; throbbed when; throbbed with; thrust; thrust backward; thrust forward; thrust into; thrust out; thrust straight; thrust toward; thrust up; thumped; tickled; tied; tied across; tied at; tied below; tied beneath; tied down; tied off; tied to; tied together; tied under; tied up; tied with; tightened; tightened around; tightened up; tilted; tilted up; tingled; tingled with; tipped; tipped forward; tipped up; told; took; took off; took up; tore through; tore up; tossed; tossed around; tottered; tottered under; touched; trailed; trailed behind; trailed beneath; trapped; trapped in; trapped under; tread; treated; trembled; trembled beneath; trembled from; trembled under; tried to; tripped; troubled; trudged; tucked below; tucked beneath; tucked in; tucked into; tucked under; tucked underneath; tucked up; turned; turned into; turned inward; turned out; turned outward; turned slightly; turned to; twined about; twined around; twisted; twisted around; twisted at; twisted beneath; twisted inward; twisted on; twisted out; twisted under; twitched; twitched apart; twitched under; uncovered; undulated; undulated upward; unfolded; united; unrolled; untied; unweaved; unwound; used; used for; used to; vanished; vanished into; varied; vaulted; vaulted over; vibrated; vibrated against; waddled; waddled around; waded; waggled; waited; waited on; walked; walked across; walked by; walked down; walked in; walked off; walked out; walked toward; wanted; warmed; wasted no time; waved; waved in; wavered; wavered in; weakened; weakened under; wedged against; wedged between; weighed; went; went about; went around; went down; went on; went out; went through; went under; went up; wet; wet from; wheeled; whined; whipped; whipped about; whipped across; whipped between; whirled; whirled around; widened; wiggled; wiggled into; willed to; windmilled; wiped; wiped down; withered; wobbled; wobbled beneath; wobbled under; wore; wore down; wore out; worked; worsened; wound; wove; wrapped; wrapped about; wrapped around; wrapped tight(ly); wrapped up; wrenched apart; wriggled; writhed; writhed on; yanked; yanked up; yanked upward.

absence of the leg(s); ache of the leg(s); action of the leg(s); aid of the leg(s); amputation of the leg(s); angle of the leg(s); appearance of the leg(s); area of the leg(s); arrangement of the leg(s); arteries of the leg(s); aspect of the leg(s); axis of the leg(s); back(s) of the leg(s); base of the leg(s); bit of leg; blur of leg(s); bone(s) of the leg(s); border of the leg(s); bottom of the leg(s); boundaries of the leg(s); calf/calves of the leg(s); center of the leg(s); churning of leg(s); circumference of the leg(s); clusters of leg(s); coldness of the leg(s); color of the leg(s); condition of the leg(s); contraction of the leg(s); control of the leg(s); couple of legs; cramp(s) in the leg(s); curvature of the leg(s); deformity of the leg(s); development of the leg(s); disease of the leg(s); display of leg(s); edge(s) of the leg(s); elevation of the leg(s); end of the leg(s); examination of the leg(s); exercise of the leg(s); expanse of the leg(s); extension of the leg(s); extremity of the leg(s); flesh of the leg(s); forest of legs; form of the leg(s); fracture of the leg(s); front of the leg(s); gangrene of the leg(s); glimpse of leg(s); growth of the leg(s); hairs of the leg(s); half of the leg; heap of legs; heaviness of the leg(s); height of the leg(s); inflammation of the leg(s); inside(s) of the leg(s); joints of the leg(s); kicking of the leg(s); kind of legs; knee of the leg; lack of leg(s); length of the leg(s); line of the leg(s); loss of the leg(s); lot of leg(s); mess of legs; mile of leg(s); motion of the leg(s); movement of the leg(s); multiplicity of legs; muscle(s) of the leg(s); nerves of the leg(s); number of legs; numbness of the leg(s); pair of legs; paralysis of the leg(s); part(s) of the leg(s); pillars of legs; placement of the leg(s); portion of the leg(s); position of the leg(s); posture of the leg(s); power of the leg(s); pressure on the leg(s); range of the leg(s); rest of the leg(s); rigidity of the leg(s); rotation of the leg(s); row of legs; scores of legs; sea of legs; section(s) of the leg(s); segment(s) of the leg(s); separation of the leg(s); series of legs; set(s) of legs; shape of the leg(s); shortness of the leg(s); show of leg(s); side(s) of the leg(s); sinews of the leg(s); size of the leg(s); skin of the leg(s); sort of legs; spasms of the leg(s); spreading of the legs; state of the leg(s); stiffness of the leg(s); stir of legs; strength of the leg(s); stretch of the leg(s); structure of the leg(s); surface of the leg(s); swelling of the leg(s); swing of the leg(s); swish of legs; tangle of legs; tendency of the leg(s); tendons of the leg(s); texture of the leg(s); thicket of legs; thickness of the leg(s); thrombosis of the leg(s); thrust of leg(s); tips of the leg(s); top(s) of the leg(s); treatment of the leg(s); tremor of the leg(s); twist of the leg(s); twitch of the leg(s); type of legs; veins of the leg(s); view of the leg(s); weakness of the leg(s); weight of the leg(s); width of the leg(s)..

USAGE EXAMPLES

His *aging legs struggled to climb* the steep staircase.

The man had *beefy legs* and a distinct limp.

Her *doughy legs floated* just above the water's surface.

He studied her *long firm legs* as they *ascended* the ladder.

The boy's *scrawny legs* managed to *carry* him across.

25
LIP(S)

Adjectives in Alphabetical Order

A - E

abused; adolescent; affectionate; African; age-thin; agitated; alert; amber; amorous; angry; anxious; apple-red; appreciative; apricot; arced; ardent; arid; aristocratic; aroused; arrogant; ashen; ashy; audible; avaricious; awful; baked; balmy; barbarous; bashful; battered; bearded; beardless; beauteous; beautiful; bee-stung; beloved; betraying; big; biting; bitter; black; blackened; blanched; bleeding; blessed; blistered; bloated; blood-drained; blood-red; blood-soaked; blood-sticky; bloodied; bloodless; bloody; blubbery; blue; blue-red; bluish; bold; bottom; bow-shaped; boyish; brazen; breathless; bright; bright-pink; brightly-colored; brittle; broad; broken; brown; bruise-colored; bruised; bubble-gum-colored; budding; bulbous; burned / burnt; burning; busted; buzzing; candy-pink; careless; carmine; Caucasian; chafed; chapped; charming; chaste; cherry-flavored; cherry-painted; cherry-red; childish; chilly; china-doll; chiseled; chubby; circular; clammy; classic; classy; clean; clean-cut; clear; cleft; clenched; closed; coarse; coconut-flavored; cold; collagen-filled; collapsed; colored; colorless; compact; complaining; compliant; compressed; confident; considerable; contemptuous; contorted; contumelious; cool; coral-tinted; cracked; craggy; creased; creepy; crimson; crimson-glossed; crinkled; crooked; cruel; crusted; cupid; cupid's-bow; curled; curved; curvy; cut; dainty; damp; dark; dark-colored; dark-red; darkened; deadly; deceitful; deep; deft; delicate; delicious; demure; desiccated; desired; dewy; diminutive; dirty; discolored; disdainful; disgusted; distended; distinct; distinguishing; distorted; divine; doll-like; doubtful; downturned; downward-curving; dried; dried-up; drooping; droopy; drunken; dry; dumb; eager; electric; elegant; eloquent; English; enigmatic; enormous; envious; European; ever-pursed; ever-silenced; exposed; expressive; exquisite; extreme.

F - Q

faint; fair; fake; faltering; familiar; famished; fat; feeble; feminine; fervent; fevered; feverish; fierce; fiery; fiery-red; fine; finely-chiseled; fire-engine-red; fire-red; firm; fish-like; flabby; flaccid; flapping; flappy; flat; flattering; flawless; fleshless; fleshy; florid; fluent; fluttering; foaming; foamy; foolish; formidable; foul; fragrant; frank; free; fresh; friendly; frost-chapped; frosted; frosty; frozen; fruit-scented; fruity; full; fullish; gaping; gashed; generous; genteel; gentle; ghastly; giant; gifted; girlish; glad; glassy; glistening; glossed; glossy; glowing; goddess-like; gorgeous; gracious; grape-flavored; grape-toned; grateful; gray; greasy; great; greedy; grim; grinning; gross; grotesque; grouchy;

gummy; haggard; half-closed; handsome; happy; hard; harsh; haughty; heavenly; hectic; high; honeyed; hooked; horny; hot; huge; humble; humid; hungry; hurt; hushed; hypocritical; icy; immobile; impassioned; imperial; impure; incredible; indifferent; indignant; indrawn; infolded; injured; inner; innocent; inviting; irresistible; jet-black; joyful; juicy; kindly; kissable; languid; large; lascivious; laughing; leathery; lifeless; lipstick-red; lipsticked; lipstickless; liquid; little; little-girl; live; liver-colored; liverish; livid; locked; loose; lovely; loving; lower; luscious; lush; mad; made-up; magnificent; maiden; manipulative; manly; maroon; masculine; massive; maternal; mauve; meaty; meek; mellifluous; melodious; melon-tinted; merciless; merry; mild; milky; misshapen; mocking; modest; moist; moistened; motionless; mournful; mustached; moving; murmuring; muted; naked; narrow; narrowed; nasty; natural; naughty; nervous; nice; noble; numb; obstinate; odorous; oh-so-perfect; old; open; opposite; orange; other; outer; outraged; outside; oval; overhanging; oversize; painted; pale; pale-pink; pallid; panting; paralyzed; parched; parted; passionate; passive; pasty; peach-colored; pendulous; perfect; persuasive; perverse; petulant; pierced; pinched; pink; pink-glossed; pink-outlined; pink-tinged; pinkish; pious; piteous; placid; pleading; pleasant; plum-colored; plump; plumped; plush; poisonous; poked-out; polished; pouted; pouting; pouty; powdered; precious; pressed; pretty; prim; prim-looking; privileged; profane; projecting; prominent; protruding; protuberant; proud; puckered; pudgy; puffed; puffy; pure; purple; purple-glossed; purple-ridged; purplish; pursed; pushed-out; quivering.

R - Z

radiant; ragged; rainforest-green; raised; rapid; ratty; razor-thin; readable; ready; red; red-glossed; red-lipsticked; red-orange; red-painted; red-stained; red-violet; refined; reluctant; resolute; responsive; restless; retracting; rhombic; rich; rigid; ripe; ripe-cherry; rose-colored; rose-petal; rose-pink; roseate; rosy; rough; round; rounded; royal; rubbery; rubied; ruddy; rude; sable; sacred; sad; salty; sandpapery; sardonic; satisfied; saucy; scab-encrusted; scalded; scalloped; scaly; scarlet; scarred; scorched; scornful; sculpted; sealed; seductive; sensitive; sensual; sensuous; serious; serrated; sexy; shadowy; shaped; shapeless; shapely; sharp; shell-pink; shining; shiny; short; shriveled; shrunken; shy; sickly; silent; silken; sinful; skeptical; skinny; slack; slackened; slanderous; sleeping; slender; slick; slight; sloping; sloppy; slow; slow-moving; slug-like; small; smeared; smiling; smoochy; smooth; snarling; snow-white; soft; soft-looking; solemn; sore; soundless; speechless; spittle-flecked; spittled; split; stained; starved; steady; stern; sticky; stiff; still-smiling; stinging; stony; straight; straining; strange; strangled; stretched; stricken; strong; stubborn; stuck-out; stunning; subtle; succulent; sugared; sulky; sullen; sun-cracked; sunburned / sunburnt; sunken; sweat-salted; sweaty; sweet; swelling; swollen; syrupy; tangerine; tangled; tasteful; taut; tempting; tender; tense; thankful; thick; thickish; thin; thirsty; thoughtful; throbbing; tight; tightened; timid; tingling; tinted; tiny; tired; toothless; top; treacherous; trembling; tremulous; truthful; tumid; tuneful; turned-up; twisted; twitching; ugly; unclosed; unkissed; unmoving; unpainted;

unresponsive; unsmiling; unwilling; unyielding; upper; upturned; velvety; venomous; vigorous; vile; violet; vivid; voiceless; voluptuous; vulgar; wan; waning; wanton; warm; waxy; weak; weary; weathered; well-curved; well-formed; well-proportioned; well-shaped; wet; whiskered; white; wicked; wide; wild; willing; wise; withered; womanish; wrinkled; young; youthful; zipped.

Verbs and Phrasal Verbs in Alphabetical Order

A - F

acted; admired; agreed; angled; announced; announced to; anointed; anointed with; answered; appeared; applied to; approached; arched; arose; aroused; arrived; articulated; asked; assumed; attached; attached to; avowed; baited; baited with; bared; bathed; became flush; belied; bent; bent into; bestowed; betrayed; bit; blanched; blazed; bled; bled from; blended; blessed; blew; blistered; blurred; bore; bracketed; breathed; brimmed with; broke into; brought; brushed; brushed against; brushed over; bubbled; bulged; bulged out; bunched; buried; buried in; burned; burnished with; burst; busted; called; came apart; came down; came together; captured; caressed; carried; caught; caught between; caught by; caused; cautioned; ceased; changed; chapped; chapped by; chattered; chilled; circled; claimed; clamped; clamped between; clamped down; clamped tight; clamped together; clasped; cleaned; cleared; clenched; closed; closed around; closed on; closed over; closed tight; clung; clung together; coated with; collapsed; collapsed into; collided; colored; complained; composed; compressed; compressed into; compressed together; concealed; confessed; connected; connected with; continued; contorted; contracted; contrasted with; conveyed; cooled; covered; covered with; cracked; creased; creased into; cried; cried; crimped; crimped into; cringed; crinkled; crooned; cuffed; cupped; cupped around; curled; curled around; curled at; curled back; curled down; curled in; curled into; curled inward; curled up; curled upward; curled with; curved; curved down; curved into; curved up; curved upward; curved with; danced; dangled; dared; darkened; darkened into; declared; decorated; decorated by; deepened; denied; descended; devoured; dipped; disappeared; disclosed; displayed; divided; divided into; dominated; downturned; drank; drew back; drew down; drew into; drew near; drew tight; drew together; drew up; dried; drifted; dripped; drooped; dropped; drove; eased back; edged; edged into; enclosed; engulfed; entered; erupted; erupted in; escaped; exaggerated; expanded; expected; exploded; exploded in; expressed; extended; extended toward; extending; extruded; faced; faltered; fastened; fastened on; fastened to; fattened; fell; fell apart; fell into; felt; filled with; firmed; fixed; flapped; flared; flared out; flashed; flattened; flattened against; flecked with; fled; flew apart; flicked; flickered; flickered in; flickered into; flirted with; flowed; fluttered; foamed; folded; folded around; folded back; folded into; followed; forced; forced upward; formed; formed into; found; framed; froze; furnished with; fused together.

G - R

gained; gaped; garnished with; gasped; gasped for; gathered; gave off; glared; gleamed; gleamed with; glided; glided against; glided over; glistened; glittered; glossed; glowed; glued to; glued together; gobbled; grazed; greased up; grew; groped for; held; held tight; held together; hesitated; hid; highlighted; hiked up; hinted at; hitched; hovered; hugged; hummed; hung; hung down; hungered; hurt; implored; impressed; imprinted; indicated; inspired; invited; issued from; jerked; jiggled; joined; joined with; jutted; jutted out; kissed; knocked against; laced; laced with; lacquered; laid; landed on; latched; latched onto; laughed; layered with; left; lengthened; lent; let; licked; lifted; lifted up; lined; lingered; lingered on; locked; locked together; looked; loosened; lost; loved; made up; managed; marked; marked with; mashed; mashed against; mashed together; masked; melted into; met; mingled with; moistened; moistened with; mouthed; moved; moved across; moved against; moved along; moved closer; moved down; moved in; moved over; moved to; moved too; moved up; moved upward; muffled; mumbled; murmured; muttered; narrowed; neared; needed; nibbled; nibbled at; notched; nuzzled; obeyed; oozed; opened; outlined; overflowed; painted on; paled; parted; passed; passed over; peeled; peeled back; perched; perspired; pierced; pierced with; pinched; pinched together; pinned together; placed; played at; plumped; poised; poked; poked out; popped out; pounced; pounced on; pouted; prepared; presented; pressed; pressed against; pressed to; pressed together; pressed up; produced; projected; prompted; pronounced; protected; protruded; puckered; puffed; puffed out; pulled away; pulled back; pursed; pursed together; pushed; pushed forward; pushed out; pushed together; pushed up; quavered; quirked; quirked upward; quivered; raised; reached; read; receded; received; reddened; reflected; refrained; refused; regained; relaxed; relaxed into; released; remained; remembered; reminded; repeated; repelled; replied; resembled; responded; rested; rested against; rested on; resumed; retained; retracted; retreated; returned; revealed; roamed; rolled; rose; rounded; rubbed; rubbed against.

S - Z

said; sang; savored; screwed up; scrunched; scuttled across; sealed; sealed tight; sealed up; searched; searched out; secured; separated; set; settled; settled into; settled on; shaped; shifted; shifted ever; shimmered; shivered; shone; shook; shook upwards; shot out; showed; shriveled; shuddered; shuddered apart; shut; shut over; shut tight; signified; skimmed; slackened; slanted; slanted upward; slapped; slathered; slathered with; slicked; slicked with; slid; slid along; slid back; slid down; slid over; slid up; slobbered; slobbered over; slowed; smacked; smeared with; smiled; snapped; snapped back; snapped into; snarled; sneered; softened; sought; sounded; spasmed; spewed; spilled; split; spoke; sported; sprang up; spread; squeezed; squeezed together; squirmed; stained with; stammered; stayed; stiffened; stirred; stitched; stitched together; stood; stood out; stood up; stopped; straightened; strained; stretched; stroked; struck; struggled; stuck against; stuck out; stuck to; stuck together; stung; sucked; sucked in; suggested; sunk; surrounded; surveyed; swarmed; swarmed around;

swelled; swooped; swooped down; talked; tasted; tasted like; teased; tensed; thickened; thinned; thrilled; thrust; thrust forward; thrust out; tickled; tightened; tilted; tilted into; tilted toward; tilted up; tinged; tinged with; tingled; tipped up; told; took; took on; touched; traced; trailed; trapped; trapped between; traveled; traveled over; trembled; trembled against; trembled in; trembled on; trembled with; tried; tucked; tucked inside; tucked into; tugged; tugged at; turned; turned down; turned downward; turned up; turned upward; twisted; twisted into; twisted up; twisted with; twitched; unfolded; united; unsealed; uttered; vanished; ventured; vibrated; vibrated with; wagged; waited; wandered; wanted; warmed; went tight; went to; wet; whispered; whitened; widened; widened in; widened into; wilted; withered; wobbled; won; wore; worked; wrapped around; wrinkled; writhed; yearned; yearned for; yielded; zipped.

Noun Phrases

angle of the lip(s); appearance of the lip(s); base of the lip(s); blueness of the lip(s); border of the lip(s); brushing of lip(s); center of the lip(s); cleft(s) of the lip; closure of the lip(s); color of the lip(s); compression of the lip(s); condition of the lip(s); contact of the lip(s); contraction of the lip(s); control of the lip(s); corners of the lip(s); curling of the lip(s); curl of the lip(s); curve of the lip(s); displacement of the lip(s); dryness of the lip(s); edge of the lip(s); expression of the lip(s); form of the lip(s); fullness of the lip(s); hue of the lip(s); kind of lip(s); kiss of lip(s); line of the lip(s); lowering of the lip(s); meeting of the lip(s); motion of the lip(s); movement of the lip(s); numbness of the lip(s); outline of the lip(s); pair of lip(s); pallor of the lip(s); parting of the lip(s); position of the lip(s); pout of the lip(s); press of lip(s); pressure of the lip(s); protrusion of the lip(s); pursing of the lip(s); quirk of the lip(s); quiver of the lip(s); redness of the lip(s); retraction of the lip(s); separation of the lip(s); set of lip(s); shape of the lip(s); side of the lip(s); skin of the lip(s); smacking of the lip(s); smack of the lip(s); smile of the lip(s); sound of the lip(s); spreading of lip(s); surface of the lip(s); sweetness of the lip(s); swipe of the lip(s); taste of lip(s); tension of the lip(s); thickness of the lip(s); thinning of the lip(s); tightening of the lip(s); tip of the lip(s); touch of the lip(s); tremor of the lip(s); twist of the lip(s); twitching of the lip(s); twitch of the lip(s); vibration of the lip(s); wetness of the lip(s).

USAGE EXAMPLES

John *claimed her apple-red lips* with a passionate kiss.

He traced her *bow-shaped lips* with the tip of his finger.

Ryan had a *bloodied lip* which he explained he got from a scuffle with Michael.

The wind further agitated her *cracked lips*.

The child's *plump lips murmured* something but it was too faint to hear.

26
MIND

Adjectives in Alphabetical Order

A - E

able; abnormal; absent; absorbent; abstract; academic; accurate; aching; acquisitive; active; acute; addled; administrative; adolescent; advanced; adventurous; affectionate; afflicted; aggressive; agile; aging / ageing; agitated; agrarian; ailing; alert; alien; almighty; almost-perfect; altered; altruistic; amazing; ambitious; amiable; ample; analytic; analytical; ancient; angelic; angry; anguished; anxious; appreciative; apprehensive; archaic; ardent; argumentative; aristocratic; arrogant; artificial; artistic; aspiring; astonishing; astral; astute; atrophied; attentive; august; austere; authoritarian; autonomous; average; awake; aware; bad; balanced; barbaric; barren; basic; beastly; beautiful; befogged; befuddled; bellicose; bemused; benevolent; besotted; best; better; bewildered; biased; big; bitter; black; blank; bleary; blind; blunted; bold; bored; boundless; bounteous; boyish; brave; bright; brightest; brilliant; broad; broken; brooding; brutal; brutish; budding; buoyant; bureaucratic; burning; busy; busying; callow; calm; candid; capable; capacious; capricious; captivating; captive; careful; careless; carnal; cautious; celebrated; changeable; changed; changing; chaotic; charitable; charming; chaste; cheerful; childish; childlike; civic; civilized; classic; clean; clear; clearest; clever; closed; clouded; cloudy; clumsy; cluttered; coarse; cobwebbed; cognitive; cold; collective; colossal; comic; commanding; commercial; common; commonplace; commonsense; communal; compassionate; competent; complete; complex; complicated; composed; comprehensive; computer-based; computerized; concentrated; conceptual; concrete; confident; confused; congenial; conquering; conscientious; conscious; consenting; conservative; considerate; consistent; constricted; constructive; contemplative; contemporary; contented; contorted; contrite; controlling; conventional; convinced; convoluted; cool; corporate; correct; corrupt; countless; courageous; covert; covetous; crafty; crazed; crazy; creative; credulous; criminal; crippled; critical; crude; cruel; cultivated; cultured; cunning; curious; cynical; damaged; damned; dangerous; daring; dark; darkened; dauntless; dazed; dazzling; dead; debased; decent; decisive; deductive; deep; deepest; defective; defenseless; definite; degenerate; dejected; deliberate; delicate; delirious; delusional; demented; dependent; depraved; depressed; deranged; despairing; desperate; despondent; desponding; destructive; detached; determined; developing; devilish; devious; devotional; devout; diabolical; different; differing; dim; diminished; dimming; diplomatic; direct; dirty; disapproving; discerning; disciplined; discontented; discriminating; diseased; disembodied; disgusting; dishonest; disinterested; disordered;

disorderly; dispassionate; distant; distempered; distinct; distinguished; distorted; distracted; distraught; distressed; disturbed; diverse; divided; divine; dizzying; docile; dogmatic; dominant; dormant; doubtful; doubtless; down-to-earth; draconic; dramatic; dreaming; dreamy; drowsy; drug-addled; drugged; drunk; drunken; dry; dualistic; dull; dullest; dynamic; eager; earnest; earthly; easy-going; eccentric; eclectic; economical; effective; efficient; elastic; elegant; elevated; embittered; eminent; emotional; empirical; empty; encyclopedic; energetic; enlightened; enormous; enquiring; enterprising; enthusiastic; entire; entrepreneurial; envious; equable; equal; errant; erratic; essential; eternal; ethereal; ethical; ever-sharp; everyday; evil; evolved; exact; exacting; exalted; excellent; exceptional; excitable; excited; exciting; exhausted; expansive; experienced; experiential; expert; extraordinary.

F - R

fading; faint; fair; faithful; fallible; false; familiar; fanciful; fantastic; fascinating; fastidious; fearful; fearless; feeble; female; feminine; fertile; fervent; fervid; fevered; feverish; fickle; fiendish; fierce; fiery; filthy; financial; fine; finest; firm; firmest; first-class; flaming; flexible; focused; fogged; foggy; foolish; forceful; foremost; forensic; forgiving; formidable; foul; fourth-rate; foxy; fractured; fragile; frank; frantic; free; frenzied; fresh; fretting; fried; friendly; frightened; frivolous; frugal; fruitful; frustrated; fuddled; full; functioning; fundamental; furious; fuzzy; general; generous; genial; gentile; gentle; genuine; giant; giddy; gifted; gigantic; girlish; gloomy; glorious; glowing; god-given; goddamn; godlike; godly; golden; good; governing; gracious; grateful; great; greatest; greedy; green; gross; growing; grown-up; guiding; guileless; guilty; gullible; habitual; half-asleep; half-awake; hallucinated; hallucinatory; happy; hard; harmonious; harried; haughty; haunted; healthy; hearty; heated; heathen; heavenly; heavy; heinous; heroic; high; higher; highest; highly-focused; holistic; holy; honest; honorable; hopeful; hospitable; hostile; human; humane; humble; humblest; humorous; hungover; hungry; hyperactive; ideal; idealistic; ideological; idle; ignoble; ignorant; ill; illiberal; illiterate; illogical; illumined; illustrious; imaginative; imitative; immature; immortal; impartial; impassioned; impatient; impenetrable; imperfect; imperial; imperious; impetuous; implant-enhanced; important; impoverished; impractical; impressible; impressionable; imprisoned; impulsive; impure; inactive; inattentive; incisive; incredible; incredulous; indecisive; indefatigable; independent; indifferent; individual; indolent; industrious; inert; inexperienced; infallible; infantile; inferior; infinite; infirm; inflamed; inflexible; influential; informed; ingenious; ingenuous; innate; inner; innermost; innocent; innovative; innumerable; inquiring; inquisitive; insane; insatiable; insightful; inspiring; instinctive; institutionalized; intact; integrated; intellectual; intelligent; intense; interested; interesting; internal; intrepid; intriguing; introspective; intuitive; inventive; investigative; invisible; ironic; irrational; irreparable; irresolute; irritable; isolated; jaded; jealous; joyful; joyous; judicial; judicious; jumbled; jumpy; just; juvenile; keen; keenest; kind; kindred; kingly; knowledgeable; laborious; labyrinthine; languid; large; lawful; lawyerly; layered; lazy; legal;

legalistic; legislative; lesser; liberal; like; limited; linear; linked; listening; listless; literal; literary; literate; little; lively; living; local; lofty; logical; lonely; lovely; loving; low; lower; lowest; lowly; loyal; lucid; lucky; luminous; lyrical; mad; maddened; magnanimous; magnificent; majestic; male; malevolent; malicious; malignant; malleable; managerial; manly; marvelous; masculine; massive; materialistic; maternal; mathematical; mature; maturing; mean; mechanical; medical; medieval; mediocre; meditative; melancholy; mental; mercenary; mercurial; mere; merged; merry; messy; metaphysical; methodical; middle-aged; mightiest; mighty; military; mired; mischievous; mistaken; mixed-up; moderate; modern; modest; moral; morbid; mortal; mournful; muddled; multiple; mundane; murderous; musical; mysterious; mystic; mystical; mythic; naive; naked; narrow; nasty; natural; naughty; negative; nervous; neurotic; neutral; new; new-age; newborn; nimble; ninety-year-old; noble; noblest; nonconscious; nonlocal; nonphysical; normal; novel; numb; obedient; observant; obsessed; obstinate; obtuse; old; omnipotent; omnipresent; omniscient; one-track; open; opposite; oppressed; optimistic; ordered; orderly; ordinary; organized; original; orthodox; other; outer; outrageous; outstanding; overactive; overall; overanalytical; overconcentrated; overheated; oversensitive; overworked; overwrought; panicked; paranoid; parental; partial; particular; passionate; passive; paternal; patient; patriarchal; patriotic; patrolling; peaceful; peculiar; pedantic; pellucid; penetrating; penetrative; pensive; perceptive; perfect; persistent; perverse; perverted; petty; phenomenal; philanthropic; philosophic; philosophical; photographic; physical; piercing; pious; placid; plain; playful; plebian; pliant; poetic; poetical; polarized; polished; political; polluted; poor; popular; positive; postmodern; potential; powerful; practical; pragmatic; precious; precise; precocious; prehistoric; prejudiced; preoccupied; prepared; prescient; present; preserved; pretty; prevailing; prideful; primal; primitive; primordial; princely; private; probing; prodigious; productive; professional; profound; progressive; prolific; prophetic; prosaic; proud; prudent; prurient; psychic; psychological; psychopathic; public; pulsing; puny; pure; purest; puzzled; questioning; quick; quickest; quiet; quirky; racing; racist; radiant; radical; raging; rambling; rancorous; rapid; rare; rational; rationalistic; razor-sharp; reactive; ready; real; reasonable; rebellious; receptive; refined; reflective; regular; relaxed; relentless; religious; reluctant; remarkable; renewed; resistant; resolute; resourceful; respective; responsible; responsive; restless; retentive; reverent; revolutionary; rich; right; righteous; rightful; rigid; ripe; rising; robust; romantic; roomy; rotted; rousing; routine; roving; royal; rude; rudimentary; rural; ruthless.

S - Y

sad; sagacious; sane; sanguine; satisfied; savage; schizophrenic; scholarly; scholastic; scientific; scintillating; seamless; seasoned; secret; secular; selective; self-conscious; self-involved; selfish; selfless; seminal; senseless; sensible; sensitive; sensual; sensuous; sentient; sentimental; separate; serene; serious; servile; shallow; sharp; sharpest; shattered; shielded; shocked; shrewd; sick; silent; silly; similar; simple; sincere; sinful; single; singular; sinless; skeptical;

slavish; sleep-deprived; sleep-logged; sleep-numbed; sleeping; sleepless; sleepy; slow; sluggish; slumbering; sly; small; smart; smug; soaring; sober; sobered; social; soggy; solid; solitary; sophisticated; sordid; sore; sorrowful; sound; sovereign; spacious; special; speculative; spellbound; spinning; spiritual; splendid; splintered; spotless; sprightly; stable; stagnant; standard; steadfast; steady; steel-trap; steely; stellar; sterile; stimulated; stimulating; stoned; stony; stout; straightforward; strange; strategic; stressed; stricken; strong; stubborn; studious; stunned; stupid; subconscious; subjective; sublime; subliminal; submissive; substantial; subtle; suffering; sufficient; suggestive; suicidal; sullen; superb; superconscious; superficial; superior; superstitious; supreme; susceptible; suspicious; sweet; swift; sympathetic; synthetic; systematic; talented; teachable; technical; technological; teeming; teenage; temperate; tenacious; tender; terrible; thankful; theological; theoretical; thick; third-rate; thirsty; thoughtful; thoughtless; thrifty; throbbing; throttled; tidy; tight; timeless; timid; timorous; tiny; tired; tiresome; tolerant; top; tormented; torn; torpid; tortured; total; totalitarian; tough; toughened; towering; traditional; trained; tranquil; transcendent; transcendental; transformed; transparent; trapped; treacherous; tribal; trivial; troubled; troubling; true; trustworthy; truthful; turbulent; twisted; two-track; ugly; ultimate; unaided; unbalanced; unbelieving; unbiased; uncanny; uncertain; unclean; unclouded; uncluttered; uncommon; unconquerable; unconscious; uncontrolled; unconventional; uncorrupted; uncritical; uncultivated; uncultured; undaunted; undecided; underemployed; undeveloped; undiminished; undisciplined; undisturbed; undivided; uneasy; uneducated; unenlightened; unfamiliar; unfettered; unforgiving; unformed; unfurnished; ungenerous; unhappy; unhealthy; unified; unimaginative; uninformed; uninstructed; unique; universal; unknown; unmatched; unoccupied; unperturbed; unphilosophical; unprejudiced; unprepared; unpretentious; unquiet; unreflective; unruffled; unschooled; unscientific; unscrupulous; unsettled; unsophisticated; unsound; unstable; unsteady; unsuspecting; unsuspicious; unswerving; untamed; unthinking; untouchable; untrained; untroubled; untutored; unusual; unwilling; urban; utilitarian; vacant; valiant; various; vast; venturesome; versatile; vicious; vigilant; vigorous; vindictive; violent; virginal; virile; virtuous; visionary; visual; vital; vivacious; vivid; volatile; voluminous; voracious; vulgar; wakeful; wandering; warlike; warped; wary; watchful; wayward; weak; weakest; weary; weird; well-balanced; well-prepared; well-trained; whimsical; whirring; whole; wholesome; wicked; wide-open; wild; willing; wine-addled; wise; wisest; wishful; witty; womanly; wonderful; wondrous; working; world-class; worldly; wormy; worried; worthy; wounded; wretched; wrong; yet-to-be-scarred; young; youthful.

Verbs and Phrasal Verbs in Alphabetical Order

A - C
abandoned; abated; abhorred; abided; abolished; absorbed; absorbed by; absorbed in; absorbed with; accepted; accommodated; accompanied by;

accompanied with; accomplished; accounted for; accused; accustomed to; ached; ached after; ached from; ached with; achieved; acknowledged; acquainted with; acquiesced; acquiesced in; acquired; acted; acted on; acted through; acted upon; acted with; actuated by; adapted; added; added to; addled; addled by; addressed; adhered; adhered to; adjusted; adjusted to; admitted; adopted; advised; affected; affected by; affected with; affirmed; afflicted with; afforded; aged; agreed; agreed with; aided by; aimed at; alerted; alerted to; alienated from; allowed; allowed for; altered; alternated; alternated between; amounted to; announced; answered; anticipated; appeared; applied; applied to; appointed; appreciated; apprehended; approached; approved; argued; argued against; arose; arose from; arose in; aroused; aroused by; arranged; arrested by; arrived; arrived at; articulated; ascended; ashamed of; asked; asked for; aspired; asserted; assigned; assimilated; assisted; associated; associated with; assumed; assured; ate up; attached; attached to; attacked; attained; attempted; attempted to; attended; attested; attested to; attracted; attributed; attuned; augmented; awaited; awakened; awakened by; awakened from; awoke; awoke from; backed away; backed out; balanced against; balked; balked at; balked over; ballooned; ballooned with; battled; battled over; beamed; beat; became; began; began to; begged; behaved; beheld; believed; believed in; belonged; belonged to; belonged with; bent; bent on; bent over; beset by; beset with; besmirched; bestowed on; bet on; betrayed; betrayed by; bit; bit off; bitched; bitched about; blanked; blanked out; blazed; blazed with; blended with; blessed with; blinded; blinded by; blistered with; blocked; blocked out; bloomed; blurred; boggled; boggled at; boiled; boiled with; bolted; bolted in; boomed; bordered on; bore; bore down; bore through; born; born of; bothered; bound; bound in; bound up; bound with; bowed down; brainwashed by; bred; bred by; bridged; brimmed with; bristled; bristled with; broadened; broadened by; broke down; broke forth; broke out; broke through; brooded; brooded on; brooded over; brought about; brought back; brought forth; brought into; brought on; brought out; brought up; brushed against; brushed out; brushed upon; bubbled; bubbled with; built; built up; burdened; burdened with; buried in; burned; burned to; burned with; burst; burst forth; busied; busied with; buzzed; buzzed with; caged; calculated; called; called for; called forth; called into; called out; called up; calmed; calmed down; came apart; came at; came back; came down; came forth; came into; came out; came over; came together; came up; came upon; captivated; captivated by; cared; careened; carried; carried away; carried back; carried on; carried out; carved out; cast; cast back; cast off; catalogued; caught; caught at; caught between; caught in; caught on; caught up; caused; caused by; caved; caved in; ceased; centered; centered on; centered upon; chanced on; changed; changed by; characterized by; charged; charged with; chased; chased down; chatted; chatted about; chatted with; chattered; checked; checked on; cherished; chipped in; choked; choked on; choked with; chose; chucked out; chugged; chugged along; churned; churned away; churned out; churned over; circled; circled around; circled back; cited; claimed; clamored; clamored for; clamped; clamped down; cleaned; cleaned up; cleansed of; cleared; cleared of; cleared up; clicked; clicked away; clicked back; clicked into; climbed; climbed up; clocked in; clocked up;

closed; closed down; closed in; closed in on; closed on; closed up; clouded; clouded by; clouded over; clouded with; clued in on; clung to; clutched at; cluttered; cluttered up; cluttered with; collapsed; collapsed in; collapsed into; collected; combed; combed over; combined; combined with; commanded; commenced; commenced on; commented on; committed; committed to; communed with; communicated; communicated with; compared; compared with; compelled; compelled to; compensated for; competed; competed for; competed in; competed with; composed; comprehended; comprised; conceived; conceived of; concentrated; concentrated in; concentrated on; concluded; conditioned; conditioned by; conducted; confabulated; confessed; confided; confided to; confined; confined within; confirmed; conformed; confounded; confounded by; confronted; confronted by; confronted with; confused; confused by; confused with; congealed; conjured; conjured up; connected; connected with; considered; consisted of; consolidated; constituted; constructed; consumed; consumed by; consumed with; contained; contained within; contemplated; continued; contradicted; contrasted with; contributed; contrived; controlled; controlled by; conveyed; convinced; convinced of; cooked up; cooled; cooperated with; coped with; corrected; corresponded; corresponded with; corrupted; corrupted by; counted; counted on; coupled with; covered; covered up; coveted; cowered from; cracked; crackled with; crammed; crammed with; craved; crawled; crazed by; created; cried; cried out; cringed; cringed at; crippled by; crumbled; crushed; cultivated; cursed; cut; cut off; cut through; cycled; cycled through.

D - G

damaged by; danced; danced over; dared; darted; dawdled; dazed; dazzled; dazzled by; deadened; deadened with; deafened by; dealt; dealt with; debilitated by; decayed; deceived; decided; declared; dedicated to; defied; degraded; deleted; deliberated on; delighted in; delivered; deluded by; delved; delved into; demanded; demanded of; demolished; demonstrated; denied; depended; depended on; depended upon; depressed by; deprived; deprived of; derived; derived from; descended; descended into; described; deserted; deserted by; deserved; designed; desired; destined; destroyed; destroyed by; detected; determined; determined to; developed; developed through; developed into; deviated from; devised; devoted; devoted to; diagnosed; dictated; died; differed; differed from; differed in; digested; diminished; diminished in; dimmed; dipped; dipped into; directed; directed toward; disabused of; disagreed; disagreed on; disagreed with; disappeared; disapproved; disbelieved in; discerned; disciplined; disclosed; discovered; discussed; disdained; diseased by; diseased through; diseased with; disengaged; disengaged from; disintegrated; disliked; displayed; displeased; dissolved; dissolved into; distinguished; distinguished between; distorted with; distracted; distracted by; distracted from; distracted with; disturbed; disturbed by; disturbed with; diverted; diverted from; divided; divided against; divided between; divided into; divided with; divorced from; dizzied; dominated; dominated by; doubted; dragged; drank in; dreamed; dreamed about; dreamed of; drew; drew back; drew from; drew in; drew to; drew toward; drew up; drifted; drifted away; drifted back; drifted in; drifted into; drifted off; drifted over; drifted through; drifted to; dripped with; droned on; dropped; dropped away; dropped off; dropped out; drove; drove for; drowned; drowned in; dulled; dulled by; dwelled; dwelled for; dwelled on; earned; eased; echoed; edged closer; edged out; edited; edited out; educated; educated in; effected; effected by; elaborated; elevated by; elucidated; emancipated from; embedded; embedded in; embodied; embodied in; embraced; emerged; emerged from; employed; employed in; emptied; emptied of; emptied out; enabled; enclosed; enclosed in; encompassed; encompassed by; encountered; encouraged; encouraged by; ended up; endowed; endowed with; endured; energized by; enfeebled; enfeebled by; enforced; engaged; engaged by; engaged in; engaged with; engrossed; engrossed by; engrossed in; engrossed with; enjoyed; enjoyed by; enriched by; enriched with; enslaved; enslaved by; entangled in; entered; entered into; entertained; enveloped; enveloped in; equipped; equipped with; erased; erred on; erupted; erupted with; escaped; escaped from; established; estranged from; evaluated; evoked; evolved; exceeded; exchanged; excused; exempted; exercised; exerted; exhausted; exhausted by; exhibited; existed; expanded; expected; experienced; experienced in; experimented; experimented with; explained; exploded; exploded with; exploited; explored; exposed; exposed to; expressed; extended; fabricated; faced; faced with; faded; fades away; failed; failed in; faltered; faltered on; fascinated by; fascinated with; fastened on; fastened onto; fastened upon; fathomed; feasted on; fed; fed on; fed upon; fell; fell apart; fell away; fell back; fell into; fell on; fell upon; felt; fetched; fiddled with; figured; figured out; filled in; filled up; filled with; filtered; filtered out; fine-tuned; finished; fired by; fired up; fired with; fit; fit for; fixated; fixated on; fixed; fixed in; fixed on; fizzed with; fizzled out; flailed; flailed about; flashed; flashed on; flashed over; flashed through; flashed to; flashed with; fled; fled back; fled in; fled to; flew; flew about; flew back; flew in; flew into; flew off; flew over; flew to; flexed; flicked; flicked back; flicked over; flickered; flickered back; flinched; flipped; flipped through; flitted; flitted back; flitted from; flitted to; floated; floated away; floated back; floated in; floated off; floated to; floated up; flocked; flocked with; flooded; flooded with; flowed; flowed back; flowed in; fluttered; focused; focused in; focused inward; focused on; focused upon; fogged; fogged by; followed; forbade; forced; foresaw; forgot; formed; formulated; fostered; fought; fought against; fought back; fought through; found; found in; founded on; freed; freed from; freed of; fretted; fretted over; froze; froze in; froze up; fugued; fulfilled; fumbled; fumbled for; fumbled through; fumbled with; functioned; furnished with; fussed with; gained; gained by; galloped; garnered; gathered; gathered together; gathered up; gave; gave up; geared; geared for; geared up; generated; glanced back; glanced off; glanced over; glowed; glowed with; gnawed at; got into; got to; governed by; grabbed; grabbed at; grabbed onto; granted; grappled; grappled for; grappled with; grasped; grasped at; grew; grew still; groaned; groaned at; groped; groped about; groped for; grounded in; guided; guided by.

H - Q

handed over; handled; harassed; harassed by; harassed with; harbored; hated; haunted by; headed; headed into; healed; heard; held; held by; held in; held off; held onto; helped; helped out; helped with; hesitated; hesitated at; hid; hid from; hijacked by; hit; hit upon; hooked; hooked on; hopped on; hovered around; hovered on; hovered over; hummed; humored; hung; hung around; hung on; hung onto; hungered for; hunted; hunted for; hurled; hurled out; hurt; hurtled; identified; ignored; illuminated; illuminated by; illustrated; imagined; imbued with; imitated; immersed; immersed in; immobilized; immobilized by; impaired; imparted; impelled; implanted in; implied; imposed; imposed on; imposed upon; impregnated with; impressed; impressed upon; imprisoned; imprisoned in; improved; improved by; included; incorporated; increased; indicated; induced; indulged in; infected with; inferred; influenced; influenced by; informed; informed by; inhabited; inhabited by; inherited; inherited from; inquired; insisted; insisted on; inspired; inspired by; inspired with; instructed; intended; intended to; interacted; interacted with; interpreted; interrupted; intoxicated with; introduced; intruded; invented; inventoried; invested; invested in; involved; involved in; isolated; itched for; jammed; jammed with; jerked; jockeyed for; joined; joined in; joined with; jostled with; journeyed; journeyed into; judged; jumbled; jumbled with; jumped; jumped ahead; jumped at; jumped from; jumped to; justified; kept; kept on; kept up; kicked; kicked in; kicked into; kindled by; kindled with; knew; knocked around; labored; labored under; labored with; lacked; lacked in; lagged; lagged behind; landed on; latched on; latched onto; launched into; leaned on; leaned toward; leaped; leaped ahead; leaped at; leaped from; leaped into; leaped to; learned; learned about; led; led astray; led by; led to; left behind; left for; left in; left off; lent; let; liberated; liberated from; lifted; lifted out; lifted up; liked; lingered; lingered on; linked to; linked with; listed; listened; listened to; lit up; lived for; lived in; lived on; loaded with; locked; locked in; locked inside; locked into; locked on; locked up; lodged in; longed for; looked; looked at; looked for; looked forward; looked over; looped; loosened; lost; lost in; lost to; loved; lugged around; lulled; lulled by; lurched; lurched from; lurched in; lurched on; lurked; made; made for; made up; magnified; maintained; mangled; manifested; manufactured; mapped; marked; marked by; marveled at; matched; matched by; matured; meant for; melded; melded to; melded together; melded with; melted; melted away; mentioned; merged; merged with; met; met in; met with; mingled with; missed; mixed; mocked; modeled; motivated by; mourned; moved; moved ahead; moved forward; moved from; moved in; moved on; moved through; moved toward; moved with; muddled; mulled over; muttered; nagged; named; needed; neglected; negotiated with; niggled; niggled at; noted; noticed; nourished by; nourished in; nourished on; nudged; numbed; numbed by; nurtured; nurtured in; nurtured on; obeyed; objected; obscured by; observed; obsessed over; obtained; occupied; occupied by; occupied in; occupied on; occupied with; occurred in; offered; offered by; offered up; opened; opened by; opened to; opened up; operated; opposed to; oppressed; ordered; organized; oriented toward; originated from; oscillated between; overcame; overflowed; overflowed with; overloaded;

overrode; overturned; overwhelmed; overwhelmed by; overwhelmed with; owed; packed with; paid attention; parted with; participated; participated in; partook of; passed; passed beyond; passed from; passed into; passed over; passed through; patterned; paused; penetrated; penetrated by; penetrated into; penetrated with; peopled with; perceived; performed; permitted; perplexed; perplexed by; perplexed with; persisted; persisted in; pervaded; petitioned; picked; picked apart; picked at; picked up; pictured; pieced together; pitched; pitched in; placed; planned; played; played back; played in; played on; played out; played over; played through; played with; pleaded; pleased; plotted; plucked; plucked at; plunged; plunged into; pointed out; poised; poised on; poisoned; poisoned against; poisoned by; poked; poked around; pondered; popped; posed; possessed; possessed by; possessed of; possessed with; pounced; pounced on; poured out; practiced; praised; preceded; precipitated; preconditioned by; predisposed to; preferred; prepared; prepared by; prepared for; prepared over; prepared with; prepossessed with; presented; preserved; pressed; presumed; presupposed; pretended; prevailed; prevailed over; prevented; prevented from; preyed on; preyed upon; probed; probed out; proceeded; proceeded in; processed; procured; prodded; produced; produced by; programmed for; progressed; projected; prompted; pronounced; protected; protected against; protested; proved; provided; prowled; pulled apart; pulled out; pulled together; pulsed; purged; purged of; purified; purified by; purified from; pursued; pushed; pushed away; pushed back; pushed for; put away; put forth; put off; put to; put together; put up; quaked; qualified; qualified for; questioned; quickened; quieted; quieted down; quietened; quit; quivered.

R - S

raced; raced after; raced ahead; raced along; raced away; raced back; raced for; raced forward; raced from; raced in; raced on; raced over; raced through; raced to; raced with; raged; railed at; raised; raised above; raised on; rambled; rambled on; rambled through; ran; ran ahead; ran along; ran away; ran down; ran forward; ran from; ran in; ran off; ran on; ran out; ran over; ran through; ran upon; ran with; ranged; raped by; rattled; re-emerged; reached; reached back; reached for; reached out; reacted; reacted against; reacted to; reacted with; read; realized; reared; reared up; reasoned; reasserted; rebelled; rebelled against; rebelled at; rebuilt; recalled; receded back; received; received from; rechecked; recognized; recoiled; recoiled at; recoiled from; recoiled in; recoiled with; recommended; recorded; recovered; recovered from; recurred; recycled; redeemed; reduced; reduced to; reeled; reeled at; reeled back; reeled from; reeled in; reeled with; referred to; reflected; reflected on; reflected upon; refreshed by; refused; refused to; regained; regarded; registered; regulated by; regurgitated; rehearsed; rejected; rejoiced; rejoiced in; rejoined; relapsed into; related; related to; relaxed; relaxed into; released; released from; relied on; relieved; relieved by; relieved from; relieved of; remained; remained in; remained on; remained still; remarked; remembered; reminded; removed; removed from; removed in; rendered; renewed; repeated; replayed; replied; reported; represented; reproduced; required; required for; reran; rescued;

resembled; reserved for; reset; resided; resided in; resisted; resolved; responded; responded to; responded with; rested; rested in; rested on; rested upon; restored; resulted from; resulted in; resumed; resurrected; retained; retaliated; retaliated by; retorted; retrained for; retreated; retreated to; returned; returned to; returned with; revealed; revealed by; revealed in; reveled in; reverberated; reverberated with; reverted; reverted back; reverted to; reviewed; revised; revived; revolted; revolted against; revolted at; revolted from; revolved; revolved around; reworked; ricocheted around; ricocheted from; riddled; ripened; roamed; roamed over; robbed of; rocked; rocked with; rocketed; roiled; roiled with; rolled; rolled along; rolled on; rolled over; rooted in; rose; rose above; rose far; rose in; rose to; rose up; rounded up; roused; roused by; roved; ruined; ruined by; ruled; ruled by; rumbled; rushed; rushed ahead; rushed back; rushed on; rushed through; sacrificed; said; said to; sampled; sang; sank; sank into; sank under; sat; satisfied with; saturated with; saved; saw; saw through; scared; scared by; scarred by; scattered; schooled in; scored; scoured; scrabbled; scrabbled around; scrabbled away; scrambled; scrambled for; scraped together; screamed; screamed at; screamed for; screamed in; screamed out; screamed with; scrolled; scrolled through; scrubbed; scurried; scurried through; scuttled; searched; searched for; seethed; seethed with; seized; seized by; seized on; seized upon; selected; selected from; sent; sent out; separated; separated from; served; served up; set; set about; set against; set at; set back; set for; set forth; set from; set in; set on; set onto; set out; set to; set toward; set up; set upon; settled; settled down; settled in; settled into; settled on; settled upon; shaped; shaped by; shared; shared by; shared with; sharpened; sharpened by; shattered; shattered by; shattered into; shied away; shied from; shifted; shifted again; shifted back; shifted from; shifted into; shone; shone forth; shook; shook off; shot back; shot from; shot through; shot to; shouted; shouted at; showed; showed off; showed through; shrank; shrank from; shrank in; shrieked; shriveled; shriveled to; shrouded in; shuddered; shuddered at; shut; shut down; shut off; shut on; shut out; shut up; signaled; skated over; skidded; skidded off; skidded through; skimmed; skimmed across; skimmed over; skipped back; skipped between; skipped from; skipped off; skipped to; skittered; skittered around; skittered away; slammed; slaved over; slid; slid away; slid back; slipped; slipped away; slipped back; slipped between; slipped from; slipped into; slipped off; slipped to; slogged through; slowed; slowed by; slowed down; slowed to; snagged on; snapped; snapped back; snapped into; snapped to; soaked in; soaked up; soared; soared above; sorted; sorted out; sorted through; sought; sought out; sounded; soured by; spanned; speculated; speculated on; speculated upon; sped; sped through; sped to; sped up; spent; spent on; spilled with; spiraled; spiraled in; spiraled with; split; split against; split in; split into; split off; spoke; spoke in; spoke out; spoke up; sprang; sprang from; spread; spread out; spread over; sprinted; sprouted; spun; spun back; spun between; spun forward; spun from; spun in; spun into; spun off; spun on; spun out; spun through; spun with; squeezed; staggered; stalked; stalled; stalled on; stared at; started; started up; starved; starved for; starved of; stated; stayed; stayed in; stayed on; stayed upon; stayed with; steadied; steeled against; steeled by; steeped in; stepped; stepped back;

stepped up; stilled; stimulated; stimulated by; stirred; stirred by; stirred up; stocked with; stole; stood; stood for; stood in; stood on; stood still; stooped; stopped; stopped at; stored; stored up; stored with; strained; strayed; strayed from; strayed to; strayed toward; strengthened; strengthened by; stretched; stretched by; stripped of; strove; strove for; struck; struck on; struck upon; struggled; struggled against; struggled for; struggled in; struggled through; struggled toward; struggled with; stuck in; stuck on; stuck with; stuffed with; stumbled; stumbled on; stumbled over; stumbled through; stung; stuttered; subjected; submerged in; submitted; submitted to; subsided; subsided from; succeeded; succeeded in; succumbed; succumbed to; suffered; suffered from; suffocated in; suffused with; suggested; suited; supervised; supplied; supported; supported by; supposed; surged; surged with; surrendered; surrounded by; survived; suspected; suspended; suspended in; sustained; sustained by; swallowed up; swam; swam in; swam with; swapped; swarmed with; swayed; swayed by; swelled with; swept; swept back; swept on; swirled; swirled inwardly; swirled with; switched; switched back; switched into; switched to; switches on; switches over; swung; swung back; sympathized with.

T - Z
tackled; tainted with; talked; talked about; tallied; tallied up; tangled; tangled up; taught; taught by; taunted; teased; teemed with; tempered by; tended to; tended toward; tested; testified; thanked; thirsted; thirsted for; thought; thought about; thought of; threaded; threatened; threw away; threw off; threw out; threw up; thrived on; throbbed with; ticked; ticked back; ticked off; ticked over; tied; tied to; tightened; tightened up; tilted; tired; tired of; told; took; took away; took in; took off; took on; took over; took to; took up; tormented by; tormented with; torn; torn between; torn by; torn with; tortured; tortured by; tortured with; tossed; tossed away; tossed out; touched; touched by; touched on; touched with; toyed with; traced; traced through; tracked; trained; trained by; trained for; trained in; trained on; trained to; transcended; transferred; transferred to; transformed; translated; transported; trapped; trapped in; trapped under; traveled; traveled back; trekked; trembled; trembled at; tricked; tried; tried to; tripped; tripped up; triumphed; triumphed over; troubled; troubled by; troubled with; trusted; tumbled; tumbled around; tumbled from; tumbled over; tuned in; tuned out; tuned to; tuned up; turned; turned against; turned away; turned back; turned from; turned inward; turned off; turned on; turned outward; turned over; turned to; turned toward; turned upon; turned with; tutored in; twisted; twittered with; unburdened by; understood; underwent; undid; unearthed; unfettered by; unfolded; unfurled; unhinged; united; united in; united with; unpacked; unraveled; unsettled; unsettled by; uploaded; urged; used; vacillated between; vanished; varied; veered; veered away; veered back; veered from; veered off; veiled by; ventured; ventured down; verged on; verified; versed in; vibrated; viewed; visited; visualized; vowed; waded through; wailed; waited; waited for; wakened; walked; wallowed; wallowed in; wandered; wandered across; wandered among; wandered around; wandered down; wandered from; wandered in; wandered off; wandered on; wandered out; wandered over; wandered

through; wandered to; wandered toward; wandered until; wandered with; wanted; warmed; warmed by; warmed with; warned; warped by; wasted; wasted away; watched; watched on; watched through; watched with; wavered; wavered between; weakened; weakened by; weakened with; wearied; wearied by; wearied with; weighed down; went around; went back; went beyond; went far; went forward; went from; went further; went into; went off; went on; went out; went over; went still; went through; went to; went up; went with; whipped; whipped out; whirled; whirled in; whirled with; whirred; whirred with; whisked; whispered; wielded; willed; wilted; wilted with; winked out; winnowed; wished; wished for; withdrew; withdrew from; woke; woke up; won out; wondered; wondered about; wondered at; wore down; wore out; worked; worked at; worked for; worked in; worked on; worked out; worked through; worried; worried about; wove; wove together; wrapped around; wrapped in; wrapped up; wrestled; wrestled between; wrestled with; writhed; yearned; yearned for; yelled; yielded; yielded to; zigzagged from; zoomed.

Noun Phrases

A - E

aberrations of the mind; ability of the mind; abnormality of the mind; absence of the mind; absorption of the mind; acceptance of the mind; accomplishment of the mind; achievement of the mind; act(s) of the mind; actions of the mind; activity of the mind; acuteness of the mind; adaptation of the mind; adherence of the mind; adhesion of the mind; adjustment of the mind; admiration of the mind; advancement of the mind; advantage of the mind; affliction of the mind; age of the mind; agency of the mind; agility of the mind; agitation of the mind; agony of the mind; agreement of the mind; aid of the mind; ailment of the mind; aim of the mind; alertness of the mind; alienation of the mind; alteration of the mind; amusement of the mind; analysis of the mind; anatomy of the mind; anguish of the mind; anticipation of the mind; anxiety of the mind; appetite of the mind; application of the mind; appreciation of the mind; apprehension of the mind; aptitude of the mind; archetypes of the mind; area(s) of the mind; arrogance of the mind; aspect of the mind; assumption of the mind; attachment of the mind; attempt of the mind; attention of the mind; attitude of the mind; authority of the mind; autonomy of the mind; aversion of the mind; awareness of the mind; back of the mind; balance of the mind; battle of the mind; beauty of the mind; behavior of the mind; belief of the mind; betrayal of the mind; bias of the mind; biology of the mind; blindness of the mind; bondage of the mind; calmness of the mind; cancer of the mind; canvas of the mind; capability of the mind; capacity of the mind; caverns of the mind; caves of the mind; center of the mind; chambers of the mind; change(s) of the mind; channels of the mind; chaos of the mind; character of the mind; characteristics of the mind; chatter of the mind; cheerfulness of the mind; chemistry of the mind; choice of the mind; clarity of the mind; cleansing of the mind; clearness of the mind; climate of the mind; clouds of the mind; cobwebs of the mind; coercion of the mind; cognition of the mind; command of the mind; commotion of the mind; communication of the mind; communion of the mind; compartments of the mind; competence of the mind; complexity of the mind; composure of the mind; comprehension of the mind; concentration of the mind; concept(s) of the mind; conceptualization of the mind; conclusion(s) of the mind; condition of the mind; confinement of the mind; conflict of the mind; conformity of the mind; confusion of the mind; connection of the mind; conscience of the mind; consciousness of the mind; consent of the mind; consideration of the mind; constructs of the mind; contemplation of the mind; contentment of the mind; contents of the mind; control of the mind; conviction of the mind; cooperation of the mind; corner(s) of the mind; corridors of the mind; corruption of the mind; courage of the mind; craving(s) of the mind; creativity of the mind; criticism of the mind; cultivation of the mind; curiosity of the mind; dance of the mind; darkness of the mind; death of the mind; decay of the mind; deception of the mind; decision of the mind; declaration of the mind; dedication of the mind; defect of the mind; deficiencies of the mind; degeneration of the mind; degradation of the mind; dejection of the mind; deliberation of the mind; delicacy of the mind; delirium of the mind; delusion(s) of the mind; denial of the mind; departure of the mind; dependence of the mind; depravity of the mind; depression of the mind; depths of the mind; derangement of the mind; descent of the mind; desire(s) of the mind; detachment of the mind; deterioration of the mind; determination of the mind; development of the mind; devotion of the mind; dialogue of the mind; dimensions of the mind; discernment of the mind; discipline of the mind; discovery of the mind; disease of the mind; disintegration of the mind; disorder of the mind; disposition of the mind; dissection of the mind; distortions of the mind; distraction of the mind; distress of the mind; disturbance of the mind; diversion of the mind; divisions of the mind; dominance of the mind; doors of the mind; dreams of the mind; drunkenness of the mind; duality of the mind; dulling of the mind; dwelling of the mind; eagerness of the mind; ecstasy of the mind; edge(s) of the mind; education of the mind; effects of the mind; efficiency of the mind; effort of the mind; elasticity of the mind; elements of the mind; elevation of the mind; emergence of the mind; emotions of the mind; employment of the mind; emptiness of the mind; endeavor of the mind; enemy of the mind; energy of the mind; engagement of the mind; engines of the mind; enjoyment of the mind; enlargement of the mind; enlightenment of the mind; enrichment of the mind; enslavement of the mind; enterprise of the mind; entertainment of the mind; enthusiasm of the mind; essence of the mind; eternity of the mind; evils of the mind; evolution of the mind; exaltation of the mind; examination of the mind; excellence of the mind; excitation of the mind; excitement of the mind; exclusion of the mind; excursions of the mind; exertion of the mind; exhaustion of the mind; exhilaration of the mind; existence of the mind; expansion of the mind; experience of the mind; exploration of the mind; expression of the mind; extension of the mind; extent of the mind; eye of the mind.

F - P

fabric of the mind; facets of the mind; facility of the mind; faculty of the mind; failure of the mind; faith of the mind; fallacy of the mind; fantasy of the mind; fatigue of the mind; fault of the mind; fear of the mind; feat(s) of the mind; feature(s) of the mind; feeling(s) of the mind; fever of the mind; fiction(s) of the mind; figment(s) of the mind; firmness of the mind; fitness of the mind; fixation of the mind; flash(es) of the mind; flexibility of the mind; flight of the mind; flow of the mind; focus of the mind; fog of the mind; forefront of the mind; form of the mind; formulation of the mind; foundation of the mind; frailty of the mind; freedom of the mind; frenzy of the mind; freshness of the mind; frontiers of the mind; function of the mind; fury of the mind; games of the mind; genius of the mind; gift(s) of the mind; glimpse(s) of the mind; gloom of the mind; goodness of the mind; gratification of the mind; greatness of the mind; growth of the mind; guidance of the mind; habits of the mind; hallucination(s) of the mind; hallways of the mind; happiness of the mind; harmony of the mind; hatred of the mind; haven of the mind; health of the mind; heart of the mind; horror of the mind; house of the mind; humor of the mind; hunger of the mind; ideals of the mind; ideas of the mind; ignorance of the mind; illness of the mind; illumination of the mind; illusion(s) of the mind; imagery of the mind; images of the mind; imagination of the mind; imbalance of the mind; immateriality of the mind; immortality of the mind; impact of the mind; impairment of the mind; impediments of the mind; importance of the mind; impression of the mind; imprint of the mind; imprisonment of the mind; improvement of the mind; impulse(s) of the mind; inability of the mind; inactivity of the mind; inclination of the mind; independence of the mind; indication of the mind; individuality of the mind; influence of the mind; information of the mind; ingenuity of the mind; insight of the mind; inspiration of the mind; instincts of the mind; instruction of the mind; instrument of the mind; integrity of the mind; intelligence of the mind; intensity of the mind; intentions of the mind; interaction of the mind; interests of the mind; interpretation of the mind; intricacies of the mind; intuition of the mind; inventions of the mind; investigation of the mind; involvement of the mind; isolation of the mind; journey of the mind; judgment of the mind; keenness of the mind; knowledge of the mind; labor of the mind; labyrinth of the mind; landscape of the mind; language of the mind; layers of the mind; laziness of the mind; levels of the mind; liberation of the mind; liberty of the mind; light of the mind; limitations of the mind; limits of the mind; location of the mind; logic of the mind; longings of the mind; loss of the mind; madness of the mind; majesty of the mind; malady of the mind; manifestations of the mind; manipulation of the mind; map of the mind; mastery of the mind; materiality of the mind; matters of the mind; maturity of the mind; mazes of the mind; mechanics of the mind; mechanism of the mind; memories of the mind; metaphysics of the mind; model of the mind; mood(s) of the mind; morality of the mind; motive(s) of the mind; movie(s) of the mind; mystery of the mind; nakedness of the mind; narrowness of the mind; nature of the mind; necessity of the mind; neglect of the mind; nerves of the mind; networks of the mind; notion of the mind; nourishment of the mind; obedience of the mind; observation(s) of the mind; obsession of the mind; occupation(s) of the mind; on account of the mind; openness of the mind; operation of the mind; opinion of the mind; organ of the mind; organization of the mind; orientation of the mind; origin of the mind; outlook of the mind; outpost of the mind; outskirts of the mind; owner of the mind; pain of the mind; paralysis of the mind; part of the mind; participation of the mind; passion of the mind; passivity of the mind; pathology of the mind; pathways of the mind; patterns of the mind; peace of the mind; peculiarity of the mind; penetration of the mind; perception of the mind; performance of the mind; perspective of the mind; perversion of the mind; phantasms of the mind; phantoms of the mind; phases of the mind; phenomena of the mind; philosophy of the mind; physics of the mind; physiology of the mind; pictures of the mind; place of the mind; plan of the mind; playground of the mind; pleasure of the mind; poetry of the mind; poise of the mind; poison of the mind; pollution of the mind; portals of the mind; portion of the mind; possession of the mind; possibilities of the mind; potential of the mind; potentiality of the mind; power of the mind; practice of the mind; preference of the mind; prejudice of the mind; preoccupation of the mind; preparation of the mind; presence of the mind; preservation of the mind; pride of the mind; principle(s) of the mind; prison of the mind; problem(s) of the mind; procedures of the mind; processes of the mind; product(s) of the mind; projection(s) of the mind; propensity of the mind; province(s) of the mind; psychology of the mind; purification of the mind; purity of the mind; purpose of the mind; pursuit(s) of the mind.

Q - Y
quality of the mind; quest of the mind; question(s) of the mind; quickness of the mind; quietness of the mind; radiance of the mind; range of the mind; rape of the mind; rapture of the mind; rationality of the mind; ravages of the mind; reach(es) of the mind; reaction of the mind; readiness of the mind; reality of the mind; realization of the mind; realm of the mind; reason of the mind; reasoning of the mind; receptivity of the mind; recesses of the mind; recognition of the mind; recoiling of the mind; recreation of the mind; rediscovery of the mind; reduction of the mind; refinement of the mind; reflection of the mind; regeneration of the mind; region(s) of the mind; rejection of the mind; relationship of the mind; relaxation of the mind; release of the mind; reliance of the mind; relief of the mind; reluctance of the mind; resistance of the mind; resolution of the mind; resourcefulness of the mind; response of the mind; rest of the mind; restlessness of the mind; restraint of the mind; revelation of the mind; revolt of the mind; revulsion of the mind; riot of the mind; sadness of the mind; sake of the mind; sanity of the mind; satisfaction of the mind; scope of the mind; scrutiny of the mind; search of the mind; secrets of the mind; section of the mind; sensation of the mind; sense of the mind; sensitiveness of the mind; separation of the mind; serenity of the mind; sharpness of the mind; sickness of the mind; silence of the mind; simplicity of the mind; skills of the mind; sluggishness of the mind; slumber of the mind; smartness of the mind; solitude of the mind; solution of the mind; sorrow of the mind; soundness of the mind; sovereignty of the mind; speculation of the mind; speed of the mind; spontaneity

of the mind; stability of the mind; stamina of the mind; state of the mind; stillness of the mind; stimulation of the mind; stirring(s) of the mind; storms of the mind; strain of the mind; strategy of the minds; strength of the mind; structure of the mind; struggle of the mind; study of the mind; subjectivity of the mind; subjugation of the mind; submission of the mind; substance of the mind; suffering of the mind; suggestion of the mind; superiority of the mind; supremacy of the mind; susceptibility of the mind; suspension of the mind; sympathy of the mind; system of the mind; talent of the mind; temper of the mind; temperament of the mind; temptations of the mind; tendencies of the mind; tension of the mind; terror of the mind; test of the mind; thirst of the mind; thoughts of the mind; torment of the mind; training of the mind; traits of the mind; tranquility of the mind; transcendence of the mind; transformation of the mind; tricks of the mind; triumph of the mind; troubles of the mind; truth of the mind; turmoil of the mind; type of the mind; understanding of the mind; uneasiness of the mind; unification of the mind; unity of the mind; utterances of the mind; vacillation of the mind; vacuum of the mind; vanity of the mind; vexation of the mind; vibrations of the mind; vices of the mind; victory of the mind; view of the mind; vigor of the mind; virtues of the mind; vision of the mind; vitality of the mind; vivacity of the mind; voices of the mind; void of the mind; walls of the mind; wanderings of the mind; war of the mind; ways of the mind; weaknesses of the mind; wealth of the mind; weariness of the mind; welfare of the mind; willingness of the mind; windows of the mind; wisdom of the mind; withdrawal of the mind; words of the mind; workings of the mind; wounds of the mind; youth of the mind.

USAGE EXAMPLES

Kate's *mind reeled* when she saw her date.

His *addled mind spun* with images of the crash.

Her *frazzled mind had finally comprehended* what he had meant.

Larry's *young mind became agitated* at the thought of spending the weekend at his grandparent's house in the country.

His *mind couldn't quite grasp* her true intent.

27
MOUTH

Adjectives in Alphabetical Order

A - L

aching; agape; aged; aggressive; aghast; agile; agreeable; amazing; ambivalent; amiable; amorous; ample; angelic; angry; arrogant; astonished; attractive; average; awful; awkward; bad; bearded; beauteous; beautiful; beckoning; bee-stung; beloved; big; birdlike; bitter; blabbering; black; blasphemous; bleeding; bloated; blood-red; bloodied; bloody; blubbering; blue; blue-tinged; bold; bountiful; bow-shaped; boyish; brazen; breathy; bright; brilliantly-painted; broad; brown; bruised; brutal; burning; busted; busy; candy-scented; capacious; cavernous; charming; chattering; cherry-red; chewing; child-sized; childish; childlike; chiselled / chiseled; circular; clammy; clamorous; clamped; clamped-shut; clean; clear; clear-lipped; cleft; clenched; clever; closed; clumsy; coarse; cold; cold-flushed; colored; comely; compressed; contemptuous; contorted; cool; covetous; cracked; crimped; crimson; crinkly; crooked; crowded; crude; cruel; crumpled; cupid-bow; cupped; curious; curved; curving; curvy; cute; cynical; dainty; damn; damned; damp; dangerous; dark; deadly; deep; deep-set; deformed; delectable; delicate; delicious; determined; devouring; dewy; dimpled; dirty; disapproving; discontented; disdainful; disgusting; distant; distended; distinct; distorted; divine; dour; down-turned; down-twisted; downcast; dreadful; dried; dried-out; drooling; drooly; drooping; droopy; dry; dumb; eager; elongated; eloquent; emaciated; empty; enormous; entire; exaggerated; expectant; exposed; expressive; exquisite; extruded; fair; faltering; fang-filled; fanged; fat; feeble; female; feminine; ferocious; festering; fetid; fevered; fierce; fiery; filthy; fine; firm; fish-like; fish-lipped; fishy; flabby; flaccid; flaming; flapping; flat; flattened; flattering; fleshy; flexible; flowering; foaming; foamy; folded-in; foolish; formidable; foul; fragrant; fresh; friendly; frightful; frothing; frothy; frowning; frozen; full; full-lipped; funny; gap-toothed; gaping; gargantuan; gasping; generous; gentle; ghastly; giant; gigantic; girlish; glossy; glowing; gnawing; goddamn; goddamned; good; gorgeous; gory; grabbing; gracious; gray; greasy; great; Grecian; greedy; Greek; grim; grimacing; grinning; grotesque; growling; guilty; gummy; hairy; half-full; half-open; half-opened; handsome; happy; hard; hard-gummed; hard-set; hard-to-open; harmless; haughty; healthy; heart-shaped; heavenly; heavy; hesitant; hidden; hideous; hollow; honest; honeyed; horrible; horrid; horseshoe-shaped; hot; howling; huge; humble; humid; humorless; humorous; hungry; ideal; ignorant; immense; impatient; imperfect; imperial; impetuous; impish; impudent; impure; incredible; incredulous; inexpressive; infinite; inner; innocent; insatiable; insistent; interesting; internal; irregular; kindly; kissable;

knife-blade; knowing; knowledgeable; large; laughing; leathery; leering; lewd; liberated; lifeless; limp; lined; lipless; lipped; lipsticked; little; little-boy; long; looming; loose; loose-lipped; lopsided; loud; lovely; loving; lower; lubricious; luscious; lush; lustful.

M - Y

maiden; male; malicious; mammoth; mangled; manly; many-toothed; marvelous; masculine; mean; meaty; meek; merry; mighty; mirthless; misshapen; misty; moaning; mocking; moist; monstrous; moody; motionless; moving; murmuring; mustachioed; mute; narrow; narrow-lipped; narrowed; nasty; natural; nervous; nice; no-nonsense; noble; noisy; normal; o-shaped; oblique; obscene; obstinate; odious; odorous; oily; old; open; opened; orange-lipsticked; ordinary; outer; outstretched; oval; over-glossed; overdrawn; overlarge; oversize; painful; painted; pale; pampered; panicked-parched; panting; papery; parched; parted; passionate; pasty; peach-colored; peevish; pencil-thin; pensive; perfect; perky; persistent; petulant; piercing; pinched; pink; pink-brown; placid; pleasant; pliant; plucked; plummy; plump; plunging; podgy; polite; poor; potty; pouting; pouty; powerful; predatory; pretty; prim; prim-looking; primal; primitive; prissy; prominent; propped-open; proud; puckered; puckish; puffing; puffy; pulsing; pungent; purple; pursed; putrid; querulous; quick; quiet; quirking; quivering; raspberry-colored; rasping; ravenous; raw; ready; rebellious; reckless; red; red-cherry; red-stained; refined; regal; relaxed; remarkable; resolute; restless; rich; rigid; ripe; ripped; roaring; rosy; rotten; rouged; rough; round; rounded; rubbery; ruddy; rude; rugged; ruined; sacrilegious; sad; sad-looking; sagging; sandy; sane; sarcastic; sardonic; sassy; saucy; savage; sawtoothed; scabrous; scarlet; scarred; scary; scornful; scowling; screaming; screwed-up; sculpted; sealed; searching; self-indulgent; selfish; sensible; sensitive; sensual; sensuous; serious; sexy; shaded; shadowy; shallow; shapeless; shapely; sharp; shaven; shining; shiny; shocked; shy; silent; silly; simpering; skillful; slack; slack-lipped; slick; slicked-up; slippery; slobbering; slobbery; sloppy; sly; small; smallish; smart; smiling; smirking; smoky; smooth; snarled; snarling; sneering; snoring; soft; soft-looking; sonorous; sore; soundless; sour; spacious; speechless; spreading; square; squared; squat; stained; startled; starving; stern; sticky; stiff; stinging; straight; strange; strong; stubborn; stupid; subtle; succulent; sucked-in; sucking; sulky; sullen; sunken; sunny; surly; surprised; suspicious; sweet; swollen; sympathetic; taut; teeny; tempting; tender; tense; terrible; thick; thick-lipped; thin; thin-lipped; thirsty; throbbing; tight; tight-lipped; tilted; tiny; tired; tobacco-darkened; tobacco-stained; too-wide; toothless; toothy; trashy; treacherous; trembling; tremendous; tremulous; troubled; turned-down; twisted; twitching; ugly; ulcerated; unbending; unclean; uneven; ungracious; unimpressive; unlined; unpleasant; unrelenting; unsmiling; unworthy; unyielding; upper; upturned; useless; vast; veiled; voluptuous; vulgar; vulnerable-looking; waiting; wanton; warm; wary; watery; weak; weary; weather-dry; wee; well-drawn; well-formed; well-meaning; well-sculpted; well-shaped; wet; whiskered; whispering; white; whole; wicked; wide; wide-lipped;

wide-open; widening; willful; willing; winsome; wise; wistful; withered; witty; womanly; wonderful; wrinkled; wry; yapping; yawning; young.

Verbs and Phrasal Verbs in Alphabetical Order

A - D

accentuated; ached; ached from; ached with; adjusted; anchored firmly; appeared; applied to; arced; arced in; arched; arched into; asked; associated with; assumed; ate; attached to; attacked; attracted; banged; banged against; bared; bared in; became; began; begged; belonged to; bent; bent in; bent upward; betrayed; bit; bit at; blasted; bled; blended; blended into; blew; blocked; blocked by; blurted; blurted out; boomed; bordered by; bordered with; bore; bowed; bowed up; bracketed by; bracketed with; breathed; broke down; broke into; brought down; brought up; bruised; brushed; brushed across; bulged; bumped; bunched; bunched in; bunched up; burned; burned from; burst into; bypassed; caked with; called; came across; came down; came forward; came open; came out; came toward; carried; cast in; caught; caused; caused by; cemented in; chafed; chafed at; changed; changed at; changed in; chapped; chapped with; chewed; chiseled; choked; choked with; cinched; cinched into; cinched tight; clacked; claimed; clamped; clamped down; clamped into; clamped onto; clamped over; clapped; cleansed; cleared; clenched; clenched against; clenched tight; clicked; clogged with; closed; closed against; closed around; closed in; closed on; closed over; closed tight(ly); clung; coated with; cocked; collapsed; combined; combined with; communicated; complained; composed; compressed; compressed into; concealed; confessed; connected; connected with; consisted of; contained; continued; contorted; contorted by; contorted downward; contorted in; contorted into; contorted with; contracted; cooed; corresponded; covered; covered by; covered in; covered with; cracked; crammed with; craved; creased; creased downward; creased upward; crept up; cried; cried out; crinkled; crinkled in; crinkled into; crinkled up; crooked up; crushed against; crushed down; curled; curled at; curled down; curled in; curled into; curled momentarily; curled sadly; curled slightly; curled up; curled upward; curled with; curved; curved back; curved down; curved downwards; curved faintly; curved in; curved into; curved slightly; curved up; curved upward; curved wryly; cut; cut on; dangled; darkened; daubed; daubed with; declared; deepened; deepened into; defined; defined by; demanded; descended; developed; devoured; differed; dipped; dipped down; dipped into; directed; disappeared; disappeared into; discovered; displayed; distended; distorted; divided; dominated; downturned; downturned at; dragged; dragged down; drank; drew; drew back; drew down; drew forward; drew into; drew inward; dribbled; dribbled with; dried; dried out; dried up; drifted; drifted to; dripped; dripped with; drooled; drooled with; drooped; dropped; dropped open.

E - O

eased; eased into; echoed; edged; edged up; edged upward; ejected; emerged; emitted; enabled; enclosed; encompassed; engulfed in; entered; erupted; erupted out; erupted with; etched by; evoked; examined; exhaled; expanded; expanded into; expelled; exploded; exposed; expressed; extended; faced; faced downward; faltered; fell; fell into; fell open; fell wide; felt; felt like; filled; filled up; filled with; fired off; fit; fitted; fitted with; fixed; fixed in; fixed on; fixed rigidly; flaked; flaked with; flapped; flashed; flashed into; flattened; flattened out; flattened to; flew open; flicked; flicked up; flickered; flickered in; flitted; flitted with; flowed; fluttered; foamed; foamed with; folded around; folded inward; followed; forced; formed; found; framed; framed by; framed with; frothed; frothed up; froze; froze in; furnished with; gagged; gaped; gargled; gasped; gasped at; gasped for; gathered; gave; gawped; gleamed; gleamed with; glinted; glinted with; glistened; glossed; glossed with; glowed; glued; gobbled; grabbed; grabbed at; grazed; grew; grew tight; grimaced; grinded; grinded against; grinned; groped; groped for; gulped; gushed; harbored; hardened; hardened into; held; held up; hid; hid behind; hinged; hinted; hinted at; hissed; hit; hovered; hovered around; hovered over; hung; hung open; hung wide; hurt; hypnotized; implied; imprinted on; inched closer; inched up; included; increased; indicated; intended to; intrigued; irritated; issued forth; jammed; jerked; jerked up; kept; kicked; kicked up; kissed; knew; labored; lacked; laid; laughed; leaped; leaped out; led; led into; leered; left; let; lifted; lifted in; lifted into; lifted slightly; liked; limited; lined; lined with; lingered; lingered in; lingered on; locked; locked in; locked onto; lolled; looked; looked like; lost; loved; lowered; lowered to; lunged; lunged forward; lurked; made; made up; managed; marked; marked from; marked with; mawed; mawed at; measured; melted; melted into; met; might; missed; moistened; mouthed; moved across; moved against; moved along; moved down; moved faster; moved in; moved into; moved like; moved silently; moved slightly; moved slowly; moved to; moved toward; moved under; moved up; moved very; moved when; muffled; muffled by; muffled with; narrowed; needed; nibbled; nibbled at; nibbled on; nipped; nipped up; nuzzled; occupied; offered; opened; opened slightly; opened slowly; opened up; opened wide; outlined; outlined with; overflowed.

P - S

painted; paled; panted; paralyzed; parted; parted in; parted into; parted slightly; passed; performed; pinched; pinched down; pinched up; pinned; placed; placed on; played; pleased; plied; plugged; plugged with; poised; poised in; poised over; poked; poked out; popped; posed; posed for; possessed; poured; pouted; pouted upward; presented; pressed; pressed against; pressed down; pressed in; pressed into; pressed together; pressed up; prevented; pried; primed; produced; projected; pronounced; protruded; provided; puckered; puckered around; puckered downward; puckered in; puckered into; puffed; puffed out; pulled; pulled back; pulled down; pulled flush; pulled in; pulled into; pulled tight; pulled up; pursed; pursed in; pursed into; pursed tight; pursed up; pushed; quirked; quirked at; quirked briefly; quirked down; quirked slightly; quirked up;

quirked upward; quivered; quivered with; raged; raged in; raised; raised in; raked; ran; rattled; reached; reached closer; reacted; reacted with; read; received; recited; recoiled; recoiled at; reflected; refused; relaxed; relaxed into; released; remained; reminded; rendered; reopened; represented; required; resembled; resisted; responded; responded warmly; responded with; rested; resumed; returned; revealed; rimmed with; ringed with; rinsed; ripped; ripped apart; roared; rolled; rolled up; rose; rose in; rose slightly; rounded; rounded into; sagged; said; salivated; sang; sank; sank to; sat; screwed up; sealed; seemed; seemed like; seemed to; seized; sensed; set; set in; set into; settled; settled in; settled into; shaped like; shifted; shook; shot off; shouted; showed; shrieked; shriveled; shrouded; shut; shut against; shut around; shut like; shut out; shut tight(ly); sighed; silenced; silenced with; sipped; slackened; slammed onto; slanted; slewed; slewed sideways; slid; slid up; slipped; slipped from; slipped into; slitted; slobbered; sloped; sloped down; sloped downward; smeared; smeared with; smelled; smelled like; smelled of; smiled; smiled at; smiled broadly; smiled down; smiled thinly; smiled with; smoldered; smooched; smothered; smudged; smudged with; snapped; snapped like; snapped tight; sneered; softened; sought; sought out; sounded; sounded like; soured; spat; spat into; spewed; splashed over; split; split in; split into; spluttered; spoke; spoke of; spoke through; sprang; spread; spread into; spurted; squeezed; squeezed in; stained with; stalled; stamped; stamped on; stank; stank of; started; stayed; stood; stopped; strained; streaked; stretched; stretched across; stretched in; stretched into; stretched tight; stretched wide; stroked; struck; struggled; struggled with; stuck out; stuffed; stuffed with; stung; stung from; sucked; sucked at; sucked in; sucked on; suckled; suctioned; suggested; suppressed; surprised; surrounded; surrounded by; surrounded with; sustained; swallowed; swayed; swelled; swelled with; swept across; swept over.

T - Z

tasted; tasted like; tasted of; tended; tensed; tensed at; thickened; thickened with; thinned; thinned with; threatened; thrilled; throbbed; throbbed with; tickled; tightened; tightened against; tightened as; tightened at; tightened in; tightened into; tightened like; tightened slightly; tightened up; tightened with; tilled; tilled with; tilted; tilted down; tilted up; tilted upward; tingled; tipped; tipped downwards; tipped into; tipped up; told; took; tore; tore at; tortured; tossed; touched; touched with; traced; traveled/travelled; trembled; trembled in; trembled into; trembled slightly; trembled with; tremored; tried; tucked; tucked down; tucked downward; tugged; tugged at; tugged upward; turned; turned down; turned downward; turned into; turned sharply; turned slightly; turned towards; turned up; turned upward; twisted; twisted down; twisted downward; twisted in; twisted into; twisted sideways; twisted slightly; twisted tight; twisted up; twisted upward; twisted with; twitched; twitched at; twitched down; twitched into; twitched nervously; twitched slightly; twitched up; twitched upward; twitched with; uncovered; unhinged; uplifted; used; used to; uttered; vanished; voiced; vomited; waited; waited for; wanted; warmed; warped; warped into; warranted; washed; washed out; watered; wavered; weakened;

went back; went down; went hard; went tight; went up; wet; wet with; wheezed; whispered; whitened; widened; widened in; widened into; withdrew; wobbled; wore; work; worked; wrapped around; wrenched; wrinkled; yawned; yearned; yearned for; zipped shut.

Noun Phrases

affection(s) of the mouth; angle of the mouth; appearance of the mouth; area of the mouth; base of the mouth; border of the mouth; boundary of the mouth; breadth of the mouth; breath of the mouth; cavity of the mouth; center of the mouth; character of the mouth; circumference of the mouth; cleanliness of the mouth; cleansing of the mouth; closure of the mouth; color of the mouth; compression of the mouth; contortions of the mouth; contour of the mouth; contraction of the mouth; corner(s) of the mouth; crease of the mouth; curve(s) of the mouth; diameter of the mouth; diarrhea of the mouth; dimensions of the mouth; direction of the mouth; drying of the mouth; dryness of the mouth; edge of the mouth; entrance of the mouth; expression of the mouth; flap of the mouth; floor of the mouth; form of the mouth; front of the mouth; gape of the mouth; heat of the mouth; height of the mouth; humming of the mouth; length of the mouth; lesions of the mouth; level of the mouth; line(s) of the mouth; lip(s) of the mouth; margin of the mouth; moisture of the mouth; motion(s) of the mouth; movement(s) of the mouth; mucus of the mouth; muscle(s) of the mouth; opening of the mouth; orifice of the mouth; outline of the mouth; palate of the mouth; part(s) of the mouth; passage of the mouth; portion of the mouth; position of the mouth; possession of the mouth; projection of the mouth; pull of the mouth; pursing of the mouth; quiver of the mouth; recesses of the mouth; region of the mouth; resonance of the mouth; rest of the mouth; rim of the mouth; roof of the mouth; saliva of the mouth; secretions of the mouth; section of the mouth; shape of the mouth; shift of the mouth; show of the mouth; side(s) of the mouth; sight of the mouth; size of the mouth; skin of the mouth; slackening of the mouth; slash of the mouth; smallness of the mouth; soreness of the mouth; sores of the mouth; sound of the mouth; speech of the mouth; stimulation of the mouth; stretching of the mouth; structure of the mouth; surface of the mouth; sweep of the mouth; taste of the mouth; temperature of the mouth; twist of the mouth; ulceration of the mouth; ulcers of the mouth; vicinity of the mouth; view of the mouth; voice of the mouth; wall(s) of the mouth; wedge of mouth; width of the mouth; word(s) of the mouth.

USAGE EXAMPLES

She had an *attractive mouth* made for kissing.

His *cavernous mouth opened wide.*

The giant's *frothing mouth gobbled up* the hapless villager.

Chris looked over at her, his *mouth grinning* with satisfaction.

Her *impetuous mouth broke into* a wide sinister smile.

28
NECK

Adjectives in Alphabetical Order

A - L

aching; ample; angled; arched; arching; aristocratic; awkward; baby-soft; bad; bald; bandaged; bare; beauteous; beautiful; beautifully-shaped; beauty-marked; beefy; bended / bent; big; birdlike; black; blazing; bleeding; blood-soaked; bloodied; bloody; blotchy; blue; blue-veined; bony; brawny; bristled; bristling; bristly; broad; broken; bronzed; brown; bruised; bulging; burly; burned / burnt; burnished; charming; child-like; chubby; circular; clammy; clean; clean-cut; coarse; cold; colored; column-like; columnar; comely; crane-like; creamy; creased; crimson; crooked; curved; cylindrical; dainty; damp; dark; defiant; delicate; delicious; dirty; discolored; dislocated; distended; distinct; doughy; downy; drooping; eager; eastern; elastic; elegant; elevated; elongated; enormous; entire; erect; excessive; exposed; exquisite; extensive; extra-long; fair; familiar; fat; feeble; female; fine; fine-haired; flabby; flat; fleshy; flexible; fractured; fragile; frail; freckled; full; furry; fuzzy; gawky; generous; gentle; giant; gleaming; glistening; glossy; glowing; golden; graceful; great; gritty; hairy; handsome; hard; haughty; heavy; high; hot; huge; immense; imperial; impressive; inflated; injured; innocent; jeweled; jittery; kingly; kissable; knife-scarred; large; lathered; lean; leathery; lifeless; limber; limp; lithe; little; lofty; lolling; long; longish; loose; lovely; low; lower; luscious.

M - Y

magnificent; male; maned; mangled; manly; marble-white; massive; mighty; muscled; muscular; naked; narrow; nice; noble; old; pale; perfect; perfumed; pillar-like; pink; pipe-thin; plain; pliant; plump; pompous; powerful; precious; pretty; prickly; prominent; prostrate; proud; pudgy; purple; quivering; rashy; red; reddish; reedy; revealed; rigid; rosy; rough; royal; rubbery; ruddy; sagging; salty; sandy; satiny; scaly; scant; scarlet; scarred; scraggy; scrawny; sculpted; serpentine; severed; shaggy; shape-long; shapely; shaved; shaven; shiny; short; silky; sinewy; sinuous; skinny; sleek; slender; slight; slim; sloping; small; smooth; snake-like; snaky; sodden; soft; solid; sore; spindly; spiny; splendid; sprained; square; stately; stiff; stooped; stout; strained; straining; streamlined; stringy; strong; struggling; stubborn; stubby; sturdy; submissive; sun-blackened; sunburned / sunburnt; superficial; supple; surrounding; swan-like; swan-white; swarthy; sweat-drenched; sweat-soaked; sweating; sweaty; sweeping; sweet; swelling; swollen; swooping; tall; tanned; tapered; tattooed; taut; tender; tense; thick; thin; tight; tiny; towering; truncated; trunk-like; tubular; twisted; ugly; unblemished; unbroken; unclean; unprotected; unshaven; unwashed; upper;

upright; upturned; vast; veined; velvety; visible; voluptuous; vulnerable; warm; weak; weary; weathered; well-shaped; wet; white; whole; wide; willing; willowy; wiry; withered; wizened; wrinkled; wrinkly; young; youthful.

Verbs and Phrasal Verbs in Alphabetical Order

A - L

ached; ached from; ached with; adorned with; appeared; arched; arched back; ascended; associated with; attached; bandaged; bared; beat; bent; bent back/backward; bent down; bent forward; bent over; bent toward; bibbed; blazed; bled; blended; blended into; blew on; blotched; bore; bothered; bounced; bounced against; bound; bowed; braced; bristled; bristled against; broke; brought out; bruised; bulged; bunched; bunched up; buried; buried in; burned; burned from; burned with; burst; burst out; came to; came up; carried; cast; caught; caused; chafed; checked for; clasped; cleaned; clicked; climbed; clothed; clotted; coated; coated in; coiled; coiled back; collapsed; complemented; connected; consisted of; contained; contracted; corresponded to/with; covered by; covered with; cracked; cramped; craned; craned forward; craned out; craned round; craned up; creaked; creased; crept up; cricked; cupped; curved; curved down; curved toward; curved up; cut; cut off; dampened by/with; danced; dangled; decorated by/with; descended; developed; dipped; disappeared; dislocated; dominated by; draped in; drenched; drew back; drew in; drew out; dripped; dripped with; drooped; dropped; dug into; edged with; elongated; embraced; emerged; encircled; encircled by/with; enclosed; enlarged; entwined; enveloped; enveloped in; erected; escaped; escaped from; exposed; extended; faced; fanned; fastened around; felt; fitted with; fixed; flailed; flared; flashed; flattered by; flew; flew back/backward; flexed; floated; flopped; flopped over; flushed; fluttered; followed; forced; formed; found; frayed; freed; freed from; froze; furnished with; gleamed; glinted; glistened; glittered; glowed; goosepimpled; got tight; grabbed; grew; grew tighter; held; held out; hidden by; hung; hung around; hung forward; hurt; inclined; included; increased; indicated; inflated; inscribed on; itched; jangled (necklace); joined; jounced; jounced up; jumped; jumped up; jutted; jutted forward; jutted out; kissed; knocked; knocked against; knotted; laced in; laid; lashed; leaned; led; lengthened; lessened; lifted; looked; loosened; lowered; lurched; lurched forward.

M - W

marked; marked with; merged into; met; moved; nestled; nuzzled; offered; ornamented by/with; passed; peeped; peeped out; pierced; pinched; pinched between; pinned; pinned to; placed; placed around; pointed down/up; popped; popped out; presented; pressed; pressed close/against; prevented; pricked; prickled; probed forward; produced; projected; protected; protested; protruded; provided; puffed; puffed up; pulled; pulled in; pulled up; pulsated; pulsed; purpled; pushed down/downwards; pushed up/upwards; quaked; radiated; raised; ran; reached; reached out; reached up; received; reclined; recoiled;

reddened; relaxed; remained; remained bent; remained tight; removed; resembled; rested; retracted; revealed; ringed with; ripped away; rippled; roped around; rose; rounded by; rubbed; sagged; sank; sat; scratched; scrubbed; seized; set; settled; settled against; severed; shaved; sheathed; sheathed in; shifted; shivered; shone; shook; shortened; shot out; showed; showed through; shrank; shrank back; slammed; slanted; slashed; sliced; slid; slit; slumped; slumped forward; smelled; smelled of; snapped; snapped back; snapped straight; soaked; softened; spasmed; sprouted; sprouted from; spun; spun around; squeezed; squeezed by; squeezed into; started; stiffened; stood; stood out; stood straight; stood up; stopped; straightened; strained; streaked with; stretched; stretched forward; stretched out; stuck out; stung; sunburned; sunk; supported; supported by; surrounded; surrounded by; suspended; swaddled; swathed in; swayed; sweat; swelled; swiveled / swivelled; swung; tapered; tapered to; tensed; tensed up; thickened; threw; threw back; threw up; throbbed; thrust; thrust forward; tickled; tied around; tied to; tied with; tightened; tilted; tinged with; tingled; tipped; tipped forward; tore off; tossed; tossed back; towered; towered over; traveled; traveled down; trembled; tucked; tucked down; turned; twinged; twisted; twitched; unbent; uncovered; vanished; vibrated; wagged; washed; wore; wore around; wound around; wrapped; wrapped around; wrapped in; wrung.

Noun Phrases

action of the neck; angle of the neck; apex of the neck; appearance of the neck; area of the neck; back of the neck; base of the neck; beginning of the neck; bone(s) of the neck; border of the neck; center of the neck; circumference of the neck; color of the neck; column of the neck; compression of the neck; condition of the neck; constriction of the neck; contour of the neck; contraction of the neck; crack of the neck; crest of the neck; curvature of the neck; curve of the neck; diameter of the neck; direction of the neck; dislocation of the neck; distension of the neck; edge of the neck; elongation of the neck; end of the neck; engorgement of the neck; enlargement of the neck; examination of the neck; exploration of the neck; exposure of the neck; extension of the neck; flesh of the neck; flexibility of the neck; folds of the neck; form of the neck; fracture of the neck; gland(s) of the neck; hair of the neck; height of the neck; hollow of the neck; inclination of the neck; inflammation of the neck; injury of the neck; insertion of the neck; irritation of the neck; joints of the neck; junction of the neck; juncture of the neck; length of the neck; line(s) of the neck; margin of the neck; motion of the neck; mouth of the neck; movement(s) of the neck; muscle(s) of the neck; musculature of the neck; nape of the neck; narrowness of the neck; nerve(s) of the neck; outline of the neck; part(s) of the neck; plane(s) of the neck; point of the neck; portion of the neck; position of the neck; posture of the neck; protection of the neck; radius of the neck; region of the neck; relaxation of the neck; remainder of the neck; rest of the neck; retraction of the neck; ridge of the neck; rigidity of the neck; rotation of the neck; section of the neck; shape of the neck; shortness of the neck; side(s) of the neck; sinews of the neck; size of the neck; skin of the neck; spasm of the neck; stiffness of the neck; strength of the neck; stretch of the neck; structure of the neck; stump of the neck; surface of the neck; sweat of the neck; swelling of the neck; tendon(s) of the neck; tension of the neck; thickness of the neck; tilt of the neck; treatment of the neck; turn of the neck; twist of the neck; underside of the neck; vein(s) of the neck; wall of the neck; weakness of the neck; width of the neck.

USAGE EXAMPLES

His *broad neck supported* Lucy's weight with ease.

She managed to *massage her stiff neck* with her index finger.

My mother applied sunscreen to my *burned neck*.

He gently caressed her *fair neck*.

Mike *twisted his neck* in the direction of the loud bang.

29
NOSE

Adjectives in Alphabetical Order

A - I

abominable; acute; African; aggressive; alcoholic; altered; always-stuffy; ample; angled; angry; angular; aquiline; arched; aristocratic; arrogant; arrow-tipped; assertive; austere; average; bad; banged-up; battered; beak-like; beaked; beaky; beautiful; bent; best; big; big-nostriled; bird-like; bleeding; bloated; blood-stained; bloodied; bloody; blue; bluish; blunt; blunt-ended; bold; bony; brazen; bridged; bridgeless; broad; broken; brown; bruised; bulbed; bulbous; bulgy; bumpy; busted; busy; buttonlike; callused; carbuncled; caricaturish; Caucasian; cavernous; charming; chilly; chiseled; classic; classical; clean; clear; clicking; clogged; coarse; coked-up; cold; colored; comical; commanding; concave; congested; conical; considerable; convex; cragged; cream-covered; crimson; crinkly; crooked; crumpled; crunched; crushed; curious; curled; curved; cute-as-a-button; dainty; damaged; damp; dangling; dark; defined; deformed; delicate; depressed; dirty; distinct; distinctive; distinguished; dominant; drippy; drooping; dry; Dutch; elegant; elevated; elongated; eminent; English; enormous; European; ever-dripping; excellent; exceptional; excessive; exposed; expressive; exquisite; extraordinary; extreme; extruded; fabulous; false; famous; fat; female; feminine; feral; fierce; fiery; fine; fine-boned; flat; flattened; flattish; fleshy; formidable; fractured; freckled; freezing; French; frozen; full; funny; funny-looking; garlic-shaped; generous; gentle; gigantic; glazed; glistening; glorious; glowing; gnarled; good; good-looking; grand; greasy; great; Grecian; Greek; grotesque; grumpy; hairy; handsome; hard; haughty; hawk-beak; hawk-like; hawkish; hideous; high; high-arched; high-bridged; honking; hooked; hooky; hot; huge; humped; hypersensitive; ice-cold; icy; immense; impeccable; imperial; imperious; impish; imposing; inflamed; injured; inner; irregular; irritated; Italian; itching; itchy.

J - Y

Jewish; jolly; jutting; keen; knobby; knotted; large; leaking; lean; lengthy; little; long; longish; lovely; luminous; lumpy; magnificent; mammoth; mangled; manly; marbled; masculine; mashed; massive; masterful; meaty; misshapen; moist; monstrous; monumental; much-broken; narrow; neat; nice; noble; noisy; Nordic; numb; oily; old; once-broken; ordinary; outer; overhanging; overlarge; oversized; overwhelming; pale; peaked; peculiar; perfect; perspiring; pert; petite; pierced; piggish; pimpled; pimply; pinched; pink; pocked; pockmarked; pocky; pointed; pointy; powdered; powerful; precious; predatory; pretty; prodigious; prominent; pronounced; protruding; protuberant; proud; prying;

pudgy; puffy; pugged; purple; purple-veined; ragged; raised; ratlike; razor-straight; red; reddened; reddish; refined; remarkable; ridged; right-shaped; rodentlike; Roman; Romanesque; roseate; rotund; round; rounded; royal; rubicund; ruddy; running; runny; scarlet; scarred; scornful; scrunching; sculpted; sensitive; serious; severe; shapeless; shapely; sharp; sharp-angled; shattered; shining; shiny; short; sizable; skewed; ski-jump; skinny; slanted; sleek; slender; slight; slim; sloped; sloping; sloppy; small; smashed; sneezy; sniffling; snotty; snoutlike; snubby; snuffly; soft; solid; sore; spectacled; spectacular; splayed; splendid; spongy; square; squashed; squat; starlit; steep; stopped-up; straight; streaming; streamlined; strong; stubby; stuffy; stumpy; sun-pink; sunburned / sunburnt; sunken; supersensitive; sweaty; swollen; tanned; tender; thick; thin; thin-bridged; thumb-like; tilted; tiny; tip-tilted; tipped-up; titanic; too-big; too-large; too-small; tremendous; triangular; turned-up; twice-broken; twitching; ugly; understated; unfortunate; unprotected; unwashed; upper; uptilted; upturned; veined; warm; warty; waxen; well-formed; well-shaped; wet; whiskered; white; whole; wide; wine-red; wonderful; wrinkled; young; youthful.

Verbs and Phrasal Verbs in Alphabetical Order

A - M

ached; aimed; aimed ahead; aimed at; aimed downward; angled; angled down; appeared; arched; attached; attached to; bandaged; banged; became red; became swollen; began dripping; began running; belonged; bent; betrayed; bit; bit off; bled; bled through; blew; blocked; bloodied; bloodied by; bloomed; bore; bothered; brightened; broke; bruised; brushed; brushed against; bubbled; bumped; bumped against; buried in; burned; burrowed; burrowed down; burst; burst out; busted; came back; came down; came up; came upon; captured; cast; caught; caught in; caused; caused by; changed; chilled; cleared; clipped; clogged; closed; cocked; collided; commanded; contained; continued; covered; covered by/with; covered in; crept out; crept upward; crimped; cringed; crinkled; crumpled; crunched; crusted with; cupped; curled; curled at; curved; cut; cut off; dabbed; dabbed at; descended; detected; dipped; directed; disappeared; discharged; dived; dominated; dotted with; dragged; dragged on; dried; dried out; dripped; drooped; dropped; dug into; dusted with; elongated; emerged; emerged from; ended in; enhanced by; entered; erupted; evoked; exploded; exposed; extended; fell; felt; festooned; festooned with; filled; filled up; filled with; flanked by; flared; flattened; flattered; followed; formed; found; freckled; froze; gained; gave; gleamed; glistened; glowed; glued to; gouged; grazed; greeted; grew; grunted; gushed; healed; held; held up; hid; hid beneath; hinted at; hit; hooked; hovered; hummed; hung; hurt; identified; immersed in; inched; inclined; indicated; inhaled; inherited from; itched; jerked; jutted; jutted out; kissed; knocked; leaked; lifted; lit up; looked; loomed; loomed over; marked; met; moved.

needed; nodded; nudged; nuzzled; nuzzled against; oozed; painted; peeled; peeped out; penetrated; peppered by/with; perched; picked; picked up; pierced; pinched; pitched down; plastered with; plowed; plugged up; plunged; pointed; pointed at; pointed down; pointed toward; pointed up; poked; poked in; poked out; poured; pressed; pressed against; pressed to; pressed up; prickled; produced; projected; pulled; punched; punctured; pushed; quivered; raised; raised toward; ran; reacted to; receded into; reddened; registered; relaxed; remained; remembered; resembled; rested against; rose; rubbed; rubbed against; rubbed into; rushed with; sat; scraped; scratched; scrunched; scrunched up; set; shaped like; shattered; shone; shoved against; showed; skewed; slanted; sloped; smashed; smashed against; smeared with; smelled; sniffed; snored; snorted; snorted up; snuffled; sought out; splattered with; sported; spread out; squashed; squashed against; squeezed; squinched; squinched up; squished; started bleeding; started running; started tightening; stood out; stopped; stopped up; straightened; streamed; stroked; struck; stuck out; stuffed; stuffed up; stung; suggested; sunk; sunk into; surmounted; swatted; swelled; swung to; tested; throbbed; thrust; thrust forward; thrust out; tickled; tilted; tipped; tipped forward; took; touched; traced; traveled; trembled; trickled; tucked into; turned; turned up; tweaked; tweaked by; twinkled; twisted; twitched; upraised; watched; went down; went up; wept; wet; whistled; whitened; widened; wiggled; wiped; wore; wrapped in; wrinkled; wrinkled up; zinced.

Noun Phrases

angle of the nose; apex of the nose; appearance of the nose; base of the nose; blockage of the nose; breadth of the nose; bridge of the nose; cartilage of the nose; cavity of the nose; center of the nose; color of the nose; congestion of the nose; contour of the nose; curve of the nose; depression of the nose; dryness of the nose; edge of the nose; end of the nose; flatness of the nose; form of the nose; fracture of the nose; front of the nose; height of the nose; infection of the nose; inflammation of the nose; irritation of the nose; jut the of nose; kind of nose; length of the nose; line of the nose; obstruction of the nose; opening(s) of the nose; outline of the nose; part of the nose; point of the nose; portion of the nose; position of the nose; profile of the nose; projection of the nose; prominence of the nose; redness of the nose; region of the nose; ridge of the nose; septum of the nose; shadow of the nose; shape of the nose; side(s) of the nose; sinuses of the nose; size of the nose; skin of the nose; slope of the nose; sort of nose; structure of the nose; style of nose; surface of the nose; tilt of the nose; tip of the nose; top of the nose; trace of the nose; type of nose; width of the nose; wrinkling of the nose.

USAGE EXAMPLES

The nobleman *raised the tip of his aristocratic nose* with an air of superiority.

His *bleeding nose dripped* all over the kitchen floor.

Beth's *exquisite nose flared* with agitation at the remark.

He had a *generous nose* with great big nostrils.

The old man *blew his ruddy nose* into a ratty gray handkerchief.

30
SHOULDER(S)

Adjectives in Alphabetical Order

A - M

able; aching; adolescent; ample; angular; arthritic; athletic; bad; bandaged; bare; bared; bearish; beautiful; beefy; bent; big; big-boned; birdlike; black; blanketed; bleeding; block-like; blockish; blocky; blood-encrusted; blood-soaked; bloody; blue; blue-jumpered; bony; bowed; brawny; bright; brittle; broad; broken; bronzed; brown; bruised; bulging; bulky; bull-like; bumpy; bunched; bundled; burly; burned / burnt; burnished; calm; capable; capacious; caped; cashmered; cherry-red; childish; chilly; chubby; chunky; clenched; cold; colored; comely; confident; cool; corduroyed; cramped; cream-colored; crimson-clad; crooked; crossed; curled; curved; dainty; damaged; damp; dandruff-covered; dark; decent; deep; defenseless; defiant; deformed; dejected; delicate; delicious; diminutive; dimpled; dislocated; distinct; drooped; drooping; dropped; elegant; elevated; enormous; excellent; expansive; exposed; expressive; exquisite; extraordinary; fabulous; fair; familiar; far; fat; feeble; feminine; fine; firm; firm-looking; flat; fleshy; football-player; fractured; fragile; frail; freckled; frozen; full; gargantuan; gaunt; gentle; giant; gigantic; girlish; glazed; gleaming; glistening; glittering; glossy; golden; good; graceful; greasy; great; hairy; handsome; hard; heavy; hefty; herculean; high; horizontal; hot; huge; hulking; humped; hunched; hurt; immaculate; immense; impatient; impertinent; inadequate; incredible; injured; inner; itching; jostling; jutting; knobby; knotted; labcoated; lacerated; large; lateral; lazy; lean; lean-muscled; left; light; limp; little; lofty; long; loose; lovely; low; lower; lowered; magnificent; manly; mannish; masculine; massive; massy; matching; meager; meaty; menacing; mighty; misshapen; moist; monumental; motionless; mountainous; muscled; muscular.

N - Y

naked; narrow; nervous; nice; noble; nude; numb; old; open; opposite; other; outer; oversized; packed; padded; painful; pale; paralyzed; partly-paralyzed; passive; paunchy; perfect; perfumed; petite; pink; pinstriped; pivoting; plump; pointed; pointy; powerful; powerful-looking; pretty; prominent; proud; raised; raw; red; red-jacketed; relaxed; resistant; resolute; rheumatic; right; rigid; ripped; rippled; rippling; robust; rocky; rolling; rough; round; rounded; rugged; sagging; sandy; scared; scarlet; scorched; scraped; scrawny; sculpted; shapeless; shapely; sharp; shifting; shining; shiny; shirtless; shivery; short; silk-covered; silk-draped; sinewy; single; skinny; sleeping; slender; slight; slim; sloped; sloping; slouched; slumping; small; smooth; snug; soaked; sodden; soft; solid; sore; spindly; sprained; square; squared; squared-off; stalwart; stately; steadfast;

steep; stiff; stiffened; stocky; stooped; stooping; stout; straight; straining; strapping; strong; stubborn; sturdy; substantial; suited; sun-browned; sunburned; suntanned; superb; supple; swarthy; swaying; sweating; sweatshirted; sweaty; sweet-smelling; sympathetic; t-shirted; tall; tanned; tattooed; taut; tender; tense; thick; thin; tight; tiny; tired; toned; trembling; tremendous; trench-coated; trim; turned; turned-away; twisted; twitchy; unblemished; unbloused; uncovered; undulating; ungainly; uniformed; unpadded; unwilling; unyielding; upper; vast; warm; weak; weary; weedy; well-defined; well-muscled; well-rounded; well-tanned; well-toned; wet; white; white-coated; white-covered; wide; wiry; wounded; young; youthful.

Verbs and Phrasal Verbs in Alphabetical Order

A - L

absorbed; accentuated; accentuated by; ached; ached from; ached with; acted up; advanced; aimed at; aligned; angled; announced; appeared; appeared above; arched; attracted; baked; bandaged; banged; banged against; bared; barged into; became; began; bent; bent forward; bent over; betrayed; blemished by; blew out; blocked; bobbed; bordered by; bounced; bounced up; bound; bowed; braced; braced against; braced for; braced on; broadened; broadened by; broke; brought up; bruised; brushed; brushed against; buckled; bulged; bulged against; bulged beneath; bulged up; bumped; bumped against; bumped together; bunched; bunched up; buried in; buried under; burned; burned beneath; burned from; burned under; burned with; burst through; butted; came down; came up; capped with; careened into; carried; cast; caught; caused; caved in; changed position; clad with; clenched; cloaked in; clothed in; collapsed; collided; collided with; connected with; contracted; contracted inward; conveyed; convulsed; covered by; covered with; cowered; cracked against; crackled with; cramped; crashed into; creaked; crept up; crunched beneath; curled; curled in; curved; curved against; curved forward; curved in; danced; danced down; darted; darted up; deflated; deflected; dipped; dipped back; disappeared; dislocated; dotted with; dragged; draped in; draped with; dressed in; dressed with; drew back; drew up; drooped; drooped forward; dropped; drove into; ducked; ducked out; dug in; dug into; eased; eased up; emerged from; exposed; extended; faced; faced down; fell; fell back; felt; felt like; felt tight; filled; filled out; fit; fit under; flapped; flapped behind; flapped out; flared; flared out; flashed; flew up; flexed; flinched; floated; flowed; flung out; folded; folded inward; followed; forced; formed; framed; framed by; freckled; freed; froze; gave out; gleamed; glistened; glowed; grabbed; grabbed at; grasped; grazed; grew; gripped; healed; heaved; held; held back; held up; hid; hiked up; hit; hit against; hovered; huddled; huddled inward; hugged; hunched; hunched forward; hunched over; hunched upward; hung; hung down; hurt; inched forward; indicated; jammed; jammed against; jerked; jolted; jumped; jumped up; knocked; knocked against; knotted; lay; lay across; leaned; leaned forward; lifted; locked up; looked; loomed; loosened; lost; lowered; lurched sideways.

M - W

managed; marked by; masked by; matted with; measured; met; moved; moved up; narrowed; nestled against; nipped; nudged; opened; passed; patted; perched on; pierced; pinched up; pinned; pinned back; pinned to; placed; pointed; pointed forward; pointed in; poised; poked; poked forward; poked up; popped; popped through; popped up; presented; pressed; pressed against; pressed together; pressed up; prevented; projected; propped against; propped up; protected; protected by; protested; protruded; pulled back; pulled up; pushed; pushed back; pushed down; quaked; quaked with; quieted; quivered; raised; raised up; ran into; reached; readied; receded; reflected; relaxed; released; remained; reset; rested; rested against; revealed; rippled; rippled with; rocked; rolled; rolled back; rolled inward; rose; rose above; rose up; rotated; rounded; roused; rubbed; rubbed against; sagged; sagged forward; sank; sat; scraped; scrunched; scrunched up; set; settled; shielded; shifted; shivered; shone; shook; shot up; shoved; showed; shrugged; shuddered; slackened; slammed into; slid down; slipped down; sloped; sloped down; slouched; slowed; slumped; slumped against; slumped down; slumped forward; smashed; smashed into; snapped; snapped straight; softened; spanned; spasmed; sprang up; spread; squared; squared up; squeezed; startled; stayed; stiffened; stilled; stood; stooped; stopped; straightened; strained; strengthened; stretched; struck; stuck out; stung; supported; swathed in; swayed; sweat; swelled; swiveled; swiveled back; swung; swung toward; tapered; tensed; tensed up; threw up; throbbed; thrust; thrust back; thrust forward; thudded against; tied; tightened; tilted; tingled; touched; trembled; tugged at; turned; twinged; twisted; twitched; unbound; unclenched; uncovered; unwound; vanished; weaved through; wedged; wedged against; wedged under; weighed down; went back; went forward; went in; went out; went up; widened; wore; worsened; wracked by; wrapped; wrapped around; wrapped in; writhed.

Noun Phrases

action of the shoulder(s); angle of the shoulder(s); appearance of the shoulder(s); area of the shoulder(s); back of the shoulder(s); base of the shoulder(s); bones of the shoulder(s); border of the shoulder(s); breadth of the shoulder(s); brush of shoulder(s); bulk of shoulder(s); center of the shoulder(s); contour of the shoulder(s); creases of the shoulder(s); crimp of shoulder(s); curve of the shoulder(s); depression of the shoulder(s); direction of the shoulder(s); dislocation of the shoulder(s); edge of the shoulder(s); elevation of the shoulder(s); end of the shoulder(s); expanse of shoulder(s); extension of the shoulder(s); feeling of shoulder(s); flesh of the shoulder(s); form of the shoulder(s); function of the shoulder(s); height of the shoulder(s); hint of shoulder(s); injury of the shoulder(s); inside of the shoulder(s); jerk of the shoulder(s); joints of the shoulder(s); length of the shoulder(s); level of the shoulder(s); line of the shoulder(s); mass of shoulder(s); mobility of the shoulder(s); motion of the shoulder(s); movement of the shoulder(s); muscles of the shoulder(s); musculature of the shoulder(s); narrowness of shoulder(s); outline of shoulder(s); pair of shoulder(s); part of the shoulder(s); portion of the shoulder(s); position of the shoulder(s); posture of the shoulder(s); power of the shoulder(s); pressure of the shoulder(s); projection of the shoulder(s); prominence of the shoulder(s); region of the shoulder(s); retraction of the shoulder(s); rotation of the shoulder(s); roundness of the shoulder(s); set of shoulder(s); shaking of the shoulder(s); shape of the shoulder(s); shrug of the shoulder(s); side of the shoulder(s); skin of the shoulder(s); slope of the shoulder(s); slump of the shoulder(s); squareness of the shoulder(s); squeeze of the shoulder(s); stability of the shoulder(s); stiffness of the shoulder(s); stoop of the shoulder(s); strength of the shoulder(s); stretch of shoulder(s); surface of the shoulder(s); swell of shoulder(s); swing of the shoulder(s); symmetry of the shoulder(s); tightening of the shoulder(s); tip of the shoulder(s); tops of the shoulder(s); trembling of the shoulder(s); twitch of the shoulder(s); view of the shoulder(s); weakness of the shoulder(s); weight of the shoulder(s); widening of the shoulder(s); width of the shoulder(s).

USAGE EXAMPLES

Jason's *broad athletic shoulders bulged beneath* his tight-fitting shirt.

She *buried her cold shoulders under* a thick blanket.

With her back facing him, she *bared her lovely lean shoulders*.

A hard shoulder drove into his ribcage, sending him flying.

Kate's *sore shoulders dipped* below the surface of the bubbling water.

31
SKIN

Adjectives in Alphabetical Order

A - F

acne-prone; acne-scarred; adolescent; adolescent-type; adverse; African; aged; ageing / aging; albino; allergic; almondy; already-raw; amazing; amber; anemic; ash-colored; ash-gray; ash-white; ashen; ashy; Asian; auburn; average; baby-smooth; bad; baggy; bald; ballooning; bare; bared; bark-brown; bark-like; barky; battered; beautiful; beige; best; better; bitter; black; black-as-midnight; blackened; blackish; blanched; blazing; bleach-white; bleached; bleeding; blemish-free; blemished; blistered; blistering; bloated; blood-rich; bloodless; bloody; blotchy; blue; blue-and-black; blue-black; blue-tinted; blue-veined; blue-white; bluish; boiled-looking; bone-white; boyish; bright; brilliant; bristly; brittle; broken; bronze-colored; bronze-tan; bronze-tinted; bronzed; bronzy; brown; browned; brownish; bruisable; bruise-dark; bruised; bubbled; bubbling; bulbous; burned / burnt; burning; burnished; buttermilk; butterscotch-colored; buttery; cadaverous; callused; caramel-colored; Caucasian; chafed; chalk-white; chalky; chapped; charred; cherubic; chilled; china-doll; china-pale; chocolate; chocolate-colored; chubby; clammy; classic; clean; clean-shaven; clear; cloud-gray; coal-black; coal-colored; coarse; coarse-grained; cocoa-brown; cocoa-colored; coffee-bean; coffee-colored; cold; colored; colored-fairish; colorless; cool; copper; copper-colored; coppery; coppery-brown; cotton-soft; cracked; cracking; crawling; cream-colored; cream-tinted; creamy; creamy-coffee; creased; Creole; crimson; crinkly; crisp; crispy; crumpled; crystal-clear; dainty; damaged; damp; dangling; dappled; dark; dark-brown; dark-coffee; darkened; darkening; darkish; dazzling; dead; dead-white; deadened; decent; deep-dark; deflated; delicate; dense; desiccated; devitalized; dewy; dimpled; dirt-stained; dirty; discolored; doughy; down-smooth; downy; dreadful; drenched; dried; drumtight; dry; dryish; dull; dusky; dust-covered; dusty; earthy; ebony-black; eczematous; elastic; English; European; excellent; excess; excessive; exfoliated; exfoliative; exotic; exposed; exquisite; extra; extraordinary; fair; fatty; faultless; female; fertile; fevered; feverish; filmy; filthy; fine; firm; fissured; flabby; flaccid; flaked; flaking; flaky; flawless; flayed; fleshy; floppy; florid; flushed; folded; forbidden; foreign; fragrant; freckled; fresh; fresh-washed; frozen; furred; furrowed; furry.

G - R

gentile; gentle; ghostly; gilded; glassy; glazed; gleaming; glistening; glittering; glittery; glossy; glowing; gold; golden; golden-brown; golden-tanned; good; goose-pimpled; goosebumped; gorgeous; gray; gray-looking; gray-white;

grayish; greasy; great; grimy; gross; hair-roughened; hairless; hairy; hairy-looking; handsome; hard; hardened; harsh; healing; healthy; heated; hereditary; hidelike; Hispanic; honey-brown; honey-colored; honeyed; horrible; hot; icy; impeccable; imperfect; incredible; Indian; inelastic; inflamed; inflated; inner; Irish; irritated; Italian; itchy; ivory-colored; ivory-hued; ivory-smooth; ivory-white; just-born; khaki-colored; lacerated; leathery; leprous; lesional; lice-covered; lickable; lifeless; light; light-brown; lilac-scented; lily-white; lined; lineless; loathsome; loose; lovely; lubricated; luminescent; luminous; lumpy; lusterless; lustrous; magnificent; male; malt-colored; mangy; manly; marbled; marked; maroon; mature; mayonnaise-colored; Mediterranean; medium-brown; Mexican; milk-white; milky; milky-white; mink-colored; miserable; mocha-brown; mocha-colored; moist; molted; mottled; muddy; mummified; muscled; muscular; musky; mutilated; naked; nasty; natural; necrotic; nice; Nubian-bronze; numb; numerous; nut-brown; nutmeg-colored; oak-brown; oak-colored; odd-smelling; oil-free; oily; old; olive; olive-colored; olive-tinted; olive-toned; once-dark; once-golden; once-ivory; once-pale; opalescent; opaque; orange; outdoor; outer; outermost; painful; painful-looking; painted; pale; pale-brown; paleish; pallid; paper-like; paper-thin; paper-white; papery; parched; parchment-colored; parchment-like; parchment-thin; pasty; pasty-white; patchy; peach-colored; peachy; peanut-colored; pearly; pebbled; pebbly; peeled; perfect; perfumed; petal-soft; picturesque; pigmented; pimpled; pimply; pink; pinkish; pinky-white; pitted; plain; plaster-like; pliant; plump; pocked; pockmarked; poor; porcelain-colored; poreless; porous; powdered; powdery; prematurely aged; pretty; prickly; psoriatic; puffy; purple; purple-black; purpled; purplish; purplish-brown; radiant; ragged; rain-soaked; raised; rashed; rashy; ravaged; raw; raw-looking; red; red-mottled; reddened; reddening; reddish; repulsive; resilient; resistant; revealing; rich; rigid; rose-colored; rose-pink; rosy; rouged; rough; roughened; royal; rubbed-raw; rubbery; ruddy; rugged; ruined; rumpled; russet; rust-colored.

S - Y

sable; sable-brown; sagging; saggy; sallow; salmon-colored; salty; sandpapery; sandy; satiny; saturated; scabby; scaly; Scandinavian; scarlet; scarred; scented; scorched; scraggy; scraped; scratchy-looking; scrubbed; sculpted; see-through; sensitive; seventeen-year-old; shaved; shaven; shimmering; shining; shiny; shiny-smooth; shredded; shriveled; sickly; silken; silky; singed; sizzling; slack; slackening; slashed; sleek; sleep-creased; sleep-lined; sleep-warmed; slender; sliced; slick; sliding; slimy; slippery; smooth; smooth-tan; snow-white; sodden; soft; soft-looking; soiled; sore; speckled; splendid; splotchy; spongy; spotted; spotty; stained; steaming; steamy; sticky; stiff; still-damp; still-tender; stretched; stretched-tight; stubbled; suede-colored; summer-brown; summer-darkened; summery; sun-beaten; sun-bronzed; sun-browned; sun-colored; sun-dark; sun-darkened; sun-drenched; sun-flushed; sun-kissed; sun-leathered; sun-ravaged; sun-roughened; sun-warmed; sunblasted; sunburned; suntanned; sunworn; supple; swarthy; sweat-drenched; sweat-sheened; sweat-shined; sweat-slicked; sweat-soaked; sweating; sweaty; sweet; swollen; syphilitic; taffy; taffy-colored;

tan; tanned; tattered; taupe-brown; taut; tea-colored; tender; tense; tepid; terrible; textured; thick; thin; tight; tight-stretched; timid; tingling; tinted; tired; tissuepaper-like; toasted; toffee-colored; tough; translucent; transparent; tropic; tropical; troublesome; ugly; ulcerated; unaffected; unattractive; unblemished; unbroken; unburned; undamaged; uneven; unexposed; unhealed; unhealthy; unlined; unlit; unmarked; unmarred; unpigmented; unprotected; unpunctured; unscarred; unscathed; unshaven; unsightly; untanned; untattooed; unwashed; unwrinkled; veined; velvety; virginal; visible; vulnerable; warm; warty; watery; wax-paper; waxen; waxy; weather-beaten; weathered; well-lined; well-tanned; wet; wheat-brown; whiskered; white; whiter-than-white; whitish; wind-burned; wind-reddened; wind-roughened; winter-sapped; winter-whitened; withered; wizened; wonderful; wounded; wretched; wrinkle-free; wrinkled; wrinkleless; wrinkly; yellow; yellow-tinged; yellow-tinted; yellow-toned; yellowed; yellowing; yellowish; yellowy-brown; young; youthful.

Verbs and Phrasal Verbs in Alphabetical Order

A - O

abraded; absorbed; ached; acquired; added; adhered; adjusted; adorned; adorned with; affected; affected by; afforded; allowed; amazed; appeared; applied to; astonished; attached; avoided; baked; bared; bathed; battered; became; began; betrayed; blackened; blanched; blazed; bleached; bled; blended with; blistered; blossomed; blotched; blotched with; blurred; blushed; bonded to; bore; breathed; bristled; broiled; broke out; browned; bruised; brushed; brushed against; bubbled; bulged; bunched; burned; burst; came away; came off; caught; caused; chafed; changed; cleaned; cleansed; cleared; clothed; clung to; coated by/with; colored; compared; concealed; connected; contacted; contrasted; cooked; cooled; covered; covered by/with; covered in; cracked; crackled; crawled; creased; crept; crimped; crinkled; curled; curved; curved into; cut; cut into; damaged; dampened; dangled; dappled; darkened; darkened by; decorated with; deepened; developed; differed; dimpled; discolored; disintegrated; dissolved; dotted with; dragged along/over; drained of; drank in; draped; draped over; dressed; dried; dripped; dripped with; dusted; dusted with; electrified by; emitted; enhanced by; erupted; erupted in; erupted with; examined; exhibited; exposed; exuded; felt; flaked; flared; flashed; flayed; flecked; flecked with; flew; flicked; flinched; flushed; flustered; fluttered; freckled; froze; gave off; gleamed; glimmered; glistened; glittered; glowed; glued to; goosepimpled; grayed; grew; hardened; healed; healed over; heated; heated up; hid; hinted at; hugged; hung; hurt; ignited; illuminated by; indicated; itched; kissed; laced with; lacked; leathered by; lightened; lined by/with; looked; loosened; lost; maintained; managed; marked; marked by/with; matted; needed; obtained; offered; ornamented with; overflowed with.

214

P - Y

painted; painted with; paled; pasted to; pebbled; peeked through; peeled; peeled off; peppered with; perspired; picked at; pierced; pierced with; pinched; pinked; pinkened; pitted; placed on; played with; pocked; popped; possessed; prepared; presented; pressed; pressed against; prevented; pricked; prickled; produced; projected; protected; protruded; proved; provided; puckered; pulled; pulsated; pulsed; pushed; quivered; radiated; ravaged by; reacted to; reddened; reddened by; reeked of; reflected; regained; removed; renewed; represented; repulsed; required; resembled; resisted; responded; responded to; rested against; resurfaced; retained; retouched; returned; revealed; ripped; rippled; rippled with; rose; rubbed; rubbed against; rubbed off; sagged; sank; sank in; scarred; scented; scented with; scraped; scraped across; scratched; scrubbed; sealed; secreted; seduced; sensitized to; shed; shimmered; shivered; shone; shook; shot over; showed; shrank; shriveled; sizzled; slapped; slid; slid against; slipped; smacked; smacked against; smarted; smeared with; smelled / smelt; smelled like; smelled of; smoldered; smoothed; smoothed by; soaked; softened; softened over; sparkled; sparkled with; spattered with; split; splotched; splotched with; spotted with; spread; spread on; spread over; sprinkled; sprinkled with; squirmed; stained; stained by; stank; steamed; stimulated; stippled; stippled with; stirred; stood; streaked by; stretched; stretched across; struck; stuck between; stuck to; studded; stung; subjected; sucked; suffered; suffocated; suffocated under; suggested; suited; sweated; swelled; tanned; tasted; tattooed; tended; tensed; tensed beneath; thickened; thinned; thrived; tightened; tinged with; tingled; tinted by; toasted by; tore; tore away; touched; touched against; toughened by; treated with; trembled; tugged; twitched; ulcerated; unveiled; vibrated; vibrated against; warmed; warmed by; warmed under; weathered; wet; whitened by; withered; wore; worked into; wrinkled; yellowed.

Noun Phrases

abrasion of the skin; amount of skin; appearance of the skin; area of skin; aspect of the skin; bag of skin; band of skin; beauty of the skin; bit of skin; blackness of the skin; blemishes of the skin; blueness of the skin; bulk of the skin; bundle of skin; care of the skin; changes of the skin; characteristics of the skin; character of the skin; circle of skin; circulation of the skin; cleanliness of the skin; cleansing of the skin; clearness of the skin; coarseness of the skin; coldness of the skin; coloration of the skin; color of the skin; complexion of the skin; condition of the skin; creases of the skin; darkness of the skin; defects of the skin; deformation of the skin; delicacy of the skin; depression(s) of the skin; discoloration of the skin; dryness of the skin; elasticity of the skin; elevation of the skin; examination of the skin; exfoliation of the skin; expanse of skin; exposure of the skin; fairness of the skin; features of the skin; fineness of the skin; flakes of skin; flap of skin; folds of the skin; greasiness of the skin; hardness of the skin; health of the skin; heat of the skin; hue of the skin; hydration of the skin; indentation of the skin; inflammation of the skin; irritation of the skin; island of skin; itchiness of the skin; layer of skin; lightness of skin; looseness of the skin; lumps of skin; moisture of the skin; oiliness of the skin; paleness of the skin; pallor of the skin; patch(es) of skin; pigmentation of the skin; pigment of the skin; plane of the skin; pores of the skin; portion of skin; quality of the skin; redness of the skin; region of the skin; response of the skin; rigidity of the skin; roughness of the skin; scaliness of the skin; sclerosis of the skin; secretion of the skin; section of skin; segment of skin; sensation of the skin; sensitivity of the skin; smoothness of the skin; softness of the skin; soreness of the skin; spots on the skin; stimulation of the skin; stretch of skin; strip of skin; surface of the skin; temperature of the skin; tenderness of the skin; tension of the skin; texture of the skin; thickness of the skin; thinness of the skin; tightening of the skin; tightness of the skin; toughness of the skin; treatment of the skin; ulceration of the skin; veins of the skin; vitality of the skin; warmth of the skin; whiteness of the skin; wrinkles of the skin; yellowness of the skin.

USAGE EXAMPLES

Her *skin crawled* at the thought of his touch.

He had *baggy skin* under his eyes which *sagged*, forming an eerie visage.

Rex *lathered his bronze-colored skin* with more sunscreen.

The *callused skin* on his palms felt rough against her own *supple skin*.

The *color of her skin turned pink* whenever he came close.

32
SPINE

Adjectives in Alphabetical Order

aching; aged; bent; bony; bowed; broken; bruised; cracked; crooked; crushed; curled; curved; curving; damaged; deformed; delicate; diseased; distorted; entire; flat; flexible; fractured; fused; grinding; hard; healthy; hidden; high; hollow; horizontal; horny; injured; inner; internal; kinked; knobby; large; little; long; lower; naked; narrow; old; osteoporotic; pliable; poor; powerful; prominent; quivering; ragged; rigid; rocky; s-shaped; saddle-hammered; saffron-robed; serrated; severed; sharp; shattered; short; slender; small; snaking; snapped; spineless; steep; stiff; stooped; stout; straight; strong; sunken; supple; sweating; thick; thin; throbbing; tingling; twisted; uneven; unrelieved; unstable; upper; upright; upstanding; vertical; warped; weak; well-trained; whole.

Verbs and Phrasal Verbs in Alphabetical Order

absorbed; ached; acquired; affected; arched; became; began; bent; bent forward; bowed; broke; buckled; bumped; busted; chipped; collapsed; compressed; consisted of; contained; cracked; crept up; curved; damaged; defied; deteriorated; developed; dipped; doubled over; drooped; electrified; examined; expanded; extended; felt; flexed; folded; formed; froze; hurt; itched; joined; jolted; leapt; leapt out; lifted; lifting; loosened; moved; moved with; placed; plastered to; plunged; pointed; popped; pressed; pressed against; prickled; produced; projected; protested; protruded; protruded from; provided; pushed; quivered; ran down; ran up; recoiled; remained; repaired; required; revealed; rippled; rippled up; rose; rubbed; sagged; shivered; showed; showed through; slackened; snapped; snapped to; splintered; split; started; stiffened; stirred; stood erect; stood up; stopped; straightened; stretched; stuck out; suffered; supported; tensed; tightened; tightened up; tingled; tingled with; trickled down; twisted; twitched; unfurled; vibrated; yielded.

Noun Phrases

area of the spine; arthritis of the spine; aspect of the spine; axis of the spine; base of the spine; bones of the spine; border of the spine; bottom of the spine; center of the spine; column of the spine; compression of the spine; condition of the spine; convexity of the spine; crest of the spine; curvature of the spine; curve of the spine; deformity of the spine; density of the spine; direction of the spine; disease of the spine; diseases of the spine; dislocation of the spine; distortion of the spine; edge of the spine; end of the spine; flexibility of the spine; fracture of the spine; fusion of the spine; inflammation of the spine; injury of the spine; instability of the spine; length of the spine; lesions of the spine; level of the spine; line of the spine; marrow of the spine; motion of the spine; movement of the spine; nerves of the spine; osteoarthritis of the spine; osteoporosis of the spine; part(s) of the spine; position of the spine; posture of the spine; projection of the spine; prominence of the spine; region of the spine; rigidity of the spine; section of the spine; segments of the spine; shape of the spine; side of the spine; snap of the spine; stability of the spine; stabilization of the spine; stiffness of the spine; tenderness of the spine; tip of the spine; top of the spine; twist of the spine; weakness of the spine.

USAGE EXAMPLES

A jolt of electricity *shot up her spine*.

The fall had *cracked her bony spine*.

Over the years, Gavin had *developed a strong spine* and could take an insult without it affecting him at all.

Her *rigid spine tingled* as he leaned closer.

Mary's *old spine began to buckle* under the pressure.

33
STOMACH

Adjectives in Alphabetical Order

A - M

aching; acidic; agonizing; amber-colored; ample; apron-covered; awful; bad; ballooning; bare; belted; best; big; bleeding; bloated; broad; brown; bruised; bulging; burning; calm; capacious; cast-iron; caved-in; churning; clean; clenched; cold; concave; considerable; contracting; corpulent; dainty; delicate; deprived; developing; digestive; dismayed; disordered; distended; distinct; double; downy; dreadful; elongated; empty; enormous; entire; excellent; excessive; expanding; exposed; extra; famished; fastidious; fat; finicky; fitful; flabby; flat; flattish; fleshy; fluttering; foul; frightened; full; furry; gaping; giant; gigantic; good; gorged; grateful; great; grizzled; growing; growling; grumbling; hairless; hairy; hard; hardy; haughty; healthy; hearty; heavy; high; hollow; hot; huge; hungry; ill; immense; inflamed; inflated; irritable; jiggly; jittery; jug-like; knotted; languid; large; lean; little; lovely; lower; manly; massive; mere; monstrous; mountainous; muscular.

N - Y

naked; nauseous; neglected; nervous; nice; nonexistent; normal; old; ordinary; oversized; padded; painful; pale; paunchy; pierced; pillowed; pink; poor; portly; pouched; pregnant; pregnant-looking; prodigious; prominent; protruding; protuberant; proud; pudgy; qualmish; queasy; rattled; ravaged; ravenous; raw; rebellious; ripe; rippled; robust; rock-hard; roiling; rolling; rotund; round; rounded; rumbling; sagging; satin-covered; sensitive; settled; shaggy; shapely; shrunken; shuddering; sick; sickly; six-pack; sizeable; slender; slight; small; smooth; soft; sore; spacious; spongy; squeamish; squishy; starved; steady; stout; strong; substantial; sunken; swelling; swollen; tanned; taut; tender; terrible; thick; thin; tight; tightened; tortured; touchy; tranquil; trim; tubular; twisted; ulcerated; undulating; uneasy; unfortunate; unprotected; upper; upset; vast; vigorous; voluptuous; warm; washboard-tight; weak; wet; white; whole; wide; wobbling; wobbly; wretched; youthful.

Verbs and Phrasal Verbs in Alphabetical Order

A - O

accentuated; accustomed; ached; acted up; announced; appeared; aspirated; awoke; balled up; bared; battled; became; began; belched; bestowed; betrayed;

bloated; boiled; bothered; bounced; brought up; brushed against; brushed by; bubbled; buckled; bulged; bumped; bumped against; bunched; bunched in; bunched into; burbled; burned; burst; calmed; came back; came down; came up; carried; caught; caused; caused by; ceased; chilled; chorused; churned; cinched; cinched up; clenched; clenched tight; clinched; clutched; clutched at; communicated; complained; consisted of; constricted; contained; continued; contracted; conveyed; convulsed; covered; covered with; cramped; cramped up; cried out; crouched down on; crouched on; curdled; curled; curled around; cut; demanded; digested; dipped; disappeared; distended; distressed; dived onto; doubled over onto; dragged; dragged against; drew in; drooped; dropped; dropped onto; eased; echoed; emitted; emptied; endured; escaped; examined; exploded; exposed; extended; faced; failed to; fed; fell; fell onto; felt; felt better; felt like; felt tight; filled; filled with; flared; flared up; flattened; flinched; flip-flopped; flipped onto; flipped over onto; flopped onto; flopped over onto; flowed from; fluttered; folded; fomented; forced; formed; fought; found; framed; frightened; furrowed; gaped; gave out; glowed; gnawed at; grazed; grew; gripped; growled; grumbled; gurgled; hardened; heaved; held; hit; hung; hung out; hung over; hurt; indented at; indicated; insisted; inspired; intensified; interrupted; jarred; jerked; jolted; jumped; kicked; knitted with; knotted; knotted up; labored; laid on; lazed on; leaped / leapt; led by; lessened; leveled; leveled off; lifted; lined; loaded; loaded with; loathed; looked; lost; lurched; mashed; moved; murmured; muttered; needed; opened.

P - W

pained; passed over; peeped out; pinched; pinched up; plummeted; plunged; pointed; pointed outwards; poked; poked out; pouched out; presented; pressed; pressed against; prevented; prickled; produced; protested; protruded; provided; puffed; puffed out; pulled in; pulsed; pumped; pumped out; punctured; pushed; pushed against; quivered; rebelled; received; recovered; reestablished; refused; rejected; relaxed; relaxes; remained; remembered; reminded; removed; required; resembled; responded; responded with; retained; returned; revolted; revolted against; revolted at; ripped; rippled; rippled beneath; roared; roiled; roiled inside; rolled; rolled over; rose; rose up; rotated onto; rumbled; sagged; sank; sat; sated; scraped; screamed; seared; seared by; secreted; seemed; seized; seized up; settled; shifted; shook; showed; showed through; shriveled up; shuddered; sickened; signaled; skittered; sliced; slid; slid across; slid on; slid onto; sloshed; slumped; slumped over; smarted; smeared on; snarled; somersaulted; sounded; sounded off; soured; sparkled; spasmed; spewed; spewed out; spilled out; spilled over; spoke; spoke up; squeezed; squirmed; stapled; started; steadied; steeled; stiffened; stirred; stopped; stuck out; stuffed; sucked in; suffered; surged; surrounded; swayed; swelled; swelled out; swelled underneath; swirled; swirled like; tensed; tensed with; thanked; threatened to; throbbed; thumped; tied; tied in; tied up; tightened; tightened up; tightened with; tilted; tingled; tolerated; took; tore; tossed; touched; trapped in; trembled; tumbled; tumbled round; turned; turned inside-out; turned onto; turned over; twisted; unclenched;

unleashed; unsettled; upset; wanted; washed; weighed; whined; worked; wound; wrenched; writhed.

Noun Phrases

acid of the stomach; amount of stomach; appearance of the stomach; area of the stomach; aspiration of the stomach; ball of the stomach; base of the stomach; billow of the stomach; border of the stomach; bottom of the stomach; bulge of the stomach; capacity of the stomach; center of the stomach; clamp of the stomach; clench(ing) of the stomach; coldness of the stomach; complaints of the stomach; compression of the stomach; condition of the stomach; congestion of the stomach; constriction of the stomach; contents of the stomach; contraction(s) of the stomach; cramp of the stomach; cravings of the stomach; curvature of the stomach; curve of the stomach; demands of the stomach; development of the stomach; digestion of the stomach; disorder of the stomach; disturbance of the stomach; edge of the stomach; emptiness of the stomach; enlargement of the stomach; feel of the stomach; fire in the stomach; flatness of the stomach; flesh of the stomach; folds of the stomach; form of the stomach; fullness of the stomach; heaving of the stomach; hold of the stomach; hollow of the stomach; hump of the stomach; inflammation of the stomach; inhalation of the stomach; irritability of the stomach; irritation of the stomach; juices of the stomach; lack of stomach; layer of stomach; layers of the stomach; length of the stomach; line of the stomach; lining of the stomach; lurch of the stomach; middle of the stomach; motion of the stomach; mound of the stomach; movements of the stomach; muscles of the stomach; musculature of the stomach; nerves of the stomach; outline of the stomach; overhang of the stomach; pain of the stomach; paralysis of the stomach; part of the stomach; paunch of the stomach; pit of the stomach; plane of the stomach; point of the stomach; portion of the stomach; position of the stomach; pouch of the stomach; pressure of the stomach; reaction of the stomach; reflux of the stomach; region of the stomach; regurgitation of the stomach; relaxation of the stomach; remainder of the stomach; response of the stomach; rest of the stomach; rise of the stomach; roll of the stomach; rolls of the stomach; rotation of the stomach; roundness of the stomach; rumble of the stomach; rumblings of the stomach; rupture of the stomach; sac of the stomach; section of the stomach; shape of the stomach; shuddering of the stomach; sickness of the stomach; side(s) of the stomach; sinking of the stomach; size of the stomach; skin of the stomach; softness of the stomach; sounds of the stomach; spasm(s) of the stomach; state of the stomach; stretch of the stomach; surface of the stomach; swell of the stomach; thickness of the stomach; tightening of the stomach; top of the stomach; ulceration of the stomach; ulcer of the stomach; uprising of stomach; volume of the stomach; wall(s) of the stomach; warmth of the stomach; washboard of the stomach; weakness of the stomach; weight of the stomach; wounds of the stomach.

USAGE EXAMPLES

His *bloated stomach drooped* over his belt buckle as he staggered out of the bar.

Her *stomach churned* with remorse at what she had cost him.

Kathleen's *fluttering stomach clenched tight* as the intruder edged nearer to her position.

The boy's *grumbling stomach communicated* that it was in desperate need of filling.

She traced her fingertips across his *lean muscular stomach.*

34
TOOTH / TEETH

Adjectives in Alphabetical Order

A - J

abnormal; abscessed; absent; aching; acute; additional; adjacent; adjoining; admirable; adult; angular; artificial; asymmetrical; authentic; avulsed; back; bad; barbed; bare; bared; beautiful; benign; best; betel-blackened; bicuspid; big; biting; black; black-edged; black-gummed; blackened; bleached; bleached-white; bleeding; blinding; blocky; blood-flecked; bloody; blue; blue-white; blunt; bone-white; bony; bottom; bright; bright-white; brilliant; brittle; broad; broken; brown; brown-stained; browned; brutal; bucked; burgeoning; burning; butter-yellow; calcified; canine; capped; carious; carnivorous; cavity-ridden; central; certain; chalk-white; chalky; chattering; chipped; chiseled; chitinous; chunky; clamped; clattery; clean; clenched; closed; closing; coarse; coffee-colored; coffee-stained; cold; colored; comical; complete; compressed; cone-shaped; conical; consecutive; conspicuous; corn-kernel; cracked; crooked; crowded; crushing; crusty; crystalline; curved; dagger-like; daggered; damaged; dangerous; dark; dazzling; dead; deadly; decayed; decaying; decimated; defective; deformed; delicate; detached; developing; dingy; dirty; disappearing; discarded; discolored; diseased; distinct; divergent; diverging; doll-sized; dreadful; eager; early; elegant; elongated; emerging; enameled; enormous; entire; equidistant; equine; eroded; even; even-sized; exaggerated; excellent; excised; existing; exposed; exquisite; extra; extra-white; extracted; fabulous; fair; fake; false; fanged; faultless; fearsome; feeble; ferocious; fierce; filed; filmy; fine; finest; flashing; flat; flat-edged; flawless; foamy; formidable; foul; fractured; fragile-looking; free; fresh; frightening; front; frosty; funny; gaping; gapped; gappy; giant; gigantic; girlish; gleaming; glinting; glistening; glittering; glorious; glossy; gnashed; gnashing; gold; gold-capped; gold-tinged; golden; good; gray; graying; grayish; great; greedy; grim; grinding; grinning; gritted; ground-down; growing; half-clenched; handsome; happy; hard; hardened; hay-colored; healthy; heavy; heavy-coated; hideous; horrible; horrid; horsey; huge; hungry; icy; immaculate; immense; imperfect; implanted; infected; inky; innumerable; interlocking; intricate; inturned; irregular; isolated; jagged; just-whitened; jutting.

K - Y

keen; knife-like; large; laser-bleached; laughing; lipstick-stained; little; locked; lonely; long; loose; lost; lousy; lovely; lower; magnificent; malformed; mammoth; massive; matching; mature; metallic; milk-white; misshapen; missing; molar; monstrous; mottled; multiple; narrow; nasty; natural; neat;

223

needle-like; needle-sharp; neighboring; nervous; never-braced; new; nice; nicotine-stained; normal; nubby; numerous; oblique; obscure; odd; off-white; offending; old; open; orange; orderly; ordinary; original; outer; overlarge; oversized; painful; pale; pale-yellow; paper-white; parted; pearl-white; pearly; peculiar; perfect; perforated; piercing; pink; pink-edged; pointed; pointy; polished; poor; porcelain-crowned; powerful; pretty; prominent; protruding; protuberant; pulled; rabbity; rabid; radiant; ragged; ravenous; razor-sharp; real; rear; red; red-stained; reddish-yellow; remaining; remarkable; repulsive; ridged; rigid; rotted; rotten; rotting; rough; rounded; rugged; ruined; sand-yellow; savage; scalloped; scissor-like; sensitive; serrated; shark-like; shark-white; sharp; sharp-looking; sharpened; shattered; shining; shiny; short; shy; significant; silver-capped; single; skewed; slender; slicing; slimy; sloppy; small; smashed; smashed-out; smiling; smooth; snaggly; snappy; snarling; snow-white; snowy; solid; sore; sparkling; sparse; spiky; splendid; sprouting; square; stained; stone-white; stout; straight; straightened; streamlined; striated; strong; stubby; stumpy; successive; superb; tangled; tawny; tea-stained; temperamental; temporary; tender; terrible; terrific; thick; thin; tiny; tobacco-stained; too-big; too-small; too-white; top; tremendous; triangular; ugly; unattractive; undamaged; uneven; unstained; unworn; upper; vertical; vicious; visible; weak; weathered; weird; well-spaced; well-whitened; white; whole; wicked; wide; wide-gapped; wide-spaced; wonderful; worn; worn-down; worn-out; yellow; yellowed; yellowing; yellowish; young.

Verbs and Phrasal Verbs in Alphabetical Order

A - K

ached; ached from; adapted to; affected by; afforded; aged; allowed; announced; appeared; approached; arranged in; ate; attached to; balanced out; bared; became; began; belonged; bit; bit down; blackened; bled; blocked; blocked out; bolstered; bounced; braced; broke; broke into; brought down; brushed; bucked; bucked out; buried; buried in; burned; burst from; buzzed; came out; came together; came toward; capped; capped with; carried; carved; caught; caused; ceased; chattered; checked; chewed; chomped; chomped down; chomped on; chomped together; clacked; clacked against; clacked together; clamped; clamped around; clamped down; clapped; clapped together; clashed; clattered; clattered together; cleaned; clenched; clenched against; clenched down; clenched together; clicked; clicked against; clicked together; clinched; clinched around; clinked; clogged up; clogged with; closed; closed down on; closed on; collided; collided with; concealed; continued; covered; covered with; cracked; cracked into; cracked together; crowded; crowded at; crumbled; crunched; crunched together; curved; curved down; cut; cut into; cut through; dangled; dangled from; dashed; dazzled; decayed; declared; developed; devoured; differed from; differed in; disappeared; discovered; displayed; disposed of; dissolved; dissolved into; drenched with; drilled into; dripped with; dropped; dropped out; drove into; embedded in; emerged; emitted; enabled; entered; eroded; erupted;

erupted from; examined; exhibited; exposed; exposed between; extended; extracted; extracted from; fastened on; fastened onto; fell; fell on; fell out; felt; filed down; filled with; fit; fixed; fixed on; flashed; flecked with; flew out; floated over; followed; formed; found; framed by; freed from; froze; fused; gleamed; glimmered; glinted; glistened; glittered; glowed; gnashed; gnawed; gnawed at; grabbed onto; grated; grated together; grazed; grazed over; grew; grinded / ground; grinned; gripped; gritted; gritted together; ground down; ground together; hammered down; held back; helped; hesitated; hid; hid behind; hung; hurt; implanted; implanted in; increased in; indicated; inserted; inserted in; irritated; jarred; joined; jumped; jutted; jutted out; kicked in; knocked; knocked out; knocked together.

L - W

lay; lay between; lifted; lined; lined up; lit up; locked; locked onto; locked together; lodged in; looked; loosened; lost; lowered; lowered down; lunged; lunged through; lurked; made; maneuvered; marked with; mashed together; matched; measured; met; missed; moved; moved in; needed; nibbled; nibbled at; nicked; nipped; nipped at; nudged; numbed; obtained; occupied; opened; opened halfway; outlined; overlapped; packed; parted; passed; peeked out; peeked through; penetrated; perched; picked; picked at; pierced; pierced through; placed on; played with; ploughed; pointed; poked; poked up; polished; popped out; possessed; prepared; presented; preserved; pressed; pressed against; pressed down; pressed into; pressed together; prevented; probed; produced; projected; projected from; protruded; protruded from; proved; provided; pulled out; punctured; pushed past; quivered; radiated; raised; raked over; ran; ran back; rattled; ravaged; reached; reflected; remained; removed; replaced; represented; required; resembled; rested; retracted; returned; revealed; reverberated; ripped; ripped at; ripped into; ripped out; rotted; rotted away; rubbed; rubbed against; sank into; scraped; scraped across; scraped against; separated; set; shaped; sharpened; sharpened with; shattered; sheared through; shifted; shivered; shone; shook; shot out; showed; showed between; shredded; shut; slammed together; slanted; slanted inward; slanted out; slashed at; slid; slid down; slipped across; slipped down; slumped; smacked; smacked together; smashed; smashed together; smeared with; smiled; smiled down; snagged on; snapped; snapped at; snapped together; sneered; soaked in; spaced; spaced unevenly; sparkled; spilled from; splayed out; splayed within; splintered; split; spread; sprung; sprung into; stabbed; stabbed into; stained with; stalked; started; startled; stood; stood out; stopped; straightened with; stretched; struck; struggled; strung with; stuck; stuck out; stuck together; suffered; suggested; supplied; surrounded by; swarmed; tangled in; tapped; tapped against; thrashed; thrashed through; threatened; throbbed; thrust; thrust into; tightened; tightened against; tilted; tingled; took out; tore; tore at; tore into; touched; treated; tugged; tugged at; twinged; twinkled; united; vanished; varied in; vibrated; went into; went up; whitened; wiggled; worked at; worked on.

Noun Phrases

absence of teeth; abundance of teeth; alignment of the teeth; angle of the teeth; appearance of the teeth; arrangement of the teeth; array of teeth; arsenal of teeth; band of teeth; base of the teeth; care of the teeth; cavities of the teeth; characteristics of the teeth; character of the teeth; chattering of teeth; cleanness of the teeth; clicking of teeth; closure of the teeth; collection of teeth; color of the teeth; columns of teeth; condition of the teeth; contour of the teeth; corners of the teeth; couple of teeth; crown of the teeth; curvature of the teeth; decay of the teeth; development of teeth; dimensions of the teeth; direction of the teeth; discoloration of the teeth; disease of the teeth; displacement of the teeth; edge of the teeth; enamel of the teeth; eruption of teeth; examination of the teeth; exposing of teeth; extraction of teeth; face(s) of the teeth; features of the teeth; flash of teeth; formation of the teeth; form of the teeth; gleam of teeth; glint of teeth; gnashing of teeth; gnawing of teeth; grinding of teeth; group(s) of teeth; growth of teeth; hardness of the teeth; health of the teeth; height of the teeth; hint of the teeth; impression(s) of the teeth; infection of the teeth; inspection of the teeth; jaw of teeth; jumble of teeth; lack of teeth; length of the teeth; line(s) of teeth; looseness of the teeth; loss of the teeth; lot of teeth; maelstrom of teeth; mark(s) of the teeth; motion of the teeth; mouthful of teeth; mouth of teeth; movement of the teeth; number of teeth; outlines of the teeth; pain of the teeth; plane of the teeth; position of the teeth; presence of teeth; pressure of the teeth; profile of the teeth; profusion of teeth; pulling of teeth; quality of the teeth; quantity of teeth; removal of teeth; resistance of the teeth; rest of the teeth; root of the teeth; row(s) of teeth; series of teeth; set of teeth; shape of the teeth; sharpness of the teeth; shock of teeth; show of teeth; size of the teeth; sliver of teeth; sound of teeth; spacing of the teeth; splinters of teeth; state of the teeth; strength of the teeth; string of teeth; stumps of teeth; succession of teeth; surface of the teeth; thickness of the teeth; tips of the teeth; type of teeth; wall of teeth; whiteness of the teeth; width of the teeth; wreckage of teeth.

USAGE EXAMPLES

His *shiny white teeth glistened* whenever he opened his mouth to speak.

Simone's *front teeth clamped down hard on* Carl's lower lip, causing him to cry out in pain.

The old man's *butter-yellow teeth clacked together* when he ate.

The doctor examined the toddler's *developing tooth* and saw that it was coming in nicely.

His *exposed teeth showed* signs of decay.

35
THROAT

Adjectives in Alphabetical Order

A - L

aching; ample; arched; ardent; bad; bare; bared; bearded; beautiful; big; bleeding; bloody; blown-out; blue; blue-veined; blushing; boozy; brawny; brazen; bright; broad; bronzed; brown; bruised; bubbling; bulbous; burning; capacious; cavernous; choked; cigarette-bitten; clamorous; clear; cleared; clearing; clefting; clenched; closed; closing; colored; constricted; convulsed; corded; creamy; crimson; cut; cylindrical; dark; deep; delicate; desperate; dignified; discordant; distended; dry; dusty; enormous; entire; expanding; exposed; fair; fat; fear-gripped; fear-strained; fearful; fearknotted; feeble; fiery; fine; flabby; fleshy; flexible; full; furry; gaping; gentle; graceful; grainy; gravelly; great; greedy; gurgling; hairy; harmonious; harsh; healthy; heavenly; hoarse; hollow; hot; huge; hungry; husky; indignant; inflamed; inflated; injured; inviting; irritable; kingly; lacerated; large; lifeless; limp; lined; little; long; loosened; lovely; lower; lucid; lusty.

M - Y

magnificent; mangled; manly; massive; mellifluous; mellow; melodious; merry; milky; moaning; monstrous; mucousy; muscular; musical; naked; narrow; nervous; noisy; old; open; oversized; painful; pale; parched; perfect; phlegmy; pimply; pink; poor; precious; pulsing; purple; quivering; rasping; raspy; ravaged; raw; red; relaxed; rigid; roughened; rubbery; ruined; sagging; scarlet; scraggy; scratched; scratchy; scrawny; severe; shaggy; shapely; short; shrill; silent; silky; sinewy; sinuous; skinny; slashed; slender; slight; slim; small; smooth; soft; sore; squeaky; stiff; still; stinging; straining; streptococcic; stringy; strong; sunburned; sweet; swelling; swollen; tattered; tattooed; tear-clogged; tender; terrible; thick; thin; thirst-parched; thirsty; throbbing; tight; tiny; too-thick; torn; tuneful; twitching; ugly; ulcerated; unprotected; unwilling; upper; upturned; veined; vulnerable; warm; wattled; waxen; weak; weary; wet; white; whitish; whole; wide; wild; windburned; wiry; withered; wrinkled; yawning; yellow; yellowish; young.

Verbs and Phrasal Verbs in Alphabetical Order

A - G

abated; accompanied by; ached; announced; appeared; associated with; backed up; beat; became; began; bent; blocked; bobbed; bothered; bound; bound by; bound in; broke; brought up; bubbled; bubbled up; bulged; burned; burst; buzzed; called; caught; caused; caused by; caved in; choked; choked up; choked with; clamped; clamped down; clasped; cleared; clenched; clenched with; clicked; climbed up; clogged; clogged up; clogged with; closed; closed around; closed off; closed up; clotted; clutched; clutched at; coated; coated with; compressed; constipated; constricted; constricted around; constricted at; constricted with; continued; contorted; contracted; convulsed; convulsed in; covered; covered with; crammed; crammed down; cried out; crushed; crushed by; crushed with; cut; cut across; disappeared; disgorged; dried; dried up; dripped; eased; encircled; encircled by; endued; engorged; examined; expanded; exploded; exposed; extended; extended out; fastened around; fell; felt; felt blocked; felt choked; felt clogged; felt tight; filled; filled up; filled with; flexed; flooded with; flushed; fluttered; followed by; formed; froze; froze with; gagged; gaped; gave; gleamed; glowed; got tight; grew; gripped; gripped around; groped; groped for; growled; gurgled.

H - W

held; held in; hissed; hummed; hung; hurt; increased; itched; jammed; killed; knocked; knotted; knotted up; labors with; lashed; leapt; left; lingered; lingered in; locked; locked up; looked; looked into; loosened; lumped; lumped up; marked; melted; melted away; met; moved; narrowed; noosed; opened; overwhelmed; packed; packed with; paralyzed; peppered by/with; pierced; pinkened; played with; prevented; pulsed; quivered; raised; rattled; reached; reached up; reddened; refused; rejected; relaxed; remained; ripped; rippled; rippled with; rose; scabbed; scarred; scarred by; sealed; sealed over; seared; seized; seized up; set; severed; shaved; shone; shone against; showed; shrank; shut; shut tight; slackened; slashed; sliced; slit; smarted; snagged; sounded; sparkled; spilled; split; squeezed; stood out; strained; strangled; stretched; stuck; stung; subsided; swallowed; swelled; tasted; tasted of; tensed; tensed up; thickened; threatened to; throbbed; tickled; tightened; tightened up; tingled; tore at; tore out; torn; tottered; touched; trembled; tried; turned; twisted; untied; vibrated; warbled; watered; went tight; wet; wheezed; widened; worked; wound around; wounded; wrapped; wrung.

Noun Phrases

appearance of the throat; area of the throat; back of the throat; base of the throat; cavity of the throat; centre of the throat; clearing of the throat; color of the throat; compression of the throat; condition of the throat; congestion of the

228

throat; constriction of the throat; contraction of the throat; convulsion of the throat; curve of the throat; depth of the throat; diameter of the throat; dryness of the throat; enlargement of the throat; entrance of the throat; flesh of the throat; hollow of the throat; infection of the throat; inflammation of the throat; irritation of the throat; length of the throat; line of the throat; movement of the throat; muscles of the throat; opening of the throat; part of the throat; passage of the throat; pit of the throat; portion of the throat; redness of the throat; region of the throat; relaxation of the throat; shape of the throat; side(s) of the throat; size of the throat; skin of the throat; soreness of the throat; spasm of the throat; surface of the throat; swelling of the throat; tightness of the throat; top of the throat; ulceration of the throat; wall of the throat; width of the throat.

USAGE EXAMPLES

She *cleared her hoarse throat.*

He ran his hand over her *fiery hot throat.*

A dreadful fear *gripped her throat.*

The words emerged from her *raspy throat.*

The young girl's *quivering throat constricted* in horror.

36
THUMB(S)

Adjectives in Alphabetical Order

absent; amputated; awkward; bad; bandaged; beleaguered; bent; big; black; bleeding; bloody; blue; blunt; bony; broad; brown; bruised; busy; calloused; careless; chapped; clumsy; coarse; cocked; cold; crimson; crooked; cruel; curved; damaged; damned; debilitated; dirty; double-jointed; dumb; eager; elevated; enthusiastic; erect; extended; fat; fickle; filthy; firm; flat; floating; free; freed; fused; gentle; giant; gleaming; gloved; good; greasy; great; green; grimy; hairy; heavy; huge; human; hurt; identical; injured; inky; jammed; large; latex-gloved; leathery; left; little; locked; long; matching; mauled; missing; mittened; moistened; moving; nervous; nice; nicotine-stained; normal; oily; old; opposable; opposing; opposite; other; outstretched; oversized; paired; pert; pinched; pink; powerful; practiced; probing; pudgy; purpled; raised; red; right; rough; rubbery; ruddy; sausage-thick; sharp; short; single; sliced; small; smooth; smudging; soaked; sore; sprained; square; stinging; stinky; strong; strong-looking; stubby; swollen; thick; throbbing; ugly; uninjured; unusual; upraised; upturned; useless; wet; white; whole; wide.

Verbs and Phrasal Verbs in Alphabetical Order

A - O

acted; aimed; aimed at; allowed; anchored; appeared; applied to; attempted to; banged; banged on; became; began; bent; bent back; bit; blackened; bled; blotted out; bore; braced; brought up; brushed; burrowed in; came down on; caressed; caught in; caught on; circled; closed; closed around; clung to; cocked; continued; contorted; covered with; crept; crossed; crushed; crushed in; curled; curled up; curved; curved around; cut; cut off; disappeared; dragged; dragged across; dragged down; drifted; dropped; dug into; eased up; extended; extended upward; fell; fell off; felt; flexed; flicked; flicked down; flicked over; floated; folded; folded over; fondled; forced; found; gouged; gouged at; gouged out; grasped; grated; grated on; grazed; heaved; held; held up; hesitated; hit; hooked; hooked around; hovered; hovered over; hurt; inched toward; inserted; jabbed; jabbed in; jammed; jammed in; jammed into; jerked; joined; jumped; jutted up; kneaded; laid; left; licked; locked; locked together; looped; loosened; marked; massaged; motioned; moved; moved across; opened.

P - W

paged through; passed over; placed on; placed over; pointed; pointed backwards; pointed down; pointed up; poised; poked; poked into; positioned; pressed; pressed against; pressed into; pressed on; pressed to; pressed together; probed; pulled; pulled back; pumped; punched; punctured; pushed; pushed against; pushed down; quivered; raised; rammed; ran through; reached; reached for; remained; rested; rested on; rested over; rubbed; rubbed against; rubbed over; sank; sank in; scraped; scraped over; shifted; shot out; shot up; skimmed; slid across; slid down; slid onto; slid over; slipped; slipped loose; slipped on; slipped out; smeared; smoothed; smudged; snapped; squeezed; stabbed; started; stayed; stayed on; stood; stopped; stretched; stretched across; stroked; stroked away; stuck in; stuck out; stuck up; sucked; switched on; tapped; throbbed; thrust; thrust into; tied; tied together; touched; traced; trailed; trailed down; tucked beneath; tucked in; tucked into; tucked under; turned; twiddled; twisted; twitched; uplifted; used to; waited; went down; wiped; wiped away; worked; wrapped; wrestled.

Noun Phrases

absence of the thumb(s); action of the thumb(s); amputation of the thumb(s); articulation of the thumb(s); aspect of the thumb(s); ball(s) of the thumb(s); base of the thumb(s); bite of the thumb(s); bone(s) of the thumb(s); border of the thumb(s); brawn of the thumb(s); breadth of the thumb(s); closing of the thumb(s); couple of thumbs; deformity of the thumb(s); direction of the thumb(s); dislocation of the thumb(s); edge of the thumb(s); end of the thumb(s); extension of the thumb(s); flick of the thumb(s); form of the thumb(s); jab of the thumb(s); jerk of the thumb(s); joint(s) of the thumb(s); kind of thumb(s); knuckle of the thumb(s); length of the thumb(s); meat of the thumb(s); mobility of the thumb(s); motion of the thumb(s); movement of the thumb(s); muscle(s) of the thumb(s); nail of the thumb(s); pair of thumbs; part of the thumb(s); point of the thumb(s); position of the thumb(s); pressure of the thumb(s); rule of thumb; side(s) of the thumb(s); size of the thumb(s); skin of the thumb(s); smoothing of the thumb(s); snap of the thumb(s); spring of the thumb(s); strength of the thumb(s); surface of the thumb(s); tendon of the thumb(s); thickness of the thumb(s); tip(s) of the thumb(s); twist of the thumb(s).

USAGE EXAMPLES

Glen's *bandaged thumb throbbed* with pain.

This guy had *broad double-jointed thumbs*, perfect for playing videogames.

With a *clumsy thumb*, he *stroked* a strand of hair out of her eye.

He had *huge hairy thumbs* that *left* an imprint on the polished table.

His *thumb probed* the small hole in the wall.

37
TOE(S)

Adjectives in Alphabetical Order

A - N

2nd; 3rd; 4th; 5th; aching; adjacent; agile; amputated; bad; bandaged; bare; beautiful; big; black; black-edged; bleeding; bloody; blue; bluish; blunt; booted; broad; broken; brown; bruised; bud-like; buried; busted-up; calloused; clammy; clawed; clean; closed; clumsy; cold; cramped; crooked; crude; curled; curled-up; curly; curved; cute; dainty; dark; deformed; delicate; dirty; distinct; divine; elongated; excellent; exposed; extra; fair; fantastic; finger-like; fire-warmed; flexible; freakish; fresh; front; frostbitten; frozen; gangrenous; giant; gleaming; glossy; gnarled; grass-stained; great; hairy; hesitant; high-heeled; hind; hurt; icy; individual; injured; inner; innermost; knobby; large; little; long; manicured; mashed; middle; misshapen; missing; moccasined; molded; muddled; muddy; nail-polished; naked; narrow; nervous; nice; nimble; normal-looking; numb.

O - Y

oily; old; open; other; outer; outermost; outside; outstretched; overlapping; painful; painted; pale; pedicured; perfect; pinched; pink; pink-painted; pliant; plump; pointed; pointy; polished; poor; principal; probing; pudgy; purple-painted; raw; red; red-polished; rosy; rounded; rubbery; salmon-colored; sandaled; sandy; scarlet; scuffed; seedy; sensitive; severed; sharp; sharp-clawed; shivering; short; silk-socked; silk-stockinged; single; skinny; slabby; slender; slippered; small; smelly; smutted; sneakered; soft; soggy; sore; splayed; square; squared; stately; stiff; stiffened; stockinged; straight; strong; stubbed; stubby; sturdy; sweaty; swollen; tangled; tanned; tapered; tender; tentative; thick; thin; throbbing; tiny; tired; unwashed; upraised; upturned; varnished; webbed; white; whole; wiggling; wild; wounded; yellow; yellowed.

Verbs and Phrasal Verbs in Alphabetical Order

A - O

ached; acted; amputated; anchored; appeared; arranged; bandaged; banged; banged against; became; began; bent; bit; bled; brushed; brushed against; burned; burned with; came down; captured in; caressed; caught; caught in; caught on; clanged; clanged against; clasped; clasped onto; clenched; clicked; clicked on; climbed; clipped; clutched; clutched at; connected with; contracted; counted; covered; covered with; cracked; crept; crimped; crimped up; crinkled;

crushed; crushed up; curled; curled around; curled into; curled over; curled round; curled up; curved; cut; cut off; danced; dangled; dangled over; darted; darted across; dipped; dipped in; displayed; dragged; dragged through; drew in; dropped; dug; dug in; dug into; emerged; encountered; exposed; extended; faced; fanned out; felt; fit; flexed; forced through; formed; fought; found; freed; freed from; froze; furnished with; gleamed; grasped; grasped between; grazed; grew; gripped; groped; groped for; held; hit; hoisted; hung; hung over; hurt; inched closer; inched up; joined; jumped; jutted; jutted out; kicked; laid; leaned against; left; lifted; lined up; linked together; linked with; looked; looked like; lost; maneuvered; missed; moved; moved against; nestled; nestled against; overlapped.

P - W

pasted with; patted; patted against; peeked; peeked from; peeked out; peeped out; pinched; placed; played with; pointed down; pointed forward; pointed in; pointed inward; pointed outward; pointed straight; pointed to; poked; poked out; poked through; polished; pressed; pressed against; protruded; protruded from; pulled; pulled back; pushed; raised; raises; reached; reached for; received; relaxed; released from; remained; rested; rested on; rose; sank; sank into; scraped; scraped along; screwed up; scrunched; scrunched up; scuffed; searched; separated; shaped; showed; showed through; showed under; skidded; skimmed; skirted; slanted; sliced; slipped; slipped over; smashed; smashed up; smothered; smothered with; snagged; soaked; soaked in; sought; sought out; splayed; splayed out; spread; spread apart; spread out; sprouted through; squashed; squashed together; squeezed; squished; started; stayed; stirred; stood; stopped; stretched; stretched apart; stretched out; struggled; stubbed; stubbed on; stuck out; stuffed; stung; sucked; swept across; tagged; tapped; throbbed; thrummed; tickled; tied; tied together; tightened; tingled; toasted; touched; traced; trailed; trembled; trembled inside; trembled on; trod; tucked in; turned inward; turned outward; turned up; twitched; united; waggled; walked; warmed; wet; whacked; wiggled; wore; worked; wriggled; wrinkled.

Noun Phrases

action of the toe(s); amputation of the toe(s); army of toes; arrangement of the toes; ball(s) of the toe(s); base of the toe(s); bridge of the toe(s); contraction of the toe(s); couple of toes; curve of the toe(s); edge of the toe(s); end of the toe(s); extension of the toe(s); extremities of the toes; extremity of the toe; joint(s) of the toe(s); length of the toe(s); movement of the toe(s); muscle(s) of the toe(s); nail(s) of the toe(s); number of toes; part of the toe(s); position of the toe(s); scratching of toes; shape of the toe(s); side of the toe(s); skin of the toe(s); sound of toes; surface of the toe(s); tap of the toe(s); tip(s) of the toe(s).

USAGE EXAMPLES

The long walk had caused her *big toe to blister.*

Aunt Mary *tickled* the baby's *cute little toes.*

The shoes *exposed her finger-like toes.*

Her *numb toes banged against* the underside of the chair.

Suzie *placed her hesitant toes* in the water.

38
VOICE

Adjectives in Alphabetical Order

A - D

abrasive; abrupt; absent; absolute; accented; accentless; accusatory; accusing; acidic; active; actorly; actressy; actual; adamant; additional; adequate; admiring; adolescent; adult; affable; affected; affectionate; aged; ageing / aging; aggressive; aggrieved; agitated; agonized; agonizing; agreeable; ailing; airy; alarmed; alarming; alcohol-soaked; alert; alien; all-business; all-knowing; all-powerful; all-surrounding; all-too-familiar; alluring; almighty; almost-imperceptible; almost-loving; alternative; alto-toned; amateur; amazed; amazing; amped; ample; amplified; amused; ancient; androgynous; angelic; angry; anguished; animated; annoyed; annoying; anonymous; answering; antagonistic; anxious; apologetic; appalled; appealing; approaching; appropriate; approving; ardent; argumentative; aristocratic; arrogant; articulate; artificial; aspirate; assertive; assured; astonished; astounded; atonal; attenuated; attractive; audacious; audible; authentic; authoritative; autocratic; automated; automatic; awed; awesome; awful; awkward; baby-talk; babyish; bad; baffled; bantering; barely-audible; bass; bassy; bawdy; beautiful; believable; bell-like; belligerent; bellowing; beloved; bemused; bereaved; beseeching; best; betrayed-sounding; better; bewildered; big; bird-like; biting; bitter; bizarre; bland; blazing; bleak; blustering; boisterous; bold; booming; boozy; bored; boring; bossy; bothered; bottomless; bouncy; boyish; brainless; brainwashed; brassy; brave; braying; brazen; breath-starved; breathless; breathy; breezy; bright; brilliant; brisk; brittle; brittle-sounding; broken; brusque; brutal; bubbly; buffoonish; bullhorned; buoyant; business-like; buttery; buzzing; cadenced; calculating; callous; calm; calming; canned; capable; captivating; careful; careless; caressing; caring; cartoonish; casual; caustic; cautionary; cautious; cavernous; cement-mix; ceremonial; challenging; chambered; changed; changeless; changing; chanting; chaotic; charismatic; charming; chattering; cheerful; cheery; chiding; child-like; childish; chilling; chipmunky; chipper; chirping; chirpy; choked; choked-up; choking; choppy; choral; chorused; chuckling; church-quiet; churning; circumspect; civil; civilized; clamoring; clamorous; clandestine; classic; clattery; clean; clear; clinical; clipped; clogged; close; closed-in; clotted; co-mingled; coarse; coaxing; cocky; cold; collected; collective; colorless; combined; come-to-mama; comfortable; comforting; commanding; common; compassionate; compelling; competing; complicated; composed; comprehensible; computer-generated; computer-simulated; computer-synthesized; computerized; concerned; conciliatory; concise; condescending; confident; confidential; confidential-sounding; confiding; conflicting; confused;

conservative; consistent; consoling; conspiratorial; constricted; contemptuous; contented; contentious; continuing; controlled; controlling; conversational; convincing; cooing; cool; cool-as-ice; corny; corporate; courteous; courtly; crabby; cracked; cracking; crackling; craggy; crazed; crazy; creaking; creaky; cream-filled; creamy; credible; creepy; crisp; critical; croaking; croaky; crooning; crotchety; crude; crusty; crying; cultivated; cultured; cursing; curt; cushion-muffled; cut-glass; cutting; cynical; dainty; damaged; damaged-sounding; dangerous; dark; dark-timbered; darkest; dazed; dead; deadened; deadest; deadly; dear; deceptive; decisive; declamatory; declarative; decrepit; deep; deep-throated; deepening; deepest; defeated; defensive; defiant; definite; dejected; deliberate; deliberative; delicate; delighted; delightful; demanding; demonic; dense; derisive; desolate; despairing; desperate; desultory; detached; determined; detested; different; diffident; digital; digitized; dignified; dim; diplomatic; direct; directionless; disappointed; disapproving; discernible; disciplined; disconcerted; disconcerting; discordant; discouraged; disdainful; disembodied; disenchanted; disgruntled; disguised; disgusted; disgusting; disinterested; dismal; dismayed; dismissive; dispassionate; disquieted; dissenting; dissident; dissonant; distance-warped; distant; distinct; distinctive; distinguished; distorted; distracted; distraught; divine; docile; doleful; dominant; door-hinge; doubtful; doubting; draconian-sounding; dragging; drained; dramatic; drawling; drawly; drawn-out; dreadful; dreamy; dried-out; droll; droning; drowsy; drugged; drunk; drunken; dry; dual; dull; dulled; dumb; dwindling.

E - M

eager; earnest; earthy; easy; ebullient; echoing; edgy; educated; eerie; effective; effeminate; efficient; effortless; eight-year-old; elated; elderly; electronic; elegant; eloquent; embarrassed; emotion-choked; emotional; emotionless; emphatic; empiric; empty; enchanting; encouraging; endearing; energetic; engaging; enhanced; enormous; enthusiastic; entreating; epic; equable; ethereal; ethnic; even; even-toned; ever-cheerful; ever-present; everyday; evil; exaggerated; exasperated; exasperating; excellent; excitable; excited; exhausted; expectant; explanatory; explosive; expressionless; expressive; exquisite; extinguished; extra; extra-soothing; extraordinary; exuberant; exultant; exulting; fabulous; faceless; factual; fading; failing; faint; faintest; fair; fake; fake-cheery; fake-disappointed; false; faltering; familiar; fanciful; fantastic; far; far-off; fateful; fatherly; fearful; feathery; feeble; female; feminine; fervent; fever-thickened; fierce; fiercest; fiery; fine; firm; firm-but-polite; firmest; flat; flattest; flawless; flirtatious; floating; fluid; flute-like; fluttery; fluty; forbidden; forbidding; forced; forceful; foreign; forgiving; forgotten; formal; formless; forthright; foxy; fractured; fragile; fragmented; frail; frantic; frayed; frenetic; frenzied; fresh; fretful; friendliest; friendly; frightened; frightening; froggy; frosty; fruity; frustrated; full; full-throated; funny; furious; fuzzy; garbled; gargled; gasping; gaspy; gathered; gay; gender-neutral; genderless; general; generic; genial; genteel; gentle; gentle-sounding; gentlest; ghostly; giant; gibbering; giddy; giggly; gin-fueled; girlish; girly; glacial; glad; glassy;

gloating; gloomy; glorious; glutinous; gnawing; god-like; goddamn; godlike; golden; good; good-natured; goofy; gracious; grainy; grand; grandest; grateful; grating; grave; gravel-laced; gravel-pit; gravelly; gravest; gravy-thick; gray; greasy; great; greatest; green-with-envy; grief-stricken; grieved; grim; grinning; grisly; gritty; grizzled; groggy; growing; growl-like; growling; growly; grown-up; gruff; gruffest; grumpy; guarded; guilty; gurgling; gushy; guttural; haggard; half-familiar; half-heard; half-lazy; half-whispered; half-whispering; halting; handsome; happiest; happy; happy-sounding; harassed; hard; hardy; harmonious; harried; harsh; hate-filled; hateful; haughtiest; haughty; haunting; hazy; healthy; heartbreaking; heartfelt; heartless; hearty; heated; heavenly; heavily-accented; heavy; heavy-sounding; hellish; helpful; helpless; hesitant; hiccupy; high; high-pitched; high-speed; hissing; hissy; hoarse; holiest; hollow; holy; honest; honey-dipped; honey-smooth; honey-sweet; honey-toned; honeyed; hopeful; hopeless; horrible; horrified; horsy; hostile; hot; huge; human; human-sounding; humane; humble; humid; humming; humorless; humorous; hungry; hurried; hurt; hushed; husky; hyper; hypnotic; hypnotized; hysteric; hysterical; icy; identical; idiosyncratic; idiotic; imagined; immediate; immoderate; impassioned; impassive; impatient; imperative; imperfect; imperious; impersonal; impish; imploring; important; impotent; impressed; impressive; inarticulate; inaudible; incisive; incoherent; incomparable; incomprehensible; incredible; incredulous; indefatigable; independent; indifferent; indignant; indispensable; indistinct; indistinguishable; individual; indolent; inelegant; inept; inexplicable; infantile; inflected; inflectionless; influential; inhuman; inner; innocent; insane; insect-squeaking; insecure; insecure-sounding; insincere; insinuating; insipid; insistent; instructive; insuppressible; intellectual; intelligent; intelligible; intense; intent; interested; intermittent; internal; interpretive; intimate; intimidating; intoxicated; intoxicating; introspective; intuitive; invisible; irascible; irate; iron-tongued; ironic; irresistible; irritable; irritated; irritating; jagged; jaunty; jealous; jeering; jocular; jokey; joking; jolly; journalistic; joy-filled; joyful; joyless; joyous; judgmental; judicious; jumbled; jumping; jumpy; just; kind; kindest; kindly; labored; lackadaisical; laconic; ladylike; lamenting; languid; languishing; large; largest; larky; latent; laughing; lavish; lazy; leaden; learned; leathery; lecturing; leisurely; lenient; lethal; level; lifeless; light; lilting; lion-like; liquid; lisping; listless; literary; little; little-bitty; little-girl; little-girlie; little-kid; little-old-lady; lively; lobotomized; lofty; logical; lone; lonely; lonesome; long-distance; long-forgotten; long-suffering; loony; looped; lost; loud; loudest; lousy; loveliest; lovely; loving; low; low-keyed; low-pitched; low-toned; lower-pitched; lowest; loyal; lucid; lucky; lugubrious; lulling; lumbering; lurid; lusty; lyrical; macho; mad; made-for-tv; magical; magisterial; magnificent; majestic; male; managerial; manic; manlike; manly; mannerly; mannish; marvelous; masculine; masterly; matching; maternal; matter-of-fact; mature; mean; measured; mechanical; mechanical-sounding; mediocre; meditative; medium-level; meek; megaphoned; melancholy; mellifluent; mellifluous; mellow; melodic; melodious; melodramatic; menacing; mental; merciless; mere; merry; mesmerizing; metallic; metaphysical; microphoned; mid-range; midwestern;

mighty; mild; mildest; military; mindless; mingled; miserable; miserable-sounding; mock-courteous; mock-earnest; mock-incredulous; mock-official; mock-petulant; mock-serious; mock-sorry; mock-tough; mocking; moderate; modern; modulated; monotoned; monotonic; monotonous; moral; moralizing; morose; motherly; motivational; mournful; much-acclaimed; muddied; muddled; muddy; muffled; multiple; mumbled; mumbling; murmured; murmuring; murmurous; musical; muted; muttering; mysterious.

N - S

nagging; nameless; nasal; nasty; native; natural; near-baritone; near-hysterical; negative; neighboring; neighborly; nervous; neutral; new; nice; nice-sounding; nicest; niggling; no-nonsense; noble; non-accusing; non-confrontational; nonsensical; normal; normal-sounding; notable; novel; now-familiar; numbed; numerous; objective; obnoxious; occasional; odd; off-camera; off-key; off-screen; offbeat; offensive; official; official-sounding; officious; oily; old; old-fashioned; old-lady; old-time; older; ominous; omnipresent; omniscient; on-screen; operatic; opining; opposing; oppositional; optimistic; ordinary; original; other; otherworldly; out-of-breath; out-of-tune; outraged; outward; over-amplified; over-solicitous; overanxious; overeager; overhead; overlapping; overpowering; pain-seared; pained; pale; panic-filled; panicked; panicky; panting; parched; parental; particular; passionate; passionless; passive; past; paternal; pathetic; patient; patriarchal; patriotic; patronizing; peaceful; pealing; pebbly; peculiar; peevish; penetrating; peremptory; perfect; perkiest; perky; perplexed; persistent; personal; persuasive; pert; pessimistic; petty; petulant; phantom; phenomenal; phlegmy; phony; physical; piercing; pinched; pipe-smoking; piqued; pissed-off; pitched; piteous; pitiful; placating; placatory; placid; plain; plaintive; plangent; playful; pleading; pleasant; pleasant-sounding; pleased; pleasing; pleasureless; poetic; pointed; polished; polite; politest; pompous; ponderous; poor; portentous; posh; positive; potent; powerful; practical; practiced; prattling; prayerful; pre-adolescent; pre-pubescent; preaching; precious; precise; prerecorded; present; pretend; pretty; prevalent; previous; prickly; priest-like; priestly; prim; primal; prissiest; prissy; pristine; private; professional; proper; prophetic; provocative; psychotic; public; puckish; pulsing; pumped-up; puny; pure; purposeful; purring; puzzled; quavering; quavery; queer; querulous; questioning; quick; quiet; quietest; quivering; quivery; racked; radical; ragged; raging; raised; rapid; rapid-fire; rasping; raspy; ratchety; rational; raucous; raw; razor-edged; razored; ready; real; reasonable; reasoned; reassuring; reciting-style; recognizable; recorded; reed-like; reed-thin; reedy; refined; reflective; regal; regretful; regular; rehearsed; reliable; relieved; remarkable; remembered; remote; repentant; reproachful; reserved; resigned; resolute; resonant; resounding; respectable; respectful; restrained; reverent; rich; ridiculous; rising; riveted; riveting; roaring; robot-like; robotic; robust; rolling; romantic; rotten; rough; rough-edged; round; rounded; rowdy; rude; rueful; rugged; rumbling; Russian-accented; rusty; sacred; sad; saddest; salty; same; sanctimonious; sandpapery; sane; sarcastic; sardonic; satiric; satisfied; saucy; savage; scandalous; scared; scariest; scary; scathing; scholastic; scolding;

scornful; scraping; scratched; scratchy; screaming; screechy; scruffy; scuffed-up; seared; searing; seasoned; secret; secretive; seductive; self-assured; self-confident; self-congratulatory; self-conscious; self-dramatizing; self-pitying; self-possessed; self-righteous; self-satisfied; semi-hysterical; semi-seductive; senatorial; sensible; sensual; sensuous; separate; serious; severe; sexiest; sexy; shabby; shaded; shaken; shaky; shallow; shared; sharp; sheepish; shifting; shimmering; shivery; shocked; short-clipped; short-order; shouted; shouting; show-offy; shrill; shrilly; shy; sibilant; sick; sickly; significant; silenced; silent; silken; silky; silly; silvery; similar; simpering; simple; simultaneous; sincere; sincere-sounding; sincerest; sing-song; sing-songy; single; singular; sinister; sinister-sounding; skeptical; sleek; sleep-clogged; sleep-deprived; sleep-logged; sleep-roughened; sleep-thickened; sleepy; slight; slogan-chanting; sloppy; slow; slow-motion; slurred; slurring; sly; small; smarmy; smart; smiling; smoke-roughened; smoky; smoldering; smooth; smoothest; smothered; smug; snarling; sneaky; sneering; snide; snooty; snotty; snowy; so-familiar; soaring; sober; socializing; soft; soft-slurred; soft-spoken; softest; sole; solemn; solicitous; solitary; somber / sombre; somnolent; sonorous; soothing; sophisticated; sore; sore-throated; sorrowful; sorry; soulful; soulless; soundless; sour; sourceless; southern; southern-sounding; speaking; special; spectral; spirited; spiritless; spiritual; spiteful; splendid; splintery; spoken; spookiest; spooky; sprightly; sputtering; squabbling; squashed; squawky; squeaking; squeaky; squealing; squealing-balloon; squealy; staccato; stammering; standard; startled; static; static-drowned; static-filled; static-streaked; staticky; steadiest; steady; steadying; steel-trap; stern; sternest; stiff; stiffening; stifled; stinging; stony; stony-hearted; strained; stranded; strange; strangled; stressed; stressed-out; stricken; strident; strong; strongest; stuffed-nose; stuffy; stunned; stunning; stupid; stylized; suave; subdued; subtle; subtly-seductive; succinct; succulent; sudden; sugar-coated; sugary; suggestive; suitable; sulky; sullen; sultriest; sultry; super-high-pitched; superb; supercilious; superhero-like; superior; supple; suppressed; sure; surly; surprised; surprising; suspicion-laden; suspicious; sustained; swaggering; sweet; sweetest; sympathetic; synthesized; synthetic; syrupy.

T - Z

take-charge; tamed; taped; tasteful; tattered; tattle-tale; taunting; taut; teacherly; teachy; tear-choked; tearful; teary; teasing; teenage; teensy; teeny; telepathic; televised; tempered; tender; tenderest; tense; tentative; tenuous; terrible; terrified; terrifying; terse; teutonic; textured; theatrical; thick; thick-accented; thickened; thin; thin-timbre; thinnest; thoughtful; threatening; thrilled; thrilling; throatiest; throaty; throbbing; thundering; thunderous; tight; timbreless; timid; tinny; tiny; tipsy; tired; tireless; tiresome; tittering; tobacco-roughened; tolerant; tolling; toneless; too-bright; too-calm; too-familiar; too-hearty; too-loud; too-perfect; too-sweet; top; top-secret; tormented; tortured; tough; tough-guy; tough-love; tragic; trailing; trained; traitorous; tranquil; translated; transmitted; treacly; treble; trembling; tremendous; tremulous; trilling; triumphant; troubled; true; trumpet-like; truncated; tuneful; tuneless; twanging; twangy; tweedy; twisted;

ugly; ultra-high; ululating; unaccented; unaggressive; unaided; unamplified; unanimous; unassuming; unbroken; uncertain; uncharitable; uncompromising; unconvincing; unctuous; understandable; understanding; underwater; unearthly; uneasy; unemotional; uneven; unexpected; unfamiliar; unflustered; unforgettable; unforgiving; unformed; unfriendly; ungentle; ungodly; unhappy; unharried; unheard; unhurried; unidentifiable; unidentified; unified; unimpressed; uninflected; unintelligible; uninvited; unique; unkind; unknown; unmistakable; unnatural; unperturbed; unpleasant; unpracticed; unprepared; unquellable; unreassuring; unrecognizable; unremarkable; unruffled; unruly; unseen; unsorry; unsteady; unstoppable; unsure; unthreatening; untoward; untrained; unusual; unwavering; unwelcome; unyielding; up-and-down; upbeat; upraised; urgent; usual; vacant; vampy; various; vast; velvety; vexed; vexing; vibrant; vicious; vigorous; violent; voiceless; volatile; voluminous; vulgar; wailing; wan; warbling; warm; warmest; wary; water-logged; watery; wavering; wavery; wayward; weak; weakened; weary; wee; weird; welcome; welcoming; well-bred; well-known; well-modulated; well-trained; wet; wheedling; wheezy; whimsical; whining; whiny; whisper-like; whisper-soft; whisper-thin; whispered; whispering; whispery; wicked; wild; windy; winning; wire-taut; wisdom-imparting; wise; wiser; wispy; wistful; withering; wobbling; wobbly; woeful; womanish; womanly; wonderful; wondering; wooden; wordless; world-weary; worn; worried; wounded; wrecked; writerly; wry; yelpy; yielding; yipping; young; younger; youthful; zombielike.

Verbs and Phrasal Verbs in Alphabetical Order

A - C

abated; abounded; abstained from; accompanied; accompanied by; accused; accustomed to; ached; ached with; achieved; acquired; acted; acted on; activated; added; added after; added to; addressed; admitted; admonished; adopted; advertised; advised; affected; agitated; agreed; aimed; aimed at; alarmed; alerted; allowed; altered; amplified; amplified by; animated; announced; announced from; announced in; announced over; annoyed; answered; answered after; answered at; answered back; answered from; answered in; answered on; answered with; apologized; apologized for; appalled; appeared; approached; arced; arched; arched with; argued; arose; arose among; arose from; arose in; aroused; aroused in; arrested; arrived; arrived over; ascended; asked; asked about; asked after; asked again; asked back; asked for; asked from; asked in; asked over; assailed; asserted; associated with; assumed; assured; attached to; attempted; attracted; awakened; awoke; bade / bid; balanced; balanced on; bantered; barked; barked above; barked at; barked behind; barked from; barked into; barked over; barked through; battled; battled with; bawled out; beat against; became (emotion); became deeper; became louder; became quieter; beckoned; beckoned from; befitted; began to; begged; belied; bellowed; bellowed above; bellowed across; bellowed at; bellowed from; bellowed somewhere; bellowed through; belonged to; belted; belted out;

beseeched; betrayed; bit back; blared; blared out; blared over; blasted; blasted out; blasted over; bleated; bleated from; bleated over; blended; blended into; blended with; blessed with; blew; blipped in; blocked; blurred; blurred with; blurted; blurted out; boomed; boomed above; boomed across; boomed back; boomed down; boomed forth; boomed from; boomed inside; boomed like; boomed out; boomed over; boomed through; boomed with; bordered on; bore; bothered; bounced back; bounced off; brayed; brayed out; breathed; breathed in; breathed out; brightened; brightened with; brimmed; brimmed with; broadcast; broadcast over; broke; broke at; broke down; broke forth; broke in; broke into; broke off; broke out; broke through; broke up; broke with; brought; brought back; brought to; brought with; brushed; brushed against; bubbled; bubbled over; bubbled up; bubbled with; built; buoyed; buoyed out; burbled; buried; buried beneath; buried inside; burned; burned through; burnished by; burrowed; burst forth; burst from; burst into; burst out; burst over; butted in; buzzed; buzzed in; buzzed over; cackled; cackled with; calculated; called; called after; called again; called at; called back; called down; called for; called from; called in; called on; called out; called over; called through; called to; called up; called upon; calmed; calmed by; calms; came; came forth; came from; came out; came over; came through; capitalized; careened on; caressed; caromed; caromed off; carped; carried; carried above; carried across; carried on; carried over; carried through; carried to; carried up; cascaded; caught; caught at; caught in; caught on; caused; cautioned; ceased; challenged; changed; changed from; changed into; changed to; chanted; chanted out; charged; charged with; charmed; chased; chatted; chatted about; chattered; checked; cheered; chided; chilled; chimed; chimed in; chimed over; chimed with; chirped; chirped on; chirped up; chirruped; choked; choked by; choked for; choked from; choked in; choked on; choked out; choked up; choked with; chopped off; chortled; chorused; chuckled; chuckled out; churned; circled; circled down; circled in; claimed; clamored; clanged; clashed; clashed with; clattered; clattered on; clawed at; cleared; clenched; climbed; climbed over; climbed with; clipped; clogged in; closed; closed in; coalesced; coaxed; coiled around; collapsed; collapsed into; collided; colored with; combined with; comforted; commanded; commandeered; commenced; commenced in; commented; commented on; commingled with; compared to; compared with; compelled; competed; competed among; competed for; complained; complained about; complained of; complemented; composed; conceded; confessed; confirmed; conflated; confused; conjured up; connected; connected with; considered; consisted of; consoled; constrained; constricted; contained; continued; continued on; contracted; contracted to; contradicted; contrasted; controlled; conversed; conveyed; convinced; cooed; cooed with; cooled; corrected; correcting; corresponded; corroded by; coughed; coughed up; counted; counted down; counted off; countered; counterpoised; coursed through; cowered; cowered in; cracked; cracked from; cracked in; cracked into; cracked out; cracked over; cracked through; cracked with; crackled; crackled a; crackled across; crackled out; crackled over; crackled through; crackled with; cranked up; crashed against; crashed through; crawled; crawled on; creaked; crept; crept closer; cried; cried at; cried for; cried from; cried in; cried out; cried over; cried through; cried to; croaked; crooned; crossed; crowded; crowded into; crowed; crowed in; cruised; cruised over; cued; culled; culled from; curdled; curdled with; cured; curled; curled like; cursed; cursed from; cut; cut above; cut across; cut in; cut into; cut off; cut out; cut over; cut through.

D - L

dared; darkened; darkened to; darted; deadpanned; deadpanned in; decided; declaimed; declared; deepened; deepened by; deepened in; deepened with; defied; degenerated into; delivered; demanded; demanded with; denied; depended on; depended upon; descended; descended from; descended into; described; destroyed by; detailed; determined; devolved into; died; died away; died down; died in; died into; died on; died out; differed from; diminished; diminished to; dipped; dipped in; dipped to; directed; disappeared; disappeared beneath; disappeared in; discomforted; discussed; disembodied; disguised; disguised by; disheartened; dismissed; disoriented; dispassioned; disputed; disrupted; dissipated; dissolved; dissolved into; distilled; distorted; distorted by; distracted; distracted by; disturbed; disturbed by; dominated; doubled; downshifted; downshifted to; dragged; drained; drawled; drenched by; drenched in; drew closer; drew nearer; drew out; dribbled; dried out; dried up; drifted; drifted away; drifted back; drifted down; drifted from; drifted in; drifted into; drifted off; drifted out; drifted through; drifted to; drifted toward; drifted up; drilled into; dripped with; drizzled; droned; droned on; dropped; dropped away; dropped in; dropped into; dropped off; dropped to; dropped toward; drove; drove away; drowned; drowned by; drowned in; drowned out; drugged with; drummed; drummed back; dulled; dwelt; dwindled; dwindled away; dwindled off; eased; ebbed; echoed; echoed above; echoed across; echoed against; echoed around; echoed back; echoed down; echoed in; echoed inside; echoed into; echoed off; echoed on; echoed out; echoed through; echoed up; edged on; edged toward; edged with; egged on; elevated; emanated from; embarrassed; embraced; emerged; emerged from; emerged in; emerged through; emitted; emphasized; emulated; encouraged; ended; ended in; ended on; enraged; enriched; entered; enunciated; enveloped; erupted; erupted from; erupted in; erupted over; escalated; escaped; escaped from; evaporated; evoked; exasperated; exceeded; exchanged; excited; exclaimed; exclaimed in; excused; exerted; exhaled; exhausted; expended; explained; exploded; exploded at; exploded in; exploded into; expressed; exuded; faded; faded away; faded in; faded into; faded off; faded out; faded to; failed; faltered; faltered at; faltered for; faltered in; faltered with; feigned; fell across; fell away; fell into; fell off; fell on; fell silent; fell to; fell upon; felt; felt like; filled up; filled with; filtered down; filtered into; filtered out; filtered through; finished; fired back; firmed; fizzled; flamed; flamed within; flared; flashed; flattened; flattened out; flavored by; flickered; flipped; floated; floated above; floated across; floated around; floated away; floated back; floated down; floated from; floated inside; floated into; floated out; floated over; floated through; floated to; floated up; floundered; flowed; flowed on; flowed over; fluttered; followed; forced; forged from; forged on; forgot; formed; fought; found; frayed; frayed out; frazzled;

fried; frightened; froze; froze up; frustrated; fueled; fumed; fumed out; fused; fussed; gabbled; gained; galvanized; garbled; gasped; gathered; gave; gave out; gentled; giggled; glided in; glistened; got deeper; got even; got hard; got inside; got into; got louder; got more; got on; got through; grabbed; graced; grated; grated in; grated like; grated on; grated out; grated with; greeted; grew; grew even; grew harder; grew in; grew into; grew less; grew louder; grew more; grew slower; grew still; grew tight; gritted; groaned; ground out; growled; growled from; growled in; growled with; grumbled; grunted; guided; gurgled; gushed; gusted; hacked; hacked out; haggled; hailed; hailed to; halted; harangued; hardened; harmed; harmonized; haunted; heaved; heaved up; heckled; hectored; held; helped; heralded; hesitated; hid; hinted at; hinted of; hissed; hissed through; hit; hoarsened; hollered; hollered out; hovered; hovered at; hovered behind; hovered over; hovered somewhere; howled; hummed; hung; hung in; hung on; hung up; hurt; hurtled down; hushed; hushed in; hushed with; hypnotized; iced over; iced up; imbued with; imitated; implied; implored; incited; increased; increased in; indicated; infiltrated; inflected by; informed; inquired; inquired after; inquired for; inquired of; insinuated; insisted; inspired; instructed; intended; intercepted; interjected; interrupted; interrupted by; interrupted over; interrupted with; interspersed with; intervened; interwoven; intimated; intoned; intoned over; intoned to; introduced; intruded; intruded into; intruded on; invaded; invited; invoked; irked; irritated; issued forth; issued from; jabbered; jabbered on; jarred; jeered; jeered at; jerked; joined; joined in; joined with; jolted; jousted; jumped; jumped out; keened; kept on; kept up; kicked in; killed; knew; knifed into; knifed through; knocked; knotted; labored; laced through; laced with; lacked; lacked in; laden with; lamented; lamented about; lapped; lashed; lashed at; lashed out; laughed; launched into; lay; lay down; layered; leached; leaked; leaked from; leaked out; leaked through; leaped; leaped out; leaped up; led; left; let out; lifted; lifted up; lightened; likened to; lilted; lilted up; lingered; lingered in; lingered over; linked; lisped; lisped with; lit; lit up; locked; locked up; loomed; loosened; lost; lost in; loved; lowered; lulled; lurched.

M - R

maintained; managed; mangled; marshaled; masked; matched; materialized; measured; melded; mellowed; mellowed with; melted; melted into; menaced; mentioned; merged; merged with; mesmerized; met; mimicked; mingled; mingled with; mirrored; mixed; mixed up; mixed with; moaned; moaned with; mocked; modulated; modulated for; modulated into; modulated to; moved; moved down; moved into; moved like; moved nearer; moved over; moved through; moved toward; muffled; muffled against; muffled by; multiplied; mumbled; murmured; mused; muttered; nagged; nagged at; named; narrated; needed; nipped; nipped at; nudged; obeyed; obliged; occupied; offered; oozed out; oozed through; oozed with; opened up; operated; ordered; originated; over-enunciated; overlapped; overpowered; overrode; overwhelmed; overwhelmed by; pained; passed; paused; pealed; pealed down; pealed out; pelted; penetrated; performed; perked up; persisted; petered out; petitioned; phoned; picked up;

pierced; pierced through; pinched; pinched with; pinged along; pinpointed; piped in; piped into; piped out; piped up; pitched above; pitched in; pitched up; played; played back; played over; pleaded; pleaded for; pleaded with; plummeted; plunged; plunged down; pointed out; poised; poked; popped out; popped through; populated; positioned; possessed; pounced; pounded; pounded hard; poured forth; poured from; poured out; poured over; poured through; powered by; powered on; practiced; praised; prayed; preached; preceded; predicted; preempted; pressed; pressed on; prevailed; prevented; pricked; prickled; prickled with; proceeded; proceeded from; proceeded with; proclaimed; produced; produced by; profaned; projected; projected into; projected off; promised; prompted; pronounced; propelled; prophesied; proposed; protested; proved; provoked; pulled; pulled at; pulsed; pulsed in; pulsed through; pulsed with; pummeled; pumped out; punctuated by; purred; purred out; pushed; pushed through; pushed upward; put forth; put in; puzzled; quacked; quaked; quaked with; quavered; quavered at; quavered on; quavered with; queried; questioned; quickened; quieted; quieted down; quietened; quit; quivered; quivered with; racked by; racked with; radiated; raged; raised; raised above; raised against; raised over; raised to; raised with; rambled; rambled on; ran down; ran on; rang; rang above; rang across; rang against; rang forth; rang out; rang over; rang through; rang with; rasped; rasped out; rasped with; rattled; rattled at; rattled into; rattled off; rattled through; raveled; raveled on; reached down; reached out; read; read out; reappeared; reassured; rebounded; rebuked; recalled; recanted; receded; recited; recommended; recomposed; recorded; recounted; recovered; reduced to; reeked of; reeked with; reeled; reflected; refused; regained; registered; registered with; rejected; rejoiced; rejoiced over; rekindled; relaxed; released; relieved; remained; remarked; remembered; reminded; removed from; rendered; repeated; replaced by; replied; reported; reported on; represented; reproved; required; resembled; reserved; resided over; resigned; resolved; resonated; resonated from; resonated in; resonated over; resonated throughout; resonated within; resounded; resounded across; resounded down; resounded from; resounded in; resounded off; resounded through; resounded throughout; responded; responded to; rested; restored; resumed; resurfaced; resurrected; retained; retorted; retreated; retreated into; returned; returned from; returned with; revealed; reverberated; reverberated from; reverberated in; reverberated inside; reverberated off; reverberated through; reverberated throughout; reverberated with; reviled; revved; ricocheted down; ricocheted off; ripped through; rippled; rippled at; rippled with; roared; roared back; roared out; roared through; rolled; rolled across; rolled on; rolled out; rolled over; rolled through; rollicked; rose; rose above; rose from; rose in; rose over; rose up; rose with; rounded in on; roused; rubbed the wrong way; ruffled; ruined; rumbled; rumbled above; rumbled against; rumbled over; rumbled through; rumbled with; rushed; rushed along; rushed on; rustled.

S – Y
sagged; said; sang; sang out; sank; sank away; sank down; saturated with; scaled upward; scared; scattered; scolded; scrambled for; scraped; scraped across;

scraped against; scraped harshly; scraped out; scratched; scratched through; scratched up; screamed; screamed above; screamed out; screamed through; screeched; seeped into; seethed; seethed with; sent back; sent forth; sent out; settled into; shadowed with; sharpened; sharpened with; shattered; shifted; shifted into; shifted to; shivered down; shocked; shook; shook with; shot back; shot out; shot through; shot up; shouted; shouted across; shouted at; shouted back; shouted down; shouted from; shouted in; shouted into; shouted out; shouted over; shrank; shredded by; shrieked; shrieked across; shrieked out; shrilled; shrilled out; shuddered; sighed; signaled; silenced; sizzled; skipped; skipped along; skipped on; sliced through; slid off; slid up; slipped; slipped into; slithered; slowed; slowed at; slowed down; slurred; smoothed; smothered; snagged on; snapped; snapped out; snarled; snorted; soaked in; soared; soared over; sobbed; sobbed out; softened; softened at; softened in; softened with; soothed; sounded; sounded above; sounded across; sounded again; sounded alike; sounded almost; sounded angrily; sounded as; sounded at; sounded out; sounded over; soured; sparked; sparkled; spat; spat back; spat out; sped; sped up; spewed; spewed forth; spewed out; spiked; spilled from; spilled out; spilled over; splintered; splintered in; split; spoke; spoke above; spoke of; spoke on; spoke out; spoke over; spoke through; spoke to; spoke up; spoke with; spoke within; spouted; sprang from; spread; spread over; spread through; sputtered; squawked; squawked out; squeaked; squeaked out; squeaked up; squealed; squealed out; squeezed; squeezed out; stabbed; stabilized; stammered; started; started up; startled; stated; stayed; steadied; steeped in; stepped up; stiffened; stifled; stifled by; stilled; stirred; stole across; stole around; stood out; stopped; strained; strained over; strained with; strangled; strangled in; strangled with; strayed; strengthened; stretched; stripped of; stroked; strove; struck; struck on; struggled; stuck; stumbled; stumbled over; stung; stunned; subdued; subjugated; submerged; subsided; suffused; suggested; suited; supplied; supported by; surfaced; surged; surged on; surpassed; surprised; surrounded; suspended; suspended on; swallowed; swallowed up; sweetened; swelled; swelled in; swelled into; swelled with; swept by; swept over; swept up; swirled; switched; switched on; swollen with; swooped; swooped up; tailed away; tailed off; talked; talked about; talked through; talked to; tangled; tapered off; taunted; teased; teetered; teetered on; tensed; tensed with; testified; thanked; thawed; thickened; thickened by; thickened with; thinned; thinned away; threatened; thrilled; thrilled with; throbbed; throbbed with; thrummed; thrummed with; thudded; thudded across; thundered; thundered across; thundered out; thundered over; tickled; tightened; tightened up; tightened with; tilted up; tinged with; tipped; tipped off; told; told of; tolled; tortured; tortured by; touched; touched on; touched with; toughened; traded; traded off; trailed; trailed away; trailed off; trailed on; trained; translated; transported; transposed; trapped; traveled; traveled down; traveled through; traveled up; trembled; trembled in; trembled with; tremored; tried; triggered; trilled; tripped; triumphed; troubled; trumpeted; tugged; tugged at; tumbled; turned; turned up; twanged; twanged with; tweaked; twined; twisted; twisted into; underlined; underscored; understood; undulated; upheld; uplifted; urged; used to; uttered; vanished; veiled; ventured; verged on;

vibrated; vibrated against; vibrated in; vibrated through; vibrated with; voiced; volunteered; wafted; wafted from; wafted in; wafted over; wailed; wailed out; wailed over; waited; wandered; wandered away; wandered off; waned; wanted; warbled; warmed; warmed with; warned; warned of; washed over; wavered; wavered with; weakened; weighed on; welcomed; went deeper; went down; went hard; went off; went on; went out; went up; wept; wept over; wheedled; wheeled; wheezed; wheezed away; whimpered; whined; whispered; whispered against; whispered behind; whispered beside; whispered into; whispered to; whistled; whooped; wilted; wobbled; wobbled with; woke up; worked; wound down; wove; yammered; yammered on; yanked; yelled; yelled at; yelled down; yelled in; yelled into; yelled out.

Noun Phrases

absence of the voice; accent of the voice; agitation of the voice; alteration of the voice; authority of the voice; balance of the voice; bass of the voice; beauty of the voice; bellow of the voice; bidding of the voice; bitterness of the voice; blur of the voice; body of the voice; boom of the voice; booming of the voice; break of the voice; breath of the voice; breathlessness of the voice; brightness of the voice; burst of the voice; cadence of the voice; calm of the voice; calmness of the voice; caress of the voice; cessation of the voice; changes of the voice; character of the voice; characteristics of the voice; charm of the voice; clarity of the voice; clearness of the voice; coldness of the voice; color of the voice; combination of voices; comfort of the voice; command of the voice; composure of the voice; condition of the voice; control of the voice; convergence of voices; countenance of the voice; crackle of the voice; cultivation of the voice; deepness of the voice; delivery of the voice; depth of the voice; description of the voice; development of the voice; difference of the voice; direction of the voice; distinction of the voice; drawl of the voice; drone of the voice; eagerness of the voice; earnestness of the voice; echo of the voice; effect of the voice; effort of the voice; elevation of the voice; eloquence of the voice; emotion of the voice; emphasis of the voice; enchantment of the voice; energy of the voice; evenness of the voice; exaltation of the voice; excellence of the voice; exertion of the voice; expression of the voice; extent of the voice; failure of the voice; fall of the voice; familiarity of the voice; fascination of the voice; feebleness of the voice; firmness of the voice; flatness of the voice; flexibility of the voice; flow of the voice; force of the voice; frequency of the voice; freshness of the voice; friendliness of the voice; gentleness of the voice; glory of the voice; grace of the voice; gravity of the voice; grip of the voice; growl of the voice; hardening of the voice; hardness of the voice; harmony of the voice; harshness of the voice; hoarseness of the voice; hollowness of the voice; hum of the voice; huskiness of the voice; imitation of the voice; impressiveness of the voice; inflection of the voice; influence of the voice; instrument of the voice; intensity of the voice; interplay of voices; intimacy of the voice; intonation of the voice; joy in the voice; kind of voice; kindness of the voice; lack of a voice; level of the voice;

lightness of the voice; loss of the voice; loudness of the voice; loveliness of the voice; lowering of the voice; lull of the voice; magnetism of the voice; majesty of the voice; mastery of the voice; mellowness of the voice; melody of the voice; mockery in the voice; modification of the voice; modulation of the voice; monotone of the voice; monotony of the voice; murmur of the voice; murmurings of the voice; music of the voice; nature of the voice; need of a voice; neutrality of the voice; noise of the voice; notes of the voice; nuance(s) of the voice; number of voices; on account of the voice; organ of the voice; parody of the voice; part of the voice; passion of the voice; peculiarity of the voice; perfection of the voice; performance of the voice; persuasion of the voice; pitch of the voice; power of the voice; presence of the voice; problems with the voice; production of voice; pull of the voice; purity of the voice; purr of the voice; qualities of the voice; quality of the voice; quaver of the voice; questioning in the voice; quietness of the voice; quiver of the voice; range of the voice; rasp of the voice; reach of the voice; recognition of the voice; recording of the voice; recovery of the voice; register of the voice; release of the voice; remnant of the voice; remorse of the voice; resolution of the voice; resonance of the voice; return of the voice; reverberation of the voice; rhythm of the voice; richness of the voice; ring of the voice; ripple of the voice; rise of the voice; roar of the voice; roughness of the voice; roundness of the voice; rumble of the voice; rush of voices; sadness of the voice; scratch of the voice; series of voices; seriousness of the voice; severity of the voice; sharpness of the voice; shrillness of the voice; sibilance of the voice; sincerity of the voice; size of the voice; slowing of the voice; smoothness of the voice; snarl of the voice; softening of the voice; softness of the voice; solemnity of the voice; sort of voice; sound of the voice; spell of the voice; state of the voice; steadiness of the voice; sternness of the voice; straining of the voice; strangulation of the voice; strength of the voice; stress in the voice; string of voices; subterfuge of the voice; surety of the voice; surface of the voice; suspension of the voice; sweetness of the voice; tenderness of the voice; terror of the voice; texture of the voice; thickness of the voice; thrill of the voice; thrust of the voice; thunder of the voice; tightening of the voice; timbre of the voice; tonalities of the voice; tone of the voice; top of the voice; transmission of the voice; tremor of the voice; tremulousness of the voice; tune of the voice; twang of the voice; type of voice; uncertainty in the voice; undertone(s) of the voice; unraveling of the voice; unsteadiness of the voice; urgency of the voice; use of the voice; utterance of the voice; variation(s) of the voice; variety of voices; vehemence of the voice; vibration of the voice; vigor of the voice; volume of the voice; warmth of the voice; waves of the voice; way of the voice; weakness of the voice; weight of the voice; whine of the voice; whisper of the voice; wishes of the voice; words of the voice.

USAGE EXAMPLES

Victor's *abrasive voice called* up to them from the kitchen.

From behind them, an *aggressive voice butted in* to their conversation.

The boy *spoke* in a *muffled voice*.

He'd *said* it in a *drawn-out voice* that made her feel sorry for him.

Upon opening the window, a *merry voice* could be heard *singing* next door.

39

WAIST

Adjectives in Alphabetical Order

ample; athletic; ballooning; bare; belted; bent; big; broad; bulging; bulky; cinched; compact; concave; corseted; curving; dainty; defined; delicate; elegant; enormous; expanded; expanding; expectant; female; fifteen-year-old; fine; flat; gaunt; generous; giant; girdled; graceful; graspable; greasy; hour-glass; immodest; jean-clad; large; lean; leather-clad; little; lovely; lower; massive; motherly; mud-covered; naked; narrow; neat; nipped-in; nonexistent; normal; perfect; petite; plump; portly; quivering; rear; rigid; roped; round; shapely; short; shrinking; slender; slight; slim; small; soft; solid; spider-slim; still-slender; stout; stretch-marked; stretched; substantial; sumptuous; supple; sweet; swollen; tanned; tapered; taut; tender; thick; thickening; thin; thirty-inch; tight; tiny; too-skinny; too-small; trim; twenty-four-inch; unyielding; virgin; warm; wasp-thin; waspish; wet; white; wide; willowy; wrinkly.

Verbs and Phrasal Verbs in Alphabetical Order

accentuated; adorned; appeared; balanced; balanced on; became; began; came over; carried; checked; cinched; cinched by; cinched tight; confined; contrasted with; disappeared; disappeared into; elongated; emphasized; emphasized by; encircled; encircled by; encountered; exceeded; expanded; exposed; fell; felt; flared; flicked; floated; formed; held; hugged; hung; looked; marked with; measured; pinched; raised; raised up; registered; remained; revealed; rolled; rolled down; rose; rotated; sat; showed; started; strained; stretched; stretched back; surrounded by; swayed; swelled; swelled above; swung; teetered; tied around; tightened; touched; tucked into; twisted; wrapped around.

Noun Phrases

back of the waist; billow of the waist; curve(s) of the waist; dip of the waist; girdle of the waist; hold of the waist; line of the waist; measure of the waist; narrowness of the waist; padding of the waist; posture of the waist; side of the waist; slenderness of the waist; slimness of the waist; slope of the waist; spin of the waist; stretch of the waist; thickness of the waist.

USAGE EXAMPLES

She lifted up her jumper, *exposing her dainty waist*.

Her *hour-glass waist flared* in all the right places.

His *jean-clad waist revealed* a body that knew the definition of hard work.

Rose's *slender waist twisted* around when she heard him call her name.

The man's *wide waist was cinched tight* in a pair of ugly brown pants.

40
WRIST(S)

Adjectives in Alphabetical Order

aching; arthritic; bandaged; bare; beating; bent; big; black; blackened; bleeding; bloodied; bloody; blue; blue-veined; bony; bound; braceleted; brawny; breakable; brittle; broken; brown; bruised; chafed; childlike; clumsy; cocked; cold; concealed; covered; crossed; cut; cylindrical; dainty; decorative; delicate; double-jointed; drooping; elastic; elegant; enormous; expensive; exposed; fabulous; fat; fine; fine-boned; flailing; flat; flexible; fractured; fragile; frail; free; full; gashed; gentle; glove-covered; gloved; golden; good; graceful; hairy; handcuffed; hot; huge; hurt; inner; knobby; lace-trimmed; lazy; left; lifeless; limp; little; liver-spotted; locked; long; loose; lovely; mangled; meager; naked; narrow; oaken; opposite; ordinary; other; outstretched; painful; pale; perfumed; pinned; powerful; pulseless; pulsing; pumped; quick; raised; rapid-beating; raw; red; reddened; relaxed; revolving; right; ropy; rotating; rubbery; scrawny; shackled; skinny; slack; slashed; slender; slight; slim; small; soft; solid; sore; spindly; sprained; stick-like; stiff; stinging; straight; strained; strong; sun-browned; sun-darkened; sunburned / sunburnt; supple; sweaty; swelling; swollen; tanned; tapered; tender; tender-boned; thick; thin; thin-boned; throbbing; tingling; tiny; tough; twisted; upper; upturned; veined; veiny; warm; watchless; weak; well-fed; white; whole; wide; wiry; wounded; wrinkled.

Verbs and Phrasal Verbs in Alphabetical Order

ached; adorned with; alighted; appeared; bandaged; became; began; bent; bled; bore; bounced; bounced around; bound; bound by; bound in; bound to; bound together; bound with; bowed; braced; braced for; branded; branded with; broke; brushed; burned; burned from; cast; caught; caught between; caused; circled; circled by; clamped; clasped; clasped together; clicked; clicked against; clinked; clinked against; closed over; cocked; cocked over; coiled; combined; crossed; crossed behind; crossed over; cuffed; cuffed in; cuffed to; cut; dangled; displayed; draped; drew up; dripped; dripped with; dropped; eased; exercised; exerted; extended; faced; fastened; fastened to; fell; felt; flapped; flexed; flicked; flickered; folded; folded over; freed; gave out; gleamed; glittered; graced with; grazed; handcuffed; held; hit; hooked; hung; hung at side; hung down; hurt; itched; jabbed; jabbed into; jingled; joined; joined together; jutted from; jutted out; laid downward; lanced; lashed; lifted; locked; locked behind; looked; managed; moved; opened; overextended; pinioned; pinned; pinned above; pinned against; played with; popped; possessed; pressed; pressed against;

pressed into; prevented; pulled; quivered; raised; reached; remained; rested; rested against; revealed; sandwiched between; scraped; secured; shackled; shook; shot out; shot up; showed; showed off; slackened; slammed; slashed; slid; slide; slit; slung; snapped; snapped back; sparkled; sported; stayed; stayed still; stiffened; stood; stood up; stopped; strained; strained against; strapped; stressed; stuck; stuck out; stuck up; stung; supported; sweat; swelled; swelled up; swiveled; swung; throbbed; throbbed with; tied; tied behind; tied to; tied together; tied with; tightened; tingled; touched; trembled; turned; turned toward; twisted; vanished beneath; wove around; wrapped; wrapped around; wrapped in; yanked.

Noun Phrases

action of the wrist(s); a hold of the wrist(s); angle of the wrist(s); arteries of the wrist(s); arthritis of the wrist(s); back of the wrist(s); bend of the wrist(s); bones of the wrist(s); center of the wrist(s); cock of the wrist(s); control of the wrist(s); crease of the wrist(s); delicacy of the wrist(s); dislocation of the wrist(s); edge of the wrist(s); end of the wrist(s); extension of the wrist(s); feel of the wrist(s); flesh of the wrist(s); flexibility of the wrist(s); flick of the wrist(s); fling of the wrist(s); flip of the wrist(s); flourish of the wrist(s); fracture of the wrist(s); grip of the wrist(s); hold of the wrist(s); hollow of the wrist(s); jerk of the wrist(s); joints of the wrist(s); knob of the wrist(s); line of the wrist(s); motion of the wrist(s); movement of the wrist(s); muscles of the wrist(s); nakedness of the wrist(s); part of the wrist(s); pivot of the wrist(s); position of the wrist(s); power of the wrist(s); reaction of the wrist(s); region of the wrist(s); roll of the wrist(s); rotation of the wrist(s); set of wrist(s)s; side of the wrist(s); skin of the wrist(s); slash of the wrist(s); snap of the wrist(s); sound of the wrist(s); sprain of the wrist(s); stiffness of the wrist(s); strength of the wrist(s); stump of the wrist(s); surface of the wrist(s); sweep of the wrist(s); tendons of the wrist(s); thinness of her wrist(s); tightening of the wrist(s); tinge of the wrist(s); top of the wrist(s); toss of the wrist(s); turn of the wrist(s); twist of the wrist(s); twitch of the wrist(s); underside of the wrist(s); veins of the wrist(s); view of the wrist(s); weakness of the wrist(s); whiteness of the wrist(s); width of the wrist(s).

USAGE EXAMPLES

A large hand clamped around her *frail wrist*, dragging her closer.

The attire she was wearing *showed off her lovely narrow wrists*.

The girl had *slashed her wrists* with a knife.

He held up her *rapid-beating wrist* to his lips and lightly embraced it.

He caught one of the old man's *veiny wrists* in his hand and squeezed.

Also by Dahlia Evans

The Dialogue Thesaurus – A Fiction Writer's Sourcebook of Dialogue Tags and Phrases

"The Book Every Aspiring Fiction Writer Needs On Their Bookshelf!"

Sometimes the word *'said'* just doesn't cut it. Sometimes a writer needs something with a little more expressive power; a word or phrase that helps the reader visualize the tonal quality or mood of the character doing the talking.

For many years, writers have been eagerly awaiting the publication of a resource to help them with this dilemma. Thankfully, that wait is finally over. Now there's a way for any writer, regardless of their experience, to craft dialogue tags that add emotion and vibrancy to their storytelling; all while avoiding tired and worn out clichés.

Dahlia Evans has compiled a dialogue thesaurus unlike anything ever published. This unique sourcebook is filled to the brim with words and phrases gathered from hundreds of bestselling novels. Finally, you will be able to open up vistas of endless inspiration and bring your dialogue to life.

Inside You'll Discover:

* Over 500 dialogue and action tags you can use instead of *'said'*.

* More than 2900 adverbs that can be used to describe speech.

* Thousands of emotion and feeling words in adjective and noun form.

* A thousand phrases to describe body language and movement.

* Tons of example sentences to help solidify your understanding.

* And best of all, words are sorted in alphabetical order, as well as by category.

The Dialogue Thesaurus is the first book of its kind; a thesaurus geared towards writers who want to frame their dialogue with compelling and expressive words and phrases.